THE EYE OF SPIRIT

THE EYE
OF SPIRIT

*An Integral Vision
for a World Gone
Slightly Mad*

THIRD EDITION
EXPANDED

Ken Wilber

SHAMBHALA
Boston & London
2001

SHAMBHALA PUBLICATIONS, INC.
Horticultural Hall
300 Massachusetts Avenue
Boston, Massachusetts 02115
www.shambhala.com

9 8 7 6 5 4 3 2

THIRD EDITION, EXPANDED
Printed in the United States of America
⊗ This edition is printed on acid-free paper that meets the
American National Standards Institute Z39.48 Standard.
Distributed in the United States by Random House, Inc.,
and in Canada by Random House of Canada Ltd

Library of Congress Cataloging-in-Publication Data
Wilber, Ken.
The eye of spirit: an integral vision for a world gone slightly mad/ Ken Wilber.—
3rd ed., expanded.
p. cm.
Includes bibliographical references and index.
ISBN 1-57062-871-8 (pbk.: alk. paper)
1. Spiritual life. I. Title.
BL624 .W53 2001
191—dc21
2001040061

Contents

78-86 science dualism
125 witness

218 obs/sub
220 total/walk
284 dualism

Preface to the Third Edition

THE EYE OF SPIRIT is an important book in my overall work, I believe, because it marked the first sustained application of my most recent and "up to date" model to particular disciplines such as psychology, art, and literature, and spirituality. This model (also called "phase-4") was first presented in detail in *Sex, Ecology, Spirituality*; a popularized version was offered in *A Brief History of Everything*, and an even more popular version in *A Theory of Everything*. But the specific application of this latest model—in cultural studies, psychology, feminism, art, science, and spirituality—was first presented in the book you now hold in your hands. Further, this book still contains my own single favorite piece of my writing ("Integral Art and Literary Theory"), and it contains the best short overview of my psychological model ("Waves, Streams, States, and Self"). For all these reasons, I believe that *The Eye of Spirit* is a cornerstone book for those wishing to understand a more integral, comprehensive, and balanced approach to the Kosmos.

As with all of the recent paperback reissues of my major books, this one is based on the edited (and revised) version that appeared in *The Collected Works of Ken Wilber,* volume 7. For this paperback, I have also added a new chapter, the aforementioned "Waves, Streams, States, and Self: An Introduction to My Psychological Model (Or, Outline of an Integral Psychology)." Combined with the Introduction, that chapter gives a fairly comprehensive overview of some of the essentials of the integral paradigm I have suggested.

The title "Waves, Streams, States, and Self" is itself a brief summary of the psychological model. Namely: there are levels or waves of consciousness, stretching from matter to body to mind to soul to spirit. Through those levels pass numerous developmental lines or streams of consciousness (the cognitive line, the moral line, the psychosexual, the interpersonal, the affective, the spiritual, etc.). These lines or streams develop in a relatively independent fashion, so that a person can be at a high level of development in some lines (e.g., the cognitive), medium in others (e.g., moral), and low in still others (e.g., spiritual). Thus, there is nothing linear about overall development. Moreover, in addition to waves and streams of consciousness, there are altered states of consciousness, and a person can have an altered state or peak experience at virtually any level or stage of development, and so once again, the nonlinear nature of overall development becomes apparent. Finally, balancing and integrating all of the waves, streams, and states of consciousness is the self (or self-system), whose job it is to navigate the various currents of the psyche from the lowest to the highest. All of those items are fully discussed in "Waves, Streams, States, and Self" (chap. 12). When added to the "quadrants"—which are fully outlined in the Introduction—the result is a fairly comprehensive overview of an integral system.

"Waves, Streams, States, and Self" also suggests that there are at least four major, different definitions of spirituality, and unless we honor all four of these definitions, we get into insuperable theoretical difficulties very quickly. Briefly, spirituality can be viewed as the highest stages in any of the lines; as a separate developmental line itself; as an altered state or peak experience; as an attitude that may or may not be present at any stage. The application of these four definitions of spirituality—which I contend are actually four aspects of overall spirituality itself—does much to further the understanding of this most important of topics.

As you will see in the following pages, the most common criticism of my model is that it is linear, a view I have not held for twenty years (i.e., the "phase-2" model). I hope that you will forgive my exasperation at some of these critics who continue to attack my model without first representing it accurately. It is, to say the least, irritating; and you will see some of this irritation in the following pages. (I could have edited these few sections out, but these ill-informed critics deserve a bit of public scolding, and it definitely livens things up!)

But what about spirituality itself? Does it necessarily unfold in stages? My answer, again, is absolutely not. Or, more precisely, of the four aspects of spirituality that I outlined, two of them tend to show developmental stages, and two of them do not. The first two aspects—spirituality as the highest stage(s) in any line, and spirituality as a separate developmental line itself—definitely show development, by definition. These developmental aspects of spirituality have been investigated by researchers from James Fowler to Daniel P. Brown, and their empirically based research needs to be honored and included in any truly integral model of spirituality. But the other two aspects of spirituality—altered states and attitude—do not necessarily show development, do not generally unfold in stages, and yet also represent some very important aspects of spiritual consciousness. The acrimonious argument about stages of spirituality—some say there are stages, some vehemently deny it—is based on a less-than-integral approach to spirituality, because the fact is, both sides of the argument are correct. In chapters 9 and 10, I focus on some of those aspects of spirituality that show stage-like development; in chapter 12, I highlight the importance of altered states and attitude—all of which need to be included in any integral theory of spirituality—and in any integral spiritual practice.

Chapters 4 and 5—"Integral Art and Literary Theory"—were originally published as a single essay (although the last section, beginning with "Take it one step further," was added when the essay was reprinted in this book.) This piece, as I said, is still my favorite of my essays. What it does theoretically can be easily stated: there are now five major theories of art and literary interpretation, and this essay suggests, quite plausibly I believe, that all five of them can be seamlessly integrated in this phase-4 model ("all-quadrant, all-level"). This approach has become known in the field as "holonic semiotics." Its reception in the art and literary world has been slow (although there are signs that this is changing). There are two major, possible reasons for this: one, the theory itself is generally wrong; two, the theory is generally correct, but integral models so threaten the established, narrow, and partial "truths" that they are immediately rejected as too unsettling. The correct answer is, of course, two.

Well, let's assume it is. In some three decades of presenting integral studies, I have found that most disciplines strenuously resist a more integral approach; four disciplines especially do so: ecology, feminism, cultural studies (including art and literary theory), and spirituality. Most ecotheorists deny holonic ecology because it does not absolutize the biosphere. Orthodox feminists are threatened by integral feminism because it distributes academic power more fairly across other disciplines (including science, which is usually demonized as patriarchal). Cultural studies go apoplectic over integral approaches, because the latter challenge the hegemony of the former. And many spiritual approaches are uneasy with integral approaches, which seem to imply that they don't have the only path to truth. Each of those topics is dealt with in the following pages, starting with the Introduction.

This unease, or even anger, at integral approaches is unfortunate, because in every case there is an integral version of the discipline that is threatened. For example, chapter 8 explores what a truly integral feminism would look like, an integral approach that has the virtue of integrating a dozen major schools of feminism. Integral ecology is described in *A Brief History of Everything*. Integral cultural studies is outlined in *Boomeritis*. And integral spirituality is elaborated in *One Taste*. In each of these cases, the particular discipline is not denied or rejected, but rather is fulfilled and completed by showing that it is actually much larger than even its advocates had realized. I hope this will become obvious in the following pages.

There is one last aspect of spirituality that I haven't mentioned. I rarely single it out as a separate item, because it is the ground of all of them; the ground, in fact, of all existence, or so countless sages have proclaimed. This aspect of spirituality—which is the essence of spirituality itself—is not a state, not a stage, not an attitude, not a line. It is the ever-present Condition of all conditions and the Nature of all natures and the Essence of all essences. It cannot be reached, attained, or grasped—because it is always already your own condition in this and every moment. You can no more attain this Ground than you can reach your lungs or acquire your feet. As Meister Eckhart said, it is closer to me than I am to myself. This book therefore ends with a chapter devoted to a meditation on this ever-present Spirit, a set of pointing-out instructions designed to help evoke or even awaken this realization in the reader. For it is indeed in the eye of Spirit that we all shall meet, never having lost it, never having found it. And with that primordial recognition, beyond the tears of joy and relief, arises the tacit understanding of who and what you really are, and the deepest desire that all sentient beings may share in this great liberation, which you alone can give.

K.W.
Spring 2001
Boulder, Colorado

What Is the Meaning of "Integral"?

JACK CRITTENDEN

Tony Schwartz, former *New York Times* reporter and author of *What Really Matters: Searching for Wisdom in America*, has called Ken Wilber "the most comprehensive philosophical thinker of our times." I think that is true. In fact, I thought that was true twenty years ago, when I founded *ReVision Journal* in large measure to provide an outlet for the integral vision that Ken was already voicing. I had just finished reading his first book, *The Spectrum of Consciousness*, which he wrote when he was twenty-three. The boy wonder was living in Lincoln, Nebraska, washing dishes, meditating, and writing a book a year. *Main Currents in Modern Thought*, which published his first essay, was just about to go out of business, and it was my desire to keep alive the integrative focus and spirit that that journal represented. This, combined with my desire to work with Ken in doing so, prompted me to drag him into the publishing business. We were both about twenty-seven at the time, and within a year or two we had *ReVision* up and running, based very much on the integral vision that we both shared and that Ken was already articulating in a powerful way.

But it is exactly the comprehensive and integral nature of Wilber's vision that is the key to the sometimes extreme reactions that his work elicits. Take, for example, his recent *Sex, Ecology, Spirituality*. The book certainly has its fans. Michael Murphy maintains that, along with Aurobindo's *Life Divine*, Heidegger's *Being and Time*, and Whitehead's *Process and Reality*, Wilber's *Sex, Ecology, Spirituality* is one of the four great books of this century. Dr. Larry Dossey proclaims it "one of the most significant books ever published," while Roger Walsh compares its scope to Hegel and Aurobindo. The most perspicuous reader of the bunch, invoking Alasdair MacIntyre's well-known choice between Aristotle and Nietzsche, claims that no, the modern world actually has three choices: Aristotle, Nietzsche, or Wilber.

The book's detractors, about some of whom you read in the following pages, are no less numerous, vocal, or determined. Feminists argue X; Jungians say Y; deconstructionists, always irritated and amazed at being outcontextualized, say Z—not to mention the generic reactions of deep ecologists, the mythopoetic movement, empiricists, behaviorists, Gnostics, neopagans, premodernists, astrologers—to name a few. Most critics have taken umbrage at Wilber's attacks on their own particular field, while they condone or concede the brilliance of his attacks on other fields. Nobody, however, has yet presented a coherent critique of Wilber's *overall* approach. The collective outrage, as it were, is astonishing, but the criticism has been little but nitpicking.

I want to focus on what is actually involved in this debate. Because, make no mistake, if Wilber's approach is more or less accurate, it does nothing less than offer a coherent integration of virtually every field of human knowledge.

Wilber's approach is the opposite of eclecticism. He has provided a coherent and consistent vision that seamlessly weaves together truth-claims from such fields as physics and biology; the ecosciences; chaos theory and the systems sciences; medicine, neurophysiology, biochemistry; art, poetry, and aesthetics in general; developmental psychology and a spectrum of psychotherapeutic endeavors, from Freud to Jung to Piaget; the Great Chain theorists from Plato and Plotinus in the West to Shankara and Nagarjuna in the East; the modernists from Descartes and Locke to Kant; the Idealists from Schelling to Hegel; the postmodernists from Foucault and Derrida to Taylor and Habermas; the major hermeneutic tradition, Dilthey to Heidegger to Gadamer; the social systems theorists from Comte and Marx to Parsons and Luhmann; the contemplative and mystical schools of the great meditative traditions, East and West, in the world's major religious traditions. All of this is just a sampling. Is it any wonder, then, that those who focus narrowly on one particular field might take offense when that field is not presented as the linchpin of the Kosmos?

In other words, to the critics the stakes are enormous, and it is not choosing sides at this point if I suggest that the critics who have focused on their pet points in Wilber's method are attacking a particular tree in the forest of his presentation. But if we look instead at the forest, and if his approach is generally valid, it honors and incorporates more truth than any other system in history.

How so? What is his actual method? In working with any field, Wilber simply backs up to a level of abstraction at which the various conflicting approaches actually agree with one another. Take, for example, the world's great religious traditions: Do they all agree that Jesus is God? No. So we must jettison that. Do they all agree that there is a God? That depends on the meaning of "God." Do they all agree on God, if by "God" we mean a Spirit that is in many ways *unqualifiable*, from the Buddhists' Emptiness to the Jewish mystery of the Divine? Yes, that works as a generalization—what Wilber calls an "orienting generalization" or "sturdy conclusion."

Wilber likewise approaches all the other fields of human knowledge: art to poetry, empiricism to hermeneutics, psychoanalysis to meditation, evolutionary theory to idealism. In every case he assembles a series of sturdy and reliable, not to say irrefutable, orienting generalizations. He is not worried, nor should his readers be, about whether *other* fields would accept the conclusions of any given field; in short, don't worry, for example, if empiricist conclusions do not match religious conclusions. Instead, simply assemble all the orienting conclusions as if each field had incredibly important truths to tell us. This is exactly Wilber's first step in his integrative method—a type of phenomenology of all human knowledge conducted at the level of orienting generalizations. In other words, assemble all of the truths that each field believes it has to offer humanity. For the moment, simply assume they are indeed true.

Wilber then arranges these truths into chains or networks of interlocking conclusions. At this point Wilber veers sharply from a method of mere eclecticism and into a systematic vision. For the second step in Wilber's method is to take all of the truths or orienting generalizations assembled in the first step and then pose this question: What coherent system would in fact *incorporate the greatest number of these truths*?

The system presented in *Sex, Ecology, Spirituality* (and clearly and simply summarized in the following pages) is, Wilber claims, the system that incorporates the greatest number of orienting generalizations from the greatest number of fields of human inquiry. Thus, if it holds up,

Wilber's vision incorporates and honors, it integrates, more truth than any other system in history.

The general idea is straightforward. It is not which theorist is right and which is wrong. His idea is that everyone is basically right, and he wants to figure out how that can be so. "I don't believe," Wilber says, "that any human mind is capable of 100 percent error. So instead of asking which approach is right and which is wrong, we assume each approach is true but partial, and then try to figure out how to fit these partial truths together, how to integrate them—not how to pick one and get rid of the others."

The third step in Wilber's overall approach is the development of a new type of *critical theory*. Once Wilber has the overall scheme that incorporates the greatest number of orienting generalizations, he then uses that scheme to criticize the partiality of narrower approaches, even though he has included the basic truths from those approaches. He criticizes not their truths, but their partial nature.

In his integral vision, therefore, is a clue to both of the extreme reactions to Wilber's work—that is, to the claims that it is some of the most significant ever published as well as to the chorus of angry indignation and attack. The angry criticisms are coming, almost without exception, from theorists who feel that their own field is the only true field, that their own method is the only valid method. Wilber has not been believably criticized for misunderstanding or misrepresenting any of the fields of knowledge that he includes; he is attacked, instead, for including fields that a particular critic does not believe are important or for goring that critic's own ox (no offense to vegetarians). Freudians have never said that Wilber fails to understand Freud; they say that he shouldn't include mysticism. Structuralists and poststructuralists have never said that Wilber fails to understand their fields; they say that he shouldn't include all those nasty other fields. And so forth. The attack always has the same form: How dare you say my field isn't the only true field!

Regardless of what is decided, the stakes, as I said, are enormous. I asked Wilber how he himself thought of his work. "I'd like to think of it as one of the first believable world philosophies, a genuine embrace of East and West, North and South." Which is interesting, inasmuch as Huston Smith (author of *The World's Religions* and subject of Bill Moyers's highly acclaimed television series *The Wisdom of Faith*) recently stated, "No one—not even Jung—has done as much as Wilber to open Western psychology to the durable insights of the world's wisdom traditions. Slowly but surely, book by book, Ken Wilber is laying the foundations for a genuine East/West integration."

At the same time, Ken adds, "People shouldn't take it too seriously. It's just orienting generalizations. It leaves all the details to be filled in any way you like." In short, Wilber is not offering a conceptual straightjacket. Indeed, it is just the opposite: "I hope I'm showing that there is more room in the Kosmos than you might have suspected."

There isn't much room, however, for those who want to preserve their fiefdoms by narrowing the Kosmos to one particular field—to wit, their own—while ignoring the truths from other fields. "You can't honor various methods and fields," Wilber adds, "without showing how they fit together. That is how to make a genuine world philosophy." Wilber is showing exactly that "fit." Otherwise, as he says, we have heaps, not wholes, and we really aren't honoring anything.

Aristotle commented that no person could judge the value of his or her life until the end of that life, that no one could determine whether he or she had led a virtuous life except by considering that life as a whole. We, of course, know the difficulty of grasping the whole, let alone of evaluating it, especially when considering, as Wilber emphasizes, that one whole is always also a part of some greater whole. We know the ardor, and often the trauma, therefore, of trying to see how the pieces of our individual lives fit together; what they amount to; and to what, and to whom, the parts are connected.

Yet Wilber is helping us with exactly that task; he is giving us a pattern that connects all of life, of the Kosmos, of Spirit. His work amounts to a guide to the secrets of life—biological, social, cultural, and spiritual life. As you will see amply displayed in the following pages, he has drawn us a detailed map, an integral vision for the modern and postmodern world, a vision that unites the best of ancient wisdom with the best of modern knowledge. Through his truly extraordinary work he gives us encouragement to continue our own work—the life journey to wholeness that none of us can avoid but that until this integral vision few could fully comprehend.

On God and Politics

THE MOST PRESSING political issue of the day, both in America and abroad, is a way to integrate the tradition of liberalism with a genuine spirituality.

Never in history have these two strands of human striving been woven together in any sort of acceptable fashion. In fact, modern liberalism (and the general movement of the European Enlightenment) came into being in large measure precisely as a force against traditional religion. Voltaire's battle cry—"Remember the cruelties!"—rang out across the continent: remember the cruelties inflicted on men and women in the name of God, and have done with those brutalities, and that God, once and for all.

This left religion, for the most part, in the hands of the conservatives. And thus, down to today, we are saddled with two heavily armed camps, each of which profoundly distrusts the other.

In one camp we have the liberals, who champion individual rights and freedoms against the tyranny of the collective, and who therefore are deeply suspicious of any and all religious movements, precisely because the latter are always ready to impose their beliefs on others, and tell you what you must do in order to save your soul. Enlightened liberalism historically came into existence to fight such religious tyranny, and it retains deep in its heart a profound distrust—amounting at times to hatred—of all things religious and spiritual, of anything vaguely divine.

Liberals have therefore tended to replace salvation by God with salvation by economics. True liberation and freedom could be found, not in some pie-in-the-sky afterlife (or any other opiate of the masses), but rather in real gains on the real earth, starting with material and economic necessities. "Progressive" and "liberal" have often been used synonymously, precisely because progress in actual social conditions—economic, material, political freedoms—defined the very heart of liberalism.

In the place of communal tyranny, liberalism has substituted what we might call "universal individualism," the call that all individuals, regardless of race, gender, color, or creed, should be treated impartially, with fairness and equal justice. Individuals set loose from communal tyranny to pursue economic and political freedoms: one of the clarion calls of liberalism.

Granted that much good has most definitely come from such liberalism. The downside, nonetheless, was that all too often, religious tyranny was simply replaced by economic tyranny, and the God of the almighty dollar replaced the God of the Pope. Your soul could no longer be crushed by God, but it could be crushed by the factory. What was of *ultimate concern* in life ceased to be your relationship to the Divine and centered instead on your relationship to your income. And thus, even in the midst of economic plenty, your soul could slowly starve to death.

In the other camp, we have the conservatives, who are wedded more to a civic humanist tradition that sees the essence of men and women dependent upon communal standards and values, including preeminently religious values. The republican and religious strands tend to be deeply interwoven in most forms of conservatism, so much so that even when conservatives boisterously champion individual rights and "freedom from government," they do so only if those "freedoms" fit their religious tenets.

The emphasis on community and family values allows conservatives to build strong nations—but often at the expense of those who do not share their particular religious orientation. A cultural tyranny is never far from a conservative smile, and liberals recoil in horror from the "love" that conservatives profess for all God's children, because the chilling fact is that if you are not one of their God's children, unpleasant days await you.

In a very simplistic sense, then, there is a "good" and a "tyranny" in both the liberal and conservative orientations, and the ideal situation would apparently be to rescue the good of each while jettisoning their respective tyrannies.

The good of liberalism is its emphasis on individual freedom and its rejection of the herd mentality. But in its zeal to protect individual freedoms, liberalism has tended to deny any communal values—including the religious and spiritual—and replace them with a focus on material and economic measures. In itself that economic focus is not bad; but it further contributes to a liberal atmosphere that allows you to worry about anything but your soul. "Religious" talk in liberal circles is always a little embarrassing. Kant spoke perfectly for the liberal Enlightenment when he said that our relation to God is now such that if someone walked in and caught you on your knees praying, you would be profoundly embarrassed.

In the liberal atmosphere of economic and political freedoms, anything spiritual or religious still tends to be quite embarrassing. I will argue in a moment that that is because we have a mythic and impoverished view of Spirit, but the point is clear enough: liberalism historically came into existence to kill God, and on balance it has succeeded quite admirably, with the result that an "antispirit tyranny" is never far from liberalism.

Can we not find a way to keep the liberal strength (of individual freedoms) and jettison the tyranny of the anti-soul?

The good of conservatism is its realization that, for all the importance of individuals and individual liberties, we are deeply confused if we imagine that individuals are islands unto themselves. Rather, we as individuals are unavoidably set in deep contexts of family, community, and spirit, and we depend for our very existence on these profound contexts and connections. In some ways, then, even as an individual, my own deepest values are dependent, not upon my relation to myself in a self-hugging stance of autonomy, but on my relation to my family, my friends, my community, and my God, and to the extent I deny those deep connections, I not only destroy the fabric of community and set it loose in a riot of hyperindividualism, I also sever the deepest connection of all, that between a human soul and a divine Spirit.

Yes, and just whose God do you mean? the liberal responds. For as undeniably true as all of those conservative points are in the abstract, when it comes to actually practicing a particular religion with a particular moral code, the witch trials historically have never been far behind. The importance of community and spiritual context and connection all too soon degenerate into my community right or wrong, my God right or wrong, my country right or wrong: and if you do not embrace my God, then you go to hell, and I will be more than glad to help you. A cultural tyranny, thinly or thickly disguised, is never far from the conservative agenda.

Can we not find a way to take the conservative strength (particularly its embrace of spirituality) and jettison its cultural tyranny? And can we not find a way to keep the liberal strength (of individual freedoms) and jettison the tyranny of the anti-soul?

In short, can we not find a spiritual liberalism? a spiritual humanism? an orientation that sets the rights of the individual in deeper spiritual contexts that do not deny those rights but ground them? Can a new conception of God, of Spirit, find resonance with the noblest aims of liberalism? Can these two modern enemies—God and liberalism—in any way find a common ground?

I believe, as I said, that there is no more pressing question, of any variety, now facing the modern and postmodern world. Traditional/conservative spirituality alone will continue to divide and fragment the world, simply because, with that agenda, you can unify people only if they convert to your particular God—and whether that God be Jehovah or Allah or Shinto or Shiva matters not in the least: those are the names in which wars are fought.

No, the gains of the liberal Enlightenment need to be firmly retained, but set in the context of a spirituality that profoundly defuses and answers the very real and very accurate objections raised by the Enlightenment. It will be a spirituality that rests on, not denies, the Enlightenment. It will be, in other words, a postliberal Spirit, which transcends and includes both liberalism and conservatism. An *integral spirituality*, embracing the best of both and moving forward.

A postliberal God depends, first and foremost, on how we answer the question: *Where do we locate Spirit?* I will return to this topic in the last chapter and discuss it at length; and subsequent books will continue to take up this theme, in even more explicit form. But the general topic of "God and politics" itself rests, I believe, on exactly the type of theoretical issues—and the integral vision—that we will be discussing in the following pages, and this discussion must come first, before the actual political contours can be described with any persuasiveness. Thus, this book will not pursue any further the explicit theme of politics and spirituality, although that is its constant background.

Rather, and more important for the time being, an integral orientation is, in the following chapters, brought to bear on such topics as psychology, philosophy, anthropology, and art. I have chosen the word *integral* to represent this overall approach because integral means integrative, inclusive, comprehensive, balanced. The idea is to apply this integral orientation to the various fields of human knowledge and endeavors, including the integration of science and spirituality. This integral approach deeply alters our conceptions of psychology and the human mind; of anthropology and human history; of literature and human meaning; of philosophy and the quest for truth—all of those, I believe, are profoundly altered by an integral approach that seeks to bring together the best of each of these fields in a mutually enriching dialogue. This book is an introduction to just that integral vision.

Over two-thirds of the following material was written specifically for this book and appears here for the first time. Into that new material I have woven a handful of earlier essays that are directly related to the various topics. Even these are reworked, however, so I consider this, for all practical purposes, a new book. Nonetheless, each chapter can still be treated as a relatively independent essay, since each takes a particular topic—from psychology to philosophy to anthropology to art and literature—and examines it from an integral perspective.

The Introduction explains the meaning of the term *integral* and outlines the overall philosophy behind it (as does the Foreword by Jack Crittenden). In some ways, the Introduction is both the most important and most challenging of all the chapters. If you find it a "bit much," then simply read through it lightly and plunge into chapter 1, which deals with integral psychology, and in much more accessible terms. Chapter 2 covers integral anthropology, and chapter 3, integral philosophy. (If, after reading this book, you wish then to reread the Introduction, that might help complete the circle of understanding.)

Chapters 4 and 5 present an integral art and literary theory, and they are perhaps my own favorite chapters. There is probably no crazier— meaning insane—field than "lit crit," overrun as it is with political agendas parading as interpretive methods, congested as it is with constructed deconstruction, postimperial imperialism, antifemale feminists, universal anti-universalists, and other assorted self-contradictions. Art and literary theory might seem a rather narrow, esoteric, and specialized field, but I consider it the absolute litmus test for any integral theory.

ReVision Journal recently carried a three-volume series devoted to my work in general and *Sex, Ecology, Spirituality* in particular. Chapters 6, 7, 8, and 9 are based in part on my response to those essays. If you read these chapters, they need to be read in order, because otherwise they won't make much sense. But they are completely self-explanatory, and there is no need to read the original *ReVision* articles to understand any of the topics. (See note 1 to chapter 8 for my assessment of that series and the book based on it.)

In these chapters, because I was asked to respond in personal ways to specific topics, I have given what amounts to a historical summary of my own work. I discuss some of my major books and the major ideas in them, give the dates and circumstances of their origin, and compare them with other approaches circulating at the time. Ordinarily I would not write in this fashion, since it strikes me as self-involved, but I could find no other way to do it in this particular case. I therefore outline the major "phases" of my work as Wilber-I, Wilber-II, Wilber-III, and Wilber-IV, thus giving a self-serving air of importance to my ramblings.

As always, I recommend that the reader save the endnotes for, and if, a second reading. They are otherwise much too disruptive.

The last two chapters, 11 and 12, are devoted to the issue *Where exactly is Spirit to be located?* Although these chapters do not specifically touch on political issues, the topic itself, once again, is a prolegomenon to exactly that. Because the fact is, *where* we locate Spirit always translates into *political agendas.* Do we locate Spirit in the patriarchy, with the Great God? Do we locate Spirit in the matriarchy, with the Great Goddess? Do we locate Spirit in Gaia? In romantic times past? In a revelation given to a particular people? Or perhaps we locate Spirit in a great Omega point toward which we are all now rushing?

I will suggest that all of those answers are off the mark. Moreover, all of those answers, without exception, will translate into a political tyranny, because they all maintain that there are places that Spirit is, and places it is not—and once you draw that line, the gas chambers stand waiting for those who do not stand on your side of the fence.

A liberal—liberated and liberating—Spirit lies down none of those roads. *Where we locate Spirit*: this is the great question of our times, is it not? And this is the central question in the search for a post-liberal God.

In the following pages I will try to suggest the one location of Spirit that damages none, embraces all, and announces itself with the simplest of clarity, which leaves no places left untouched by care nor cuts its embrace for a chosen few; neither does it hide its face in the shadows of true believers, nor take up residence on a chosen piece of real estate, but rather looks out from the very person now reading these words, too obvious to ignore, too simple to describe, too easy to believe.

In the eye of Spirit we will all meet, and I will find you there, and you me, and the miracle is that we will find each other at all. And the fact that we do is one of the simplest proofs, no doubt, of God's insistent existence.

K.W.
Boulder, Colorado
Spring 1996

THE EYE OF SPIRIT

An Integral Vision

THE GOOD, THE TRUE,
AND THE BEAUTIFUL

To understand the whole, it is necessary to understand the parts. To understand the parts, it is necessary to understand the whole. Such is the circle of understanding.

We move from part to whole and back again, and in that dance of comprehension, in that amazing circle of understanding, we come alive to meaning, to value, and to vision: the very circle of understanding guides our way, weaving together the pieces, healing the fractures, mending the torn and tortured fragments, lighting the way ahead—this extraordinary movement from part to whole and back again, with healing the hallmark of each and every step, and grace the tender reward.

This introductory chapter is a short survey of the whole—the whole of this book, that is. As such, some of it might not make total sense until all the parts—the succeeding chapters—unfold. But starting in chapter 1, the parts are carefully laid out, simply and clearly, and the circle of understanding will, I believe, begin to come alive, and the integral vision clearly shine forth.

Thus, if this introductory survey is a "bit much," simply read it lightly and then jump into chapter 1. As you continue to read, I believe the integral vision will come upon you slowly but surely, carefully but fiercely, deliberately but radiantly, so that you and I will find ourselves sharing in the same circle of under-

standing, abiding in the eye of Spirit, dancing in the freedom of the whole, expressed in all its parts.

THE BIG BANG has made idealists out of almost anybody who thinks. First there was nothing, and then in less than a nanosecond the material universe blew into existence. These early material processes were apparently obeying mathematical laws that themselves, in some sense, existed prior to the Big Bang, since they appear to be operative from the very beginning. Of the two great and general philosophical orientations that have always been available to thoughtful men and women—namely, materialism and idealism—it appears that, whatever else the Big Bang did, it dealt something of a lethal blow to materialism.

But this idealistic trend in modern physics goes back at least to the twin revolutions of relativity and quantum theory. In fact, of the dozen or so pioneers in these early revolutions—individuals such as Albert Einstein, Werner Heisenberg, Erwin Schroedinger, Louis de Broglie, Max Planck, Wolfgang Pauli, Sir Arthur Eddington—the vast majority of them were idealists or transcendentalists of one variety or another. And I mean that in a rather strict sense. From de Broglie's assertion that "the mechanism demands a mysticism" to Einstein's Spinozist pantheism, from Schroedinger's Vedanta idealism to Heisenberg's Platonic archetypes: these pioneering physicists were united in the belief that the universe simply does not make sense—and cannot satisfactorily be explained—without the inclusion, in some profound way, of mind or consciousness itself. "The universe begins to look more like a great thought than a great machine," as Sir James Jeans summarized the available evidence. And, using words that few of these pioneering physicists would object to, Sir James pointed out that it looks more and more certain that the only way to explain the universe is to maintain that it exists "in the mind of some eternal spirit."[1]

It's interesting that "mental health" has always been defined as, in some basic sense, being "in touch" with reality. But what if we look to the very hardest of the sciences in order to determine the nature of this bedrock reality—the reality that we are supposed to be in touch with—and we are rudely told that reality actually exists "in the mind of some eternal spirit"? What then? Does mental health mean being directly in touch with the mind of some eternal spirit? And if we don't believe these physicists as to the nature of ultimate reality, then whom are we to believe? If sanity is the goal, then exactly what reality are we supposed to be in touch with?

THE GHOST IN THE MACHINE

One of the great problems with this "spiritual" line of reasoning is that, unless one is a mathematical physicist wrestling daily with these issues, the conclusions sound too tenuous, too speculative, too "far-out" and even spooky. Not to mention the fact that all too many theologians, Eastern as well as Western, have used the stunning loopholes in the scientific account of nature to shove their version of God into the limelight.

Which is why most modern working scientists, physicians, psychologists, and psychiatrists go on about their business without much of this strange "idealistic speculation" clouding their horizons. From cognitive behaviorism to artificial intelligence, from psychological connectionism to biological psychiatry—most researchers have simply remained very close to a materialistic explanation of mind, psyche, and consciousness. That is, the fundamental reality is assumed to be the material or physical or sensorimotor world, and mind is therefore believed to be nothing much more than the sum total of representations or reflections of that empirical world. The brain itself is said to be a biomaterial information processor, explainable in scientific and objective terms, and the information it processes consists of nothing but *representations* of the *empirical* world ("no computation without representation"). A material and objective brain simply processes a material and objective world, and the subjective domain of consciousness is, at best, an epiphenomenon generated in the wake of the physiological fireworks. The mind remains, hauntingly, the ghost in the machine. And whether that machine be computer or biomaterial processor or servomechanism matters not the least. The plaintive call of the dead and ghostly mind echoes down the imposing corridors of today's scientific research.

Typical of these objectivist approaches is Daniel Dennett's widely esteemed *Consciousness Explained*, which, others have less charitably pointed out, might better have been entitled *Consciousness Explained Away*. In all of these approaches, objective representations are sent scurrying through *connectionist networks*, and the only item that differs in most of these accounts is the exact nature of the objective network through which information bits hustle in their appointed rounds of generating the illusion of consciousness. All of these accounts—quite apart from certain undeniably important contributions—are nonetheless, in the final analysis, attempts by consciousness to deny the existence of consciousness, which is an extraordinary amount of causal activity for what after all is supposed to be an ineffectual vapor, a ghostly nothingness.

But say what we will, these empirical and objectivist accounts—analog and digital bits scurrying through information networks, or neurotransmitters hustling between dendritic pathways—are not how we *actually experience* our own interior consciousness. For when you and I introspect, we find a different world, a world not of bites and bits and digital specs, but a world of images and desires, hungers and pains, thoughts and ideas, wishes and wants, intentions and hesitations, hopes and fears. And we know these interior data in an immediate and direct fashion: they are simply given to us, they are simply there, they simply show up, and we witness them to the extent we care to. These interior data might indeed be part of extensive chains of mediated events—that is very likely true—but at the moment of introspection, that doesn't matter in the least: my interior states are simply given to awareness, immediately, whenever I take the time to look.

And thus, even if we attempt to agree with the cognitivists and functionalists and behaviorists, even if we attempt to think of consciousness as nothing but information bits hopping through neuronal networks, nonetheless that *idea itself* is known to me only in an interior and direct apprehension. I experience that idea in an interior and immediate way; at no point do I actually experience anything that even remotely looks like an information bit dashing through a connectionist pathway. That is simply a concept, and I know that concept, as I know all concepts, in an interior and conscious apprehension. The objectivist approach to experience and consciousness, in other words, cannot even account for its own experience and consciousness: cannot account for the fact that digital bits are experienced, not as digital bits, but as hopes and fears.

INTERIOR AND EXTERIOR

In short, my interior and subjective experience is given to me in terms that simply do not match the objectivistic and empirical terms of functionalism or cognitivism or neuronal connectionism. My *subjective* and interior world, known by many names—consciousness, awareness, mind, psyche, qualia, idea, idealism—definitely appears to be at odds with my *objective* and exterior description of the world, also known by many names—material, biophysical, brain, nature, empirical, materialism. Inside vs. outside, interior vs. exterior, mind vs. brain, subjective vs. objective, idealism vs. materialism, introspection vs. positivism, hermeneutics vs. empiricism. . . .

Small wonder that, almost from the inception of the human knowledge quest, theorists have generally fallen into these two rather different and apparently conflicting approaches to knowledge—interior vs. exterior. From psychology to theology, from philosophy to metaphysics, from anthropology to sociology, the human knowledge quest has almost universally consisted of these two broad paths.

(And, as we will soon see, one of the main tasks of an *integral* approach is to honor and incorporate both of these general paths, and to explain how both can be *equally* significant and important in the understanding of human consciousness and behavior.)

On the one hand are those paths that start with objective, empirical, and often quantifiable observables. These overall approaches—let us call them "exterior" or "naturalistic" or "empiric-analytic"—take the physical or empirical world as most fundamental, and all theorizing must then be carefully tied to, or anchored in, empirical observables. In *psychology*, this is classical behaviorism, and more recently, cognitive behaviorism (cognitive structures are granted reality only to the extent they manifest in observable behavior). In *sociology*, this is classical positivism (as with the founder of sociology itself, Auguste Comte); but also the extremely influential structural-functionalism and systems theory (from Talcott Parsons to Niklas Luhmann to Jeffrey Alexander), where cultural productions are taken to be significant to the extent that they are aspects of an objective social action system. And even in *theology* and *metaphysics*, this naturalistic approach starts from certain empirical and material givens, and then attempts to *deduce* the existence of spirit on the basis of empirical realities (the argument from design, for example).

Arrayed against these naturalistic and empirical approaches are those that start with the immediacy of consciousness itself—let us call them the "interior" or the "introspection and interpretation" approaches. These approaches do not deny the importance of empirical or objectivist data, but they point out, as William James did, that the definition of the word "data" is "direct experience," and the only genuinely direct experience each of us has is his or her own immediate and interior experience. The primordial data, in other words, is that of consciousness, of intentionality, of immediate lived awareness, and all else, from the existence of electrons to the existence of neuronal pathways, are deductions away from immediate lived awareness. These secondary deductions may be very true and very important, but they are, and will always remain, secondary and derivative to the primary fact of immediate experience.

Thus, in *psychology*, where the objectivist approach produces varieties of behaviorism, the subjectivist approach shows up in the various schools of depth psychology, such as psychoanalysis, Jungian, Gestalt, phenomenological-existential, and humanistic—not to mention the vast number of contemplative and meditative psychologies, East and West alike. All of these traditions take, as their starting point, immediately apprehended interior states and direct experiential realities, and they anchor their theories in those immediate data.

These schools are thus interested not so much in *behavior* as in the *meaning* and *interpretation* of psychological symbols and symptoms and signs. Freud's first great book says it all: *The Interpretation of Dreams*. Dreams are an interior and symbolic production. But all *symbols* must be *interpreted*. What is the *meaning* of *Hamlet*? of *War and Peace*? of your dreams? of your life? And the introspective and interpretive schools of psychology are attempts to help men and women interpret their interiors more accurately and more authentically, and thus to gain an understanding and a meaning for their actions, their symptoms, their distresses, their dreams, their lives.

In *sociology*, the subjectivist approach shows up in the immensely influential schools of hermeneutics and interpretive sociology (hermeneutics is the art and science of interpretation). And once again, in contrast to the objectivist approaches, which are interested in *explaining* empirical behavior, the interpretive approaches in sociology are interested in *understanding* symbolic productions. Not "How does it *work*?" but "What does it *mean*?"

Take the Hopi Rain Dance, for example. A typical objective functionalist approach attempts to explain the existence of the Dance by seeing it as a necessary aspect of the integration of the social action system. The Dance, in other words, is performing a behavioral function in the social system as a whole, and this function—which is generally unknown to the natives—is said to be the preservation of the autopoietic self-maintenance of the social action system (e.g., Parsons).

The hermeneutic approach to sociology, on the other hand, seeks instead to take the view of the cultural native and to understand the Dance *from within*, as it were, in a sympathetic stance of mutual understanding. And what the interpretive sociologist (as "participant observer") finds is that the Dance is a way to both honor Nature and sympathetically influence Nature. The interpretive sociologist thus concludes that, phenomenologically, the Dance is a pattern of connecting with a realm felt to be sacred. (Recent examples of hermeneutic sociology and anthropology include such influential theorists as Charles Taylor, Clifford Geertz, Mary Douglas; they often trace part of their lineage to Heidegger's hermeneutic ontology and Hans-Georg Gadamer's hermeneutic philosophy, and further back to such pioneers as Wilhelm Dilthey and Friedrich Schleiermacher.)

In *theology* and *metaphysics*, the exterior and interior approaches likewise tend to diverge sharply. The objectivist approach starts with certain empirical and material facts, and attempts to deduce the existence of transcendental realities from those facts. Saint Thomas Aquinas takes this approach when he gives most of his various arguments for the existence of God. He starts from certain natural facts and then attempts to show that these facts demand an Author, as it were. And right down to today, many physicists and mathematicians use the "argument from design" to conclude that there must be some sort of Designer. This approach includes the recent (and quite popular) Anthropic Principle, which maintains that, because the existence of humans is incalculably improbable, and yet they exist, then the universe simply must have been following a hidden design from the start.

The subjective and introspective approach, on the other hand, does not attempt to prove the existence of Spirit by deduction from empirical or natural events, but rather turns the light of consciousness directly onto the interior domain itself—the only domain of direct data—and looks for Spirit in the disclosures of that data. Meditation and contemplation become the paradigm, the exemplar, the actual practice upon which all theorizing must be based. The God within, not the God without, becomes the beacon call. (In the West, this is the path laid out preeminently by Plotinus and Saint Augustine, which is why the great and enduring theological tension in the West has been between Augustine and Aquinas.)

In *philosophy* itself this is, of course, the colossal divide between the modern Anglo-Saxon and Continental approaches, a difference which both camps happily announce (while just as happily denouncing each other). The typical Anglo-Saxon (British and American) approach is empiric-analytic, begun principally by John Locke and David Hume, but made most famous in that Cambridge triumvirate of G. E. Moore, Bertrand Russell, and (early) Ludwig Wittgenstein. "We make pictures of (empirical) facts" announces Wittgenstein's *Tractatus*, and the aim of all genuine philosophy is the analysis and clarification of these empirical pictures of the empirical world. No empirical pictures, no genuine philosophy.

Which always struck the great Continental philosophers as impossibly naive, shallow, and even primitive. Beginning most notably with Immanuel Kant—and running, in various ways and different guises, through Schelling, Hegel, Nietzsche, Schopenhauer, Heidegger, Derrida, and Foucault—a dramatically different theme was announced: the so-called "empirical" world is in many important ways not just a *perception* but an *interpretation*.

In other words, the allegedly simple "empirical" and "objective" world is not simply lying around "out there" waiting for all and sundry to see. Rather, the "objective" world is actually set in subjective and intersubjective contexts and backgrounds that in many ways govern what is seen, and what *can* be seen, in that "empirical" world. Thus, genuine philosophy, they would all maintain in their various ways, is not merely a matter of making pictures of the objective world, but rather of investigating the structures in the subject that allow the making of the pictures in the first place. Because, put bluntly, the mapmaker's fingerprints are all over the maps he makes. And thus the secret to the universe is not just in the objective maps but in the subjective mapmaker.

The fact that both of these approaches—the exterior and the interior, the objectivist and the subjectivist—have aggressively and persistently existed in virtually all fields of human knowledge ought to tell us something—ought to tell us, that is, that both of these approaches are profoundly significant. They both have something of incalculable importance to tell us. And the integral vision is, beginning to end, dedicated to honoring and incorporating both of these profound approaches in the human knowledge quest.

To Honor These Truths: An Integral Approach

If we look at all the examples that I just gave of the different types of approaches to the knowledge quest, we will find that they actually fall into not just two but four large camps. Because both the *interior* and the *exterior* approaches can be subdivided into *individual* and *collective*.

In other words, any phenomenon can be approached in an interior and exterior fashion, and also as an individual and as a member of a collective. And there are, already in existence, major and quite influential schools in each of those four large camps. I have included a table (see figure 1) with some well-known theorists in each of these four camps. The Upper Left is the interior of the individual (e.g., Freud). The Upper Right is the exterior of the individual (e.g., behaviorism). The Lower Left is the interior of the collective (e.g., the shared cultural values and worldviews explored by interpretive sociology). And the Lower Right is the exterior of the collective (e.g., the objective social action system studied by systems theory).

As an example covering all four of these domains, let us take a single thought, say the thought of going to the grocery store. When I have that thought, what I actually experience is the thought itself, the interior

	LEFT-HAND PATHS	RIGHT-HAND PATHS
	· Interpretive	· Monological
	· Hermeneutic	· Empirical, positivistic
	· Consciousness	· Material form
INDIVIDUAL	Freud C. G. Jung Piaget Aurobindo Plotinus Gautama Buddha	B. F. Skinner John Watson John Locke Empiricism Behaviorism Physics, biology, neurology, etc.
COLLECTIVE	Thomas Kuhn Wilhelm Dilthey Jean Gebser Max Weber Hans-Georg Gadamer	Systems Theory Talcott Parsons Auguste Comte Karl Marx Gerhard Lenski

FIGURE 1

thought and its meaning—the symbols, the images, the idea of going to the grocery store. That's the Upper Left, the interior of the individual.

While I am having this thought, there are, of course, correlative changes occurring in my brain—dopamine increases, acetylcholine jumps the synapses, beta brainwaves increase, or whatnot. Those are observable behaviors in my brain. They can be empirically observed. And that's the Upper Right.

Notice that, even though my brain is "inside" my organism, it is still not part of my actual interior awareness. In fact, I can't even see my brain without cutting open my skull and getting a mirror. My brain is an objective, physical, biomaterial organ, known in an objective and empirical manner (Upper Right). But I know my mind, my consciousness, in an immediate and direct and interior fashion (Upper Left). When I experience the thought of going to the grocery store, I do not say, "Wow, what a dopamine day"; rather, I experience the thought in its own terms, with its own contours. The brain is seen objectively, the mind is experienced subjectively. We might eventually find that they are indeed two different aspects of the same thing, or that they are parallel, or dualist, or interactionist, or whatever, but the crucial point for now is that, in any case, neither can be reduced to the other without remainder, because whatever else might be said, they each have a drastically different phenomenology.

To return to the internal thought itself (Upper Left): notice that it only makes sense in terms of my cultural background. If I spoke a different language, the thought would be composed of different symbols and have quite different meanings. If I existed in a primal tribal society a million years ago, I would never even have the thought "going to the grocery store." It might be, "Time to kill the bear." The point is that my thoughts themselves arise in a *cultural background* that gives texture and meaning and context to my individual thoughts, and indeed, I would not even be able to "talk to myself" if I did not exist in a community of individuals who also talk to me.

So the cultural community serves as an *intrinsic background* and *context* to any individual thoughts I might have. My thoughts do not just pop into my head out of nowhere; they pop into my head out of a cultural background, and however much I might move beyond this background, I can never simply escape it altogether, and I could never have developed thoughts in the first place without it. The occasional cases of a "wolf boy"—humans raised in the wild—show that the human brain, left without culture, does not produce linguistic thoughts on its own.

In short, my individual thoughts only exist against a vast background of cultural practices and languages and meanings and contexts, without which I could form virtually no individual thoughts at all. And that's the Lower Left, the interior of the collective, the intersubjective space of shared cultural contexts.

But my culture itself is not simply disembodied, hanging in idealistic midair. It has *material components*, much as my own individual thoughts have material brain components. All *cultural* events have *social* correlates. These concrete social components include types of technology, forces of production (horticultural, agrarian, industrial, etc.), concrete institutions, written codes and patterns, geopolitical locations, and so on. That's the Lower Right, the social action system. And these concrete material components—the actual *social system*—are crucial in helping to determine the types of cultural worldview, within which my own thoughts will arise.

So my supposedly "individual thought" is actually a phenomenon that intrinsically has (at least) these four aspects to it—intentional, behavioral, cultural, and social. And around the holistic circle we go: the social system will have a strong influence on the cultural worldview, which will set limits to the individual thoughts that I can have, which will register in the brain physiology. And we can go around that circle in any direction. They are all interwoven. They are all mutually determining. They all cause, and are caused by, the others, in concentric spheres of contexts within contexts indefinitely.

I am not going to make a long and drawn-out argument for this, but simply take it as plain fact that the persistent existence of these four large camps in the knowledge quest is evidence enough that none of them can be totally reduced to the others. Each approach is giving us, as it were, one corner of the Kosmos. Each is telling us something very important about various aspects of the known world. And none can be reduced to the others without aggressive and violent rupture, distortion, dismissal.

In my opinion, these four large camps of human knowledge exist precisely because these four aspects of human beings are very real, very persistent, very profound. And one of the aims of an integral approach (and what we might call *integral studies* in general) is to honor and incorporate each of these extraordinary domains—intentional, behavioral, cultural, and social.[2]

As we will continue to see, the integral approach is an "all-level, all-quadrant" approach.

The Four Faces of Truth

Each of these "four quadrants," in fact, has its own particular type of truth or type of "validity claim"—the ways in which it goes about accumulating and validating its data and its evidence. I have given a brief summary of these in figure 2. And to say that none of these quadrants can be reduced to the others is to say that none of their respective truths can be dismissed or reduced, either.

Here are some quick examples of the different validity claims or "types of truth," going around the four quadrants in figures 1 and 2.

Truth

The type of truth found in the Upper-Right quadrant is known variously as representational, propositional, or correspondence. In propositional truth, a statement is said to be true if it matches an objective fact. "It is

	INTERIOR Left-Hand Paths	EXTERIOR Right-Hand Paths
	SUBJECTIVE	OBJECTIVE
INDIVIDUAL	*truthfulness* sincerity integrity trustworthiness	*truth* correspondence representation propositional
	I | it	
	we | its	
COLLECTIVE	*justness* cultural fit mutual understanding rightness	*functional fit* systems theory web structural-functionalism social systems mesh
	INTERSUBJECTIVE	INTEROBJECTIVE

FIGURE 2

raining outside" is said to be a *true* statement if it actually matches the facts at that moment. Propositions are tied to single, empirical, objective observables, and if the propositions match, they are said to be true. In other words, if the *map* matches the *territory*, it is said to be a true representation or a true correspondence ("We make pictures of facts"). Most people are quite familiar with this type of truth. It guides much of empirical science, and indeed much of our everyday lives. So common is propositional truth that it is often just called "truth" for short.

Truthfulness

In the Upper-Left quadrant, on the other hand, the question is not, "Is it raining outside?" The question here is, When I tell you it is raining outside, am I telling you the truth or am I lying? Not, does the map match the territory? but can the mapmaker be trusted?

Because here, you see, we are dealing not so much with exterior and observable behavior but with interior states, and the *only* way you and I can get at each other's interiors is by dialogue and interpretation. If I want to actually know, not simply your behavior, but how you are feeling, or what you are thinking, then I must talk to you, and I must interpret what you say. And yet, when you report to me your inner status, you might be lying to me. Moreover, *you might be lying to yourself.*

And with the fact that you might be lying to yourself, we step into the whole realm of depth psychology in general. The validity claim here is not so much whether my statements match exterior facts, but whether I can *truthfully* report on my own inner status.

For, according to virtually all schools of depth psychology, "neurosis" is, in the broadest sense, a case of being out of touch with one's true feelings, or one's actual desires, or one's authentic inner state. At some point in development, most of these schools maintain, the person began to deny, repress, distort, conceal, or otherwise "lie" to himself about his own interior status; he began to *mis*-interpret his subjective condition. And these misinterpretations, these concealments, these fictions, begin to cloud awareness in the symbolic form of painful symptoms, telltale traces of the telltale lie.

And thus for these schools, therapy is first and foremost an attempt to get in touch with—and more accurately and *truthfully interpret*—one's interior states, one's symptoms, symbols, dreams, desires. A more accurate and faithful *interpretation* of the person's distresses helps the person to understand his otherwise baffling symptoms, helps him to see their *meaning.* And thus the person can become less opaque to himself, more transparent and open and undefended.

Thus, according to the schools of depth psychology, the individual's painful symptoms were generated by a misinterpretation, a concealing, a dynamic and forceful hiding, a "lying" about one's interior state; and a more truthful, faithful, and appropriate interpretation opens the depths in an individual in a more meaningful and transparent fashion, thus lessening the painful symptoms. Not so much *objective truth* as *subjective truthfulness*: and there is the validity claim of the Upper-Left quadrant.

(Incidentally, when it comes to therapy, an integral or "all-level, all-quadrant" approach would certainly not neglect the behavioral and pharmacological therapies of the Upper-Right quadrant. We are simply, at the moment, discussing each quadrant in turn, with its distinctive validity claim and type of truth.)

Notice also that, for example, the phenomenology of meditative states depends entirely upon the validity claim of subjective truthfulness, which is a totally different approach from the objective physiology of meditative states. That is, if you are interested in the neurophysiological changes that occur during meditation, you can hook me up to an EEG machine and monitor my brain states, no matter what I say about them. You simply use empirical and objective truth to map my brain physiology; you don't even have to talk to me. The machine will faithfully record what is happening in my brain.

But if you want to know what is actually going on in my awareness, in my mind, then you are going to have to ask me and talk to me—the approach is dialogical and intersubjective, not monological and merely empirical. When the needle jumps on the EEG machine, what am I experiencing? Am I seeing a brilliant interior illumination that seems to carry a compassionate depth and warmth? Or am I thinking of new ways to rob the local liquor store? The EEG machine will not, and cannot, tell you.

And in the quest for this type of interior truth, the validity claim is truthfulness, trustworthiness, sincerity (Upper Left). If I am being insincere in my reports, you will not get an accurate phenomenology of my interior states at all, but only a series of deceptions and concealments. Moreover, if I have already thoroughly *lied to myself*, I will honestly believe I'm telling the truth, and absolutely nothing on the EEG machine will be able to spot this. So much for empirical tests.

Thus, meditative physiology relies on objective data guided by the yardstick of propositional truth, whereas meditative phenomenology relies on subjective data guided by the yardstick of truthfulness; and we can see a striking example of the Upper-Right and Upper-Left approaches to consciousness, with their different but equally important validity claims.

Functional Fit

The two lower quadrants (interior-collective and exterior-collective) deal not merely with the *individual* but with the *collective* or communal. As we saw with the example of the Hopi Rain Dance, the Lower-Right camps approach the communal from an exterior and objective stance, and attempt to explain the status of the individual members in terms of their *functional fit* with the objective whole. That is, this approach attempts, with its validity claim, to situate each and every individual in an objective network that in many ways determines the function of each part. The truth, for these Lower-Right approaches, is found in the objective intermeshing of individual parts, so that the objective, empirical whole—the "total system"—is the primary reality. And it is the objective behavior of the overall social action system, considered from an empirical stance, that forms the yardstick by which truths in this domain are judged. Its validity claim, in other words, is *functional fit*, so that each proposition must be tied to the intermeshing of the total system or network.

We all know this as standard systems theory, in its many guises. And when we hear theories about Gaia (and usually the Goddess), or about global networks and systems, or about "new paradigms" that emphasize "holistic networks," or dynamic processes all interwoven into the great empirical Web of Life—these are all approaches that emphasize the Lower-Right quadrant: observable and empirical processes seamlessly intermeshed in functional fit.

Justness

Where the Lower-Right approaches attempt to explain how objects fit together in a functional whole or total web of empirical processes, the Lower-Left approaches attempt instead to understand how *subjects* fit together in acts of *mutual understanding*.

In other words, if you and I are going to live together, we have to inhabit, not just the same empirical and physical space, but also the same intersubjective space of mutual recognition. We are going to have to fit not just our bodies together in the same objective space, but our subjects together in the same cultural, moral, and ethical space. We are going to have to find ways to recognize and respect the rights of each other and of the community, and these rights cannot be found in objective matter, nor are they simply a case of my own individual sincerity, nor are they a matter of functionally fitting together empirical events: they are rather a matter of fitting our minds together in an intersubjective space that allows each of us to recognize and respect the other. Not necessarily *agree* with each other, but *recognize* each other—the opposite of which, put simply, is war.

We are interested, that is, not only in the truth, not simply in truthfulness, and not merely in functional fit: we are interested in justness, rightness, goodness, and fairness.

This *intersubjective space* (our commonly shared background contexts and worldviews) is a crucial component of the human being, without which our individual subjective identities could not even exist, and without which objective realities could not even be perceived. Moreover, this intersubjective strand develops and unfolds, just as the other quadrants do. (And thus a comprehensive theory of human consciousness and behavior will want to take all of these quadrants—and their development—into careful account. And this, I will argue, is a crucial aspect of integral studies.)

Notice that both of the collective approaches are equally *holistic*, but the social sciences tend to approach the whole from without in an objective or empirical stance, whereas cultural hermeneutics tend to approach the whole from within in an empathetic grasp. The former have a validity claim of functional fit or systems-mesh, an interobjective fit of each and every objective process with each and every other. The latter have a validity claim of cultural fit or mutual recognition, the intersubjective mesh that leads not to objective systems interlinking, but to human beings reaching mutual understanding. In other words, exterior and interior holism.

(It might be obvious that most theorists who call themselves "holistic" are ironically only exterior holists, an imbalance we need not champion. As of yet, there has historically been no "holism" that actually embraces all four quadrants in all their levels, and I will argue that this is one of the central aims of the integral approach.)

THE VALIDITY OF INTEGRAL KNOWLEDGE

The significant point is that each of these four validity claims has its own type of evidence and data, and thus particular assertions within each claim can be *adjudicated*—that is, can be confirmed or denied, justified or rebuffed, validated or rejected. Accordingly, each of these claims is open to the all-important *fallibilist criterion* of genuine knowledge.

We are all familiar with how fallibilism works in empirical sciences: maps and models and pictures that do not match empirical facts can eventually be dislodged by further facts. But the same fallibilism is at work in all of the genuine validity claims, which is precisely why *learning* can occur in all four quadrants: mistakes are dislodged by further evidence in those quadrants.

For example, *Hamlet* is an interpretive, not an empirical, phenomenon, and yet the statement "*Hamlet* is about the joys of war" is a false statement—it is a bad interpretation, it is wrong, and it can be thoroughly *rejected* by the community of those who:

1. perform the *injunction* or the *experiment* (namely, read the play called *Hamlet*);
2. gather the interpretative *data* or apprehensions (study the meaning of the play in light of the total available evidence); and
3. compare this data with others who have completed the experiment (*consensual* validation or rejection by a community of the adequate).

Those three strands of all genuine knowledge accumulation (injunction, data, confirmation) are present in all of the validity claims, which themselves are *anchored* in the very real intentional, behavioral, cultural, and social domains of human beings. In other words, these very real domains ground our quests for truthfulness, truth, justness, and functional fit, each of which proceeds by the checks and balances of injunction, data, and confirmation. (We will return to this topic in chapter 3.)

Thus, the epistemological claims of integral studies are, like any other valid knowledge claims, thoroughly grounded in experiment, data accumulation, and consensual justification.

Fortunately, there is a very easy way to simplify all of this!

I, We, and It

You can see all four of these equally important validity claims or "types of truth" listed in figure 2. And you might also notice that I have written the words "I," "we," "it" (and "its") in the corners of the four quadrants. The reason is that *each of these quadrants is described in a different language.* That is, they each have a different but quite valid phenomenology, and thus each of them is natively described in a distinct language.

Thus, the events and data found in the Upper-Left quadrant are described in "I" language. The events and data of the Lower-Left quadrant are described in "we" language. And both of the Right-Hand quadrants, because they are empirical and exterior, can be described in "it" language. Thus, the four quadrants can be simplified to three basic domains: I, we, and it.

Because none of the quadrants can be reduced to the others, likewise none of these languages can be reduced to the others. Each is vitally important, and forms a crucial part of the universe on the whole—not to mention a vital part of a comprehensive understanding of the psychology and sociology of human beings. Here are just a few of the important ingredients of these three major domains of I, we, and it:

> I (Upper Left)—consciousness, subjectivity, self, and self-expression (including art and aesthetics); truthfulness, sincerity; first-person accounts
>
> We (Lower Left)—ethics and morals, worldviews, common context, culture; intersubjective meaning, mutual understanding, appropriateness, justness; second-person accounts
>
> It (Right Hand)—science and technology, objective nature, empirical forms (including brain and social systems); propositional truth (in both singular and functional fit); third-person accounts

Science—empirical science—deals with objects, with "its," with empirical patterns. Morals and ethics concern "we" and our intersubjective world of mutual understanding and justness. Art and aesthetics concern the beauty in the eye of the beholder, the "I."

And yes, this is essentially Plato's the *Good* (morals, the "we"), the *True* (in the sense of propositional truth, objective truths or "its"), and the *Beautiful* (the aesthetic dimension as perceived by each "I").

These three domains are also Sir Karl Popper's rather famous distinction of three worlds—objective (it), subjective (I), and cultural (we).

Many people, myself included, consider Jürgen Habermas the world's foremost living philosopher, and these three great domains correspond exactly with Habermas's three validity claims: objective truth, subjective sincerity, and intersubjective justness.

Of enormous historical importance, these three domains showed up in Kant's immensely influential trilogy—*The Critique of Pure Reason* (objective science), *The Critique of Practical Reason* (morals), and *The Critique of Judgment* (aesthetic judgment and art).

Even into the spiritual levels of development, these three domains show up as, to give only one example, the Three Jewels of Buddhism, namely: *Buddha*, *Dharma*, and *Sangha*. Buddha is the enlightened mind in each and every sentient being, the I that is no-I, the primordial awareness that shines forth from every interior. Buddha is the "I" or the "eye" of Spirit. Sangha is the community of spiritual practitioners, the "We" of Spirit. And Dharma is the spiritual truth that is realized, the "It" or "isness" or "thusness" or "suchness" of every phenomenon.

Dozens of other examples could be given, but that's the general picture of these great domains of I, we, and it. And this is obviously crucial for integral studies, because any comprehensive theory of human consciousness and behavior will want to honor and incorporate all four quadrants, or simply these three great domains, each possessing a different validity claim and a quite different language. This is simply another example of the pluralistic, multimodal, and multidimensional attitude that is a defining hallmark of an integral approach: all-level, all-quadrant.

FLATLAND

Despite the resiliency of what we might call the Left-Hand approaches of introspection and interpretation and consciousness (approaches that honor the "I" and the "we" domains), nonetheless there has been in the West, for the last three hundred years or so, a profound and aggressive attempt by modern science (and the exclusively Right-Hand approaches) to reduce the entire Kosmos to a bunch of "its." That is, the I and we domains have been almost entirely colonized by the it-domains, by scientific materialism, positivism, behaviorism, empiricism, and objectivistic-exterior approaches in general.

This entire Right-Hand imperialism, which in so many ways has been the hallmark of Western modernity, is known generally as *scientism*, which, as I would define it, is the belief that the entire world can be fully explained in it-language. It is the assumption that all subjective and intersubjective spaces can be reduced, without remainder, to the behavior of objective processes, that human and nonhuman interiors alike can be thoroughly accounted for as holistic systems of dynamically interwoven its.

Gross reductionism we all know about: it is the reduction of all complex entities to material atoms, which is gross indeed. But *subtle reductionism* is all the more widespread, insidious, and damaging. Subtle reductionism simply reduces every event in the Left Hand to its corresponding aspect in the Right Hand. That is, subtle reductionism reduces all "I's" and all "we's" to their corresponding empirical correlates, reduces them to "its." Mind is reduced to brain; praxis is reduced to techne; interiors are reduced to bits of digital its; depth is reduced to endless surfaces roaming a flat and faded system; levels of quality are reduced to levels of quantity; dialogical interpretation is reduced to monological gaze—in short, the multidimensional universe is rudely reduced to flatland.

But precisely because human beings do indeed have these four different aspects—intentional, behavioral, cultural, and social—this "scientific" approach can seem to make a great deal of sense, because every interior event does indeed have an exterior correlate. (Even if I have an out-of-the-body experience, it registers in the empirical brain!) And thus it initially makes all the sense in the world to try to simplify the knowledge quest by allowing only empirical data and objective its.

But when you have finally finished reducing all I's and all we's to mere its, when you have converted all interiors to exteriors, when you have turned all depth into shiny surfaces, then you have perfectly gutted an entire Kosmos. You have completely stripped the universe of all value, meaning, consciousness, depth, and discourse—and delivered it up dried and desiccated, laid out on the marble slab of a monological gaze.

Consciousness indeed becomes the ghost in the machine, precisely because it has just committed suicide.

And thus we end up with Whitehead's famous summary of the modern scientific worldview (of subtle reductionism): "a dull affair, soundless, scentless, colorless; merely the hurrying of material, endlessly, meaninglessly." To which, incidentally, he added: "Thereby, modern philosophy has been ruined."

It doesn't help that this subtle reductionism is often "holistic," because with subtle reductionism, the holism is always of the exterior variety alone: holistic and dynamically interwoven its! Open any textbook on holistic systems theory or the new holistic scientific paradigm, and you will find an endless discussion of chaos theory, cybernetic feedback mechanisms, dissipative structures, complexity theory, global networks, systems interactions—all described in process it-language. You will find nothing substantial on aesthetics, poetry, beauty, goodness, ethical dispositions, intersubjective development, interior illumination, transcendental intuition, ethical impulses, mutual understanding, justness, or meditative phenomenology (so much for being "holistic"). All you will find, in other words, is a monochrome world of interwoven its, without so much as an acknowledgment of the equally important and equally holistic domains of the I and the we, the subjective and intersubjective spaces that allow objective systems to be perceived in the first place.

Thus, systems theory admirably fights gross reductionism, but is itself the prime example of subtle reductionism, of the "it-ism" that has so defined modernity. "Thereby, modern philosophy has been ruined." So has modern psychology and psychiatry and cognitive science, to the extent they continue to reduce all I's and all we's to info-its running through neuronal it-pathways carried by it-neurotransmitters to it-goals. Your presence, your existence, your consciousness is not required. That these are often holistic and systems-oriented approaches is no solace at all: that's simply subtle reductionism at its worst: a flatland web of interwoven its.

But the existence of these objectivistic, empirical, systems it-approaches is not the problem. These approaches accurately and importantly report on the exteriors of various phenomena, and they are indispensable in that regard! I fully support them in that regard. The difficulty is when these approaches attempt to corner the market on truth, and to claim that the empirical it-domain is the only significant domain in existence. It is this aggressive imperialism and colonization of the I and the we domains by the monological it-approaches that we must everywhere resist, and resist in the name of other and equally honorable truths.

And remember: "In the mind of some eternal Spirit" simply gives us fair warning that a world of mere "its" is no world at all. Consciousness and form, subjective and objective, interior and exterior, Purusha and Prakriti, Dharmakaya and Rupakaya, are the warp and woof of a wondrous universe that makes precisely no sense if either is dismissed.

THE PAIN OF DENIAL

In fact, it is fast becoming quite obvious that if any system of thought (from philosophy to sociology to psychology to religion) attempts to ignore or deny any of the four validity claims, then those ignored truths actually *reappear* in the system as an internal and massive self-contradiction.

In other words, if I refuse reality to any of these truths, then that denied quadrant will in fact *sneak into my system*—I will smuggle it into my philosophy—and there it will eat away at my system from within, until it eventually gnaws its way to the surface as a jolting contradiction.

We can go around the quadrants and see what happens to our theories of knowledge if we deny any of the quadrants. This is very important, I think, because not only orthodox but "postmodern" as well as "new paradigm" approaches have often been plagued by many of these lopsided fads, which an integral approach would criticize in the name of wider and more inclusive occasions.

Scientism

As we have seen, empiricists (and positivists and scienticians in general) deny constitutive reality to virtually all Left-Hand dimensions; only the Right Hand is real. All Left-Hand occasions are at best reflections or representations of the sensorimotor world, the world of simple location, the world of its, detected by the human senses or their extensions.

But "empirical objective knowledge" arises only because of, and in the space of, an intersubjective structure that allows the differentiation of subject and object in the first place. In Thomas Kuhn's now-famous formulation, scientific facts are embedded in cultural practices or paradigms. This does *not* deny the objective component of the knowledge; it denies that the knowledge is merely objective or innocently empirical. In other words, in order to *assert* that all truth is "strictly empirical," empiricists have to stand in intersubjective structures that their own theories cannot account for. The linguistic assertion that all valid knowledge is empirical is not itself empirical, and thus in asserting their own position, they contradict themselves; the denied intersubjective quadrant retaliates with a sneak attack! (This intersubjective component of empirical knowledge is the basis of many influential critiques, not just Thomas Kuhn's attack on simple empiricism, but also Piaget's cognitive-structural revolution and Heidegger's notion of the "background"—to name a very few.)

Cultural Constructivism

More recently we have the reverse attempt: to deny any form of objective truth and dissolve it into *cultural constructivism*. (This approach is also called "social constructivism," but the technical meaning is always cultural constructivism.) That is, with the extreme versions of postmodern constructivism, there is an aggressive attempt to reduce all quadrants to the Lower-Left quadrant (i.e., an attempt to reduce all knowledge claims to intersubjective constructions). This backfires immediately and spectacularly. In fact, not even Derrida and Foucault accept this extreme constructivism (although their American followers often claim that they do). Derrida now concedes the existence of transcendental signifieds; without them, he says, we couldn't even translate between various languages. And Foucault's own archaeology is a series of universal constants in human knowing, within which culturally relative variations are constructed.

But extreme constructivists claim that there is no such thing as objective *truth* at all, because our ideas are simply *constructed* according to various *interests*—usually power, but also various "isms" and various ideologies (sexism, racism, speciesism, logocentrism, etc.).

Yet the constructivists themselves claim that their stance is *true*. And this they cannot do without asserting a theory of truth that is not itself distorted by power or ideology. In other words, they will have to acknowledge and admit the Right-Hand aspects of existence that ground correspondence claims of truth, for that is also an important aspect of all knowledge.[3] Instead, they are simply claiming that it is objectively true that there is no objective truth at all.

Aspects of knowledge are indeed intersubjectively constructed; but those constructions are set in networks of subjective, objective, and interobjective realities that *constrain* the construction. We will never, for example, find a shared cultural worldview where apples fall upward or men give birth: so much for arbitrary constructivism.

No wonder that John Searle's most recent book is an aggressive attack on mere constructivism. He calls it *The Construction of Social Reality*, as opposed to "the social construction of reality," the point being that social reality is in part constructed on a given sensorimotor world that is then reflected in correspondence, so that it itself is not socially constructed. His point is that we can't even get to the constructed aspects of reality without also having a foundation in correspondence: both are irreplaceable.

Systems Theory Reductionism

Whereas cultural constructivists attempt to reduce all reality to the Lower Left, systems theory attempts to reduce all reality to the Lower Right. That is, social reductionism attempts to reduce all truth to functional fit, to the dynamic interplay of holistic its. All I's and we's dissolve in the dynamic web of mutually interwoven its.

Of course, that dynamic web is indeed real—it is the Lower-Right quadrant of the Kosmos—but it is a partial truth that, when expanded into a complete "wholism," takes the entire Left Half of the Kosmos with it into oblivion.

In functional fit, all reality is ultimately reduced to Lower-Right terms (the social system), and so all other validity claims (from propositional truth to cultural meaning to personal integrity) are judged ultimately in terms of their capacity to *serve the holistic functioning of the social system*. All qualitative distinctions are thus reduced to terms of expediency and efficiency; nothing is "true," because all that enters the equation is usefulness (i.e., "truth" becomes anything that furthers the autopoietic regime of the self-organizing social system; such theories dissolve their own truth value in the functional fit of that which they describe).

And yet, of course, those of the social theorists, ecoholists, ecofeminists, and deep ecologists who use systems theory want to claim that their approach has a *moral superiority* to the alternatives. But this moral value cannot even be stated, let alone explained, in the terms of their own systems theory, because, in this theory, all existing things and events are equally strands in the total web of life, and so there is simply no way to say that one of them is right and one of them is wrong. Whatever happens is what the total system is actually doing, and we do not and cannot challenge the overall system because we are all equally strands in that web. What looks like evil to us is simply something the overall system is doing, and thus all ethical drives dissolve in the flatland web of dynamically interwoven its.

Of course, many systems theorists immediately attempt to sneak or smuggle moral and normative claims into their theory by saying, in effect: that which furthers the system is good, and that which harms the system is bad. But to even be able to make that claim is to actually step outside of the system in order to comment on it, and this, according to systems theory, is impossible. Thus, to the extent that systems theorists claim to offer a moral or normative direction, to just that extent they have ceased to be systems theorists. They have moved from descriptive it-language to normative I and we language, terms which systems theory does not and cannot comprehend, and terms which therefore have to be smuggled into their overall view. To just that extent, the banished I and we domains reassert themselves as formal contradictions in the flatland and exterior holism of the systems approach.

Systems theory definitely has its important (if limited) place, yet it is now, by virtue of its extensive subtle reductionism, one of the great modern enemies of the I and the we domains, of the individual lifeworld and of cultural richness—what Habermas refers to as "the colonization of the lifeworld by the imperatives of functional systems that externalize their costs on the other . . . a blind compulsion to system maintenance and system expansion."

These approaches have a wonderfully noble intent, which I believe we can all applaud, but somewhere on the way to the global wedding they took a wrong turn and found themselves deep in the flatland of subtle reductionism, which effectively perpetuates exactly the fragmentation they so nobly desire to overcome.[4] Thus, we wish to honor systems theory and its truth, but set in its own much larger context of other and equally honorable truths.

Cultural Relativity

Those theorists who focus exclusively on the Lower-Left or cultural quadrant tend to fall into various types of extreme relativism, which, in denying other quadrants, ends up self-contradictory. Cultural relativists, extreme pluralists, and multiculturalists are all caught in a similar contradiction: The claim is made that all truths are relative, that there are and can be no universal truths.

Unfortunately, that view itself is claiming to be universally true. It is making a series of *strong claims* that it insists are true for *all* cultures (the relative nature of truth, the contextuality of claims, the social relativity of all categories, the historicity of truth, and so on). This view thus claims that there are no universal truths of any sort—except for its own, which are universal and superior in a world where nothing is supposed to be universal or superior at all.

This is yet another attempt to reduce all objective truth to intersubjective agreement, and it suffers the same fate: it cannot assert its own position without contradicting itself. It is maintaining that there are several objectively true things about all cultures—and this is correct, but only if we fully acknowledge some aspect of objective truth. Otherwise, the denied quadrant once again sneaks back into the system and explodes it from within.

Some aspects of culture are most definitely constructed, and some aspects are both relative and historically bound. But many features of the human bodymind show universal commonalities across cultures. The human body everywhere has 206 bones, one heart, two kidneys. And the human mind everywhere has the capacity to produce images, symbols, concepts, and rules. The sturdy conclusion is that the human body and mind cross-culturally share certain *deep features* that, when they appear, are everywhere quite similar, but the *surface features*—the actual manifestations of these common traits—are indeed relative, culturally bound, marked by historicity, and determined contingently. The human body might indeed have 206 bones wherever it appears, but not all cultures use those bones to play baseball.

The integral approach fully acknowledges and honors the richness of cultural diversity in surface features, while also pinpointing the common deep features of the human family: neither monolithic universalism nor incoherent pluralism, but rather a genuinely universal pluralism of commonality-in-difference.

Aesthetics Only

We have recently seen a flurry of merely aesthetic theories of truth: whatever you happen to like, that is the final arbiter of truth. All objective, interobjective, and intersubjective truths are cheerfully reduced to subjective inclinations (all quadrants are reduced to the Upper Left). Personal taste alone is the arbiter of reality. I do my thing, you do yours. Nietzsche is always (incorrectly) accused of advocating this.

Integrating the aesthetic judgment (Upper Left) with truth and justness is certainly important, but a theory of knowledge that is merely aesthetic is simply inarticulate. Not only does it fail to deal with intersubjective goodness and justness, it trashes any objective aspects of any sorts of truths. And once again, as long as this aesthetic theory is totally silent and never utters its own views, it is fine. But as soon as it tries to explain why aesthetics alone works, it will smuggle in the other quadrants and end up contradicting itself. It will claim, at least implicitly, that what it is doing is true, and moreover, *better* than your view, thus sneaking in both objective and intersubjective judgments, where they explode from within, scattering the landscape with performative contradictions.

Conclusion

And so on around the four quadrants. The point is that every human being has a subjective aspect (sincerity, truthfulness), an objective aspect (truth, correspondence), an intersubjective aspect (culturally constructed meaning, justness, appropriateness), and an interobjective aspect (systems and functional fit), and our different knowledge claims are *grounded* in these very real domains. And thus, whenever we attempt to deny any of these insistent domains, we simply end up, sooner or later, smuggling them into our philosophy in a hidden and unacknowledged fashion: the empiricists use interpretation in the very act of denying its importance; the extreme constructivists and relativists use universal truth in order to universally deny its existence; extreme aestheticians use beauty alone to claim moral goodness—and on and on and on. To deny any of these domains is, as it were, to be hoist with our own petard and end up in a severe self-contradiction.

A more integral vision attempts instead to include the moment of truth in each of those approaches—from empiricism to constructivism to relativism to aestheticism—but, in stripping them of their claims to be the only type of truth in existence, releases them from their contradictions—and places them, as it were, into a genuine rainbow coalition.

THE SPECTRUM OF CONSCIOUSNESS

Integral studies in general are dedicated to an "all-level, all-quadrant" view of human consciousness and behavior. But if for the moment we focus on the Upper-Left quadrant—the interior of the individual, the site of consciousness itself—what do we find?

Biological and medical scientists are now in the midst of intensive work on the Human Genome Project, the endeavor to map all of the genes in the entire sequence of human DNA. This spectacular project promises to revolutionize our ideas of human growth, development, disease, and medical treatment, and its completion will surely mark one of the great advances in human knowledge.

Not as well known, but arguably more important, is what might be called the Human Consciousness Project, the endeavor, now well under way, to *map the entire spectrum of the various states of human consciousness* (including, as well, realms of the human unconscious). This Human Consciousness Project, involving hundreds of researchers from around the world, involves a series of multidisciplinary, multicultural, multimodal approaches that together promise an exhaustive mapping of the entire range of consciousness, the entire sequence of the "genes" of awareness, as it were.

These various attempts are rapidly converging on a "master template" of the various stages, structures, and states of consciousness available to men and women. By comparing and contrasting various multicultural approaches—from Zen Buddhism to Western psychoanalysis, from Vedanta Hinduism to existential phenomenology, from Tundra Shamanism to altered states—these approaches are rapidly piecing together a master template—*a spectrum of consciousness*—using the various approaches to fill in any gaps left by the others.

Although many of the specifics are still being intensively researched, the overall evidence for the existence of this spectrum of consciousness is already so significant as to put it largely beyond serious dispute. We will examine this spectrum in more detail in chapter 1. For the moment, we will simply note that this spectrum appears to range from instinctual to egoic to spiritual modes, from prepersonal to personal to transpersonal experiences, from subconscious to self-conscious to superconscious states, from body to mind to spirit itself.

The field that has perhaps most carefully and meticulously studied this extraordinary spectrum of consciousness is the discipline known as *transpersonal psychology*. Transpersonal psychology is sometimes called "the fourth force," after the first three of behavioristic, psychoanalytic, and humanistic schools. The word "transpersonal" itself simply means "personal plus." That is, the transpersonal orientation explicitly and carefully includes all of the facets of personal psychology and psychiatry, but then *adds* those deeper or higher aspects of human experience that transcend the ordinary and the average—experiences that are, in other words, "transpersonal," or "more than the personal," or personal plus. Thus, in the attempt to more fully and accurately reflect the entire range of human experience, transpersonal psychology and psychiatry take, as their basic starting point, the entire spectrum of consciousness.

The integral approach that I am advocating acknowledges and honors this all-inclusive spectrum of consciousness as being perhaps the best available map of the Upper-Left quadrant in general, a map that is the direct result of this extraordinary Human Consciousness Project.

But the integral approach does not stop there. The point, of course, is that *if the entire spectrum of consciousness is acknowledged and taken into account, it will dramatically alter each and every discipline it touches*—from anthropology to ecology, from philosophy to art, from ethics to sociology, from psychology to politics.

This is why we can say that integral studies in general are dedicated to an "all-level, all-quadrant" view of human consciousness and behavior—covering not just all of the quadrants, but all of the various levels and dimensions in each of those quadrants—the entire spectrum of levels in the intentional, behavioral, cultural, and social aspects of human beings.

In the following chapters, we will specifically look at examples of each of those branches of integral studies, including integral psychology (chapters 1, 9, 10), integral anthropology (chapter 2), integral philosophy (chapter 3), integral art and literary theory (chapters 4 and 5), integral feminism (chapter 8), and integral spirituality (chapters 9, 10, 11).

These are the parts that we will attempt to weave into the integral vision as a whole, thus completing, at least for this round, that extraordinary circle of understanding.

THE GREAT WISDOM TRADITIONS

Men and women, as the Christian mystics are fond of saying, have (at least) three eyes of knowing: the eye of flesh, which apprehends physical events; the eye of mind, which apprehends images and desires and concepts and ideas; and the eye of contemplation, which apprehends spiritual experiences and states. And that, of course, is a simplified version of the spectrum of consciousness, reaching from body to mind to spirit.

Indeed, the Upper-Left quadrant has historically been studied as the *Great Chain of Being*, a concept which, according to Arthur Lovejoy, "has been the dominant official philosophy of the larger part of civilized humankind through most of its history." Huston Smith, in his remarkable book *Forgotten Truth*, has demonstrated that all of the world's great wisdom traditions, from Taoism to Vedanta, Zen to Sufism, Neoplatonism to Confucianism, are based on the Great Chain—that is, based on some version of the overall spectrum of consciousness, with its levels of being and knowing.

Some postmodern critics, however, have claimed that the very notion of the Great Chain, since it is hierarchical, is somehow oppressive; it is supposed to be based on unpleasant "ranking" instead of compassionate "linking." But this is a rather unfair complaint. First, the antihierarchical and antiranking critics are themselves engaged in hierarchical judgments of ranking—namely, they claim their view is *better* than the alternatives. In other words, they themselves have a very strong ranking system—it's just hidden and inarticulate (and self-contradictory).

Second, the Great Chain is actually what Arthur Koestler called a *holarchy*: a series of concentric circles or nests, with each senior level *transcending* but *including* its juniors. This is a ranking, to be sure, but a ranking of increasing inclusiveness and embrace, with each senior level including more and more of the world and its inhabitants, so that the upper or spiritual reaches of the spectrum of consciousness are absolutely all-inclusive and all-embracing.

Of course, any hierarchy—including the feminist hierarchy that values "linking" as better than "ranking"—can be put to severe abuse, repressing or marginalizing certain values. But this condemns not hierarchies in general, but merely pathological or dominator hierarchies. As Riane Eisler has reminded us, there is a big difference between actualization hierarchies and dominator hierarchies; and the Great Nest of Being was from its inception a profound actualization holarchy, quite apart from the abuses to which it was occasionally put. (We will return to the Great Nest in chapter 1, and examine its importance more carefully.)

But apart from such abuses, the great wisdom traditions *even at their best* still neglected several crucial items, items that the early investigators of the spectrum of consciousness could not, or at any rate did not, know. Two deficiencies in the wisdom traditions especially deserve mention, because integral studies, to be genuinely integral, must directly and forthrightly address these serious inadequacies.

The first is the recognition that the very earliest stages of human development can play a decisive role in subsequent growth—Freud's pioneering work, for example. The great contemplative traditions excelled in tracing human growth from mental and egoic modes to transmental and spiritual modes, but they were extremely weak in their understanding of the stages leading up to the mental-ego itself. In Jack Engler's memorable phrase, "You have to be somebody before you can be nobody." That is, you must develop a strong and secure ego before you can transcend it; and whereas the great traditions were superb at the latter, they often failed at the former. And a truly "full spectrum" approach to psychiatry and psychology would rigorously embrace both: the move from instinct to ego, as well as from ego to spirit.

Precisely because the spectrum of consciousness develops, modern-day researchers can bring to bear the vast arsenal of developmental research techniques to help elucidate the various developmental lines of consciousness itself. That is, we can now begin to trace the developmental unfolding of such lines as cognition, affect, moral sense, object-relations, self-identity, modes of space and time, motivations, needs, and so on—and not just from pre-egoic to egoic modes, but also from egoic to transegoic modes. This gives integral studies the chance historically to be the first genuinely "full spectrum" model of human growth and development.

Likewise for integral psychotherapy. Precisely because the spectrum of consciousness develops, various "misdevelopments" can occur at any stage of this unfolding. As with any living entity, pathology can occur at any point in growth. Thus, the spectrum of consciousness is also a spectrum of different types of possible pathologies: psychotic, neurotic, cognitive, existential, spiritual. And a "full-spectrum" approach to psychology and psychiatry is devoted to a full range of treatments that address these different types of pathologies (we will return to this topic in chapters 6 and 7).

The second major weakness of the great traditions is that they did not clearly recognize that the various levels of interior consciousness *have correlates in the other quadrants*. In other words, it is not simply, as the great traditions assume, that human beings have different levels—body, mind, soul, and spirit, for example—but *also* that *each* of those levels has four aspects—intentional, behavioral, cultural, and social. This multidimensional grid—not simply "all-level" but "all-level, all-quadrant"—opens the study of human beings in a profound fashion. That, of course, is part of integral studies.

We can now, for example, begin to correlate states of meditative awareness with types of brainwave patterns (without attempting to reduce one to the other). We can monitor physiological shifts that occur with spiritual experience. We can follow the levels of neurotransmitters during psychotherapeutic interventions. We can follow the effects of psychoactive drugs on blood distribution patterns in the brain. We can trace the social modes of production and see the corresponding changes in cultural worldviews. We can follow the historical unfolding of cultural worldviews and plot the status of men and women in each period. We can trace the modes of self that correlate with different modes of techno-economic infrastructure. And so on around the quadrants: not simply "all-level," but "all-level, all-quadrant."

Thus, modern-day integral studies can do something at which the great traditions generally failed: trace the spectrum of consciousness not just in its intentional but also in its behavioral, social, and cultural manifestations, thus highlighting the importance of a multidimensional approach for a truly comprehensive overview of human consciousness and behavior.

Finally, with these broader and more sophisticated tools of behavioral, developmental, and cultural analysis, we will also be able to more clearly spot those areas where the great traditions were all-too-embedded in the social injustices of the day, from sexism to speciesism to militarism to ethnocentrism.

In short, modern-day integral studies have reconnected with the world's great wisdom traditions, honoring and incorporating many of their essential and pioneering insights, while, at the same time, adding new methodologies and techniques previously unavailable. This is multiculturalism in its best and deepest sense, cherishing cultural differences, but set in a truly universal context.

CONCLUSION

An integral approach is dedicated to an all-level, all-quadrant program, honoring the entire spectrum of consciousness, not just in the I-domain, but also in the we and the it domains, thus *integrating* art, morals, and science; self, ethics, and environment; consciousness, culture, and nature; Buddha, Sangha, and Dharma; the beautiful and the good and the true.

In the following chapters, we will see very concrete examples of each of these many facets of the Kosmos, as we attempt to weave them into a blanket of many colors.

And who knows, we might, you and I just might, in the upper reaches of the spectrum of consciousness itself, directly intuit the mind of some eternal Spirit—a Spirit that shines forth in every I and every we and every it, a Spirit that sings as the rain and dances as the wind, a Spirit of which every conversation is the sincerest worship, a Spirit that speaks with your tongue and looks out from your eyes, that touches with these hands and cries out with this voice—and a Spirit that has always whispered lovingly in our ears: Never forget the Good, and never forget the True, and never forget the Beautiful.

The integral vision is the modern and postmodern attempt to honor just that pledge.

1

The Spectrum of Consciousness

INTEGRAL PSYCHOLOGY AND
THE PERENNIAL PHILOSOPHY

Biological and medical scientists are now in the midst of intensive work on the Human Genome Project, the endeavor to map all of the genes in the entire sequence of human DNA. This spectacular project promises to revolutionize our ideas of human growth, development, disease, and medical treatment, and its completion will surely mark one of the great advances in human knowledge.

Not as well known, but arguably more important, is what might be called the Human Consciousness Project, *the endeavor, now well under way, to map the entire spectrum of human consciousness (including, as well, realms of the human unconscious). This Human Consciousness Project, involving hundreds of researchers from around the world, includes a series of multidisciplinary, multicultural, multimodal approaches that together promise an exhaustive mapping of the entire range of consciousness, the entire sequence of the "genes" of awareness, as it were.*

These various attempts are rapidly converging on a "master template" of the various stages, structures, and states of consciousness available to men and women. By comparing and contrasting various multicultural approaches—from Zen Buddhism to Western psychoanalysis, from Vedanta Hinduism to existential phenomenology, from Tundra Shamanism to altered states—these approaches are rapidly piecing together a master template—a spectrum of consciousness—using the various approaches to fill in any gaps left by the others.)

Although many of the specifics are still being intensively researched, the overall evidence for the existence of this spectrum of consciousness is already so significant as to put it largely beyond serious dispute.

(Moreover, in a rather stunning fashion, it has increasingly become obvious that this overall spectrum is quite consistent with the essential core of the world's great wisdom traditions.)

The "master template" that is emerging from this modern research is therefore able to honor and connect with the essence of the world's wisdom traditions, while simultaneously attempting to update and modernize their insights where appropriate. (The goal of an integral approach is thus a judicious blend of ancient wisdom and modern knowledge.)

Let us start with the basics, with those items from the great traditions that seem to have withstood the test of time with flying colors, so much so that they are even making a remarkable comeback in many modern and scientific disciplines.

And they all hinge on this extraordinary spectrum of consciousness.

WHAT IS THE WORLDVIEW that, as Arthur Lovejoy pointed out, "has been the dominant official philosophy of the larger part of civilized humankind through most of its history"? The worldview that "the greater number of the subtler speculative minds and of the great religious teachers [both East and West] have, in their various fashions, been engaged in"? What is the worldview that led Alan Watts to state flatly that "we are hardly aware of the extreme peculiarity of our own position, and find it difficult to realize the plain fact that there has otherwise been a single philosophical consensus of universal extent. It has been held by [men and women] who report the same insights and teach the same essential doctrine whether living today or six thousand years ago, whether from New Mexico in the Far West or from Japan in the Far East."

And why is it of interest to anyone living in today's world?

Known as the "perennial philosophy"—"perennial" precisely because it shows up across cultures and across the ages with many similar features—this worldview has, indeed, formed the core not only of the world's great wisdom traditions, from Christianity to Buddhism to Taoism, but also of many of the greatest philosophers, scientists, and psychologists of both East and West, North and South. So overwhelmingly widespread is the perennial philosophy—the details of which I will explain in a moment—that it is either the single greatest intellectual error ever to appear in humankind's history—an error so colossally widespread as to literally stagger the mind—or it is the single most accurate reflection of reality yet to appear.

Central to the perennial philosophy is the notion of the *Great Chain of Being*. The idea itself is fairly simple. Reality, according to the perennial philosophy, is not one-dimensional; it is not a flatland of uniform substance stretching monotonously before the eye. Rather, reality is composed of several *different* but *continuous* dimensions. Manifest reality, that is, consists of different grades or levels, reaching from the lowest and most dense and least conscious to the highest and most subtle and most conscious. At one end of this continuum of being or spectrum of consciousness is what we in the West would call "matter" or the insentient and the nonconscious, and at the other end is "spirit" or "godhead" or the "superconscious" (which is also said to be the all-pervading ground of the entire sequence, as we will see). Arrayed in between are the other dimensions of being arranged according to their individual degrees of reality (Plato), actuality (Aristotle), inclusiveness (Hegel), consciousness (Aurobindo), clarity (Leibniz), embrace (Plotinus), or knowingness (Garab Dorje).

Sometimes the Great Chain is presented as having just three major levels: matter, mind, and spirit. Other versions give five levels: matter, body, mind, soul, and spirit. Still others give very exhaustive breakdowns of the Great Chain; some of the yogic systems give literally dozens of discrete yet continuous dimensions. For the time being, our simple hierarchy of matter to body to mind to soul to spirit will suffice.

The central claim of the perennial philosophy is that *men and women can grow and develop (or evolve) all the way up the hierarchy to Spirit itself*, therein to realize a "supreme identity" with Godhead—the *ens perfectissimum* toward which all growth and evolution yearns.

But before we get to that, the first thing that we can't help but notice is that the Great Chain is indeed a "hierarchy"—a word that has fallen on very hard times. Originally introduced by the great Christian mystic Saint Dionysius, it essentially meant "governing one's life by spiritual principles" (*hiero-* means sacred or holy, and *-arch* means governance or rule). But it soon became translated into a political/military power play, where "governance by spirit" came to mean "ruled by the Catholic Church"—a spiritual principle mistranslated into a despotism.

But as used by the perennial philosophy—and indeed, as used in modern psychology, evolutionary theory, and systems theory—a hierarchy is simply a ranking of orders of events *according to their holistic capacity.* In any developmental sequence, what is whole at one stage becomes merely a part of a larger whole at the next stage. A letter is part of a whole word, which is part of a whole sentence, which is part of a whole paragraph, and so on. Arthur Koestler coined the term "holon" to refer to that which, being a whole in one context, is a part of a wider whole in another. With reference to the phrase "the bark of a dog," for example, the word "bark" is a whole with reference to its individual letters, but a part with reference to the phrase itself. And the whole (or the context) can determine the meaning and function of a part—the meaning of "bark" is different in the phrases "the bark of a dog" and "the bark of a tree." The whole, in other words, is more than the sum of its parts, and that whole can influence and determine, in many cases, the function of its parts.

Hierarchy, then, is simply an order of increasing holons, representing an increase in wholeness and integrative capacity. This is why hierarchy is so central to systems theory, the theory of wholeness or holism ("wholism"). And it is absolutely central to the perennial philosophy. Each expanding link in the Great Chain of Being represents an increase in unity and wider identities, from the isolated identity of the body through the social and communal identity of the mind to the supreme identity of Spirit, an identity with literally all manifestation. This is why the great hierarchy of being is often drawn as a series of concentric circles or spheres or "nests within nests." As we will see, the Great Chain is actually the Great Nest of Being.

And finally, hierarchy *is* asymmetrical (or a "higher"-archy) because the process does not occur in the reverse. For example, there are first letters, then words, then sentences, then paragraphs, but not vice versa. And that *not vice versa* constitutes an unavoidable hierarchy or ranking or asymmetrical order of increasing wholeness.

All developmental and evolutionary sequences that we are aware of proceed in large measure by hierarchization, or by orders of increasing holism—molecules to cells to organs to organ systems to organisms to societies of organisms, for example. In cognitive development, we find awareness expanding from simple images, which represent only one thing or event, to symbols and concepts which represent whole groups or classes of things and events, to rules which organize and integrate numerous classes and groups into entire networks. In moral development (in both male and female), we find a reasoning that moves from the isolated subject to a group or tribe of related subjects, to an entire network of groups beyond any isolated element. And so on.

These hierarchical networks necessarily unfold in a sequential or stagelike fashion, because you first have to have molecules, *then* cells, *then* organs, *then* complex organisms—they don't all burst on the scene simultaneously. In other words, growth generally occurs in *stages*, and stages, of course, are *ranked* in both a logical and chronological order. The *more holistic* patterns appear *later* in development because they have to await the emergence of the parts that they will then integrate or unify, just as whole sentences emerge only *after* whole words.

And some hierarchies do involve a type of control network—the lower levels (which means, less holistic levels) can influence the upper (or more holistic) levels, through what is known as *upward causation*. But just as important, the higher levels can exert a powerful influence or control on the lower levels—so-called *downward causation*. For example, when you decide to move your arm, and you do so, all the atoms and molecules and cells in your arm move with it—an instance of downward causation.

In any developmental or growth sequence, as a more encompassing stage or holon emerges, it *includes* the capacities and patterns and functions of the previous stage (i.e., of the previous holons), and then adds its own unique (and more encompassing) capacities. In that sense, and that sense only, can the new and more encompassing holon be said to be "higher" or "wider." Whatever the important value of the previous stage, the new stage has *all* of that plus something extra (more integrative capacity, for example), and that "something extra" means "extra value" *relative* to the previous (and less encompassing) stage. This crucial definition of a "higher stage" was first introduced in the West by Aristotle and in the East by Shankara and Lieh-Tzu; it has been central to the perennial philosophy ever since.

Let me give one example. In cognitive and moral development, in both the boy and the girl, the stage of preoperational or preconventional thought is concerned largely with the individual's own point of view ("narcissistic"). The next stage, the operational or conventional stage, still takes account of the individual's own point of view, but *adds* the capacity to take the view of others into account. Nothing is lost; something is added. And so in this sense it is properly said that this stage is higher or wider, meaning more valuable and useful for a wider range of interactions. Conventional thought is *more valuable* than preconventional thought in establishing a balanced moral response (and postconventional is even more valuable, and so on). As Hegel first put it, and as developmentalists have echoed ever since, each stage is adequate and valuable, but each higher stage is more adequate, and, in that sense only, more valuable (which always means, more holistic).

It is for all these reasons that Koestler, after noting that all complex hierarchies are composed of holons, or increasing orders of wholeness, pointed out that the correct word for "hierarchy" is actually *holarchy*. He is absolutely right, and so from now on I will refer to hierarchy in general, and the Great Chain—the Great Nest—in particular, as holarchy.

So that is normal or natural holarchy, the stagelike unfolding of larger networks of increasing wholeness, with the larger or wider wholes being able to exert influence over the lower-order wholes. And as natural, desirable, and unavoidable as that is, you can already start to see how holarchies might turn *pathological*. If the higher levels can exert control over the lower levels, they can also overdominate or even repress and alienate the lower levels. That leads to a whole host of pathological difficulties, in both the individual and society at large.

It is precisely *because* the world is arranged holarchically, precisely because it contains fields within fields within fields, that things can go so profoundly wrong, that a disruption or pathology in one field can reverberate throughout an entire system. And the "cure" for this pathology, in all cases, is essentially the same: rooting out the pathological holons so the holarchy itself can return to harmony. The cure does not consist, as the reductionists maintain, in getting rid of holarchy per se, since, even if that were possible, it would simply result in a uniform, one-dimensional flatland of no value distinctions at all (which is why those critics who toss out hierarchy in general immediately replace it with a new scale of values of their own, i.e., with their own particular hierarchy).

(Rather, the "cure" of any diseased system consists in rooting out any holons that have usurped their position in the overall system by abusing their power of upward or downward causation.) This is exactly the "cure" we see at work in psychoanalysis (shadow holons refuse integration), democratic social revolutions (monarchical or fascist holons oppress the body politic), medical science interventions (cancerous holons invade a benign system), critical social theory (opaque ideology usurps open communication), radical feminist critiques (patriarchal holons dominate the public sphere), and so on. It is not getting rid of holarchy per se, but arresting (and integrating) its arrogant holons.

As I said, all of the world's great wisdom traditions are basically variations of the perennial philosophy, of the Great Holarchy of Being. In his wonderful book *Forgotten Truth*, Huston Smith summarizes the world's major religions in one phrase: "a hierarchy of being and knowing." Chögyam Trungpa Rinpoche pointed out, in *Shambhala: The Sacred Path of the Warrior*, that *the* essential and background idea pervading all of the philosophies of the East, from India to Tibet to China, lying behind everything from Shintoism to Taoism, is "a hierarchy of earth, human, heaven," which he also pointed out is equivalent to "body, mind, spirit." And Coomaraswamy noted that the world's great religions, bar none, "in their different degrees represent a hierarchy of types or levels of consciousness extending from animal to deity, and according to which one and the same individual may function on different occasions."

Which brings us to the most notorious paradox in the perennial philosophy. We have seen that the wisdom traditions subscribe to the notion that reality manifests in levels or dimensions, with each higher dimension being more inclusive and therefore "closer" to the absolute totality of Godhead or Spirit. In this sense, Spirit is the summit of being, the highest rung on the ladder of evolution. But it is also true that Spirit is *the wood out of which the entire ladder and all its rungs are made*. Spirit is the suchness, the isness, the essence of each and every thing that exists.

The first aspect, the highest-rung aspect, is the *transcendental* nature of Spirit—it far surpasses any "worldly" or creaturely or finite things. The entire earth (or even universe) could be destroyed, and Spirit would remain. The second aspect, the wood aspect, is the *immanent* nature of Spirit—Spirit is equally and totally present in all manifest things and events, in nature, in culture, in heaven and on earth, with no partiality. From this angle, no phenomenon whatsoever is closer to Spirit than another, for all are equally "made of" Spirit. Thus, Spirit is *both* the highest *goal* of all development and evolution, and the *ground* of the entire sequence, as present fully at the beginning as at the end. Spirit is prior to this world, but not other to this world.

Failure to take both of those paradoxical aspects of Spirit into account has historically led to some very lopsided (and politically dangerous) views of Spirit. Traditionally, the patriarchal religions have tended to overemphasize the transcendental nature of Spirit, thus condemning earth, nature, body, and woman to an inferior status. Prior to that, the matriarchal religions tended to emphasize the immanent nature of Spirit alone, and the resultant pantheistic worldview equated the finite and created Earth with the infinite and uncreated Spirit. You are free to identify with a finite and limited Earth; you are not free to call it the infinite and unlimited.

Both matriarchal and patriarchal religions, both of these lopsided views of Spirit, have had rather horrible historical consequences, from brutal and large-scale human sacrifice for the fertility of the earth Goddess to wholesale war for God the Father. But in the very midst of these outward distortions, the perennial philosophy (the esoteric or inner core of the wisdom religions) has always avoided any of those dualities— Heaven or Earth, masculine or feminine, infinite or finite, ascetic or celebratory—and centered instead on their union or integration ("nondualism"). And indeed, this union of Heaven and Earth, masculine and feminine, infinite and finite, ascending and descending, wisdom and compassion, was made explicit in the "tantric" teachings of the various wisdom traditions, from Neoplatonism in the West to Vajrayana in the East. And it is this nondual core of the wisdom traditions to which the term "perennial philosophy" most applies.

The point, then, is that if we are to try to think of Spirit in mental terms (which necessarily involves some difficulties), then at least we should remember this transcendent/immanent paradox. Paradox is simply the way nonduality looks to the mental level. Spirit itself is not paradoxical; strictly speaking, it is not characterizable at all.

This applies doubly to hierarchy (holarchy). We have said that when transcendental Spirit manifests itself, it does so in stages or levels—the Great Holarchy of Being. But I'm not saying Spirit or reality itself is hierarchical. Absolute Spirit or reality is not hierarchical. It is not qualifiable at all in mental terms (lower-holon terms)—it is *shunyata*, or *nirguna*, or *apophatic*—unqualifiable, without a trace of specific and limiting characteristics at all. But it manifests itself in steps, in layers, dimensions, sheaths, levels, or grades—whatever term one prefers—and that is holarchy. In Vedanta these are the *koshas*, the sheaths or layers covering Brahman; in Buddhism, these are the eight *vijnanas*, the eight levels of awareness, each of which is a stepped-down or more restricted version of its senior dimension; in Kabbalah these are the *sefirot*, and so on.

The whole point is that these are levels of the manifest world, of *maya*. When maya is not recognized as the play of the Divine, then it is nothing but illusion. Hierarchy is illusion. There are levels of illusion, not levels of reality. But according to the traditions, it is exactly (and only) by understanding the hierarchical nature of samsara that we can in fact climb out of it, a ladder discarded only after having served its extraordinary purpose.)

(We can look now at some of the actual levels or spheres of the holarchy, of the Great Nest of Being, as it appears in the three largest wisdom traditions: Judeo-Christian-Muslim, Buddhism, and Hinduism, although any mature tradition will do.)

(*Let me remind you that these are the levels in the Upper-Left quadrant*, the levels in the spectrum of consciousness itself. We will, in the following chapters, see how this spectrum plays itself out in the other quadrants as well, cultural and social and behavioral—from anthropology to philosophy to art and literature. But for now we are concentrating on the spectrum of consciousness as it appears in the individual human being, the Upper-Left quadrant.)

The Christian terms are the easiest, because most of us are familiar with them: matter, body, mind, soul, and spirit. *Matter* means the physical universe as it appears in our own physical bodies (e.g., those aspects of our existence covered by the laws of physics); and whatever else we might mean by the word "matter," it means in this case the dimension with the least amount of consciousness (some would say no consciousness, and you can take your pick). *Body* in this case means the emotional body, the "animal" body, sex, hunger, vital life force, and so on (e.g., those aspects of existence studied by biology). *Mind* is the rational, reasoning, linguistic, and imaginative mind (studied by psychology). *Soul* is the higher or subtle mind, the archetypal mind, the intuitive mind, and the essence or the indestructibleness of our own being (studied by theology). And *spirit* is the transcendental summit of our being, our Godhead (studied by contemplative mysticism).

According to Vedanta Hinduism, the individual person is composed of five "sheaths" or levels or spheres of being (the koshas), often compared to an onion, so that as we peel away the outer layers we find more and more the essence. The lowest (or most outer) is called the annamayakosha, which means "the sheath made of food." This is the physical sphere. Next is the pranamayakosha, the sheath made of prana. *Prana* means vital force, bioenergy, élan vital, libido, emotional-sexual energy in general—the sphere of the emotional body (as we are using the term). Next is the manomayakosha, the sheath of manas or mind—

rational, abstract, linguistic. Beyond this is the vijnanamayakosha, the sheath of intuition, the higher mind, the subtle mind. Finally there is the anandamayakosha, the sheath made of ananda, or spiritual and transcendental bliss.

Further—and this is important—Vedanta groups these five sheaths into three major realms: gross, subtle, and causal. The gross realm is correlated with the lowest level in the holarchy, the physical body (annamayakosha). The subtle realm is correlated with the three intermediate levels: the emotional-sexual body (pranamayakosha), the mind (manomayakosha), and the higher or subtle mind (vijnanamayakosha). And the causal is correlated with the highest level, the anandamayakosha, or archetypal spirit, which is also sometimes said to be largely unmanifest, or formless. Further, Vedanta relates these three major *realms of being* with the three major *states of consciousness*: waking, dreaming, and deep dreamless sleep. Beyond all three of these states is absolute Spirit, sometimes called turiya, "the fourth," because it is beyond (and includes) the three states of manifestation; it is beyond (and thus integrates) gross, subtle, and causal.[1]

So the Vedanta version of five sheaths is almost identical to the Judeo/ Christian/Muslim version of matter, body, mind, soul, and spirit, as long as we understand "soul" to mean, not just a higher self or higher identity, but higher or subtler mind and cognition. And soul also has the meaning, in *all* the higher mystical traditions, of being a "knot" or "contraction" (what the Hindus and Buddhists call the ahamkara), which has to be untied and dissolved before the soul can transcend itself, die to itself, and thus find a supreme identity with and as absolute Spirit (as Christ said, "He cannot be a true disciple who hateth not his own soul").

So "soul" is both the highest level of individual growth we can achieve, and also the final barrier, the final knot, to complete enlightenment or supreme identity, simply because as transcendental witness it stands back from everything it witnesses. Once we push through the witness position, then the soul or witness itself dissolves and there is only the play of <u>nondual awareness, awareness that does not look at objects but is completely one with all objects</u> (Zen says "it is like tasting the sky"). The gap between subject and object collapses, the soul is transcended or dissolved, and pure spiritual or nondual awareness—which is very simple, very obvious, very clear—arises. You realize that your intrinsic being is vast and open, empty and clear, and everything arising anywhere is arising within you, as intrinsic spirit, spontaneously.

The central psychological model of Mahayana Buddhism is the eight vijnanas, the eight levels of consciousness. The first five are the five senses. The next is the manovijnana, the mind that operates on sensory experience. Then there is manas, which means both higher mind and the center of the illusion of the separate self. It is the manas that looks at the alayavijnana (the next higher level, that of supraindividual consciousness) and mistakes it for a separate self or substantial soul, as we have defined it. And beyond these eight levels, as both their source and ground, is the pure alaya or pure empty Spirit.

(I don't mean to minimize some of the very real differences between these traditions. I'm simply pointing out that they share certain deep structure similarities, which testifies eloquently to the genuinely universal nature of many of their insights.)

(And so we can end on a happy note: After being temporarily derailed in the nineteenth century by a variety of materialistic reductionisms (from scientific materialism to behaviorism to positivism), the Great Nest of Being, the Great Holarchy of Being, is making a stunning comeback.) That temporary derailment—an attempt to reduce the holarchy of being to its lowest level, matter—was particularly galling in psychology, which first lost its spirit, then lost its soul, then lost its mind, and was reduced to studying only empirical behavior or bodily drives, a restriction that at any other time or place would be considered a precise definition of insanity.

But now evolutionary holarchy—the holistic study of the development and self-organization of fields within fields within fields—is once again a dominant theme in many scientific and behavioral disciplines (as we will see), though it goes by many names (Aristotle's "entelechy," to give only one example, is now known as "morphogenetic fields" and "self-organizing systems"). This is not to say that the modern versions of the Great Holarchy and its self-organizing principles offer no new insights, for they do, particularly when it comes to the actual evolutionary unfolding of the Great Nest itself. Each glimpse of the Great Holarchy is adequate; each advancing glimpse is more adequate. . . .

But the essentials are unmistakable. Ludwig von Bertalanffy, the founder of General System Theory, summarized it perfectly: "Reality, in the modern conception, appears as a tremendous hierarchical order of organized entities, leading, in a superposition of many levels, from physical and chemical to biological and sociological systems. Such hierarchical structure and combination into systems of ever higher order, *is characteristic of reality as a whole* and of fundamental importance especially in biology, psychology and sociology."

Thus, for example, in modern psychology, holarchy is the dominant *developmental* and *process* paradigm, cutting across the actual (and often quite different) content of the various schools. Every school of developmental psychology acknowledges some version of hierarchy, or a series of discrete (but continuous), irreversible stages of growth and unfolding. This includes the Freudians, the Jungians, the Piagetians, Lawrence Kohlberg, Carol Gilligan, and the cognitive behaviorists. Maslow, representing both humanistic and transpersonal psychology, put the "hierarchy of needs" at the center of his system—to mention only a few.

From Rupert Sheldrake and his "nested hierarchy of morphogenetic fields" to Sir Karl Popper's "hierarchy of emergent qualities" to Birch and Cobb's "ecological model of reality" based on "hierarchical value"; from Francisco Varela's groundbreaking work on autopoietic systems ("it seems to be a general reflection of the richness of natural systems to produce a hierarchy of levels") to the brain research of Roger Sperry and Sir John Eccles and Wilder Penfield ("a hierarchy of nonreducible emergents") to the social critical theory of Jürgen Habermas ("a hierarchy of communicative competence")—the Great Nest is back.

And the only reason *everybody* doesn't realize this is that it is hiding out under a variety of different names.

But no matter; realized or not, it is already well under way. And the truly wonderful thing about this homecoming is that modern theory can now reconnect with its rich roots in the perennial philosophy, reconnect with not only Plato and Aristotle and Plotinus and Maimonides and Spinoza and Hegel and Teresa in the West, but also with Shankara and Padmasambhava and Chih-i and Fa-tsang and Abinavagupta and Lady Tsogyal in the East—all made possible by the fact that many aspects of the perennial philosophy do indeed seem to be perennial—or essentially universal wherever they appear—thus cutting across times and cultures alike to point to the heart and soul and spirit of the family of humankind (indeed, all sentient beings as such).

There is, really, only one major thing left to be done, one fundamental item on the homecoming agenda. While it is true, as I said, that one of the unifying paradigms in modern thought, from physics to biology to psychology to sociology, is evolutionary holarchy (see, for example, Laszlo, Jantsch, Habermas, Lenski, Dennett), nonetheless most orthodox schools of inquiry admit the existence only of matter, body, and mind.[2] The higher dimensions of soul and spirit are not yet accorded quite the same status. We might say that the modern West has still only acknowledged three fifths of the Great Holarchy of Being. The agenda, very simply, is to reintroduce the other two fifths (soul and spirit).

Once we recognize and honor *all* the levels and dimensions of the Great Nest, we simultaneously acknowledge all the corresponding modes of knowing—not just the eye of flesh, which discloses the physical and sensory world, or just the eye of mind, which discloses the linguistic and symbolic world, but also the eye of contemplation, which discloses the soul and spirit. (We will return to this important topic in chapter 3.)

And so there is the agenda: Let us take the last step and reintroduce the eye of contemplation, which, as a sound and repeatable methodology, discloses soul and spirit. And that integral vision is, I submit, the final homecoming, the reweaving of our modern soul with the soul of humanity itself—the true meaning of multiculturalism—so that, standing on the shoulders of giants, we transcend but include, which always means honor, their ever-recurring presence. Uniting ancient wisdom with modern knowledge is thus the clarion call of the integral vision, a beacon in the postmodern wilderness.

An acknowledgment of the full spectrum of consciousness would alter the course of every one of the modern disciplines it touches—and that, of course, is an essential aspect of an integral approach.

But indeed the first and most immediate impact would be on the field of psychology itself. I have explored this full-spectrum psychology in a number of books (including The Spectrum of Consciousness, No Boundary, The Atman Project, Transformations of Consciousness, *and* A Brief History of Everything). [See Integral Psychology *for the most recent and most comprehensive treatment.]*

These books present a view of human development that attempts to incorporate the entire spectrum of consciousness, from instinct to ego to spirit, from prepersonal to personal to transpersonal, from subconscious to self-conscious to superconscious. If nothing animal, human, or divine is alien to me, then no state of consciousness can be dismissed from the generous embrace of a truly integral psychology. In the Preface to the new edition of The Atman Project, *I try to suggest why such an integral and inclusive stance is so important.*

The Atman Project was, as far as we can tell, the first psychology that suggested a way of uniting East and West, conventional and contemplative, orthodox and mystical, into a single, coherent, and plausible framework. In so doing, it incorporated a good number of approaches, from Freud to Buddha, Gestalt to Shankara, Piaget to Yogachara, Kohlberg to Krishnamurti.

I began writing *The Atman Project* in 1976, along with its sister volume, *Up from Eden*—one covering ontogeny, the other phylogeny. In the almost two decades since writing *Atman*, I have found its basic framework to be as sturdy and solid as ever, and thus I believe that its general tenets, with a little fine tuning here and there, will continue to be valid for a long and fruitful time.

A few critics complained that I had simply used various sources in a literary fashion, that my approach wasn't based on clinical or experimental evidence. But this is perhaps a bit disingenuous: the vast majority of theorists that I relied on were exactly those who had pioneered direct clinical and experimental evidence, from Jean Piaget's *méthode clinique* to Margaret Mahler's exhaustive videotaped observations to Lawrence Kohlberg's and Carol Gilligan's groundbreaking moral investigations—not to mention the vast phenomenological evidence presented by the contemplative traditions themselves. *The Atman Project* was directly based on the evidence of over sixty researchers from numerous approaches, and hundreds of others in an informal way.

(We will return to, and carefully explore, this integral psychology in chapters 6, 9, 10, and 11.)

The Atman Project also ended my flirtation with Romanticism and its attempt to make regression into a source of salvation. I had in fact begun to write both *Atman* and *Eden* as a validation of the Romantic view: men and women start out in an unconscious union with the Divine—an unreflexive immersion in a type of heaven on earth, a paradisiacal Eden, both ontogenetically and phylogenetically; then they break away from that union, through a process of alienation and dissociation (the isolated and divisive ego); then return to the Divine in a conscious and glorious union.

Human development thus proceeds, so to speak, from unconscious Heaven to conscious Hell to conscious Heaven. I started writing both books to validate that Romantic notion.

But the more I worked on those books, the more it became obvious that the Romantic view was hopelessly muddled. It combined one or two very important truths with some outrageous confusions, and the result was a theoretical nightmare. Untangling this mess was a constant preoccupation with me for several years—almost a decade, actually—

and marked one of the most turbulent theoretic times of my life. The reason that I have authored so many essays about fallacies—such as the pre/trans fallacy and the single boundary fallacy—is that the Romantics committed many of them, and I, being a good Romantic, had committed them royally; and thus understanding these fallacies from the inside, up close and very personal, I could write some very strong criticisms of them. You are never so vicious toward a theory as toward one that you yourself recently embraced.

But the crucial error of the Romantic view is fairly easy to understand. Take childhood, for example. The Romantic view, as we said, is that the infant starts out in a state of *unconscious Heaven*. That is, because the infant self isn't yet differentiated from the environment around it (or from the mother), the infant self is actually one with the dynamic Ground of Being—but in an unconscious (or "un-self-conscious") fashion. Thus, unconscious Heaven—blissful, wonderful, mystical, the paradisiacal state out of which it will soon fall, and to which it will always long to return.

And indeed, the Romantic view continues, sometime in the first few years of life, the self differentiates from the environment, the union with the dynamic Ground is lost, subject and object are separated, and the self moves from unconscious Heaven into conscious Hell—the world of egoic alienation, repression, terror, tragedy.

But, the happy account continues, the self can make a type of U-turn in development, sweep back to the prior infantile union state, reunite with the great Ground of Being, only now in a fully conscious and self-actualized way, and thus find conscious Heaven.

Hence, the overall Romantic view: one starts out in unconscious Heaven, an unconscious union with the Divine; one then *loses* this unconscious union, and thus plunges into conscious Hell; one can then regain the Divine union, but now in a higher and conscious fashion.

The only problem with that view is that the first step—the loss of the unconscious union with the Divine—is an absolute impossibility. All things are one with the Divine Ground—it is, after all, the Ground of all being! To lose oneness with that Ground is to cease to exist.

Follow it closely: there are only two general stances you can have in relation to the Divine Ground: since all things are one with Ground, you can either be aware of that oneness, or you can be unaware of that oneness. That is, you can be conscious or unconscious of your union with the Divine Ground: those are the only two choices you have.

And since the Romantic view is that you start out, as an infant, in an unconscious union with Ground, you *cannot then lose that union*! You have *already* lost consciousness of the union; you cannot then further lose the union itself or you would cease to be! So if you are unconscious of your union, it can't get any worse, ontologically speaking. That is already the pits of alienation. You are already living in Hell, as it were; you are already immersed in samsara, only you don't realize it—you haven't the awareness to recognize this burning fact. And so that is more the actual state of the infantile self: unconscious Hell. The infant self already suffers hunger, pain, rudimentary fear, and thirst—all the signs of samsara. But it registers them dimly.

What does start to happen, however, is that you begin to wake up to the alienated world in and around you. You go from unconscious Hell to *conscious* Hell, and being conscious of Hell, of samsara, of lacerating existence, is what makes growing up—and being an adult—such a nightmare of misery and alienation. The infant self is relatively peaceful, not because it is living in Heaven, but because it isn't aware enough to fully register the flames of Hell all around it. The infant is most definitely immersed in samsara, it just doesn't know it, it isn't aware enough to realize it, and enlightenment is certainly not a return to this infantile state! Or a "mature version" of this state! Neither the infant self nor my dog writhes in guilt and angst and agony, but enlightenment does not consist in recapturing dog-consciousness (or a "mature form" of dog-consciousness!).

As the infant self grows in awareness and consciousness, it slowly becomes aware of the intrinsic pain of existence, the torment inherent in samsara, the mechanism of madness coiled inherently in the manifest world: it begins to suffer. It is introduced to the first Noble Truth, a jolting initiation into the world of perception, whose sole mathematics is the torture-inducing fire of unquenched and unquenchable desire. This is not a desire-ridden world that was lacking in the infant's previous "wonderful" immersion state, but simply a world that dominated that state unconsciously, a world which the self now slowly, painfully, tragically becomes aware of.

And so, as the self grows in awareness, it moves from unconscious Hell to conscious Hell, and there it may spend its entire life, seeking above all else the numbing consolations that will blunt its raw and ragged feelings, blur its etchings of despair. Its life becomes a map of morphine, and folding itself into the anesthetic glow of all its compensations, it might even manage to convince itself, at least for an endearing blush of rose-tinted time, that the dualistic world is an altogether pretty thing.

But alternatively, the self might continue its growth and development into the genuinely spiritual domains: transcending the separate-self sense, it uncoils in the very Divine. The union with the Divine—a union or oneness that had been present but unconscious since the start—now flares forth in consciousness in a brilliant burst of illumination and a shock of the unspeakably ordinary: it realizes its Supreme Identity with Spirit itself, announced, perhaps, in nothing more than the cool breeze of a bright spring day, this outrageously obvious affair.

(And thus the actual course of human ontogeny: from unconscious Hell to conscious Hell to conscious Heaven. *At no point does the self lose its union with the Ground,* or it would utterly cease to be! In other words, the Romantic agenda is right about the second and third steps (the conscious Hell and the conscious Heaven), but utterly confused about the infantile state itself, which is not unconscious Heaven but unconscious Hell.)

Thus, the infantile state is not unconscious transpersonal, it is basically prepersonal. It is not transrational, it is prerational. It is not transverbal, it is preverbal. It is not transegoic, it is pre-egoic.[3] And the course of human development—*and evolution at large*—is from subconscious to self-conscious to superconscious; from prepersonal to personal to transpersonal; from under-mental to mental to over-mental; from pre-temporal to temporal to trans-temporal, by any other name: eternal.

The Romantics had simply confused pre with trans, and thus elevated the pre states to the glory of the trans (just as the reductionists would dismiss the trans states by claiming they were regression to pre states). These two confusions—the *elevationist* and the *reductionist*—are the two main forms of the pre/trans fallacy, which was first outlined and identified in the following pages. And the crucial point was that development is not regression in service of ego, but evolution in transcendence of ego.

And thus ended my Romantic fascination.

Now, there is indeed a *falling away* from Godhead, from Spirit, from the primordial Ground, and this is the truth the Romantics are trying to get at, before they slip into their pre/trans fallacies. This falling away is called *involution*, the movement whereby all things fall away from a consciousness of their union with the Divine, and thus imagine themselves to be separate and isolated monads, alienated and alienating. And once involution has occurred—and Spirit becomes unconsciously involved in the lower and lowest forms of its own manifestation—then *evolution* can occur: Spirit unfolds in a great *spectrum of consciousness*, from the Big Bang to matter to sensation to perception to impulse to image to symbol to concept to reason to psychic to subtle to causal occasions, on the way to its own shocking self-recognition, Spirit's own self-realization and self-resurrection. And in each of those stages—from matter to body to mind to soul to spirit—evolution becomes more and more conscious, more and more aware, more and more realized, more and more awake—with all the joys, and all the terrors, inherently involved in that dialectic of awakening.

At each stage of this process of Spirit's return to itself, we—you and I—nonetheless remember, perhaps vaguely, perhaps intensely, that we were once consciously one with the very Divine itself. It is there, this memory trace, in the back of our awareness, pulling and pushing us to realize, to awaken, to remember who and what we always already are.

In fact, all things, we might surmise, intuit to one degree or another that their very Ground is Spirit itself. All things are driven, urged, pushed, and pulled to manifest this realization. And yet, prior to that divine awakening, all things seek Spirit in a way that actually prevents the realization: or else we would be realized right now! We seek Spirit in ways that prevent it.

We seek for Spirit in the world of time; but Spirit is timeless, and cannot there be found. We seek for Spirit in the world of space; but Spirit is spaceless, and cannot there be found. We seek for Spirit in this or that object, shiny and alluring and full of fame or fortune; but Spirit is not an object, and it cannot be seen or grasped in the world of commodities and commotion.

In other words, we are seeking for Spirit in ways that prevent its realization, and force us to settle for substitute gratifications, which propel us through, and lock us into, the wretched world of time and terror, space and death, sin and separation, loneliness and consolation.

And that is the Atman project.

The Atman project: the attempt to find Spirit in ways that prevent it and force substitute gratifications. And, as you will see in the following pages, the entire structure of the manifest universe is driven by the Atman project, a project that continues until we—until you and I—awaken to the Spirit whose substitutes we seek in the world of space and time and grasping and despair. The nightmare of history is the nightmare of the Atman project, the fruitless search in time for that which is finally timeless, a search that inherently generates terror and torment, a self ravaged by repression, paralyzed by guilt, beset with the frost and fever of wretched alienation—a torture that is only undone in the radiant Heart when the great search itself uncoils, when the self-contraction relaxes its attempt to find God, real or substitute: the movement in time is undone by the great Unborn, the great Uncreate, the great Emptiness in the Heart of the Kosmos itself.

And so, as you read this book, try to remember: remember the great event when you breathed out and created this entire Kosmos; remember the great emptying when you threw yourself out as the entire World, just to see what would happen. Remember the forms and forces through which you have traveled thus far: from galaxies to planets, to verdant plants reaching upward for the sun, to animals stalking day and night, restless with their weary search; through primal men and women, yearning for the light, to the very person now holding this book: remember who and what you have been, what you have done, what you have seen, who you actually are in all those guises, the masks of the God and the Goddess, the masks of your own Original Face.

Let the great search wind down; let the self-contraction uncoil in the immediateness of present awareness; let the entire Kosmos rush into your being, since you are its very Ground; and then you will remember that the Atman project never occurred, and you have never moved, and it is all exactly as it should be, when the robin sings on a glorious morning, and raindrops beat on the temple roof.

2

In a Modern Light

INTEGRAL ANTHROPOLOGY AND
THE EVOLUTION OF CULTURES

An integral approach is committed to the full spectrum of consciousness as it manifests in all its extraordinary diversity. This allows an integral approach to recognize and honor the Great Holarchy of Being first elucidated by the perennial philosophy and the great wisdom traditions in general.

At the same time, Spirit moves on. Evolution continues to unfold, leaving nothing in the manifest world untouched. And the great traditions are just that—traditions—some of whose insights have stood the test of time, and some of which most definitely have not.

A truly integral approach must therefore fight on two fronts, as it were: against a modernity that is slow to recognize the full spectrum of consciousness, and against a traditionalism that refuses to recognize any substantial advances made by modernity itself.

In the previous chapter, we took the side of the great traditions against modernity, and argued for a recognition of the full spectrum of consciousness, the Great Holarchy of Being. In this chapter, we will take the side of modernity against traditionalism, and argue that, as evolution continues, new truths emerge, new insights spring forth, new realizations unfold, and therefore the great traditions are in desperate need of a modern touch as well.

The integral vision embodies an attempt to take the best of both worlds, ancient and modern. But that demands a critical stance willing to reject unflinchingly the worst of both as well.

THOUGHTFUL MEN AND WOMEN, throughout the ages, have always found the perennial philosophy a grounding and balancing influence, being, like Dr. Watson, that one constant in a changing world. It is especially appropriate, then, in these times of rapid transition and uncertain change, that we look to the ancient wisdom for some stability and guidance, since, at its core, it has always purported to represent timeless and eternal truths, beyond the ravages and turmoils of space and time. "I am come as Time, waster of peoples, ready for the hour that ripens to their ruin." And the perennial philosophy is come as antidote, balm for the wearied soul, ready for the hour that sounds its great salvation.

But, indeed, there has always been something of a problem in integrating "ancient" wisdom with "modern" times—even the terms "ancient" and "modern" sound mutually incompatible. What I therefore would like to review is exactly what we mean by the term "ancient" or "perennial," and how those "ancient" teachings can in fact be reconciled with "modern" or "progressive" society.

To begin with, when we speak of the "Ancient Wisdom" as the *philosophia perennis*, there can properly be only one correct meaning, namely, those truths—or rather, That Truth—which is radically *timeless* or *eternal*, one and whole, only and all. That Truth—using "Truth" in the broadest sense as the ultimately Real or Spirit itself—is the essence of the perennial philosophy. In other words, the perennial philosophy is not, at its core, a set of doctrines, beliefs, teachings, or ideas, for all of those are *of* the world of form, of space and time and ceaseless change, whereas very Truth is radically formless, spaceless, and timeless, encompassing all space and time but limited to none. That One—the radical Truth—is not *in* the world of space and time, except as *all* space and time, and thus it could never be enunciated in formal or doctrinal fashion. We cannot make a statement about the *whole* of Reality, because any conceivable statement is itself merely *part* of that Reality, and thus the perennial philosophy, as a direct insight-union with that Reality itself, could never be adequately captured in any set of doctrines or ideas, all of which are partial, finite, and limited. Radical Truth can be *shown* (in contemplative awareness) but never exhaustively *said* (in discursive language).

There is, in other words, an important distinction between Truth and *forms* of Truth. Radical Truth itself is formless, timeless, spaceless, changeless; its various forms, however, the various ideas, symbols, images, and thoughts we use to represent it, ceaselessly change and evolve. Radical Truth is timeless; its various forms exist in the world of time, and are subject to time's laws. Radical Truth is spaceless, whereas its various forms are space-bound, finite, and contingent. Radical Truth is not one condition among other conditions, but the very Condition of all conditions, the Nature of all natures, the suchness or thatness or isness of all phenomena and all forms, and is therefore not itself any particular phenomenon or form.

Now we can never know *all* the forms of Truth—psychological truth, sociological truth, economic truth, biological truth, and so on. These forms ceaselessly advance and evolve, alter and complexify. And although we can never know all these forms of Truth, we can know Truth itself, or the absolute reality of which all these forms are but partial and approximate reflections. In other words, although we can never know all the facts of existence, we can know the Fact of Existence which underlies and grounds all possible and relative facts, just as, once we know the ocean is wet, we know all waves are wet, even though we may never know each and every wave.

So that is one meaning of the words *ancient wisdom* or *perennial philosophy*—that absolute Truth which is timeless, formless, and spaceless, radically whole and complete, outside of which nothing exists—a Truth that can be known (via direct and formless intuition-identity), but which can never be adequately or fully captured in any form, doctrine, system, philosophy, proposition, thought or idea (all of which are merely partial, temporal, and finite reflections).

Now another meaning of the word *ancient* is "old," "archaic," "primitive." And, indeed, many individuals who speak glowingly of "ancient wisdom" mean "wisdom of past ages." And it is this "past wisdom" we are supposed to bring into the present culture as a source of meaning, stability, and salvation.

But already, you can see, there is a confusion of *past forms* of Truth with Truth itself. Once this confusion is made, then "timeless Truth" comes to mean "what the old folks said." There is a whole tendency to glorify yesterday; to see a greater "wisdom" available in the past than in the present; to eulogize ancient Egypt, China, India; to romanticize our ancestors and denigrate our contemporaries; and, on the whole, to see in the manifest realm not an *evolution* of increasing wisdom but a *devolution* of increasing ignorance. And all of this, I believe, is rather muddle-headed.

My point is that when we say "our present culture needs ancient wisdom," we must be very careful to specify exactly what we mean by "ancient wisdom." If by "ancient" we mean "timeless," then of course our culture is in desperate need of such wisdom (as have all cultures been in such need). But if by "ancient" we mean "past forms of Truth," then I believe nothing but a reactionary, antiprogressive, antiliberal, anti-evolutionary stance could ever result from such an importation.

Indeed, those who maintain that our present culture needs the "wisdom of past ages" can only mean one of two things: that the *past forms* of Truth were more adequate than the present forms; or that individuals in past ages intuited the Truth itself more clearly than we of today do or even can—and I believe both of those propositions are fundamentally incorrect.

The simplest examination of spiritual and cultural anthropology will, I believe, easily bear this out. If we believe even adequate forms of the "perennial" philosophy existed throughout all primal cultures, we are in for a rude surprise. There is, for example, precious little evidence that Paleolithic cultures had a sophisticated version of the perennial philosophy; even the central (and simplest) notion that there is one reality behind multiple phenomena was grasped, if at all, by a minuscule number of souls. And in any event, virtually all scholars agree that, as we move from Paleolithic and Mesolithic into Neolithic and Bronze Age periods, there is an unprecedented explosion of spiritual and cultural understanding, infinitely richer and more sophisticated than any of its predecessors. And then, starting around the sixth century BCE, we have the extraordinary emergence of the "axial sages"—Zoroaster, Gautama Buddha, Plato, Lao Tzu, Confucius, Moses, Socrates—whose insights clearly showed an even deeper realization of spiritual Truth and Reality.

There is a tendency among Romantics (lovers of "ancient wisdom" as "what the old folks said") to see spiritual development going straight downhill after the axial period, resulting eventually in our decadent-secular-scientific modern society. But again, I think this romantic fallacy comes precisely from confusing Truth with past forms of Truth, and that a clearer examination of the historical record shows, if anything, a continuing evolution and deepening of spiritual understanding, past the axial period and right up to (and including) modern times.

There is, first, the magnificent growth of Mahayana Buddhism in India, beginning around the second and third centuries CE; the extraordinary growth of Ch'an, T'ien T'ai, and Hua Yen Buddhism in China, especially beginning in the sixth, seventh, and eighth centuries; the exquisite Vajrayana in Tibet, which didn't even get started until the eighth century; Tantric Buddhism in India, which was developed between the eighth and eleventh centuries; and Zen in Japan, where the great Hakuin wasn't born until 1685! In Vedanta, Shankara doesn't arrive on the scene until 800 CE; Ramanuja until 1175; Ramakrishna until 1836; and the greatest of all Vedantic sages, Sri Ramana Maharshi, and the greatest of all Vedantic philosophers, Sri Aurobindo, both died only a few decades ago!

(I could go on like this, building what I think is an absolutely airtight case: both the *quality* of humanity's spiritual understanding, and the *form* of its presentation, are deepening and becoming *more* adequate in modern times, not less.)

There is one point in particular I would like to single out and stress, namely, the notion of evolution. It is common to assume that one of the doctrines of the perennial philosophy (i.e., one of the more common forms of radical Truth) is the idea of involution-evolution. That is, the manifest world was created as a "fall" or "breaking away" from the Absolute (involution), but that all things are now returning to the Absolute (via evolution). In fact, the doctrine of a progressive temporal return to Source (evolution) does not appear anywhere, according to such scholars as Joseph Campbell, until the axial period (i.e., a mere two thousand years ago). And even then, the idea was somewhat convoluted and backwards. The doctrine of the yugas, for example, sees the world proceeding through various stages of development, but the direction is *backward*: yesterday was the Golden Age, and time ever since has been a devolutionary slide downhill, resulting in the present-day Kali Yuga. Indeed, this notion of a *historical* fall from Eden was ubiquitous during the axial period; the idea that we are, at this moment, actually *evolving toward* Spirit was simply not conceived in any sort of influential fashion.

(But sometime during the *modern* era—it's almost impossible to pinpoint exactly—the idea of history as devolution (or a fall from God) was slowly replaced by the idea of history as evolution (or a growth toward God). We see it explicitly in Schelling (1775–1854); Hegel (1770–1831) propounded the doctrine with a genius rarely equaled; Herbert Spencer (1820–1903) made evolution a universal law, and his friend Charles Darwin (1809–1882) applied it to biology. We next find it appearing in Aurobindo (1872–1950), who gave perhaps its most accurate and profound spiritual context, and Pierre Teilhard de Chardin (1881–1955), who made it famous in the West.

But here is my point: we might say that the idea of evolution as return-to-Spirit is part of the perennial philosophy, but the idea itself, in any adequate form, is no more than a few hundred years old. It might be "ancient" as timeless, but it is certainly not ancient as "old."

(With this whole shift in the understanding of evolution, the form of the perennial philosophy took on an entirely new look: there is still That One, or the timeless and absolute Spirit of which the entire universe is but a manifestation, but that world of manifestation is not now devolving away from Spirit, it is evolving toward Spirit. God does not lie in our collective past, God lies in our collective future; the Garden of Eden is tomorrow, not yesterday; the Golden Age lies down the road, not up it.)

This fundamental shift in the sense or form of the perennial philosophy—as represented in, say, Aurobindo, Hegel, Adi Da, Schelling, Teilhard de Chardin, Radhakrishnan, to name a few—I should like to call the "neoperennial philosophy." And it is the neoperennial philosophy—not "old wisdom"—that our present culture so desperately needs.

Thus, at the core of the neoperennial philosophy is the same Radical and Formless Truth glimpsed by the wisdom cultures of the past (and given such culture-specific and temporal names as Tao, Buddha Mind, Brahman, Goddess, Keter, etc.); but its outward *form*, its clothing cut in the relative and manifest world, has naturally changed and evolved to keep pace with the progressive evolution of the manifest world itself—and that includes, of course, the very idea of evolution. (And whereas "ancient wisdom"—meaning in this case the outward doctrines, ideas, and symbols used in past ages to metaphorically represent inward and Radical Truth—is by and large outdated, outmoded, anachronistic, or simply wrong (even though they were, for their earlier time and place, perfectly phase-specific and culture-appropriate), the form of the neoperennial philosophy is much more finely tuned to present-day needs, ideas, and advances in science. There is a new koan for our age, and only the neoperennial philosophy can answer it: Does a computer have Buddha-nature?)

(Here is what we have: The "perennial" or "primordial" or "ancient" wisdom can have two different meanings. One, it can mean radically timeless, spaceless, formless Truth, the Ground of all Being, primordial Emptiness, pure unmanifest Spirit, the Condition of all conditions, the State of all states, the Nature of all natures, the noumenon transcendent to, but immanent in and as, all phenomena, <u>known or realized in a timeless state of contemplative unity or identity with all manifestation</u>. When we descend from this plane of formless, imageless, timeless union-samadhi, we naturally clothe that Realization of formless Truth in the various forms and truth-symbols available to our particular sociocultural milieu. The particular outward forms and symbols used by past wisdom cultures has led to the second widespread meaning of "ancient wisdom"—namely, the actual doctrines, words, theories, metaphors, symbols, and models used by ancient or past cultures to express and embody their own realization of that Radical Truth. And whereas radical and formless Truth, to the extent it is clearly recognized, is necessarily one and identical in all times and places, nonetheless the forms of its expression are and can only be judged according to their appropriateness for the particular sociocultural context in which they live, and from which their very metaphors and models are drawn.

Now if we use "Ancient" (with a capital A) to represent radical, timeless, and formless Truth, and if we use "ancient" (small a) for the particular past forms and expressions of radical Truth—then we can summarize our major point thus: modern culture needs Ancient truth, not ancient truth. And our corollary point: the best and most appropriate form of Ancient Truth is now the neoperennial philosophy, and not a blind allegiance to "what the old folks said." Modern culture is by and large incompatible with ancient culture, and their forced fit could never benefit more than a small percentage of the nostalgically oriented. Formless or Ancient Truth, we would all agree, is a perfect union-identity with the entire manifest world; but our *present*-day manifest world includes computers, global politics, the idea of evolution, molecular engineering, human-machine interfacing, radical medical advances, and so on. In short, the *form* of Ancient Wisdom can no longer be ancient. The neoperennial philosophy, with its adaptability to modern needs and desires, is and must now be God's witness to the new and rising wisdom culture.

We said that past forms of Truth arose in response to the needs and desires of past cultures, and that they were, for the most part, perfectly adequate during those times. Of course, some of those past forms might still find a partial and limited use in our present society (just as we still use the wheel)—but, by definition, they then become merely part of our *present* forms of Truth, adapted and fitted into a more comprehensive structure (as, for instance, Aurobindo fitted spirituality and evolution, and Vivekananda initiated the dialogue between physics and spirituality). The point is that the evolution of the *forms* of Truth clearly show a succession of *increasingly adequate* and *more comprehensive* structures for truth's expression and representation. (The notion of each developmental stage being adequate, but each successor being *more adequate*, was first elucidated by Hegel, one of the first great neoperennial philosophers.) The past had the Great Religions. The future will have the Greater Religions.

I realize that tends to yank our vision in a direction opposite to what we usually think; but what if I had made that statement in, say, 500,000 BCE? It would obviously be true. Has evolution stopped with us, giving us and not our descendants privileged status? Fact is, our so-called Great Religions will be reduced, by future spiritual evolution, to footnotes on the developmental history of Spirit, of the same status we now accord to, say, voodoo and sympathetic magic. The greater and more adequate forms of the Ancient Wisdom will appear *tomorrow*, and tomorrow and tomorrow and tomorrow again, just as they always have in the past.

Now the foregoing does not mean that any particular individuals have to wait for future evolution in order to find transcendence. Any individual, now as in the past, is perfectly free, via contemplative-meditative practices, to pursue transcendence in his or her own case. Radical Truth, being formless, does not have to await the arrival of future forms nor lament the loss of past forms. Our exclusive reliance on the future or the past simply perpetuates the confusion of Truth with its temporal forms. Radical Truth, as always, is completely and entirely available only in the timeless present. It is simply that, as consciousness on the whole continues to evolve and develop, in a now planetary fashion, then global awareness (which is a transcendence of any narrow parochialism) becomes increasingly easier, more obvious, more appealing—and therefore, I believe, more likely. We might speculate, with Sheldrake, that this is the effect of a morphic field; in any event, the evolutionary accumulation seems undeniable.

Thus, the idea that present-day rational-secular society is somehow antispiritual comes, I believe, largely from a misunderstanding of the actual nature of evolution, which, according to the neoperennial philosophers, is nothing but Spirit-in-action, or the stages of Spirit's return to Spirit as Spirit. One of those stages—according to neoperennial philosophers from Aurobindo to Hegel to Adi Da—is exactly a humanistic-scientific-rational stage, which, far from being antispiritual, is actually a necessary and intermediate form of Spirit-in-action. It is only when, failing that understanding, we make the nostalgic comparison of the present form of Spirit-in-action with its old and past forms, that we arrive at the romantically dismal conclusion that the modern era is a sorry spiritual production compared with, say, Mesopotamia (most of whose religious practices were, in fact, of the most barbaric variety imaginable).

It is time, then, to have done with our sickly yearning for yesteryear, our morbid fixation to Mother Past, our preposterous groveling at any doctrine whose only authority comes from the fact that it was uttered by a really really ancient sage, centuries or preferably millennia ago. For, ironically enough, our fixation to the past comes only from our fear of death in the present: unable to die to our egos, we latch onto the permanence and fixity of the past as a substitute immortality project. The corpse of yesteryear becomes our morbid refuge, our rancid immortality.

Let us instead appreciate the past, honor it, be thankful for its successes, upon whose base our present consciousness rests—but let us release its hold on us. When we look at the past sages, and marvel at their insight, and fall in love with some one or the other of them, what is it we really see and feel? What can it be but our own highest Self or Spirit, since Spirit is one and timeless? Our loyalty to the past is just this misplaced intuition of absolute Spirit, diverted from a present Realization onto a past idolization by the inability to fall now into timeless transcendence. So let us relax our death-grip on ancient wisdom so that Ancient Wisdom may dawn, ever new and ever renewing, pointing home ahead.

Spiritual evolution, cultural evolution, evolution itself: the past wisdom traditions rarely acknowledge any aspect of this liberal and progressive and evolutionary view. And yet, who can really blame them? How can any of us possibly subscribe to such notions as spiritual evolution when faced with the searing signs of Auschwitz, Hiroshima, Wounded Knee, Gulag, Chernobyl; where the names of Hitler, Mussolini, Stalin, Pol Pot, Amin are burned into the flesh of modernity, their scars still there for all to see?

In a book called Up from Eden: A Transpersonal View of Human Evolution, *I attempted to come to terms with these most difficult of issues. Although* Up from Eden *has increasingly gained a general acknowledgment, it originally generated an enormous controversy, for reasons I address in the Preface to the new edition, where I focus on one of the foremost problems (and central nightmares) of modern sociology and anthropology:* How can we speak of cultural evolution with Auschwitz on the horizon?

This question is crucial, because unless we can plausibly answer it, there is absolutely no way whatsoever that we can reconcile ancient and modern worldviews (since the former deny evolution while the latter embrace it). What is required, then, is a way to see evolution in a radically new light, where both the ups and downs of Spirit's journey in time can be fully honored and acknowledged.

But in order to see evolution as Spirit-in-action, certain stern objections must be answered, because, in my opinion, neither the traditionalists nor the liberal modernists have fully come to terms with the profound meaning of evolution itself. If evolution is operating throughout the universe, then it must be operating in humans as well, which means human cultures must also evolve, which means progressively advanced forms of interaction must be emerging . . . which runs smack into the contradiction known as Auschwitz.

The future of an integral vision, in other words, hinges fatefully on the precise stance we take toward evolution itself: in what domains does evolution operate, and what does it actually mean? And if we are to see evolution as Spirit-in-action, then how can we answer the Gulag?

I began work on *Up from Eden* in 1977, when it was very fashionable to believe that evolution touched all domains of the universe *except the human.* That is, the Kosmos labored mightily some twelve billion years, with every aspect of it operating under evolutionary principles, an extraordinary and all-encompassing developmental process that eventually brought forth the first human cultural productions, whereupon it promptly ceased operating.

Evolution was felt to be working in the rest of the universe, but not in humans! This rather extraordinary opinion was held by traditional religious thinkers, by retro-Romantics, and by liberal social theorists: virtually the entire pantheon of influential writers and theorists from across the spectrum of social studies.

Most religious traditionalists allowed that individual humans show development, but not a collective and cultural humanity. Traditionalists displayed this intense antipathy to cultural evolution mostly because modern history had rather thoroughly rejected traditional mythic religion, and thus if history were really being driven by evolution, then evolution had rudely passed right over them and their beliefs.

No doubt about it, modernity by and large has thoroughly rejected religion: liberal modernity does not accept traditional mythic religion in its governing and political bodies, does not accept mythic-religious explanations for scientific facts and truths, and does not accept specific mythic-religious tenets in public discourse and public morality. And thus, as well they might, traditionalists look at modernity as a largely antispiritual movement, the horrible movement of secularization and rationalization: modernity is the great Satan. And if evolution produced *this*, then please, give us less of it. More strongly: evolution is not operating in the human domain!

The retro-Romantics and neopagans fully agreed that evolution operated in the rest of the universe but not in humans; in fact, the Romantics added, in the case of humans, evolution started *running backwards*! In the general Romantic view, humans, both phylogenetically and ontogenetically, started out in a type of primal Eden, a great paradise, an original Heaven on earth, and then things promptly started going downhill from there. The massive forces operating in the Kosmos for billions and billions of years—forces that produced ants from atoms and apes from amoebas, colossal forces that propelled galaxies and quasars into planetary configurations, and from there into cells with sensations, and organisms with perceptions, and animals that could see and feel and even think—all of those forces, once humans were produced, simply came to an abrupt and crashing halt—they simply stopped working!—and for no other apparent reason than that they didn't fit with the retro-Romantics' ideas of the way the world should run. Evolution for the rest of the Kosmos; downhill for humans. What an extraordinary and vicious dualism!

This hostility to cultural evolution was also shared by liberal social theorists, and for some very understandable and even noble reasons. Social Darwinism in its most common forms was so crude and so cruel—not to mention based on the most dubious aspects of Darwinian theory—that it came to mean not much more than a colossal lack of compassion for one's fellow men and women. And thus liberal social theorists, of virtually every variety, collectively decided that instead of trying to tease apart the valid from the grotesque aspects of cultural evolution, it was better to avoid and even deny the topic altogether.

The thesis of *Eden* was thus, at the time, rather daring, certainly controversial. Various grand theorists from Teilhard de Chardin to Aurobindo and Hegel had already advanced the idea that evolution itself was actually a *spiritual unfolding*, with each stage transcending but including its predecessor. But none of them had combined that philosophical notion with an actual hard look at anthropological data, and none of them had advanced any of the specific stages of this evolution based on any sort of extensive empirical and anthropological evidence. In this regard, *Eden* was, I believe, a major advance.

At the time I was writing *Eden*, the researches of two other theorists, working in the same general area, were just becoming available to the English-speaking world: Jean Gebser and Jürgen Habermas. What I knew of Gebser was obtained from one long article published in *Main Currents* (which was then the only such article available in English), but it was enough to show me unmistakably that Gebser and I had hit upon essentially identical stages in the broad evolution of human consciousness. Out of respect and deference to the pioneering work of Gebser (he had been working on this for decades before I was even born), I immediately annexed his terminology to mine, so that the various cultural stages had names like magical-typhonic and mental-egoic.

In other words, these were *the stages of the evolution of cultural worldviews* (the stages of the evolution of the Lower-Left quadrant), stages which Gebser's pioneering studies had already identified as archaic, magic, mythic, mental, and integral-aperspectival. My research had led me to similar, almost identical, stages, which I termed uroboric, typhonic, membership, egoic, and existential. (And thus, when I annexed Gebser's terms, I would often refer to magical-typhonic, mythic-membership, and so on.)

But in my approach, beyond the integral-existential stage—Gebser's highest—there are then the further or deeper stages of spiritual and transpersonal development itself, moving from psychic to subtle to causal to nondual, stages that Gebser does not clearly recognize. But up to that point, Gebser is the unsurpassed master and one of the primary innovators in the understanding of the evolution of cultural worldviews.

(Integral studies as a discipline includes a careful investigation of the entire spectrum of cultural worldviews as they develop and evolve, because what appears in individuals as a spectrum of consciousness [the Upper Left] appears in cultures as a spectrum of worldviews [the Lower Left]. Tracing the correlations between the ontogenetic and phylogenetic formation of the human species is thus a central task of integral anthropology.)

This ties in directly with the work of Jürgen Habermas and his associates. Habermas exploded on the scene with *Knowledge and Human Interests*, a devastating attack on mere positivism and empiricism; and, by

1976, he had released *Communication and the Evolution of Society*, a succinct but altogether brilliant outline of what he saw as the universal stages of consciousness development. I came upon Habermas's work just as I was finishing *Eden*, and could only acknowledge him briefly, but it was quite obvious that Habermas, coming from a very different starting point, had also hit upon the same general stages as Gebser and myself. Habermas went on to become what many people, myself included, consider the world's greatest living philosopher, and in subsequent books I would draw heavily, and gratefully, on Habermas's unending genius.

But what Gebser and Habermas both lacked was a genuinely spiritual dimension. Gebser vigorously attempted to include the spiritual domain in his work, but it soon became obvious that he simply was not aware of—or did not deeply understand—the contemplative traditions that more readily penetrate to the core of the Divine. As I said, beyond the integral-aperspectival, which is Gebser's highest stage, there are actually several stages of transpersonal or spiritual development, which Gebser clumsily collapses into his integral stage. And Habermas, being essentially a German rationalist, did not (and still does not) understand any God higher than Reason.

What was needed, then, was something of a cross between Aurobindo, Teilhard de Chardin, Gebser, and Habermas—in other words, some sort of framework that could actually accommodate the strengths of each of their approaches. And looking back on it, I believe that is what *Up from Eden* managed to do. I have since refined the categories given in *Eden*, and I have expanded the quadrants of analysis (interested readers might consult *Sex, Ecology, Spirituality* and *A Brief History of Everything*). But the essential framework is given here, and is still as valid as ever, I believe. In fact, recent research, evidence, and theory have, if anything, substantially increased the validity of *Eden* and its central conclusions.

(The crucial issue was this: In order for cultural evolution to be embraced as an explanatory principle in human history, it faces exactly those profound objections that led traditionalists, Romantics, and liberal social theorists aggressively and thoroughly to reject it. In other words, if evolution is operating in the human domain, how can we account for Auschwitz?) And how dare we make judgments about some cultural productions being more evolved than others? How dare we make such value rankings? What kind of arrogance is that?

Thus, even though I started this preface by chiding the anti-evolutionary theorists, they do in fact raise several profound and significant objections, and these objections need to be taken most seriously and addressed as fairly as possible.

The traditionalists, for example, cannot believe in cultural evolution because of such modern horrors as Auschwitz, Hiroshima, Chernobyl. How can we say evolution is at work in humans when it produces such monsters? Better to deny evolution altogether than to get caught up in having to explain those obscenities.

And the Romantics are responding to what seems to be a universal human sympathy for a time prior to today's turmoils. Primal men and women, on the whole, did not suffer the disasters of modernity—no industrial pollution, little slavery, few property disputes, and so on. By any scale of quality, haven't we in fact gone downhill? Isn't it time to get back to nature, back to the noble savage, and thus find a truer self, a fairer community, a richer life?

The liberal social theorists likewise have every reason to recoil in horror from the notion of cultural evolution. Its unbelievably crude forms, such as Social Darwinism, are not just lacking in compassion; much more sinister, this type of crass "evolutionism," pressed into the hands of moral cretins, would produce exactly the type of ruinous and barbaric notions of the superman, the master race, the coming human demigods, who would chillingly goose-step their way into history, who would in fact inscribe their beliefs on the tortured flesh of millions, would press their ideology into the gas chambers and let it all be settled there. Liberal social theorists, reacting to such horrors, naturally tend to look upon any sort of "social hierarchy" as a prelude to Auschwitz.

Obviously, if consciousness evolution is to be used as any sort of explanatory principle, it faces several stern difficulties. What is therefore required is a set of tenets that can explain *both* advance and regression, good news and bad news, the ups and downs of an evolutionary thrust that is nonetheless as active in humans as it is in the rest of the Kosmos. Otherwise, we face the extremely bizarre situation of driving a virulent wedge right through the middle of the Kosmos: everything nonhuman operates by evolution; everything human does not.

What are the principles that can rehabilitate cultural evolution in a sophisticated form, and thus reunite humanity with the rest of the Kosmos, and yet also account for the ups and downs of consciousness unfolding? Here are some of the central explanatory principles that I believe we need:

1. *The dialectic of progress.* (As consciousness evolves and unfolds, each stage solves or defuses certain problems of the previous stage, but then adds new and recalcitrant—and sometimes more complex and more difficult—problems of its own.) Precisely because evolution in all domains (human and otherwise) operates by a process of differentiation and integration, then each new and more complex level necessarily faces problems not present in its predecessors. Dogs get cancer; atoms don't. But this doesn't damn evolution altogether! It means evolution is good news, bad news, this dialectic of progress. And the more stages of evolution there are—the greater the depth of the Kosmos—the more things that *can* go wrong!

So evolution inherently means that new potentials and new wonders and new glories are introduced with each new stage, but they are invariably accompanied by new horrors, new fears, new problems, new disasters. And *Up from Eden* is a chronicle of the new wonders and the new diseases that unfolded in the unrelenting winds of the evolution of consciousness.

2. *The distinction between differentiation and dissociation.* Precisely because evolution proceeds by differentiation and integration, something can go wrong at each and every stage—as I said, the greater the depth of the Kosmos, the more diseases there can be. And one of the most prevalent forms of evolutionary pathology occurs when *differentiation* goes too far into *dissociation.* (In human evolution, for example, it is one thing to differentiate the mind and body, quite another to dissociate them. It is one thing to differentiate culture and nature, quite another to dissociate them.) Differentiation is the prelude to integration; dissociation is the prelude to disaster.

As we will see in the following pages, human evolution (like evolution everywhere else) is marked by a series of important differentiations, which are absolutely normal and altogether crucial for the evolution and integration of consciousness. But at each stage, these differentiations can go too far into dissociation, which converts depth into disease, growth into cancer, culture into nightmare, consciousness into agony. And *Eden* is a chronicle not only of the necessary differentiations of consciousness evolution, but also of the pathological dissociations and distortions that all too often followed in their wake.

3. *The difference between transcendence and repression.* To say that evolution proceeds by differentiation and integration is to say that it proceeds by transcendence and inclusion. That is, each stage of evolu-

tion (human and otherwise) *transcends and includes* its predecessors. Atoms are parts of molecules, which are parts of cells, which are parts of complex organisms, and so on. Each stage thus includes its predecessor(s), and then adds its own defining and emergent qualities: it transcends and includes.

(But for just that reason, with *pathology*, the senior dimension doesn't transcend and include, it transcends and represses, denies, distorts, disrupts. Each new and higher stage has exactly this choice: transcend and include, befriend, integrate, honor; or transcend and repress, deny, alienate, oppress.) And *Eden* is a chronicle of the great transcendent occasions of human evolution, as well as of the grotesque repressions, oppressions, brutalities. The brighter the light, the darker the shadow, and *Eden* stares into the eyes of each.

4. *The difference between natural hierarchy and pathological hierarchy.* During the evolutionary process, that which is whole at one stage becomes a part of the whole of the next. Each and every thing in the Kosmos is thus what Arthur Koestler called a "holon," a whole that is simultaneously a part of some other whole, indefinitely. Whole atoms are parts of molecules, whole molecules are parts of cells, and so on. Each is a whole/part, a holon, existing in a *natural hierarchy*, or an order of increasing wholeness and holism.

For this reason, Koestler pointed out that normal hierarchy ought really to be called *holarchy*, and he's quite right. All processes of evolution (human and otherwise) proceed in part by hierarchization (holarchization)—each senior dimension transcends and includes its juniors: each level is a whole that is part of another whole, indefinitely, which is exactly why each unfolding stage transcends and includes its predecessor(s), and thus the Kosmos unfolds in embrace after embrace after never-ending embrace.

(But that which transcends can repress. And thus normal and natural hierarchies can degenerate into pathological hierarchies, into dominator hierarchies. In these cases, an arrogant holon doesn't want to be both a whole and a part; it wants to be a whole, period. It does not want to be a mutual part of something larger than itself; it does not want to share in the communions of its fellow holons; it wants to dominate them with its own agency. Power replaces communion; domination replaces communication; oppression replaces reciprocity.) And *Eden* is a chronicle of the extraordinary growth and evolution of normal hierarchies, a growth that ironically allowed a degeneration into pathological hierarchies, which left their marks burned into the tortured flesh of untold millions, a trail of terror that accompanied the animal who can not only transcend but repress.

5. *Higher structures can be hijacked by lower impulses.* Tribalism, when left to its own devices, is relatively benign, simply because its means and its technologies are relatively harmless. You can only inflict so much damage on the biosphere, and on other humans, with a bow and arrow (and this lack of means does not necessarily mean presence of wisdom). (The problem is that the advanced technologies of rationalization, when hijacked by tribalism and its ethnocentric drives, can be devastating.)

Auschwitz is not the result of rationality. Auschwitz is the result of the many products of rationality being used in irrational ways. Auschwitz is rationality hijacked by tribalism, by an ethnocentric mythology of blood and soil and race, rooted in the land, romantic in its dispositions, barbaric in its ethnic cleansing. You cannot seriously attempt genocide with a bow and arrow; but you can attempt it with steel and coal, combustion engines and gas chambers, machine guns and atomic bombs. These are not rational desires by any definition of rational; these are ethnocentric tribalisms commandeering the tools of an advanced consciousness and using them precisely for the lowest of the lowest motives. Auschwitz is the endgame, not of reason, but of tribalism.

Those are a handful of the distinctions that, I believe, are necessary to reconstruct the evolution of human consciousness in a much more satisfactory and compelling fashion, a fashion that can clearly account for the undeniable advances as well as the undeniable disasters of human history. And finally, this gives us a way to approach the objections of the anti-evolutionary theorists, who in many ways still dominate the theoretical discourse in this area.

To the traditionalists, we can say: You have not understood the dialectic of progress. You have included all the bad news of modernity, but you carefully leave out the good news, and so you damn the rise of modernity and its rational-secularization, failing to see that modernity is actually the form of Spirit's unfolding as the Presence of today's world. And so you worship the previous mythic-agrarian age, when the whole world bowed to the mythic God or Goddess, and religion everywhere smiled on this fair earth, and every man and woman devoutly embraced your beloved God, and all was wonderfully enchanted and alive with spiritual portent.

And let us conveniently ignore the fact that, as recent evidence has made abundantly clear, 10 percent of foraging and 54 percent of agrarian societies had slavery; 37 percent of foraging and 64 percent of agrarian societies had bride price; 58 percent of foraging and an astonishing 99 percent of horticultural societies engaged in frequent or intermittent warfare. The temples to this beloved God and Goddess were built upon the broken backs of millions of enslaved and tortured humans, who were not accorded even the simplest of human dignities, and who left their trail of blood and tears as the altar to that beloved God.

(The traditionalists have reminded us of the nightmares of modernity; let them not so easily forget the nightmares of yesteryear. And as for the good news of modernity, about which the traditionalists are strangely silent, let us remind them: the great liberation movements—the freeing of slaves, of women, of the untouchables—these great emancipation movements were brought into the modern world precisely by rationality, which was—make no mistake!—the form of Spirit's unfolding in the modern world.) The positive aspects of modernity—including medical advances that have single-handedly relieved more pain and suffering than any other advance in history—are exactly the Eros and the Agape of Spirit's present unfolding: the liberal democracies are Spirit's compassion manifested, not in some cruelly promised mythic heaven but right here and now on earth, in the actual lives of a vast humanity that heretofore had lived on this dear earth as slaves, as the property of another, and almost always the property of another who devoutly believed in the glories of the great and wondrous God.

And so we say to the traditionalists: You have not seen the dialectic of progress, you have not seen that the higher can be hijacked by the lower, you have not seen that the form of Spirit in the present world is precisely the good news of modernity—in these ways and more, you have lost touch with the pulse of Spirit's ongoing evolution and unfolding, the miracle of evolution as self-realization through self-transcendence.

To the retro-Romantics, we say: You have confused differentiation and dissociation, you have confused transcendence and repression. And thus, every time evolution introduces a new and necessary differentiation, you scream downfall! nightmare! horror upon horrors! devolution! the loss of Eden, the alienation of humankind, the trail of misery written on the winds of history.

The acorn has to differentiate in order to grow into an oak. But if you see every differentiation as a dissociation—if you thoroughly confuse the two—then you are forced to see the oak as a terrible violation of the acorn. And thus your solution to any problem faced by the oak is: we must get back to our wonderful acornness.

The solution, of course, is just the opposite: find those factors that prevent acorns from self-actualizing as oaks, and remove those obstacles, so that differentiation and integration can occur naturally instead of drifting into dissociation and fragmentation. We can agree with the Romantics that horrible pathologies have often crept into the ongoing march of development and evolution—there is no argument there!—but the solution is not an idealization of acornness, but a removal of the obstacles that prevent the acorn's growth to its own self-actualized oakness.

To the liberal social theorists, we say: You have not understood the difference between natural hierarchy and pathological hierarchy, and thus in your understandable zeal to erase the latter, you have destroyed the former: you have tossed the baby with the bathwater.

(Value ranking—hierarchy in the broadest sense—is inescapable in human endeavors, simply because we are all holons: <u>contexts within contexts forever</u>, and each broader context pronounces judgment on its less encompassing contexts.) And thus, even when the egalitarian social theorists assert their rejection of hierarchy, they do so using hierarchical judgments: they assert that nonranking is *better* than ranking. Well, that's a hierarchical judgment, which puts them in the embarrassing position of contradicting themselves, of secretly embracing that which they vocally condemn. They have a hierarchy that denies hierarchy, a ranking that hates ranking.

What they are trying to do, of course, is get rid of pathological hierarchies, and in this endeavor I believe we can all follow them. But the only way to get rid of pathological hierarchy is by embracing normal and natural hierarchy—that is, embracing normal holarchy, which integrates the arrogant holon back into its rightful place in a mutual reciprocity of care and communion and compassion. But without holarchy you have heaps, not wholes, and no integration is possible at all.

And thus, with this approach, and with these five or so distinctions, we can reunite humanity with the rest of the Kosmos, and not be saddled with a truly bizarre and rigid dualism: humanity over here, everything else over there.

(No, we are part and parcel of a single and all-encompassing evolutionary current that is itself Spirit-in-action, the mode and manner of Spirit's creation, and thus is always going beyond what went before—

that leaps, not crawls, to new plateaus of truth, only to leap again, dying and being reborn with each new quantum lurch, often stumbling and bruising its metaphysical knees, yet always getting right back up and jumping yet again.)

And do you remember the Author of this Play? As you look deeply into your own awareness, and relax the self-contraction, and dissolve into the empty ground of your own primordial experience, the simple feeling of Being—right now, right here—is it not obvious all at once? Were you not present from the start? Did you not have a hand to play in all that was to follow? Did not the dream itself begin when you got bored with being God? Was it not fun to get lost in the productions of your own wondrous imagination, and pretend it all was other? Did you not write this book, and countless others like it, simply to remind you who you are?

And so, looking back on it, *Eden* was one of the first sustained attempts, based on actual anthropological evidence, to reunite humanity with the rest of the Kosmos, to see the same currents running through our human blood that run through swirling galaxies and colossal solar systems, that crash through the great oceans and course through our own veins, that move the mightiest of mountains as well as our own glorious moral aspirations—one and the same current moves throughout the All, and drives the entire Kosmos in its every lasting gesture, and refuses to surrender until you remember who and what you are, and that you were carried to this realization by that single current of an all-pervading Love, and here "there came fulfillment in a flash of light, and vigor failed the lofty fantasy, but now my will and my desires were moved like a wheel revolving evenly, by the Love that moves the sun and other stars."

3

Eye to Eye

INTEGRAL PHILOSOPHY AND
THE QUEST FOR THE REAL

*An acknowledgment of the full spectrum of consciousness
would profoundly alter the course of every one of the modern
disciplines it touches—and that, of course, is an essential aspect
of integral studies.*

*We have seen this full-spectrum approach applied to psychol-
ogy, anthropology, and sociology. We will soon see it applied to
art and literature, feminist theory, cultural studies, and spirituality. But now we look briefly to philosophy, which traditionally
has been the queen of the mental sciences, simply because its
defining heart is the love of wisdom, in all its wondrous forms.*

*A full-spectrum approach to human consciousness and be-
havior means that men and women have available to them a
spectrum of knowing—a spectrum that includes, at the very
least, the eye of flesh, the eye of mind, and the eye of spirit.
What would happen if we took this integral vision and applied
it to philosophy? Eye to Eye took exactly that approach, and in
the Preface to its new edition, I outline the reasons why I believe
this integral approach is so profoundly important.*

THE VAST MAJORITY OF THE great philosophers of the West have
maintained that there does indeed exist some sort of Absolute, from

the Good to God to Geist. That has never seriously been doubted by the vast majority. The burning question, rather, has always been this: What is the relation of the absolute One to the world of the relative Many?

This crucial question has, like many of the most profound questions in Western philosophy, generated a series of utterly intractable difficulties, paradoxes, absurdities. Like the mind/body problem and the question of free will versus determinism, the absolute/relative issue has been a bloody thorn in the side of the Western tradition, a thorn that has refused to either go away or have the good sense to be solved.

And, more intriguingly, all of these central issues—mind/body, mind/brain, free will/fate, absolute/relative, noumenon/phenomena—are, we will see, precisely the same problem.

And they all have precisely the same answer.

BUT WHERE IS GOD?

Aristotle gave the classic statement of a God that has nothing substantial to do with the relative world. Aristotle's God is a God of pure Perfection, and for such a God to dirty its hands with the relative world—to be involved with relative and finite creatures—would surely indicate a lack of fullness, a lack of completeness, and thus a lack of self-contained perfection. Since God requires nothing, there is certainly no reason for God to produce or create a relative world. In fact, if God actually created the relative world, that would indicate that God lacked something in its own being, which obviously is not possible (you don't get to be God by lacking something!). Thus, God is "in" the relative world only as final cause: the Good toward which all relative creatures strive but never, never reach.

Aspects of Plato's writing could certainly be interpreted to support Aristotle's notion of an untouchable, uninvolved, totally self-contained God. This world, after all, could be seen as nothing but the fleeting and shadowy reflection of the real world, a world utterly transcendent to the relative world of sense and confused opinion.

But that is only half of Plato, so to speak. The other (and less noted) half confirms in the strongest way that the entire relative world is a production, an emanation, a mark of the Plenitude of the Good. Thus, in the *Timaeus*—arguably the most influential book of Western cosmology—an Absolute that cannot create a world is described as decidedly inferior to an Absolute that can. Contrary to Aristotle's conclusion—

that God must be totally self-contained to be perfect—the conclusion of the *Timaeus* is that a God that cannot create is no God at all. (It is even implied that a God who cannot create is envious of a God who can!) Thus, through the Absolute's *creative outflowing*, the entire manifest realm issues forth, so that all things are essentially the Plenitude of the Good. Therefore this very earth Plato describes as a "visible, sensible God."

Thus would begin this version of the West's most intractable dualism: the Absolute versus the relative, and what exactly is their relation?

The great difficulty with Aristotle's position is that it simply leaves the dualism as it finds it. Aristotle's God creates nothing; all things are driven by their desire to reach up to that God, but none of them make it. And however "clean" this might be logically, it leaves the Kosmos with a divisive wedge driven violently into its heart. God over there, us over here, and the two meet only in perpetually unrequited love.

And yet the other side of the attempted solution—God is present in the world as Plenitude—also had its own grave difficulties, at least as it was usually presented. Namely, if we intellectually picture the Absolute as substantially creating the relative world, then how do we account for the existence of evil? If God has His, Her, or Its hand in this world, then doesn't God get blamed for Auschwitz? If so, what kind of grotesque monster is that God?

This dualism between the Absolute and the relative—and their relation, if any—would split the entire tradition of Western philosophy and theology into two warring and largely irreconcilable camps: those who saw God strongly (or even totally) in this world versus those who saw God strongly (or even totally) out of this world: this-worldly versus other-worldly, the Descenders versus the Ascenders, the immanentists versus the transcendentalists, empiricists versus rationalists, one flavor or another.

The Aristotelian tradition simply stood back from the commotion of the relative world, and refused to have its God dirty its fingers. God is a self-contained and unitary perfection, and thus that God has no need to create the world or anything else. How could anything so utterly Perfect do anything further without falling away from Perfection? To create implies that something is lacking, and God lacks nothing; hence God does not create. Where the world came from, and why, is thus left literally hanging, though buried deep in the relative world's heart is the burning desire to reach the state of God-perfection, which would actually mean, for this autistic God, to simply be done with all its neighbors and disappear into its own self-contained absoluteness, basking in the wonders of its unending specialness.

But the alternative intellectual position—that the Perfect One nonetheless got itself involved with imperfect creatures—is scarcely more attractive. If the Perfect One steps down into imperfect evil, something has gone terribly wrong somewhere, and the blame for that can only rest with the One itself.

Christian theologians would, for the most part, maintain that God's Will creates the world, and since freedom is a good component of that world, God allows, but does not create, evil. The Gnostics headed in the other direction: this world is so obviously evil (as in the famous Gnostic line, "What kind of God is this?") that they maintained the entire world was created, not by the real Absolute, but by a Demiurge, an evil or at least inferior spirit. This tricky attempt to keep God out of the world! Because if we let God into the world, something has gone horribly, wretchedly wrong.

Approaching the dualism in this intellectual fashion does little to ameliorate it. If, as the Gnostics maintain, this world is phenomenal, illusory, evil, the product of the Demiurge and not of the real Godhead, then the Demiurge itself comes perilously close to absolute status, and indeed some Gnostics would simply claim that the Demiurge itself creates but is not created, and that is in fact a definition of the Absolute. So now we have two absolutes: an absolute Good, and an absolute Evil, and we have reintroduced exactly the dualism we set out to overcome.

This intractable dualism, I maintain, is the central dualism in the Western tradition, and it would appear and reappear in numerous disguises: it would show up as the dualism between noumenon and phenomena, between mind and body, between free will and determinism, morals and nature, transcendent and immanent, subject and object, ascending and descending. That these are essentially the same dualism is a theme I carefully pursued in *Sex, Ecology, Spirituality* (and its popular version, *A Brief History of Everything*), and the interested reader might consult those sources for a more detailed look.

But what I would like to emphasize here is simply that, buried in the Western tradition—and in the Eastern—is a *radical and compelling solution to these massive dualisms*, a literal solution to the West's most intractable philosophical problems, from the absolute/relative to the mind/body dilemma. But this solution—appropriately known as "nondualism"—has an unbelievably awkward characteristic: namely, its compelling answer cannot be captured in words, a type of metaphysical catch-22 that absolutely guarantees to solve all your problems as long as you don't ask it to.)

And that is where *Eye to Eye* comes in.

THE EYES OF KNOWING

The premise of *Eye to Eye* is that there is a great spectrum of human consciousness; and this means that men and women have available to them a *spectrum of different modes of knowing*, each of which discloses a different type of world (a different worldspace, with different objects, different subjects, different modes of spacetime, different motivations, and so on).

(Put in its simplest form, there is, at the very least, the eye of flesh, the eye of mind, and the eye of spirit (or the eye of contemplation). An exclusive or predominant reliance on one of these modes produces, for example, empiricism, rationalism, and mysticism.)

The claim of *Eye to Eye* is that each of these modes of knowing has its own specific and quite valid set of referents: *sensibilia*, *intelligibilia*, and *transcendelia*. Thus, all three of these modes of knowing can be validated with similar degrees of confidence; and thus all three modes are perfectly valid types of knowledge. (Accordingly, any attempt at a comprehensive and graceful understanding of the Kosmos will most definitely include all three types of knowing; and anything less comprehensive than that is gravely suspect on its own merits.)

Once we allow that the Kosmos is an altogether big and wondrous thing, and once we allow that at least these three types of knowing are necessary to get a decent taste of this miracle of existence, then we very well might find that some of our most recalcitrant philosophical problems are not so recalcitrant after all. And that includes, yes, the most aggravating dualism of all—the absolute and the relative—and its dozen or so bastard offspring, from the mind/body problem to fate and free will to consciousness and brain.

THE PROBLEM OF PROOF

But is the knowledge gained by the three eyes of knowing valid knowledge? How can we confirm or justify this knowledge? How do we know we are not mistaken, confused, or even hallucinating?

(*Eye to Eye* suggests that all valid knowledge (in any level and any quadrant) has the following strands:)

1. *Instrumental injunction.* This is generally of the form, "If you want to *know* this, *do* this."
2. *Intuitive apprehension.* This is an immediate experience of the domain disclosed by the injunction; that is, a direct experience or data-apprehension. (Even if the data is mediated, at the moment of experience it is immediately apprehended.) In other words, this is the direct apprehension of the data brought forth by the particular injunction, whether that data be sensory experience, mental experience, or spiritual experience.
3. *Communal confirmation* (or rejection). This is a checking of the results—the data, the evidence—with others who have *adequately completed* the injunctive and apprehensive strands.

In order to see the moons of Jupiter, you need a telescope. In order to understand *Hamlet*, you need to learn to read. In order to see the truth of the Pythagorean Theorem, you must learn geometry. In other words, valid forms of knowledge have, as one of their significant components, an *injunction*—if you want to *know* this, you must *do* this.

The injunctive strand of valid knowledge leads to an *apprehension* or an *illumination*, a direct disclosing of the data or referents in the world-space brought forth by the injunction, and this illumination is then *checked* (confirmed or refuted) by those who have adequately performed the injunction and thus disclosed the data.

Science, of course, is often taken as *the* model of genuine knowledge; and the philosophy of science is now dominated by three major approaches, which are generally viewed as mutually exclusive: that of empiricism, Thomas Kuhn, and Sir Karl Popper.

The strength of empiricism is its demand that all genuine knowledge be grounded in experiential evidence, and I agree entirely with that demand. But not only is there sensory experience, there is mental experience and spiritual experience. In other words, there is direct data, direct experience, in the realms of sensibilia and intelligibilia and transcendelia. And thus, if we use "experience" in its proper sense as direct apprehension, then we can firmly honor the empiricist demand that *all genuine knowledge be grounded in experience*, in data, in evidence. The empiricists, in other words, are highlighting the importance of the apprehensive or *illuminative strand* in all valid knowledge.

But evidence and data are not simply lying around waiting to be perceived by all and sundry, which is where Kuhn enters the picture.

Thomas Kuhn, in one of the greatly misunderstood ideas of our time, pointed out that normal science proceeds most fundamentally by way of what he called *paradigms* or *exemplars*. A paradigm is not merely a concept, it is an *actual practice*, an injunction, a technique taken as an exemplar for generating data. And Kuhn's point is that genuine scientific knowledge is grounded in paradigms, exemplars, injunctions, which bring forth new data. New injunctions disclose new data, and this is why Kuhn maintained *both* that science is progressive and cumulative, and that it also shows certain breaks or discontinuities (new injunctions bring forth new data). Kuhn, in other words, is highlighting the importance of the *injunctive strand* in the knowledge quest, namely, that data are not simply lying around waiting for anybody to see, but rather are *brought forth* by valid injunctions.

The knowledge brought forth by valid injunctions is indeed genuine knowledge precisely because paradigms in some ways disclose data, they do not merely invent it. And the validity of this data is demonstrated by the fact that bad data can be rebuffed, which is where Popper enters the picture.

Sir Karl Popper's approach emphasizes the importance of falsifiability: genuine knowledge must be open to disproof, or else it is simply dogma in disguise. Popper, in other words, is highlighting the importance of the *confirmation/rejection strand* in all valid knowledge; and, as we will see, this falsifiability principle can be operative in every domain, sensibilia to intelligibilia to transcendelia.

Thus, this integral approach acknowledges and incorporates the moments of truth in each of these important contributions to the human knowledge quest (evidence, Kuhn, and Popper), but without the need to reduce these truths to sensibilia alone. The mistake of the empiricists is the failure to see that, in addition to sensory experience, there is mental and spiritual experience as well. The mistake of the Kuhnians is the failure to see that injunctions apply to all forms of valid knowledge, not just sensorimotor science. And the mistake of the Popperians is the attempt to restrict falsifiability to sensibilia alone and thus make "falsifiable-by-sensory-data" the criterion for mental and spiritual knowledge, whereas bad data in those domains are indeed falsifiable, but only by further data *in those domains*, not by data from lower domains! The Popperians are right about falsifiability, wrong about sensory only.

For example, a bad interpretation of *Hamlet* is falsifiable, not by any empiric-scientific data, but by further interpretations, further mental data, generated in a community of interpreters. *Hamlet* is not about the search for a sunken treasure buried in the Pacific. That is a bad interpretation, a false interpretation, and this falsifiability can easily be demonstrated by a community of researchers who have completed the first two strands (read the play, apprehend its various meanings).

As it is now, the Popperian falsifiability principle has one widespread and altogether perverted use: it is implicitly restricted *only to sensibilia*, which, in an incredibly hidden and sneaky fashion, *automatically bars all mental and spiritual experience from the status of genuine knowledge*. This unwarranted restriction of the falsifiability principle claims to separate genuine knowledge from the dogmatic, when all it is actually accomplishing, in this shrunken form, is a silent but vicious reductionism, a reductionism that cannot even be supported by its own falsifiability principle!

On the other hand, when we free the falsifiability principle from its restriction to sensibilia, and set it free to police the domains of intelligibilia and transcendelia as well, then it most definitely becomes an important aspect of the knowledge quest in all domains, sensory to mental to spiritual. And in each of those domains, it does indeed help us to separate the true from the false, the demonstrable from the dogmatic, the dependable from the bogus.

ENGAGE THE SPIRITUAL INJUNCTION

(In short, all valid forms of knowledge have an *injunction*, an *illumination*, and a *confirmation*; and this is true whether we are looking at the moons of Jupiter, the Pythagorean Theorem, the meaning of *Hamlet*, or . . . the nature of the Absolute.)

And where the moons of Jupiter can be disclosed by the eye of flesh (by the senses or their extensions—sensibilia), and the Pythagorean Theorem can be disclosed by the eye of mind and its inward apprehensions (intelligibilia), the nature of the Absolute can only be disclosed by the *eye of contemplation* and its directly disclosed referents—its transcendelia, its spiritual data, the brought-forth facts of the spiritual worldspace.

But in order to gain access to any of these valid modes of knowing, I must be *adequate* to the injunction—I must successfully complete the injunctive strand. This is true in the physical sciences, the mental sciences, and the spiritual sciences. If we want to *know* this, we must *do* this. And where the exemplar in physical sciences might be a telescope, and in the human sciences might be linguistic interpretation, in the spiritual sciences the exemplar, the injunction, the paradigm, the practice is: meditation or contemplation. It too has its injunctions, its illuminations, and its confirmations, all of which are generally repeatable, verifiable, or falsifiable—and all of which therefore constitute a perfectly valid mode of knowledge acquisition.

But in all cases, we must engage the injunction. We must take up the exemplary practice, and this is certainly true for the spiritual sciences as well. If we do not take up the injunctive practice, then we will not have a genuine paradigm, and therefore we will never see the data of the spiritual worldspace. We will in effect be no different from the Churchmen who refused to follow Galileo's injunction and look through the telescope itself.

And that is where the catch-22 comes in.

THE EYE OF CONTEMPLATION

(As I will argue in the following pages, *we cannot solve the absolute/ relative problem using the eye of flesh or the eye of mind*. This deepest of problems and mysteries directly yields its resolution only to the eye of contemplation. And, as both Kant and Nagarjuna forcefully demonstrated, if you try to state this solution in intellectual or rational terms, you will generate nothing but antinomies, paradox, contradiction.)

In other words, we cannot solve the absolute/relative problem empirically, using the eye of flesh and its sensibilia; nor can we solve it rationally, using the eye of mind and its intelligibilia. The solution, rather, involves the direct apprehension of transcendelia, which are disclosed only by the eye of contemplation and are most definitely verifiable or falsifiable in that domain, using what are in fact quite *public* procedures—public, that is, to all who have completed the injunction and disclosed the illumination.

(And likewise again with fate and free will, the one and the many, noumenon and phenomena, mind and brain. *Eye to Eye* argues that only with the higher stages of consciousness development—part and parcel of the meditative or contemplative unfolding—does the solution to these dilemmas become obvious. But that is not an empirical discovery nor a rational deduction; it is a contemplative apprehension.)

To the question, what is the relation of mind and body—or mind and brain—typical Western answers include the *identity thesis* (they are two different aspects of the same thing), *dualism* (they are two different things), *interactionism* (they are different but mutually causal), *parallelism* (two different things that never speak to each other), *epiphenomenalism* (one is the byproduct of the other). And, despite what their adherents claim, not one of those positions has been able to carry the day, simply because they are all basically flawed in one way or another.

The reason they are inadequate, a more integral philosophy would maintain, is that the mind/body problem cannot be satisfactorily solved with the eye of flesh or the eye of mind, since those are exactly the two modes that need to be integrated, something neither of them could accomplish on its own.

Thus, the only acceptable response to the question, What is the relation of the mind and body?, is to *carefully explain the actual contemplative injunctions*—the contemplative practices or paradigms or exemplars—and invite the questioners to take up the practice and see for themselves. If you want to *know* this, you must *do* this. Although both the empiricist and the rationalist will not find this answer satisfactory—they wish only to engage their own paradigms and exemplars—nonetheless this is the only technically acceptable answer and course of action.

Both the rationalist and the empiricist press us: they want us to state our contemplative conclusions and let them check these conclusions *against their own injunctions*. That is, they want our words without our injunctions. They want to try to follow our words without the pain of having to follow our exemplars. And so we must remind them: Words without injunctions are meaningless. Words without injunctions have no means of verification whatsoever. Words without injunctions are the stuff of doggerel, dogma, and delusions. Our words and our conclusions can indeed be carefully justified—verified or rejected—but only if the injunctions are engaged.

And so when the empiricist and the rationalist demand our conclusions without the injunctions, they have guaranteed a *meaningless* answer—and they blame us for the meaninglessness! Our data cannot be generated by their particular paradigms and exemplars, and so they scratch their heads. They will *not* do this, and therefore they will *not* know this. They circle in the orbit of their self-imposed blindness, and they call this blindness reality.

SPIRITUAL TRAINING AND TRANSCENDENTAL DATA

In the East, Zen would handle the problem of the One and the Many in the following way. The question might be, as a famous Zen koan has it, "If all things return to the One, to what does the One return?" This is, of course, that intractable dilemma: what is the relation of the absolute and the relative, the One and the Many, Emptiness and Form?

But Zen, of course, will reject every intellectual response. A clever student might respond, "To the Many!" which is a perfectly good intellectual answer, yet it will earn only a sharp blow from the Master. Any intellectual response will be radically rejected, no matter what its content!

Rather, the student must take up an *injunction*, a paradigm, an exemplar, a practice, which in this case is zazen, sitting meditation. And—to make a very long and complex story brutally short—after an average of five or six years of this exemplary training, the student may begin to have a series of profound illuminations. And you will simply have to trust me that no one would go through this extended hell in order to be rewarded only with an epileptic fit or a schizophrenic hallucination.

No, this is Ph.D. training in the realm of transcendelia. And once this injunctive training begins to bear fruit, a series of illuminations—commonly called kensho or satori—begins to flash forth into direct and immediate awareness, and this data is then checked (confirmed or refuted) by the community of those who have completed the injunctive and the illuminative strands. At this point, the answer to the question "To what does the One return?" will become extremely clear and straightforward—and I will give that answer in a moment.

(But the point is, the actual *answer* to the question, What is the relation of the One and the Many, the absolute and the relative, free will and fate, consciousness and form, mind and body?—the technically correct and precise answer is: satori. The technically correct answer is: take up the injunction, perform the experiment, gather the data (the experiences), and check them with a community of the similarly adequate.)

We can't *state* what the answer is other than that, because if we did, we would have merely words without injunctions, and they would indeed be utterly meaningless. It's very like baking a pie: you follow the recipe (the injunctions), you bake the pie, and then actually taste it. To the question, "What does the pie taste like?" we can only give the person the recipe, and let them make it and taste it themselves. We *cannot* theoretically or verbally or philosophically or rationally describe the answer in any other satisfactory fashion: if you want to *know* this, you must *do* this.

And thus: take up the injunction or paradigm of meditation; practice and polish that cognitive tool until awareness learns to discern the incredibly subtle phenomena of transcendelia; check your observations with others who have done so, much as mathematicians will check their proofs with others who have completed the injunctions; and thus confirm or reject your results. And in the verification of that transcendelia, the relation of the One and the Many will become perfectly clear—at least as clear as rocks are to the eye of flesh and geometry is to the eye of mind—and thus will that most intractable of dualisms quite literally come unglued.

The answer to the relation of the Absolute and the relative is therefore most definitely *not*: the Absolute created the world. It most definitely is *not*: the world is illusory and the Absolute alone is real. It is *not*: we perceive only the phenomenal reflection of a noumenal reality. It is *not*: fate and free will are two aspects of one and the same process. It is *not*: all things and events are different aspects of a single interwoven web-of-life. It is *not*: the body alone is real and the mind is a reflection of that only reality. It is *not*: mind and body are two different aspects of the total organism. It is *not*: mind emerges from hierarchical brain structure. In fact, it is not even: noumenon and phenomena are not-two and nondual.

Those are all merely *intellectual symbols* that purport to give the answer, but the real answer does not lie in sensibilia or intelligibilia, it lies in transcendelia, and that domain only discloses itself after the meditative exemplar is engaged, whereupon every single one of those intellectual answers is seen to be inadequate and off the mark; each generates nothing but more insolvable and insuperable difficulties, dilemmas, and contradictions. The answer is not more talk; the answer is satori, by whatever name we wish to use to convey valid contemplative awareness.

And, much more to the point, even if this answer could be stated in words—and in fact, the answer can be stated in words, because Zen masters talk about it all the time!—nonetheless, it would make no sense to anybody who had not also performed the injunction, just as mathematical symbols can be seen by anybody but understood only by those who have completed the training.

But open the eye of contemplation, and the answer is as obvious, as perfect, as unmistakable as the play of sunlight on a crystal clear pond, early on a cool spring morning.

You see, that was the answer.

CONCLUSION

We have seen that the Western tradition has been plagued, from its inception, with a series of brutal dualisms, and that virtually all forms of Western philosophy, right up to today, have come to rest finally on one or another of these dualisms (mind/body, truth/appearance, noumenon/phenomenon, transcendental/immanent, ascending/descending, subject/object, signified/signifier, consciousness/brain).

But these dualisms, and the root issues surrounding them, cannot finally be solved by the eye of flesh and its empiricism, nor by the eye of mind and its rationalism, but only, finally, by the eye of contemplation and its radical experiential mysticism (satori by whatever name).

In the West, since Kant, metaphysics has fallen on hard times. I maintain that it has done so precisely because it attempted to do with the eye of mind that which can only be done with the eye of contemplation. Because the mind could not actually deliver the metaphysical goods, and yet kept loudly claiming that it could, somebody was bound to blow the whistle sooner or later and demand real evidence. Kant made the demand, and metaphysics collapsed—and rightly so, in its typical form.

Neither empiricism, nor pure reason, nor practical reason, nor any combination thereof can see into the realm of Spirit (and "real metaphysics"). In the smoking ruins that Kant left, the only possible conclusion is that all future metaphysics, to be genuine, must offer direct experiential evidence and data of the spiritual domain itself. And that means, in addition to sensory experience and its empiricism (scientific and pragmatic), and mental experience and its rationalism (pure and practical), there must be added spiritual experience and its mysticism (spiritual practice and its experiential data).

The possibility of the direct experience of sensibilia, intelligibilia, and transcendelia radically defuses the Kantian objections, and sets the knowledge quest firmly on the road of evidence, with each of its validity claims (truth, truthfulness, justness, functional fit) guided by the three strands of genuine knowledge accumulation (injunction, apprehension, confirmation) at every level (sensory, mental, spiritual—across the entire spectrum of consciousness, however many levels we wish to invoke).

In short, the three strands of genuine knowledge accumulation operate for all levels, in each quadrant. The application of the three strands (with their built-in demand for exemplars, evidence, and falsifiability) does indeed help us in our quest to separate the wheat from the chaff, the true from the false, the demonstrable from the dogmatic, the dependable from the bogus. Guided by the three strands, the validity claims of every quadrant can indeed be redeemed. They carry cash value. And the cash is experiential evidence, sensory to mental to spiritual.

(With this approach, metaphysics regains its proper warrant, which is not sensory or mental but finally contemplative. With the eye of Spirit, God can be seen. With the eye of Spirit, the universe unfolds its innermost contours. With the eye of Spirit, noumenon announces its pure Presence. With the eye of Spirit, the Kosmos delivers its deepest secrets. And with the eye of Spirit, the intractable nightmares of the sensory and mental dilemmas yield to the radiance of Emptiness itself.)

Integral philosophy cannot replace any of the other modes or functions of knowing—it cannot replace empirical science, or contemplative meditation, or even the other mental modes, from literature to poetry to history to psychoanalysis to mathematics to linguistics.

(But integral philosophy is there, at the very heart of the mental world, coordinating and elucidating all of these modes of knowing, dimensions of value, levels of being. Integral philosophy itself is of the mental domain, and cannot by itself, with its mental devices alone, step beyond that sphere. But it firmly acknowledges the role of contemplation in generating data, and it takes that data into account in its own coordinating and elucidating activities. If it does not itself deliver meditative data, it firmly acknowledges the existence and importance of that data.[1] It is mandalic reason at its finest and most encompassing. It knows the difference between relative truth, which it can divulge, and absolute truth, for which it must yield to the eye of contemplation.)

Integral philosophy thus mentally coordinates the Good, and the True, and the Beautiful, weaving a mandala of the many faces of Spirit, and then invites us to take up spiritual practice itself, and thus finally meet Spirit face to face.

(And as for the final answer to the great Western dualism? The final answer to the mind/body problem? To the One and the Many? God and creation? Was God at Auschwitz? Are we fated or free-willed? It's all the same question, you see, so here is another perfectly complete answer:)

> This slowly drifting cloud is pitiful!
> What dreamwalkers we all are!
> Awakened, the one great truth:
> Black rain on the temple roof.

Integral philosophy attempts to include and coordinate the many faces of the Good (the "we"), and the True (the "it"), and the Beautiful (the

"I"), as all of them evolve across the entire spectrum, from their sensory forms (seen with the eye of flesh) to their mental forms (seen with the eye of mind) to their spiritual forms (seen with the eye of contemplation)—a pluridimensional Kosmic mandala of unending embrace.

(With science we touch the True, the "It" of Spirit. With morals we touch the Good, the "We" of Spirit. What, then, would an integral approach have to say about the Beautiful, the "I" of Spirit itself? What is the Beauty that is in the eye of the Beholder? When we are in the eye of Spirit, the I of Spirit, what do we finally see?)

4

Integral Art and Literary Theory

PART I

In the process of understanding and interpretation, part and whole are related in a circular way: in order to understand the whole, it is necessary to understand the parts, while to understand the parts it is necessary to have some comprehension of the whole.

—DAVID COUZENS HOY

Thus the movement of understanding is constantly from the whole to the part and back to the whole. Our task is to extend in concentric circles the unity of the understood meaning. The harmony of all the details with the whole is the criterion of correct understanding. The failure to achieve this harmony means that understanding has failed.

—HANS-GEORG GADAMER

INTRODUCTION

WITH THE DEATH of the avant-garde and the triumph of irony, art seems to have nothing sincere to say. Narcissism and nihilism battle for a center stage that isn't even there; kitsch and camp crawl all over each other in a fight for a representation that no longer matters anyway; there seems to arise only the egoic inclination of artist and critic alike, caught in halls of self-reflecting mirrors, admiring their image in a world that once cared.

The aim of this essay is to step out of the narcissistic and nihilistic endgame that has so often overtaken the world of postmodern art and literature, and to introduce instead the essentials of a genuinely integral art and literary theory—what might be called *integral hermeneutics*.

I will cover both art and literature, but with an emphasis on visual art, which is actually a "trickier" and in some ways more difficult case, since it usually lacks narrative structure to help guide the interpretation. (A subsequent essay focuses specifically on an "all-level, all-quadrant" analysis of literary signification and semiotics in general.)[1]

It is no secret that the art and literary world has reached something of a cul-de-sac, a dead end. Postmodern literary theory is a stark example of the "babble of interpretations" that has overcome the art world. It used to be that "meaning" was something the author created and simply put into a text, and the reader simply pulled it out. This view is now regarded, by all parties, as hopelessly naive.

Starting with psychoanalysis, it was recognized that some meaning could be unconscious, or unconsciously generated, and this unconscious meaning would find its way into the text even though the author was unaware of it. It was therefore the job of the psychoanalyst, and not the naive reader, to pull this hidden meaning out.

The "hermeneutics of suspicion," in its many forms, thus came to view artworks as repositories of hidden meaning that could be decoded only by the knowing critic. Any repressed, oppressed, or otherwise marginalized context would show up, disguised, in the art, and the art was thus a testament to the repression, oppression, marginalization. Marginalized context was hidden subtext.

The Marxist variation was that the critics themselves existed in the context of capitalist-industrial social practices of covert domination, and these hidden contexts and meanings could be found in (and therefore pulled out of) any artwork created by a person in *that* context. Similarly, art would be interpreted in the context of racism, sexism, elitism, speciesism, jingoism, imperialism, logocentrism, phallocentrism, phallologocentrism (batteries not included).

Various forms of structuralism and hermeneutics fought vigorously to find the "real" context which would, therefore, provide the real and final *meaning*, which would undercut (or supersede) all other interpretations. Foucault, in his archaeological period, outdid them both, situating both structuralism and hermeneutics in an *episteme* that was itself the cause and context of the type of people who would even want to do hermeneutics and structuralism in the first place.

In part in reaction to some of this, the New Criticism had said, basically, let us ignore all of those interpretations. The artwork, in and by itself, is all that really matters. Ignore the personality (conscious or unconscious) of the author, ignore the historical setting, the time, the place, and look solely at the structural integrity of the artwork itself (its regime, its code, its internal pattern). "Affective stylistics" and "reader-response" theory reacted strongly to all that, and maintained that since meaning is only generated in reading (or in viewing) the artwork, then the *meaning* of the work is actually found in the *response* of the viewer. The phenomenologists (e.g., Iser, Ingarden) had tried a combination of the two: the text has gaps ("spots of indeterminacy"), and the meaning of the *gaps* can be found in the reader.

(And deconstruction came along and said, basically, you're all wrong. (It's very hard to trump that.) Deconstruction maintained that all meaning is context-dependent, and contexts are boundless. There is thus no way to control, or even finally to determine, meaning—and thus both art and criticism spin endlessly out of control and into the space of unrelenting ambiguity, never to be seen or heard from again.)

Postmodern deconstruction, it has finally been realized, leads more often than not to nihilism: there is no genuine meaning anywhere, only nested deceptions. And this leaves, in the place of art as sincere statement, art as anarchy, anchored only in egoic whim and narcissistic display. Into the vacuum created by the implosion that is so much of postmodernism, rushes the ego triumphant. Meaning is context-dependent, and contexts are boundless, and that leaves art and artist and critic alike lost in aperspectival space, ruled only by the purr of the selfcentric engine left driving the entire display.

The laments are loud and well known. Painter and critic Peter Fuller:

> I feel that we are living through the epilogue of the European professional Fine Art tradition—an epilogue in which the context and subject-matter of most art is art itself.[2]

And art historian Barbara Rose:

> The art currently filling the museums and galleries is of such low quality generally that no real critical intelligence could possibly feel challenged to analyze it. . . . There is an inescapable sense among artists and critics that we are at the end of our rope, culturally speaking.[3]

But who knows? Perhaps meaning is in fact context-dependent, and perhaps contexts are indeed boundless. Is there any way that this state of affairs can be viewed so as to actually restore a genuine sense of meaning to art and its interpretation? Is there any way to ground the babble of interpretations that has finally self-deconstructed? Is there any way that the nested lies announced by postmodernism could in fact be nested truths? And could this spell the endgame of the narcissism and nihilism that had so proudly announced their own ascendancy?

Could, in short, an integral orientation save art and literary theory from itself?

CONTEXTS WITHIN CONTEXTS ENDLESSLY

We live in a world of holons. "Holons": the word was coined by Arthur Koestler to indicate *wholes* that are simultaneously *parts* of other wholes: a whole quark is part of a whole atom; a whole atom is part of a whole molecule; a whole molecule is part of a whole cell; a whole cell is part of a whole organism. . . . In linguistics, a whole letter is part of a whole word, which is part of a whole sentence, which is part of a whole paragraph . . . and so on.

In other words, we live in a universe that consists neither of wholes nor of parts, but of whole/parts, or holons. Wholes do not exist by themselves, nor do parts exist by themselves. Every whole simultaneously exists as a part of some other whole, and as far as we can tell, this is indeed endless. Even the whole of the universe right now is simply a part of the next moment's whole. There are no wholes, and no parts, anywhere in the universe; there are only whole/parts.

As I have tried to suggest in *A Brief History of Everything*, this is true in the physical, emotional, mental, and spiritual domains. We exist in fields within fields, patterns within patterns, contexts within contexts, endlessly. There is an old joke about a King who goes to a Wiseperson and asks, "How is it that the Earth doesn't fall down?" The Wiseperson replies, "The Earth is resting on a lion." "On what, then, is the lion resting?" "The lion is resting on an elephant." "On what is the elephant resting?" "The elephant is resting on a turtle." "On what is the. . . ?" "You can stop right there, your Majesty. It's turtles all the way down."

Holons all the way down, in a dizzyingly nested fashion, without ever hitting a foundation. The "postmodern poststructuralists"— usually associated with such names as Jacques Derrida, Michel Foucault, Jean-François Lyotard, and stretching back to Georges Bataille and Friedrich Nietzsche—have been the great foes of any sort of systematic theory or "grand narrative," and thus they might be expected to raise stern objections to any overall theory of "holons." But a close look at their own work shows that it is driven precisely by a conception of holons within holons within holons, of texts within texts within texts (or contexts within contexts within contexts), and it is this sliding play of texts within texts that forms the "foundationless" platform from which they launch their attacks.

Georges Bataille, for instance. "In the most general way"—and these are his italics—"*every isolable element of the universe always appears as a particle that can enter into composition with a whole that transcends it. Being is only found as a whole composed of particles whose relative autonomy is maintained* [a part that is also a whole]. These two principles [simultaneous wholeness and partness] dominate the uncertain presence of an *ipse* being across a distance that never ceases to put *everything* in question."[4]

Everything is put into question because everything is a context within a context forever. And *putting everything in question* is precisely what the postmodern poststructuralists are known for. And so in a language that would soon become quite typical (and by now quite comical), Bataille goes on to point out that "putting everything into question" counters the human need to arrange things violently in terms of a pat wholeness and smug universality: "With extreme dread imperatively becoming the demand for universality, carried away to vertigo by the movement that composes it, the *ipse* being that presents itself as a universal is only a challenge to the diffuse immensity that escapes its precarious violence, the tragic negation of all that is not its own bewildered phantom's chance. But, as a man, this being falls into the meanders of the knowledge of his fellowmen, which absorbs his substance in order to reduce it to a component of what goes beyond the virulent madness of his autonomy in the total night of the world."[5] Um, and so forth.

The point is *not* that Bataille himself was without any sort of system, but simply that the *system is sliding*—holons within holons forever. So the claim to simply have "no system" is a little disingenuous. Which is why André Breton, the leader of the surrealists at the time, began a counterattack on this part of Bataille, also in terms that are echoed by today's critics of postmodernists: "Bataille's misfortune is to reason: admittedly, he reasons like someone who 'has a fly on his nose,' which allies him more closely with the dead than with the living, but *he does reason*. He is trying, with the help of the tiny mechanism in him which is not completely out of order, to share his obsessions: this very fact proves that he cannot claim, no matter what he may say, to be opposed to any system, like an unthinking brute."[6]

Both sides are correct, in a sense. There is system, but the system is sliding. It is unendingly, dizzifyingly, holonic. This is why Jonathan Culler, perhaps the foremost interpreter of Jacques Derrida's deconstruction, can point out that Derrida does *not* deny truth per se, but only insists that truth and meaning are *context-bound* (each context being a whole that is also part of another whole context, which itself . . .). "One could therefore," says Culler, "identify deconstruction with the twin principles of the *contextual determination of meaning* and the *infinite extendability of context.*"[7]

Turtles all the way up, all the way down. What deconstruction puts into question is the desire to find a final resting place, in either wholeness or partness or anything in between. Every time somebody finds a final interpretation or a foundational interpretation of a text or artwork (or life or history or cosmos), deconstruction is on hand to say that the final context does not exist, because it is also unendingly a part of yet another context forever. As Culler puts it, any sort of final context is "unmasterable, both in principle and in practice. *Meaning is context bound, but context is boundless.*"[8]

Even Jürgen Habermas, who generally takes Breton's position to Derrida's Bataille, agrees with that particular point. As Habermas puts it, "These variations of context that change meaning cannot in principle be arrested or controlled, because contexts cannot be exhausted, that is, they cannot be theoretically mastered once and for all."[9]

That the system is sliding does *not* mean that meaning can't be established, that truth doesn't exist, or that contexts won't hold still long enough to make a simple point. Many postmodern poststructuralists have not simply discovered holonic space, they have become thoroughly lost in it. Georges Bataille, for example, took a good, long, hard look at holonic space and went properly insane, though which is cause, and which effect, is hard to say.

As for our main topic, we need only note that there is indeed system, but the system is sliding: The universe is composed of holons—contexts within contexts within contexts—all the way up, all the way down.

MEANING IS CONTEXT-DEPENDENT

The word "bark" means something very different in the phrases "the bark of a dog" and "the bark of a tree." Which is exactly why all meaning is context-bound; the identical word has different meanings depending upon the context in which it is found.

(This context-dependency seems to pervade every aspect of the universe and our lives in it.) Take, for example, a single thought, say the thought of going to the grocery store. When I have that thought, what I actually experience is the thought itself, the interior thought and its meaning—the symbols, the images, the idea of going to the grocery store. (This is the Upper-Left quadrant, the intentional.)

Now the internal thought only makes sense in terms of my cultural background. If I spoke a different language, the thought would be composed of different symbols and have quite different meanings. If I existed in a primal tribal society a million years ago, I would never even have the thought "going to the grocery store." It might be, "Time to kill the bear." The point is that my thoughts themselves arise in a *cultural background* that gives texture and meaning and context to my individual thoughts, and indeed, I would not even be able to "talk to myself" if I did not exist in a community of individuals who also talk to me. (This is the Lower-Left quadrant, the cultural.)

So the cultural community serves as an *intrinsic background* and *context* to any individual thoughts I might have. My thoughts do not just pop into my head out of nowhere; they pop into my head out of a cultural background, and however much I might move beyond this background, I can never simply escape it altogether, and I could never have developed thoughts in the first place without it. The occasional cases of a "wolf boy"—humans raised in the wild—show that the human brain, left without culture, does not produce linguistic thoughts on its own.

In short, my individual thoughts only exist against a vast background of cultural practices and languages and meanings and contexts, without which I could form virtually no individual thoughts at all. But my culture itself is not simply disembodied, hanging in idealistic midair. It has *material components*, much as my own individual thoughts have material brain components. All *cultural* events have *social* correlates. These concrete social components include types of technology, forces of production (horticultural, agrarian, industrial, etc.), concrete institutions, written codes and patterns, geopolitical locations, and so on (the Lower-Right quadrant). And these concrete material components—the actual *social system*—are crucial in helping to determine the types of cultural worldview within which my own thoughts will arise.

(So my supposedly "individual thought" is actually a holon that has all these various aspects to it—intentional, behavioral, cultural, and social.) And around the holonic circle we go: the social system will have a strong influence on the cultural worldview, which will set limits to the individual thoughts that I can have, which will register in the brain physiology. And we can go around that circle in any direction. They are all interwoven. They are all mutually determining. They all cause, and are caused by, the other holons, in concentric spheres of contexts within contexts indefinitely.

And this fact bears directly on the nature and meaning of art itself.

WHAT IS ART?

The simplest and perhaps earliest view of the nature and meaning of art (and thus of its interpretation as well) is that art is *imitative* or *representational*: it copies something in the real world. The painting of a landscape copies or represents the real landscape. Plato takes this view of art in the *Republic*, where he uses the example of a bed: the painting of a bed is a copy of a concrete bed (which is itself a copy of the ideal Form of a bed). Notoriously, for Plato, this puts art in a rather bad position: it is making copies of copies of the Ideal, and is thus doubly removed and doubly inferior. Later theorists would "upgrade" this Platonic conception by maintaining that the true artist is actually copying the Ideal Forms directly, seen with the mind's eye, and thus is performing a "perfectionist" artistry—as Michelangelo said, "The beauty which stirs and carries up to heaven every sound intellect."

Aristotle likewise takes the view of art as imitative or copying the real world, and in one form or another this notion of art as *mimesis* has had a long and profound influence: the *meaning* of art is that which it represents.

The grave difficulty with this view, taken in and by itself, is that it unmistakably implies that the better the imitation, the better the art, so that a perfect copy would be perfect art, which lands art squarely in the province of *trompe l'oeil* and documentary photography: a good likeness on a driver's license photo would be good art. Moreover, not all art is representative or imitative: surrealist, minimalist, expressionist, conceptual, and so forth. So while some art has representative aspects, *mimesis* alone can account for neither the nature nor the value of art.

With the rise of the Enlightenment in Europe, two other major theories of the nature and meaning of art gained prominence, and they are both still quite influential today. Not surprisingly, these theories would spring respectively from the great rational and great romantic currents that were set in motion in the seventeenth and eighteenth centuries, and which, translated into the artistic domain, came to be known generally as formalist and expressivist (rational and romantic!).

And at this point, the question became, not so much *what* is art, but *where* is art?

ART IS IN THE MAKER

If the nature, meaning, and value of art are not simply due to art's imitative capacity, perhaps the essence of art lies in its power to *express* something, and not simply to *copy* something. And indeed, in both the theory and practice of art, emphasis often began to turn from a faithful copying and representing and imitating—whether of religious icons or of a realistic nature—to an increasingly expressionistic stance, under the broad influence of the general currents of Romanticism. This view of art and its value was given strong and quite influential voice by theorists such as Benedetto Croce (*Aesthetics*), R. G. Collingwood (*Principles of Art*), and Leo Tolstoy (*What Is Art?*).

The basic conclusion of these Romantic theorists: art is, first and foremost, the *expression* of the feelings or intentions of the artist. It is not simply the imitation of an external reality, but the expression of an internal reality. We therefore can best *interpret* art by trying to understand the *original intention* of the maker of the artwork itself (whether painter, writer, composer).

Thus, for Tolstoy, art is the "contagion of feeling." That is, the artist expresses feeling in the artwork which then evokes that feeling in us, the viewers; and the quality of the art is best interpreted by the quality of the feelings it expresses and "infects" us with. For Croce—arguably the most influential aesthetician of the 1900s—art is the expression of emotion, itself a very real and primal type of knowledge, often cosmic in its power, especially when expressed and evoked by great works of art. And Collingwood made the original intention of the artist so utterly primary that the inward, psychological vision of the artist was itself said to be the actual art, whether or not that vision ever got translated into public forms.

This view of art as the expression of an original intention or feeling or vision in the artist gave rise to what is still perhaps the most widespread school of the *interpretation* of art. Modern "hermeneutics"—the art and science of interpretation—began with certain Romantically inspired philosophical trends, notably in Friedrich Schleiermacher and then Wilhelm Dilthey, and continued down to this day in such influential theorists as Emilio Betti and E. D. Hirsch. This approach, one of the oldest and in some ways the most central school of hermeneutics, maintains that the key to the correct interpretation of a text—considering "text" in the very broadest sense, as any symbol requiring interpretation, whether artistic, linguistic, poetic—the key to correct interpretation is *the recovery of the maker's original intention*, a psychological *reconstruction* of the author's (or artist's) intentions in the original historical setting.

In short, for these approaches, since the *meaning* of art is the maker's original intention, a *valid* interpretation involves the psychological reconstruction and recovery of this original intention. The hermeneutic gap between the artist and viewer is closed to the extent there is a "seeing eye to eye" with the artist's original meaning, and this occurs through the procedures of valid interpretation based on original recovery and reconstruction.

It is no accident that the *theory* of art as expression was historically paralleled by the broad trends of expressionism in the *practice* of art itself. The nineteenth-century expressionists and Postimpressionists, including Van Gogh, Gauguin, and Munch, directly opposed the Realist and Impressionist imitation of nature (Van Gogh: "Instead of trying to reproduce exactly what I have before my eyes, I use color more arbitrarily so as to express myself more forcibly"); from there to the Cubists and Fauves (Matisse: "What I am after above all is expression"); to Kandinsky and Klee and the abstract expressionism of Pollock, Kline, and de Kooning. In its various manifestations, expressionism was not just a stylistic or idealizing alteration of external representation, but an almost complete and total break with the tradition of imitation.

No sooner was this theory (and practice) of art as expression put forth than another offshoot of the broad Romantic movement—psychoanalysis—pointed out that many human *intentions* are in fact *unconscious*. And further, these intentions, even though unconscious, nonetheless can make their way in disguised forms into everyday life, perhaps as neurotic symptoms, or as symbolic dreams, or as slips of the tongue, or, in general, as compromise formations expressing the conflict between a forbidden desire and a censoring or repressing force. The psychoanalyst, trained to spot the symbolic expression of these hidden desires, could thus *interpret* these symbols and symptoms to the individual, who in turn would thus gain, it was duly hoped, some sort of understanding and amelioration of his or her distressing condition.

In the sphere of art and literature, this inevitably meant that the original maker (artist, writer, poet) would, like everybody else, have various unconscious intentions, and these intentions, in disguised forms, *would leave traces in the artwork itself*. It followed then with mathematical precision: (1) if the meaning of art is the original intention expressed in the work, and (2) if the correct interpretation of art is therefore the reconstruction of this intention, but (3) if some intentions are unconscious and leave only symbolic traces in the artwork, then (4) an important part of the correct interpretation of an artwork is the unearthing and interpreting of these unconscious drives, intentions, desires, wishes. The art critic, to be a true critic, must also be a psychoanalyst.

ART IS IN THE HIDDEN INTENT: SYMPTOMATIC THEORIES

This soon opened a Pandora's box of "unconscious intentions." If the artwork expressed the unconscious Freudian desires of the artist, why limit it to Freudian themes? There are, after all, several different types of unconscious structures in the human being, the list of which soon exploded. The artist exists in a setting of techno-economic structures, the Marxists pointed out, and a particular artwork will inexorably reflect the "base" of economic realities, and thus the correct interpretation of a text or work of art involves highlighting the class structures in which the art is produced. Feminists soon caught the fever, and avidly tried to suggest that the fundamental and hidden structures were primarily those of gender, so that even Marxists were driven by the unconscious or thinly disguised intentions of patriarchal power. Womanists (feminists of color) very rapidly outflanked the mainstream feminists with a criticism whose opening line was, in effect, "We can't blame everything on the patriarchy, white girl. . . ." And so the list would go: racism, sexism, elitism, speciesism, anthropocentrism, androcentrism, imperialism, ecologism, logocentrism, phallocentrism.

All of those theories might best be called *symptomatic theories*: they view a particular artwork as symptomatic of larger currents, currents the artist is often unaware of—sexual, economic, cultural, ideological. They generally grant that the meaning of art is the expression of an original feeling, intention, or vision of the artist. But they immediately add that the artist might have, or exist in, structures of unconscious intention, and these unconscious structures, generally not available to the awareness of the artists themselves, would nonetheless leave symbolic traces in their works of art, and these traces could be spotted, decoded, deciphered, and interpreted by the knowing critic. A *valid* interpretation is thus one that decodes and exposes the hidden intentions, whether individual or cultural.

ART IS IN THE ARTWORK

While there may be much truth to each of those positions—and we will shortly return for an assessment—nonetheless, few critics would concede that intentions alone, conscious or unconscious, define the nature and value of art.

In part as a reaction to these originally Romantic and expressivist versions of art, there arose various more "formal" interpretations of art and literature; and this, as I suggested, was in large measure a legacy of the more *rational* side of the Enlightenment agenda.

This Enlightenment rationalism had several profound influences on art theory and practice. The general atmosphere of Enlightenment scientific realism soon translated almost directly to the realist trends in literature and painting (Zola, Balzac, Flaubert, Courbet), and from there to the Impressionists, who repudiated so much of the Romantic-expressionist trends and sought instead to capture "immediate visual impressions" rendered intensely and impersonally, the emotions of the artist being quite secondary at best (Monet, Renoir, Manet, Pissarro, Degas), as well as the objective rendering of contemporary and actual experience, sometimes verging on the documentary, and always in sympathy with a realist attitude.

But Enlightenment rationalism also entered art theory and practice in a rather strict and dry sense, namely, in the view that the nature and value of art is to be found in the *form* of the artwork itself. Much of this *formalism* had its modern origin in Kant's immensely influential *Critique of Judgment*, but it would soon be powerfully expressed in music theory by Eduard Hanslick and in the visual arts by Roger Fry and Clive Bell. Formalism would likewise find its way into literary theory, most significantly with the Russian formalists (Jakobson, Propp); the American New Critics (Wimsatt and Beardsley); the French structuralists

(Lévi-Strauss, Barthes), neo-structuralists (early Foucault), and post-structuralists (Derrida, Paul de Man, Hartman, Lyotard).

For formalism in general, the *meaning* of a text or an artwork is found in the formal relationships between elements of the work itself. A valid interpretation of the work, therefore, involves the elucidation of these formal structures. In many cases, this was (and is) coupled with an aggressive denial of the importance or significance of the maker's original intention. Indeed, the artist or the author or the subject was pronounced "dead"—totally irrelevant to the work—as in Barthes's famous "death of the author" ("amputate the art from the artist"). Language itself replaced the author as the producer of the text, and structural analysis (in its original, neo-, or post-forms) became the only sure method of artistic interpretation. The "death of the subject" meant as well the death of the subject's original intention as a source of valid interpretation, and "What comes after the subject?" became the new rallying call.

In the rather influential American New Criticism, this view was expressed most forcefully by Monroe Beardsley and William Wimsatt, Jr. In their now famous essay, "The Intentional Fallacy," they conclude bluntly that the *maker's intention* is "neither available nor desirable as a standard for judging the success of a work" of art.[10] It was to the *artwork itself* that the interpreter and critic must essentially look. After all, they maintained, how can you know the intent of the artwork if it is not expressed in the art itself? Where else could you possibly look? Intentions that don't make it into the artwork might be interesting, but they are not, by definition, part of the artwork. And thus interpretation should center first and foremost on elements intrinsic to the artwork considered as a whole in itself.

Similar formalist theories of art were put forth in music by Eduard Hanslick (*The Beautiful in Music*), who maintained that the meaning of music was in its internal forms (melody, rhythm, harmony); and in the visual arts by Roger Fry (*Vision and Design*) and Clive Bell (*Art*), who both maintained that the nature and meaning of art was to be found in its "significant form" (Cézanne, for both of them, being the great exemplar).

In all of these versions of formalism, the locus and meaning of art is *not* in the intention of the artist, nor does it lie in what the artwork might *represent*, nor what it might *express*. Rather, the nature and meaning of art lies in the formal or structural relationship of the elements manifested in the artwork itself. And thus *valid* interpretation consists primarily in the elucidating of these forms and structures.

ART IS IN THE VIEWER

As the modern world of the Enlightenment and its Romantic rebellion gave way to the postmodern world, yet another extremely influential trend in art and literary criticism emerged. Just as formalist theories killed the artist and centered solely on the artwork, this new trend further killed the artwork itself and centered solely on . . . the viewer of the art.

For these various theories of "reception and response," the meaning of art is not found in the author's original intention, nor is it found in any specific features of the artwork itself. Rather, these theories maintain, since the only way we actually get to know a work of art is by viewing it (looking, listening, reading), then the primary locus of the meaning of the artwork can only be found in the *responses* of the viewers themselves.

Thus, according to this view, the nature and meaning of art is to be found in the history of the reception and response to the artwork; and likewise, a *valid* interpretation of the artwork consists in an analysis of these responses (or the cumulative history of these responses). As Passmore summarizes it, "The proper point of reference in discussing works of art is an interpretation it sets going in an audience; that interpretation—or the class of such interpretations—is the work of art, whatever the artist had in mind in creating it. Indeed, the interpreter, not the artist, creates the work."[11]

These theories trace much of their lineage to the work of Martin Heidegger, whose hermeneutic philosophy broke with the traditional conception of truth as an unchanging and objective set of facts, and replaced it with the notion of the *historicity* of truth: human beings do not have an unchanging *nature* so much as a changing *history*, and thus what we call "truth" is, in important ways, historically situated. Moreover, we come to understand the historicity of truth not so much through scientific empiricism but rather through *interpretation* (through "hermeneutics"), just as, if you and I want to understand each other, we must interpret what we are saying to each other ("What do you mean by that? Oh, I see"). Interpretation lies at the very heart of the historicity of truth.

Heidegger's hermeneutic philosophy has had an immense influence on art and literary theory, principally through two major students of his work: Hans-Georg Gadamer and Jacques Derrida. We briefly mentioned Derrida in connection with structuralist and poststructuralist theories, which locate the meaning of a text in chains of formal signifiers (and according to "poststructuralism," the chains of signifiers are endlessly "sliding"). Gadamer's influence has been equally widespread; he is now arguably the foremost theoretician of aesthetics.

For Gadamer, even a "purely" aesthetic event, such as looking at an abstract painting, is not merely a simple sensory occasion. The moment we start to ask what the painting means, or how it affects us, or what it might be saying—the moment the mute stare gives way to meaning— then we are inexorably stepping out of the "merely sensory" and into language and history. We are stepping into the linguistic world, which itself can only be understood by *interpretation*: What does that *mean*? And all meaning exists in history; that is, all meaning is marked by historicity. What a painting means to us, today, will be different from what that painting means to, say, people a thousand years from now (if it means anything at all). In other words, for these theorists, we cannot isolate meaning from the ongoing sweep of history.

The work of art, accordingly, exists in this historical stream, which brings forth new receptions, elicits new responses, gives new interpretations, unfolds new meanings as it flows. And, according to this view, the artwork is, so to speak, the sum total of its particular historical stream. The artwork is not something that exists by itself, outside of history, isolated and self-regarding, existing only because it looks at itself; rather, the only way we know the artwork is by viewing and interpreting it, and it is those interpretations, grounded in history, that constitute the overall art.

AND SO *WHERE*, EXACTLY, IS ART?

We have seen that the major theories of art disagree sharply on the nature, locus, and meaning of art. Intentional theories locate art in the original intent or feeling or vision of the maker. Formalist theories locate the meaning of art in the relationships among elements of the artwork itself. Reception-and-response theories place the nature and meaning of art in the viewer. And symptomatic theories place the locus of art in larger currents operating in a mostly unconscious fashion in the artist and viewer alike.

In fact, the whole of art theory can be seen as a spirited attempt to decide exactly what the *locus* of art is, and therefore where we can find or locate the *meaning* of an artwork—and thus, finally, how we can develop valid *interpretations* of that art. In short: What and where is art?

And I am saying, the nature and meaning of art is thoroughly *holonic*. Like every other entity in the universe, art is holonic in its nature, its locus, its structure, its meaning, and its interpretation. Any specific artwork is a holon, which means that it is a whole that is simultaneously a part of numerous other wholes. The artwork exists in contexts within contexts within contexts, endlessly.

Further—and this is the crucial point—*each context will confer a different meaning on the artwork*, precisely because, as we have seen, all meaning is context-bound: change the context, you elicit a different meaning.

Thus, all of the theories that we have discussed—representational, intentional, formalist, reception-and-response, symptomatic—are basically correct; they are all true; they are all pointing to a *specific context* in which the artwork subsists, and without which the artwork could not exist, contexts that therefore are genuinely *constitutive* of the art itself—that is, part of the very being of the art.

And the only reason those theories disagree with each other is that each of them is trying to make its own context the only real or important context: paradigmatic, primal, central, privileged. Each theory is trying to make its context the only context worth serious consideration.

But the holonic nature of reality—contexts within contexts forever—means that each of these theories is part of a nested series of truths. Each is true when highlighting its own context, but false when it tries to deny reality or significance to other existing contexts. And an integral art and literary theory—covering the nature, meaning, and interpretation of art—will of necessity be a holonic theory: concentric circles of nested truths and interpretations.

The study of holons is the study of nested truths. And now we can see exactly how postmodernist deconstructionists took a wrong turn at holons and got hopelessly, helplessly lost. They looked clearly at holonic space and then, rather like Bataille, went properly insane: reality consists not of nested truths but of nested lies, deceptions within deceptions forever, precisely the features of a psychotic break. They have it exactly backwards, the photographic negative of a reality they no longer trust. And once having stepped through that inverting mirror and into Alice's Wonderland, nothing is ever what it seems, which leaves only the ego to impose its will, and nothing real to resist it—leaves the nausea of nihilism and narcissism to define a world that no longer cares.

Not nested lies, but nested truths. A comprehensive art and literary theory can more gracefully, more accurately, and more beautifully be viewed as concentric circles of enveloping truths and interpretations. We can now very briefly follow the story of art from its original impulse forward, honoring and including each of the truths in this development that is envelopment, as each whole becomes part of another whole, endlessly, miraculously, inevitably.

5

Integral Art and Literary Theory

PART 2

*We can now very briefly follow the story of art from its original
impulse forward, honoring and including each of the truths in
this development that is envelopment, as each whole becomes
part of another whole, endlessly, miraculously, inevitably. . . .*

*(And who knows? Proceeding thus, searching for the source
of art, we might eventually find ourselves residing in the eye of
Spirit, the Beauty in the eye of the Beholder, delivered unto a
luminous Kosmos that, in its entirety, is the extraordinary Artwork of our own highest Self—so that the final meaning of Art
will reveal its own Original Face, exquisite to infinity, obvious
in the ordinary, the entire canvas of the Kosmos as its radiant
vision, always and even now.)*

THE PRIMAL ART HOLON

WITHOUT IN ANY WAY ignoring the other numerous contexts that
will determine the artwork, in many important ways we can date
its beginning with an event in the mind and being of the artist: an interior perception, feeling, impulse, concept, idea, or vision. From exactly
where, nobody knows, the creative impulse bubbles up. Many contexts
no doubt precede it; many more will follow. But let us start the story
here, with the primal artistic perception or impulse, and let us call that
the *primal holon* of art.

This primal holon may in fact represent something in the external world (the basis of imitative or representational theories). But it might also express an interior state, whether a feeling (expressionism) or an idea (conceptualism). Around that primal holon, like the layers of a pearl growing around an original grain of sand, will develop contexts within contexts of subsequent holons, as the primal holon inexorably enters the historical stream that will govern so much of its subsequent fate.

The primal artistic holon itself, even when it first bubbles up in the consciousness of the artist, nonetheless arrives into numerous contexts that *already* exist, contexts into which the primal holon is instantly subsumed: perhaps unconscious structures in the artist; perhaps structures in the artist's culture; perhaps larger currents in the universe at large, about which the artist might know little. And yet those larger holons have their fingerprints all over the primal holon from the very first instant of its existence: they indelibly stamp the primal holon with the codes of the larger currents.

But the theories that focus on the primal holon are, of course, the expressivist theories. For these theories in general, the *meaning* of art is the primal holon—the original intent of the maker—and therefore a correct *interpretation* is a matter of the accurate *reconstruction* and *recovery* of that original intent and meaning, that primal holon. Thus, we are to *understand* the artwork by trying to accurately understand the original meaning that the artwork had for the artist.

And this makes sense to most of us. After all, when we read Plato's *Republic*, we want to know, as best we can, what Plato originally meant. Most of us do not want to know what the *Republic* means to my grandmother; we want to know what it means for Plato.

In this task of recovering the original meaning, these *traditional hermeneutic theories* do indeed rely, to some extent, on other contexts. They might look at other works by the same maker (which often show a pattern that helps to explain individual works); at other works in the same genre (which might highlight originality); and at the expectations of the original audience (e.g., the fools in Shakespeare's comedies are always jousting and punning in ways that most moderns find tiresome and dull, but Elizabethans—the original audience—enjoyed and expected comedies to have this structure, and thus this expectation would be a part of the original intention of the author, which helps us to understand and interpret it). All of these other contexts will help the interpreter determine and recover the original meaning of the artwork (the text, the book, the painting, the composition). But, for these intentional theories, all of these contexts are, in a sense, secondary to—and none of them constitutive of—the primal holon.

No doubt that attempting to "reconstruct" and "recover" this original intent is a very delicate, difficult, and in some ways endless task. And it might even be that this attempt is, in the last analysis, more of an ideal than a pragmatic possibility. But this is no warrant to simply dismiss this original intent as if it did not exist at all, which is what virtually every subsequent theory of art and its interpretation has done. Art certainly cannot be limited and confined to the primal holon; but neither can it ignore it. And the idealized attempt to recover as much of the original, primal holon as is pragmatically possible: this will always be part of an integral theory of interpretation in general—including, of course, art and literary interpretation as well.

Nonetheless, the attempt to pin art down to just the primal holon and its expression is precisely where the trouble begins. All of the definitions that attempt to limit art to the original intention and its expression have failed in very significant ways. The reason, of course, is that the primal holon is a whole that is *also* a part of other wholes, and so the story unavoidably continues. . . .

For example, even if we agree that art is found first and foremost in the original intention of the artist, it is now widely acknowledged, as we were saying, that the artist can have unconscious intentions: patterns in his or her work that can be clearly spotted by others but might not be consciously known to the artists themselves.

Unconscious Intentions

No doubt, as the primal holon bubbles up, it bubbles up through structures of the artist's own being, some of which are unconscious. Freud himself was perhaps the first to dwell on these unconscious structures and their influence on the actual features of the artwork, most famously in his essay on Leonardo da Vinci (an essay which, interestingly, Freud always said was his own favorite work). As Freud points out, Leonardo da Vinci had suggestively recalled, "This writing distinctly about the vulture seems to be my destiny, because among the first recollections of my infancy it seemed to me that as I lay in my cradle a vulture came to me and opened my mouth with its tail and struck me many times with its tail inside my lips."[1]

In the psychoanalytic interpretation, this fantasy is a key to both Leonardo's infancy and the origins of his homosexuality (a fellatio fantasy), and is therefore also a key to interpreting much of his artistic endeavors. That is, whatever primal artistic holons that might well up in Leonardo's psyche, they well up through the structures of his unconscious desires. The primal holon therefore inexorably arrives on the scene already set in contexts of this unconscious wish. And thus, if the meaning of art is to be found in the original intent of the maker, then some of this meaning is unconscious because some of the intentions are unconscious. It is, therefore, the job of the psychoanalytic interpreter to discern and elucidate these deeper contexts, these background holons, within which the primal holon arises.

And that is surely true enough, and surely part of the overall story we wish to tell. Although, equally surely, it is not the entire story, nor is it the entire locus, of the artwork. To begin with, once we acknowledge that there are unconscious structures in the artist (as well as viewer and critic), we are immediately allowed to ask, What is the actual nature and extent of this unconscious? Are there no other unconscious structures besides the narrowly Freudian? When we look into the depths of the psyche of men and women, is sex and aggression really all that we will find?

The answer, of course, is no. Subsequent psychological and sociological research has demonstrated a plethora of largely unconscious structures, patterns, codes, and regimes, each of which has a hand in governing the shape of our conscious intentions. We already mentioned several of these background structures, these deeper and wider holons: linguistic, economic, cultural, historical, and so on. It is these background holons, these wider contexts, to which all of the "symptomatic theorists" look in order to discern deeper and wider meanings in the particular artwork, because, once again, context determines meaning, and thus wider contexts will disclose deeper meanings, meanings and patterns perhaps not obvious in the artist or the artwork alone.

THE SPECTRUM OF CONSCIOUSNESS

I will return to these larger symptomatic theories in a moment. Let me first point out that, even in the "individual psyche," research has unearthed, in addition to the Freudian unconscious, several important *levels* of usually unconscious contexts. In particular, the schools of existential-humanistic and transpersonal psychology—the so-called "third" and "fourth" forces of psychology (in addition to behaviorism and psychoanalysis)—have discovered and confirmed numerous "realms of the human unconscious," realms that are in many cases the very key to understanding conscious life.

The human being, like all entities in existence, is a holon, a compound individual, in this case composed of physical, emotional, mental, existential, and spiritual or transpersonal dimensions. All of those structures serve as background contexts through which our surface consciousness moves. And just as an unconscious "Freudian" structure can color and shape our conscious intentions, so any of these deeper realms can ride hidden in the Trojan horse of our everyday awareness.

(We need not go into all the detailed evidence; for our simpler purposes it is enough to note that, according to transpersonal psychology, there is in fact a *spectrum of consciousness*, reaching from the isolated and individual ego, at one end, to states of "unity consciousness" and "spiritual union" at the other. This overall spectrum of consciousness consists of at least a dozen levels of awareness, each with a very recognizable structure (including instinctual, Freudian, linguistic, cognitive, existential, and spiritual levels).)

The essential point is that any or all of these dimensions can contribute—consciously or unconsciously—to the artist's overall intention which eventually finds expression in the artwork. And thus a familiarity with the spectrum of consciousness would give the discerning critic a palette of interpretations quite beyond the shallower Freudian array, by elucidating deeper and wider contexts of awareness.

Thus, part of an integral or holonic theory of art interpretation and literary criticism would include all of these various realms of the human unconscious as they manifest in the intention of the primal holon and its subsequent public display (the artwork and its reception). Human intentionality is indeed "onionlike": holons within holons of intentionality in an extraordinary spectrum of consciousness. (I will later return to this spectrum of intentionality and give several examples of how it can effectively guide interpretation.)

The various schools of intentionality—covering the entire spectrum of consciousness—are most definitely on the trail of a very important aspect of the nature and meaning of art. But again, these theories—whether focusing on conscious or unconscious realms—are still, by their very nature, partial and limited. They tend to ignore the technical and formal features of the artwork itself, and thus cannot account for, say, the importance of the structure of musical harmony and melody, or plot structure and function in a narrative, or the technical applications of types of paint, or the structural conditions for various artworks, and so forth.

For all these reasons and more, many theorists began to look more closely at the actual structure and function of the artwork itself, divorced from either maker or viewer. For the fact is, when the artist attempts to express the primal holon in an actual work of art, that primal holon runs smack into the material conditions of its medium: the rock of a sculpture, the actual paint and canvas of a painting, the various instruments and their players in a musical composition, the actual grammar and syntax of a narrative: the primal holon is instantly clothed in a medium that has its own structure, follows its own rules, imposes its own limits, announces its own nature. The primal holon is now a part of another whole, the overall artwork itself.

THE ARTWORK HOLON

Art theories have historically gone back and forth in a wave of action and reaction between two extremes: trying to determine the artist's original meaning, or, tiring of that seemingly *endless* task, looking elsewhere for a way to interpret the meaning of art. The most common is to focus on the artwork itself, that is, on the *public piece of artwork* (the painting, the book, the performed play, the musical), which we will simply call the *artwork holon*.

The great strength—and great weakness—of this approach is that it intensely focuses on only one context: the public artwork as it is immediately perceived. All other contexts are bracketed or basically ignored: the maker's intentions (conscious or unconscious), the historical set and setting, the original audience expectations, the history of reception and response—all are bracketed, removed from the story, thrown out of court when it comes to judging the success or failure of the artwork.

These theorists have their reasons for these exclusions. How are we to know, they ask, what the artist's original intentions for the artwork are, except to look at the artwork itself? If the artist had intentions that didn't make it into the artwork, well then, the artist has simply failed in that regard; intentions that didn't make it into the artwork are, by definition, not part of that artwork, so they can and should be ignored (to assume otherwise is the "intentional fallacy"). And why should we even ask the artist what he or she *really* meant? Just as you and I are not always the best interpreters of our own actions (as our friends will attest), so artists are not always the best interpreters of their own works. Thus, in all cases, we must simply look to the artwork itself, and judge it on its own terms, as a whole unto itself: the artwork holon.

And that is what all artwork theories do. They judge the art as an intrinsic whole, and the meaning of the artwork is to be found in the *relationships among the elements or features of the work itself* (i.e., the relations among the "sub-holons" constituting the artwork). We already looked briefly at many variations on this theme: formalism, structuralism, neo-structuralism, post-structuralism, New Criticism—applied to music, visual arts, poetics, linguistics, and literary theory.

However limited, the merits of this approach are nonetheless obvious. There are indeed features of artworks that stand, relatively, on their own. True, the artwork is actually a whole that is *also* a part of other wholes. But the "wholeness" aspect of any holon can indeed be focused on; the wholeness aspect is very real, very genuine. Various formalist and structuralist theories have rightly gained a permanent foothold in the repertoire of legitimate interpretive tools precisely by focusing on the wholeness aspect of any holon. Doing so, such theorists have offered a list of qualities that many find valuable in the artwork: criteria such as coherence, completeness, harmony of elements within the whole; but also uniqueness, complexity, ambiguity, intensity.

All of which tell us something interesting about the artwork holon itself; none are to be excluded. Still, we cannot in the last analysis forget that every whole is also a part; it exists in contexts within contexts within contexts, each of which will confer a new and different meaning on the original whole, a meaning that is *not* obvious, and *cannot* be found, by looking at the individual holon itself.

Imagine, for example, you are watching a game of cards, perhaps poker. All of the cards are being used according to rules, but the interesting fact is that none of these rules are written on the cards themselves—none of the rules can be found anywhere on the cards. Each card is actually set in a larger context which governs its behavior and meaning, and thus only by taking a larger perspective can the actual rules and meanings of the card in that game be discovered and correctly interpreted. Focusing merely on the card itself will completely miss the rules and meanings it is obeying.

Just so, the very *content* of an artwork itself will be determined in part by the various *contexts* in which the primal holon arises and in which the artwork holon exists. Here's a quick example, which pinpoints the inadequacy of focusing on the artwork holon alone:

A Pair of Worn Shoes

In his essay entitled "The Origin of the Work of Art," Heidegger interprets a painting of a pair of shoes by Van Gogh in order to suggest that art can disclose truth. And however much we might agree with that general conclusion, Heidegger's path, in this particular case, is a prime example of what can go so horribly wrong when holonic contexts are ignored.

The painting to which Heidegger refers is simply of a pair of rather worn shoes, facing forward, laces undone, and that is pretty much all; there are no other discernible objects or items. Heidegger assumes they are a pair of peasant shoes, and he tells us that he can, with reference to the painting alone, penetrate to the essence of its message:

> There is nothing surrounding this pair of peasant shoes in or to which they might belong, only an undefined space. There are not even clods from the soil of the field or the path through it sticking to them, which might at least hint at their employment. A pair of peasant shoes and nothing more. And yet.

And yet, Heidegger will reach deeply into the form of the artwork, all by itself, and render the essence of its meaning:

> From the dark opening of the worn insides of the shoes the toilsome tread of the worker stands forth. In the stiffly solid heaviness of the shoes there is the accumulated tenacity of her slow trudge through the far-spreading and ever-uniform furrows of the field, swept by a raw wind. On the leather there lies the dampness and saturation of the soil. Under the soles there slides the loneliness of the field-path as the evening declines. In the shoes there vibrates the silent call of the earth, its quiet gift of the ripening corn and its enigmatic self-refusal in the fallow desolation of the wintry field. This equipment is pervaded by uncomplaining anxiety about the certainty of bread, the wordless joy of having once more withstood want, the trembling before the advent of birth and shivering at the surrounding menace of

death. This equipment belongs to the *earth* and it is protected in the *world* of the peasant woman. From out of this protected belonging the equipment itself rises to its resting-in-self.[2]

That is a beautiful interpretation, beautifully expressed, lodging itself carefully in the details of the painting, which makes it all the sadder that virtually every statement in it is wildly inaccurate.

To begin with, these are Van Gogh's shoes, not some peasant woman's. He was by then a town and city dweller, not a toiler in the fields; under its soles there are no corn fields, no slow trudging through uniform furrows, no dampness of the soil and no loneliness of the field-path. Not an ounce, nary a trace, of enigmatic self-refusal in the fallow of the desolation of the wintry field can be found. "Van Gogh's painting is the disclosure of what the equipment, the pair of peasant shoes, *is* in truth," exclaims Heidegger.

Perhaps, but Heidegger has not come near that truth at all. Instead— and while not in any way ignoring the relevant features of the artwork holon itself—we must go outside the artwork, into larger contexts, to determine more of its meaning.

Let us go first to the maker's intent, as Van Gogh himself described it, or rather, talked generally about the circumstances leading up to the painting. Paul Gauguin shared a room with Van Gogh in Arles, in 1888, and he noticed that Vincent kept a pair of badly worn shoes which seemed to have a very important meaning for him. Gauguin begins the story:

> In the studio was a pair of big hob-nailed shoes, all worn and spotted with mud; he made of it a remarkable still life painting. I do not know why I sensed that there was a story behind this old relic, and I ventured one day to ask him if he had some reason for preserving with respect what one ordinarily throws out for the rag-picker's basket.[3]

And so Vincent begins to recount the tale of these worn-out shoes. "My father," he said, "was a pastor, and at his urging I pursued theological studies in order to prepare for my future vocation. As a young pastor I left for Belgium one fine morning, without telling my family, to preach the gospel in the factories, not as I had been taught but as I understood it myself. These shoes, as you see, have bravely endured the fatigue of that trip."

But why exactly were these shoes so important to Vincent? Why had he carried them with him for so long, beaten and worn as they were? It turns out, Gauguin continues, that "Preaching to the miners in the Borinage, Vincent undertook to nurse a victim of a fire in the mine. The man was so badly burned and mutilated that the doctor had no hope for his recovery. Only a miracle, he thought, could save him. Van Gogh tended him forty days with loving care and saved the miner's life."

It must have been an extraordinary forty days, deeply etched on Van Gogh's soul. A man so badly burned, so horribly in pain, that the doctor had abandoned him to certain and gruesome death. For more than a month, Vincent at his side. And then a vision came upon Vincent, a vision that he disclosed to his friend Gauguin, a vision that explains why this incident was so important to him.

Gauguin begins at the beginning: "When we were together in Arles, both of us mad, in continual struggle for beautiful colors, I adored red; where could one find a perfect vermilion? He, with his yellowish brush, traced on the wall which suddenly became violet:

I am whole in Spirit
I am the Holy Spirit

"In my yellow room—a small still life: violet that one. Two enormous wornout misshapen shoes. They were Vincent's shoes. Those that he took one fine morning, when they were new, for his journey on foot from Holland to Belgium. The young preacher had just finished his theological studies in order to be a minister like his father. He had gone off to the mines to those whom he called his brothers. . . .

"Contrary to the teaching of his wise Dutch professors, Vincent had believed in a Jesus who loved the poor; and his soul, deeply pervaded by charity, sought the consoling words and sacrifice for the weak, and to combat the rich. Very decidedly, Vincent was already mad."

"Vincent was already mad"—Gauguin repeats this several times, thick with irony; that we all should be graced enough to touch such madness!

Gauguin then tells of the explosion in the mine: "Chrome yellow overflowed, a terrible fiery glow. . . . The creatures who crawled at that moment . . . said 'adieu' to life that day, goodbye to their fellow-men. . . . One of them horribly mutilated, his face burnt, was picked up by Vincent. 'However,' said the company doctor, 'the man is done for, unless by a miracle. . . .'

"Vincent," Gauguin continues, "believed in miracles, in maternal care. The madman (decidedly he was mad) sat up, keeping watch forty days, at the dying man's bedside. Stubbornly he kept the air from getting into his wounds and paid for the medicines. A comforting priest (decidedly, he was mad). The patient talked. The mad effort brought a dead Christian back to life."

The scars on the man's face—this man resurrected by a miracle of care—looked to Vincent exactly like the scars from a crown of thorns. "I had," Vincent says, "in the presence of this man who bore on his brow a series of scars, a vision of the crown of thorns, a vision of the resurrected Christ."

At this point in telling Gauguin the story, Vincent picks up his brush and says, referring to the "resurrected Christ": "And I, Vincent, I painted him."

Gauguin finishes: "Tracing with his yellow brush, suddenly turned violet, Vincent cried:

I am the Holy Spirit
I am whole in Spirit

"Decidedly, this man was mad."

Psychoanalysis, no doubt, would have some therapeutic interpretations for all of this. But psychoanalytic interpretations, relatively true as they might be, do not in themselves touch any deeper "realms of the human unconscious," such as the existential or the spiritual and transpersonal. And thus, as I earlier pointed out, if we look to the school of transpersonal psychology for a finer and more comprehensive account of the deeper dimensions of human awareness, we find a compelling amount of evidence that human beings have access to higher or deeper states of consciousness quite beyond the ordinary egoic modes—a spectrum of consciousness.

And at the upper reaches of the spectrum of consciousness—in the higher states of consciousness—individuals consistently report an awareness of being one with the all, or identical with spirit, or whole in spirit, and so on. The attempt of shallower psychologies, such as psychoanalysis, to merely pathologize *all* of these higher states has simply not held up to further scrutiny and evidence. Rather, the total web of cross-cultural evidence strongly suggests that these deeper or higher states are potentials available to all of us, so that, as it were, "Christ consciousness"—spiritual awareness and union—is available to each and every one of us.

A transpersonal psychologist would thus suggest that, whatever other interpretations we wish to give to Vincent's vision, the overall evidence most clearly suggests that it was very probably a true vision of the radical potential in all of us. These higher states and visions are sometimes intermixed with personal pathologies or neuroses, but the states themselves are not pathological in their essence; quite the contrary, researchers consistently refer to them as extraordinary states of *well-being*. Thus, Vincent's central vision itself most likely was not pathological, not psychotic, not madness at all—which is why Gauguin keeps poking fun at those who would think that way: decidedly, he was mad. Which means, decidedly, he was plugged into a reality that we should all be so fortunate to see.

Thus, when Vincent said he saw the resurrected Christ, that is exactly what he meant, and that is very likely exactly what he saw. And thus he carried with him, as a dusty but dear reminder, the shoes in which this vision occurred.

And so, you see, an important part of the primal meaning of the painting of these shoes—not the only meaning, but a primal meaning—is very simple: these are the shoes in which Vincent nursed Jesus, the Jesus in all of us.

THE VIEWER HOLON

Whatever one might think of that interpretation, one thing is certainly obvious: a merely formal or artwork approach—Heidegger's, for example—would miss important meanings of Van Gogh's painting. Many moderns will stop short of my transpersonal interpretation—would it help if I pointed out that Gauguin finishes his account with this?: "And Vincent took up his palette again; silently he worked. Beside him was a white canvas. I began his portrait. I too had the vision of a Jesus preaching kindness and humility."

Are we moderns too jaded for this? Ah, well, whether we accept this transpersonal aspect of the interpretation, we can easily accept the rest of the account—the mining accident, nursing the man, and so on—as providing some very crucial contexts which confer various added meanings to the artwork holon itself (since meaning, as always, is context-bound).

Thus, the various artwork approaches (which are true but partial) suffer by overlooking the primal holon (the maker's intent in all its levels and dimensions). But they also attempt to ignore the viewer's response. These theories consequently cannot account at all for the role that interpretation itself plays in helping to *constitute* the overall nature of the art.

The artist did not parachute to earth, antiseptic and isolated and hermetically sealed. Both art and artist exist only in a stream of history, and thus the primal holon itself *never* arrives in a *tabula rasa*, a clear and blank slate formed only by the artist's isolated intention. Rather, the primal holon itself is shaped, *even as it is forming*, by a cultural background. And this cultural background is historical through and through—it is itself unfolding in history.

Thus, without in any way denying any of the other meanings of the artwork, from the primal intention of the maker to the formal elements of the artwork itself, nonetheless the fact remains: when I view the artwork, it has *meaning for me*. Each and every time a viewer sees a work and attempts to understand it, there is what Gadamer so unerringly calls a "fusion of horizons"—as I would also put it, a *new holon emerges*, which itself is a new context and thus carries new meaning.

Obviously, *the* meaning of an artwork does not reside solely in my particular response to it. Other people might have different responses. But the general point is that the meaning of an artwork cannot be divorced from the overall impact it has on viewers. And in a stronger version, "the viewer" simply means the entire cultural background, without which meaning would not and could not exist in the first place. This great intersubjective background, this cultural background, provides the ocean of contexts in which art, artist, and viewer alike necessarily float.

Even when the artist is first starting to work on a piece, he has somebody in mind; some sort of viewer looms in his awareness, however briefly or fleetingly; the *intersubjective* background is already a *context* within which his subjective intentions arise. The viewer response is thus *already* at work in shaping the art. The cultural background of interpretations is *already* a part of the very makeup of the artwork. And as the artwork goes public, it will enter a stream of further historical interpretations, each of which will form yet another layer in that temporal and historical pearl. And each new, emerging, historical context will confer a new meaning on the pearl, a new layer to the pearl which will in fact be an intrinsic part of the pearl itself, a whole that becomes part of yet other wholes and is changed in the process itself.

To give a crude example, think of the controversy today surrounding Columbus's voyage of 1492. If, as an example, we pretend that his voyage is an artwork, then what is the meaning of that art? Even a few decades ago, the meaning was something like this: Columbus was a rather brave fellow who, against some very difficult odds, made a perilous voyage that discovered the Americas—the New World—and thus brought culture and civilization to a fairly primitive and backward people.

Today, many people would give the meaning more like this: Columbus was a sexist, imperialist, lying, rather cowardly low-life, who went to the Americas on a voyage of plunder and pillage, in the process of which he brought syphilis and other scourges to the peace-loving peoples he everywhere met.

The meaning of the original artwork not only looks different, it *is* different, based on its subsequent history of reception and response. There is no way to avoid this *historicity*, this constitutive nature of interpretations. Subsequent contexts will confer new meaning on the art, because meaning is always and inevitably context-bound. And the viewer-response theories, in their various forms, focus on this history of response as constitutive of the art.

Thus, these reception-and-response theories maintain, as one critic explains it, that artistic meaning "is not a function of its genetic origin in an author's psyche [the primal holon], nor of purely intrinsic relations between the printed marks on a page [formalist theories], but of its reception in a series of readings constituting its history of influence, [which] stresses the temporality and historicity of understanding and interpretation."[4]

The partial truths of viewer response are surely part of any holonic theory of art and its interpretation. And yet, as with every other approach we have seen, the true but partial notions of viewer response, when they pretend to be the whole story, become not only distorting but outright comical.

And it is the *viewer-response theories*, coupled with the *symptomatic theories*, that have almost totally dominated the postmodern art scene—in theory and in practice—thus leading, as we earlier suggested, into increasingly narcissistic and nihilistic ramblings.

Start with viewer response.

THE WONDER OF BEING ME

Art critics have always been in a slightly awkward situation: the unkind word is "parasitic." Flaubert's view was typical: "Criticism occupies the lowest place in the literary hierarchy: as regards form, almost always; and as regards 'moral value' incontestably. It comes after rhyming games and acrostics which at least require a certain inventiveness."[5]

Couple this parasitism with another awkward fact: more than one social commentator has seen the baby boomer generation defined by a rampant narcissism, and if one item marks narcissism, it is a refusal to take a back seat to anybody.

From which it follows, art and literary theory in the hands of the boomers was going to be a wild affair. As parasitic collided with grandiose, something would have to give. The critic needed desperately to get out of the back seat and into the driver's seat.

The means for this glorious promotion were provided, as I began to suggest, by viewer-response theories coupled with symptomatic theories, together parading under the broad banner of poststructural postmodernism. If the nature and meaning of art lies solely in the viewer—"the interpreter, not the artist, creates the work"—and if only knowing interpretation is valid, then *voilà*: the critic alone creates all art.

And so it came about that the viewer response—that is to say, me—became the alpha and omega of art, which placed the critic—that is to say, me—in the very center of the creative act, not to mention at the very heart of the artworld. Thus Catherine Belsey in her *Critical Practice*: "No longer parasitic on an already given literary text, criticism constructs its object, produces the work."[6]

Which, of course, comes as news to most artists. The partial truths of viewer response became a platform from which the critic as sole creator gained (and still has) enormous currency. The embarrassing dilemma for this brand of postmodernism is that it completely and totally erases the artwork itself, and thus it ends up with a viewer-response theory that—oops!—has nothing to actually respond to.

If the artwork is not there to respond to, my ego alone remains. All of this has played precisely into the two trends, barely concealed, of extremist postmodernism—namely, nihilism and its hidden core of narcissism—as the more observant critics have recently begun to note. David Couzens Hoy points out that "freeing criticism from its object"—that is, erasing the artwork by emphasizing viewer response—"may open it up to all the possibilities of rich imaginations; yet if . . . there is now no truth of the matter, then nothing keeps it from succumbing to the sickness of the modern imagination's obsessive self-consciousness." Criticism thus becomes "only the critic's own ego-gratification." The culture of narcissism. "Then a sheer struggle for power ensues, and criticism becomes not latent but blatant aggression," part of "the emergent nihilism of recent times."[7]

These viewer-response theories, as I said, were particularly coupled with symptomatic theories—the most influential being Marxist, feminist, racist, and imperialist (postcolonial studies). The idea being, recall, that the meaning of art is found in the background social and economic contexts, contexts that are often masquerades for power and ideology, and contexts that therefore confer a specific meaning on art produced in those contexts, meanings that the knowing critic can pull out by highlighting and elucidating the particular background structures.

All true enough; and all terribly partial, lopsided, and distorted when taken in and by themselves. These views have promoted the notion, given currency by Foucault's early work, that truth itself is culturally relative and arbitrary, grounded in nothing but shifting historical tastes, or power and prejudice and ideology. Since truth is context-dependent, the argument goes, then it is completely relative to changing contexts. All truth is therefore *culturally constructed*—the social construction of gender, the social construction of the body, the social construction of pretty much everything—and because all truth is culturally constructed, there are and can be no universal truths.

Unfortunately, that view itself is claiming to be universally true. It is making a series of strong claims that it insists are true for *all* cultures (the relative nature of truth, the contextuality of claims, the social construction of all categories, the historicity of truth, and so on). This view thus claims that there is no universal truth at all—except for its own, which is universal and superior in a world where nothing is supposed to be universal or superior at all. It's not simply that this stance is hypocritical, concealing its own structures of power and domination; as an added bonus, the sheer narcissism of the stance once again rears its wonderful horrible head.

But *contextualism*, on which these symptomatic theories are all based, means neither arbitrary nor relativistic. It means determined by contexts that constrain the meaning. In other words, "context" means "constraints," not chaos. These contexts are neither arbitrary, subjective, idiosyncratic, merely constructed, nor radically relative, contrary to the abuse to which these theories have been subjected by extreme postmodernists.

Thus, even Foucault abandoned this "merely constructivist" approach to knowledge; he called it "arrogant." And even a foremost interpreter of Gadamer's very strong version of the historicity of truth could explain that "since no context is absolute, different lines of interpretation are possible. But this is not radical relativism, since not all contexts are equally appropriate or justifiable. . . . Contextualism demands justifying reasons for interpretations, and these reasons can be assumed to be as factual or 'objective' as any objectivist could produce. [Therefore] the choice of context or framework is far from arbitrary."[8]

Thus, meaning is indeed context-dependent (there are only holons!), but this means neither arbitrary nor relative, but firmly anchored in various contexts that *constrain* the meaning. And, of course, these contexts—whether in artist, artwork, viewer, or world at large—must themselves be real contexts, actually existing contexts. We are not allowed to arbitrarily dream up contexts; any ole context will not do. Rather, the context that is being used for interpretation must itself be justified according to the total web of available evidence.

And this puts many symptomatic theories at a great disadvantage, because too many of these approaches take a rather specific and often quite narrow context and make it the sole, dominating, hegemonic context within which all interpretations must be registered, whether imperialist, racist, capitalist, ecologist, feminist.

The results, as I said, have become more often than not quite comical, as minor truths are blown up to cosmic proportions. Alfred Kazin, recently called "the greatest literary critic in America" by *The New Republic*, reports on a typical scene, a session on Emily Dickinson organized by the Modern Language Association in 1989. The session was entitled "The Muse of Masturbation," and, says Kazin, "it was thronged," the point being "that the hidden strategy of Emily Dickinson's poetry is in her use of 'encoded images of clitoral masturbation to transcend sex-role limitations imposed by the nineteenth-century patriarchy.' " Kazin: "The basic idea was that Dickinson loaded her work with references to peas, crumbs, and flower buds in order to broadcast secret messages of forbidden onanistic delights to other female illuminati."[9]

It is one thing to expose a context; quite another to impose one. And too much of symptomatic theory is, alas, the imposition of the critic's pet context and ideology, bereft of confirming truth or evidence or justification (since, after all, there is no truth, only social constructions, why bother with evidence in the first place?).

And thus, from the uncontested fact that all truth is context-dependent, and that contexts are boundless, we have finally arrived, slipping and sliding, at the dizzy notion that all truths are merely subjective and relative, arbitrary and constructed. Truth is whatever you want, which leaves us nothing at all, except that shell of nihilism filled with the thickest of narcissism, a postmodern pastry from hell.

CONCLUSION

Let us realign the postmodern scene more adequately: Contexts are boundless means, not nested lies and arbitrary constructions depending only on egoic whim, but nested truths anchored in wider and deeper realities. The nihilistic and narcissistic spin is dismantled right at the beginning, and meaningless relativism gives way to richly textured contexts of value and meaning that ground sound interpretations. That all things are holons means that all things are contexts within contexts forever, and each context confers a new and genuine meaning upon the original holon itself.

Thus, to *locate* art is to situate it in its various contexts. Art includes, in its development that is envelopment:

- the primal holon or original intent of the maker, which may involve numerous levels of the psyche, both conscious and unconscious, reaching from the individual self to the transpersonal and spiritual dimensions (the spectrum of consciousness)
- the artwork holon itself, the public work materialized, in both its form and content
- the history of reception and response (the numerous viewer holons) that in important ways are constitutive of the overall work
- the wider contexts in the world at large, economic and technical and linguistic and cultural contexts, without which specific meanings could not be generated in the first place

Each of those are wholes that are parts of other wholes, and the whole confers meaning on the parts which the parts themselves do not possess. Each wider whole, each broader context, brings with it a new meaning, a new light in which to see the work, and thus constitute it anew.

Thus, any particular *meaning* of an artwork is simply the highlighting of a particular context. The *interpretation* of an artwork is the evoking and elucidating of that highlighted context. *Justifiable* interpretation means verifying that a particular context is indeed real and significant, a justification procedure that, like any other, involves a careful look at the total web of evidence.

And the *understanding* of an artwork means to hermeneutically enter, to actually enter as far as possible, the contexts determining the art, a "fusion of horizons"—the emergence of a new holon—in which the understanding of a work of art is simultaneously a process of self-understanding, liberating in its final effect. To understand the art I must to some degree enter its horizon, stretch my own boundaries, and thus grow in the process: the fusion of horizons is a broadening of self.

Thus, the validity criteria for justifiable interpretations of art and literature rest, in the last analysis, on what the critic thinks is the nature and locus of meaning in an artwork. And I am saying, it is holonic. There is no single correct interpretation because no holon has only one context. There are as many legitimate meanings as there are legitimate contexts, which does not lead to nihilism but cornucopia. This is far from arbitrary and relative, because while there is no one right interpretation, there are plenty of wrong ones (the necessary and important fallibilist criterion is most definitely part of artistic interpretation).[10]

"Interpretation is dependent upon the circumstances in which it occurs. . . . A strategy for finding a context may be essential to all interpretation as a condition for the very possibility of interpretation," points out Hoy.[11] Indeed so, but not just as a condition for the possibility of interpretation, but rather of existence itself: there are only holons.

(An integral theory of art and literary interpretation is thus the multidimensional analysis of the various contexts in which—and by which—art exists and speaks to us: in the artist, the artwork, the viewer, and the world at large.[12] Privileging no single context, it invites us to be unendingly open to ever-new horizons, which broaden our own horizons in the process, liberating us from the narrow straits of our favorite ideology and the prison of our isolated selves.)

CONTEMPLATING ART

Let me return to what art is finally all about. When I directly view, say, a great Van Gogh, I am reminded of what all superior art has in common: the capacity to simply take your breath away. To literally, actually, make you inwardly gasp, at least for that second or two when the art first hits you, or more accurately, first enters your being: you swoon a little bit, you are slightly stunned, you are open to perceptions that you had not seen before. Sometimes, of course, it is much quieter than that: the work seeps into your pores gently, and yet you are changed somehow, maybe just a little, maybe a lot; but you are changed.

No wonder that for the East and West alike, until just recent times, art was often associated with profound spiritual transformation. And I don't mean merely "religious" or "iconographic" art.

(Some of the great modern philosophers, Schelling to Schiller to Schopenhauer, have all pinpointed a major reason for great art's power to transcend. When we look at any beautiful object (natural or artistic), we suspend all other activity, and we are simply aware, we only want to contemplate the object. While we are in this contemplative state, we do not want anything from the object; we just want to contemplate it; we want it to never end. We don't want to eat it, or own it, or run from it, or alter it: we only want to look, we want to contemplate, we never want it to end.)

(In that contemplative awareness, our own egoic grasping in time comes momentarily to rest. We relax into our basic awareness. We rest with the world as it is, not as we wish it to be.) We are face to face with the calm, the eye in the center of the storm. We are not agitating to change things; we contemplate the object as it is. Great art has this power, this power to grab your attention and suspend it: we stare, sometimes awestruck, sometimes silent, but we cease the restless movement that otherwise characterizes our every waking moment.

(It doesn't matter what the actual *content* of the art is; not for this. Great art grabs you, against your will, and then suspends your will. You are ushered into a quiet clearing, free of desire, free of grasping, free of ego, free of the self-contraction. And through that opening or clearing in your own awareness may come flashing higher truths, subtler revelations, profound connections. For a moment you might even touch eternity; who can say otherwise, when time itself is suspended in the clearing that great art creates in your awareness?)

You just want to contemplate; you want it never to end; you forget past and future; you forget self and same. The noble Emerson: "These roses under my window make no reference to former roses or to better ones; they are for what they are; they exist with God today. There is no time for them. There is simply the rose; it is perfect in every moment of its existence. But man postpones or remembers; he does not live in the present, but with reverted eye laments the past, or heedless of the riches that surround him, stands on tiptoe to foresee the future. He cannot be happy and strong until he too lives with nature in the present, above time."[13]

Great art suspends the reverted eye, the lamented past, the anticipated future: we enter with it into the timeless present; we are with God today, perfect in our manner and mode, open to the riches and the glories of a realm that time forgot, but that great art reminds us of: not by its content, but by what it does in us: suspends the desire to be elsewhere. And thus it undoes the agitated grasping in the heart of the suffering self, and releases us—maybe for a second, maybe for a minute, maybe for all eternity—releases us from the coil of ourselves.

That is exactly the state that great art pulls us into, no matter what the actual content of the art itself—bugs or Buddhas, landscapes or abstractions, it doesn't matter in the least. In this particular regard—from this particular context—great art is judged by its capacity to take your breath away, take your self away, take time away, all at once.

And whatever we mean by the word "spirit"—let us just say, with Tillich, that it involves for each of us our ultimate concern—it is in that simple awestruck moment, when great art enters you and changes you, that spirit shines in this world just a little more brightly than it did the moment before.

Take it one step further: What if we could somehow manage to see *everything* in the entire universe as being exquisitely beautiful, like the finest piece of great art? What if we right now saw every single thing and event, without exception, as an object of extraordinary beauty?

Why, we would be momentarily frozen in the face of that vision; all of our grasping and avoiding would come quickly to rest; we would be released from the self-contraction and ushered into the choiceless contemplation of all that is. Just as a beautiful object or artwork momentarily suspends our will, so the contemplation of the universe as an object of beauty would open us to the choiceless awareness of that universe, not as it should be or might be or could be, but simply as it is.

Could it then be possible, just possible, that when the beauty of all things without exception is perceived, we are actually standing directly in the eye of Spirit, for which the entire Kosmos is an object of Beauty, just as it is, precisely because the entire Kosmos is in fact the radiant Art of Spirit itself?

(In this extraordinary vision, the entire Kosmos is the Artwork of your own highest Self in all its shining creativity, which is exactly why every object in the universe is in truth an object of radiant Beauty when perceived with the eye of Spirit.)

(And conversely: if you could right here, right now, actually see every single thing and event in the entire universe as an object of sheer Beauty, then you would of necessity be undone as ego and stand instead as Spirit. You would want nothing from the Kosmos at that moment except to contemplate its unending Beauty and Perfection. You would not want to run from the universe, or grasp it, or alter it at all: in that contemplative moment you will neither fear nor hope, nor move at all. You will want nothing whatsoever, except to Witness it all, contemplate it unendingly, you want it never to end. You are radically free of will, free from grasping, free from all mean motion and commotion. You are a center of pure and clear awareness, saturated in its Being by the utter Beauty of everything it contemplates.)

(Not a single particle of dust is excluded from this Beauty; no object whatsoever, no matter how "ugly" or "frightening" or "painful"—not a single thing is excluded from this contemplative embrace, for each and every thing is radically, equally, unendingly the brilliant radiance of Spirit. When you behold the primordial Beauty of every single thing in the universe, then you behold the glory of the Kosmos in the eye of Spirit, the I of Spirit, the radical I-I of the entire universe. You are full to infinity, radiant with the light of a thousand suns, and all is perfect just as it is, always and eternally, as you contemplate this, your greatest Artwork, the entire Kosmos, this thing of Beauty, this object of unending joy and bliss radiant in the Heart of all that arises.)

Think of the most beautiful person you have ever seen. Think of the exact moment you looked into his or her eyes, and for a fleeting second you were paralyzed: you couldn't take your eyes off that vision. You stared, frozen in time, caught in that beauty. Now imagine that *identical* beauty radiating from every single thing in the entire universe: every rock, every plant, every animal, every cloud, every person, every object, every mountain, every stream—even the garbage dumps and broken dreams—every single one of them, radiating that beauty. You are quietly frozen by the gentle beauty of everything that arises around you. You are released from grasping, released from time, released from avoidance, released altogether into the eye of Spirit, where you contemplate the unending beauty of the Art that is the entire World.

That all-pervading Beauty is not an exercise in creative imagination.

It is the actual structure of the universe. That all-pervading Beauty is in truth the very nature of the Kosmos right now. It is not something you have to imagine, because it is the actual structure of perception in all domains. If you remain in the eye of Spirit, every object is an object of radiant Beauty. If the doors of perception are cleansed, the entire Kosmos is your lost and found Beloved, the Original Face of primordial Beauty, forever, and forever, and endlessly forever. And in the face of that stunning Beauty, you will completely swoon into your own death, never to be seen or heard from again, except on those tender nights when the wind gently blows through the hills and the mountains, quietly calling your name.

6

The Recaptured God

THE RETRO-ROMANTIC
AGENDA AND ITS LIABILITIES

Transpersonal psychology is the major school in psychology today that takes spiritual experience seriously. There are perhaps five major approaches in transpersonal psychology that are particularly influential: systems theory, altered (or discrete) states of consciousness, Stan Grof's holotropic model, various forms of Jungian psychology (including Michael Washburn's "neo-Jungian" view), and my own spectrum or integral approach. I maintain not only that the integral model incorporates the essentials of the other models, but that it includes many significant areas ignored by the others—and thus it can account for considerably more research and evidence.

In this and the next chapter we will explore this claim, dialoguing with each of the major theorists of these alternative models.

A BRIEF SUMMARY OF MY CONSCIOUSNESS MODEL

WE BEGIN WITH the work of Michael Washburn and his notion of the Dynamic Ground.[1] Washburn is a very clear and careful writer, whose formulations I have always appreciated, even when we disagree. I never fail to learn something interesting from his presentations, and I have always been a staunch supporter of his publications. It is therefore rather disappointing that he tends to misrepresent my overall model. Since this misunderstanding is fairly common, I will be as careful as I can in summarizing my view.

As explained in *Transformations of Consciousness* and *Brief History* [and most recently in *Integral Psychology*], the overall consciousness system (the Upper-Left quadrant) has, I believe, at least *three main components:* the basic levels, the developmental lines, and the self.

The Basic Levels or Waves

The basic levels are simply the basic levels in the spectrum of consciousness—matter to body to mind to soul to spirit. The basic levels are essentially the traditional Great Holarchy of Being (as presented by, say, Plotinus or Asanga or Aurobindo), refined with numerous contributions from the modern cognitive sciences and developmental psychology. In chapter 1, I explained that this overall spectrum can be divided and subdivided in many different but valid ways. In *The Atman Project,* I give seventeen basic levels or basic structures in the overall spectrum of consciousness, including: matter, sensation, perception, impulse, image, symbol, concept, rule, formal, vision-logic, psychic, subtle, causal, and nondual. I usually simplify this to nine or ten of the most central and most important basic structures, which are, I believe, the minimum that we need to adequately characterize the overall spectrum and its development. These are: sensorimotor, vital-emotional, representational, rule/role, formal, vision-logic, psychic, subtle, causal, and nondual.

I refer to these as the basic levels, structures, or waves of consciousness. Each of those terms implies something important. *Level* means that these are qualitatively different dimensions of being and consciousness. *Structure* means that they are relatively stable patterns. And *wave* indicates that, like the colors in a rainbow, these basic dimensions shade and grade into each other. The basic levels or waves are simply the basic colors in the spectrum of consciousness. As I said, this spectrum is sometimes simplified to *matter* (sensorimotor), *body* (vital-emotional), *mind* (rep, rule, formal, vision-logic), *soul* (psychic, subtle), and *spirit* (causal, nondual). And even that is sometimes simplified to just body, mind, and spirit (or gross, subtle, and causal). But for this presentation, I will use those nine or ten basic levels as the most important colors in the overall spectrum of consciousness.

One other item about the basic levels: they are relatively permanent or *enduring structures*. Once they emerge in development, they tend to remain in existence, even though they are often subsumed or incorporated in later waves.[2] Unlike many of the stages of the developmental lines, which are temporary, the developmental levels of consciousness are permanent acquisitions. Once they emerge, matter, body, mind, soul, and spirit are all enduring patterns in consciousness, and they form the basic levels through which the many developmental lines will pass: the basic waves in the river of life through which its many streams will flow.

THE DEVELOPMENTAL LINES OR STREAMS

Through the basic levels of consciousness, numerous different developmental lines progress. Some of the more important developmental lines include cognitive, moral, aesthetic, psychosexual, self-identity, worldviews, needs, motivation (and several others we will discuss later). Thus, for example, cognition can move from body (sensorimotor cognition) to mind (concrete and formal operational cognition) to soul (subtle and archetypal consciousness) to spirit (formless and nondual). Morals can develop from body (egocentric and preconventional impulses) to mind (conventional rules and postconventional meta-rules) to soul (saintly compassion) to spirit (nondual liberation). Likewise, one's sense of self-identity unfolds from body (the narcissistic bodyego) to mind (the pluralistic ego) to soul (the pure witness) to spirit (the nondual self), not in a rigid sequence but in flowing waves of consciousness. And so on.

Of course, those examples are using just four of the basic levels of the spectrum (body, mind, soul, and spirit), but you can easily expand that to the nine or ten basic waves through which each of the developmental streams flows. For example, you can do this for *worldviews* (e.g., archaic, magic, mythic, mental, existential, psychic, subtle, causal, and nondual; cf. Gebser); *self-needs* (e.g., physiological, safety, belongingness, self-esteem, self-actualization, self-transcendence into subtle, causal, nondual; cf. Maslow); *self-identity* (e.g., pleroma, uroboros, typhon, persona, ego, centaur, soul, spirit; cf. Loevinger); and so forth.[3] The point is that through some nine or ten basic waves pass some two dozen relatively independent developmental streams, and a comprehensive or integral model would attempt to take all of those facets of consciousness into account.

"Relatively independent" means that each of the developmental lines flows through the spectrum of consciousness in a fairly independent manner. *Thus, a person can be at a relatively high level of development in some lines, a medium level of development in others, and a low level in still others.* A substantial amount of research continues to confirm that each developmental line itself (cognitive, moral, psychosexual, etc.) tends to unfold in a sequential or stage-like manner. Nonetheless, because the lines themselves develop in a relatively independent fashion—some high, some medium, some low, with no overall sequence—there is absolutely nothing "linear" about overall development. Each person's growth through the spectrum of consciousness, with its many waves and streams, will be a radically unique and individual affair.

Whereas the basic levels of development tend to be relatively permanent or enduring (once they emerge they remain in existence), the stages in the lines of development tend to be relatively temporary or transitional. For example, as a person moves from moral stage 1 to 2 to 3 to 4 to 5, each of those stages is not so much incorporated into subsequent stages as replaced by subsequent stages. With the basic levels, if you have access to a relatively high level of consciousness (say, vision-logic), you still have *full access* to all the lower basic levels (including sensorimotor, images, symbols, concepts, and so on). But when you are at, say, moral stage 5, you do not have full access to moral stages 1, 2, or 3. A person acting from postconventional moral compassion does not simultaneously act from a narcissistic self-glorifying stance.[4] Those earlier stages are not incorporated but mostly replaced, as consciousness continues its ever-expanding growth and development.

THE SELF AND ITS FULCRUMS

Navigating all the various waves and streams is the *self-system* or *self-sense* (or just the *self*), which is the third major component. The self-system is, in many ways, the most important of the three, because it is "where the action is." I have suggested that the self-system is the locus of several crucial capacities and operations, including: *identification* (the locus of self-identity), *organization* (that which gives cohesiveness to the psyche), *will* (the locus of choice within the constraints of the present developmental level), *defense* (the locus of defense mechanisms, phase-specific and phase-appropriate, hierarchically organized), *metabolism* (the "digestion" of experience), and *navigation* (developmental choices).[5]

Because the self is the locus of identification, each time the self identifies with a basic level of consciousness, that identification generates (or is the support of) a corresponding series of developmental streams. Thus, for example, when the self identifies with preoperational thought (symbols and concepts), this supports a preconventional moral stance (Kohlberg), a set of safety needs (Maslow), and a protective self-sense (Loevinger). When higher basic structures emerge (say, concrete operational rules), then the self (barring arrest) will eventually switch its central identity to this higher and wider organization, and this will help to generate a new moral stance (conventional), a new set of self-needs (belongingness), a new self-sense (conformist persona), and so forth.[6]

As the self-system negotiates each basic wave in the unfolding spectrum of consciousness, it will switch from a narrower to a wider identity, and thus it undergoes a *fulcrum* or milestone in its own development. That is, each time the self rides a new wave of consciousness (each time it identifies with a new and wider basic structure), it will go through a process of (1) merger or fusion or embeddedness, (2) differentiation or transcendence or disembedding, and (3) incorporation or integration. This 1-2-3 process is a fulcrum of self-development, and there are as many fulcrums of self-development as there are basic structures to negotiate.

Thus, at any given level of development, the self starts out identified with (or in fusion with, or embedded in) the basic structure of that level. Its locus of identification—or its *center of gravity*—circles around that basic structure: it is identified with it. But if development continues, the self will begin to disidentify, or differentiate, or "let go of," or transcend that structure, and then identify with the next higher stage while integrating the previous basic structure into the new organization. The *exclusive* identity with the lower structure is dissolved (disembedded, transcended, or negated), but the capacities and competences of that basic structure itself are incorporated and integrated (preserved and included) in the new and higher organization. The center of gravity of the self is now predominantly *identified* with a higher basic level or wave of consciousness, and this identification and embeddedness will then help to generate many of the developmental streams at *that* stage (a new moral stance, new self-needs, new self-identity, etc.). For each basic level or wave of consciousness unfolding, there is thus a corresponding fulcrum of self-development, a process of (1) fusion-merger-identification-embeddedness, (2) differentiation-disidentification-disembedding-transcendence, and (3) integration-incorporation-inclusion. Again, not in a rigid or set fashion, but in flowing waves of unfolding consciousness.

We can, of course, divide and subdivide development in numerous and virtually endless ways, but, as I said, I have found that we need at least nine or ten basic structures or levels of the spectrum of consciousness in order to account for the most pertinent facts of overall development. To each of these ten basic structures or waves there corresponds a fulcrum of self-development, that 1-2-3 process of fusion/differentiation/integration that occurs each time the self-system steps up to a new wave in the expanding spheres of consciousness.

I have also suggested that the preponderance of clinical evidence strongly suggests that each fulcrum can, if disturbed, generate a specific level of pathology—psychotic, borderline, neurotic, script, identity, existential, psychic, subtle, and causal.[7] In several publications I have given extensive examples of these developmental levels of pathology, and I have also suggested the types of therapy that seem best suited to dealing with each of them.[8] It certainly seems to make sense that a "spectrum of pathology" has a corresponding "spectrum of treatment modalities."

This model also specifically includes *states of consciousness*. States of consciousness include both *natural* states (such as waking, dreaming, and deep sleep) and *altered* or *nonordinary* states (such as religious experiences, peak experiences, meditative states, holotropic experiences, drug-induced states, etc.). An altered state (including various spiritual or peak experiences) *can occur at virtually any stage of development*. The idea that spiritual or transpersonal experiences can only occur in the higher stages of development is thus incorrect. Nevertheless, in order for these temporary states to become permanent traits, growth and development must occur (the conversion of states to structures). Focusing merely on nonordinary states tends to divert attention away from the necessary process of permanent realization. We will further explore this in later discussions.[9]

With that brief summary, we can now look at certain common misunderstandings of this model.

Wilber's model is rigidly linear, which ignores all the amorphous and nonlinear aspects of life.

This is incorrect on many counts. Overall development, as we have seen, follows no set sequence at all. The various streams flow through the waves of consciousness in a relatively independent fashion, so a person can have many different streams simultaneously all over the spectrum of consciousness.

Further, we have seen that a person can have a peak experience or an altered state of consciousness at virtually any stage of development, and there is nothing linear about that, either.

Likewise, when it comes to the self, much of its journey is radically nonlinear as well. In fact, the self can roam all over the spectrum of consciousness (or the spectrum of basic structures). This is why the self is "where the action is." It can jump ahead, regress, spiral, go sideways, or otherwise dialetically spin on its heels. As Plotinus pointed out long ago, *precisely because the basic levels themselves have no inherent self-sense, the self can identify with any of them.*[10] And, in my model, each time the self does so, it will generate a new series of developmental streams. It will see the world from its presently-identified-with basic structure (which acts as its center of gravity), and the basic limiting principles of that wave of consciousness will govern what it sees, and what it can see, from that vantage point. Growth will involve the relinquishing of a narrower and shallower level of awareness in favor of an expansion into wider and deeper and higher modes.

Nonetheless, an extraordinary amount of evidence has continued to indicate that most of the separate developmental lines *themselves* tend to unfold in a sequential or stage-like or "linear" fashion. In the cognitive line, for example, images emerge before symbols, which emerge before concepts, which emerge before rules. This is equally true in both genders; we know of no society where that sequence is bypassed; there is no amount of societal conditioning that can reverse that order; and we know of no major exceptions. In other words, research has consistently demonstrated that these important stages, when they emerge, are basically gender-neutral, cross-cultural, invariant, and holarchical ("holarchy" means "nested hierarchy"—see chapter 1).

Just as an acorn grows into an oak in a series of linear, developmental, irreversible stages, so the basic components of the human psyche unfold in a holarchical sequence of differentiation-and-integration. Letters come before words which come before sentences, because each incorporates and builds upon its predecessors, which become components in its own being (each senior holon envelops or nests its junior holons). And, of course, you cannot have sentences before you have letters. The higher and wider holons will come later in development because they will integrate and unify the earlier and more partial elements.

"Linear" is often used in a very derogatory fashion, which is contrasted with the nice holistic alternative, which is somehow supposed to be "not linear." But most organic and holistic systems actually unfold in irreversible stages of increasing inclusiveness and envelopment—acorn to oak, seed to rose—and they unavoidably do so in the linear stream of time's arrow (a point Prigogine is always emphasizing about dissipative structures).

That is the meaning of "linear" in developmental studies (irreversible nested envelopment), and some aspects of human development (including the basic structures and most developmental streams) are indeed linear, as enormous amounts of experimental and clinical evidence have made more than obvious. In fact, those theories that fail to take these linear aspects into account are severely deficient and inadequate theories.

Even so, all of the developmental stages themselves are fairly fluid in their unfolding. For example, research shows that somebody who is at, say, moral stage 3, actually only gives 50 percent of her responses from that level; 25 percent of her responses are from a *higher* level, and 25 percent are from a *lower* level. In other words, her center of gravity is at moral stage 3, but the self is still quite fluid in its growth.

Likewise, although the basic structures unfold in a holarchical fashion, with each senior wave nesting and enfolding and including its juniors, the self's journey through those expanding spheres of consciousness is nowhere near that "linear." As we said, the self can be, and usually is, all over the place—regressing, temporarily leaping forward, spiraling back and forth, immersed in all sorts of altered states from all sorts of realms (prepersonal, personal, and transpersonal). This means that, on the long view, there will be a discernible progression of the self's center of gravity from narrower to wider, from shallower to deeper—an overall expansion of identity from matter to body to mind to soul to spirit. Nonetheless, in the short view, the self's journey is altogether tumultuous, much more of a roller coaster than a linear ladder.

Thus, in terms of "linearity," we have this: the basic levels and the major streams tend to unfold in a holarchical, stage-like fashion, as research continues to confirm. But because they do so in a relatively independent fashion, there is nothing linear about overall development—a person can be highly evolved in some lines, medium in others, and low in still others. And, just as important, the self can experience altered states of consciousness at virtually any level of development, and altered states are not linear.

All of those components—basic levels, relatively independent lines, the roaming self, and nonlinear states—need to be included in any truly integral psychology, especially if we wish to honor, acknowledge, and incorporate the substantial amounts of evidence from clinical, meditative, phenomenological, altered-states, and empirical studies, both East and West.

Wilber doesn't give much attention to conflict in the pre-egoic stages.

Washburn makes this claim, and I find it incomprehensible. "The main theme of the pre-egoic period, for Wilber, is the development of lower-level basic structures."[11] Actually, as we have just seen, that is only one-third of the story. The other two-thirds of the story concern the developmental lines and the self-system with its fulcrums, which is where "all the action is."

The pre-egoic period covers roughly the first four fulcrums of self-development (fulcrum-0, or the pre- and perinatal period; fulcrum-1, roughly the first eighteen months; fulcrum-2, generally one to three years; and fulcrum-3, around three to six years). These fulcrums are perhaps the most crucial in all of self development, for they set the foundation for all that is to follow. Moreover, they are the essential etiological fulcrums for some truly severe pathologies (psychotic, borderline, neurotic).

It is the self-system, as I earlier indicated, that is the locus of defense mechanisms (including introjection, projection, splitting, denial, reaction formation, repression proper, etc., arrayed in a hierarchical pattern). Thus, any specific aspects of any of the structures of consciousness can be dissociated, in one form or another, from the ongoing sweep of consciousness unfolding, if they are sensed as a threat to the self-system.[12]

These sealed-off (or otherwise dissociated) components act as *lesions in awareness* that then tend to sabotage consciousness with symptomatic expressions (i.e., various pathologies). The self cannot genuinely disembed and transcend these alienated aspects of its own being, because they are now hidden and sealed off—they remain as pockets of unconscious attachment, unconscious identification, unconscious embeddedness, unconscious intentionality—they are not "died to" and "let go of." They are "little subjects" that refuse to be differentiated, transcended, and *thereby genuinely integrated*, and instead carry on terrorist activities from the basement, from the locus of their unconscious attachment and fixation. This is self-alienation, repression, and pathology.

Because most defense mechanisms are quite common and normal (and phase-specific), virtually nobody escapes early development totally intact; on that point Washburn and I are in general agreement. *Our disagreement concerns only the nature of what exactly is being repressed or dissociated in these early stages.*

For Washburn, it is nothing less than the Dynamic Ground that is being fundamentally repressed or *forced out of the consciousness* of the infant. In my opinion, what is being repressed is basically various affects, emotions, diffuse bodily feelings, sensuality, and emotional-sexual energies in general—the overall domain of prana, or life vitality.

Washburn believes that certain pre-egoic capacities and the Dynamic Ground itself are *necessarily* lost, and that the *recapture* of these lost capacities is the *prerequisite* for transpersonal development. The individual must regress to the earliest infantile stages, spiraling back to contact the lost Dynamic Ground, and then develop forward into transcendence. In virtually all cases, significant regression is necessary for transpersonal growth.

I believe that regression is common and *sometimes* necessary, not because the Dynamic Ground is lost at age one, but because repression itself tends to cripple further growth in any case. The greater the repression in the earlier stages, then the more higher growth is crippled. In my view, "regression in service of ego" is thus a return to, and a recontacting of, the alienated feelings, emotions, affects, or emotional-sexual energies that were dissociated in the early fulcrums. Once these are integrated into the self-system, then growth can more easily move forward into the higher and transegoic realms. Thus, regression in service of ego is sometimes a prerequisite for transcendence of ego, but it is not the actual mechanism of transpersonal growth itself.

The major difference, then, is whether something like a Dynamic Ground is actually forced out of the consciousness of the infant in the first year of life, as Washburn maintains. I will argue that such a stance is incoherent on its own terms (even if we include the bardo or "in between" realms, which I do, and which I will explain below). In the meantime, my own model more than accounts for the massive conflicts in the earliest years of life.

Wilber's model totally negates the self instead of including it.

Several critics have maintained that I give the self virtually no importance or even relative existence. This is difficult to maintain, in that the self-system has at least the six characteristics I listed (from identification to defense to will). That is quite a lot of activity for a nonentity. In fact, the self-system is an inherent functional capacity of the psyche. It develops and unfolds its own identity from matter to body to mind to soul to spirit, in a great holarchy of increasing inclusion and embrace.

Most of this misunderstanding stems from a colossal semantic confusion. The question is, "Does any form of the ego exist in the higher stages of development?" And the answer is, "It depends entirely on what you mean by 'ego.' " If by "ego" you mean an *exclusive* identity with the individual bodymind, then clearly that ego is largely deconstructed with the emergence of the Supreme Identity, where one's center of gravity switches from the organism to the All. The self-system no longer exclusively identifies with the basic structures of the mind (thus generating the transitional self-sense known as the ego), but instead identifies with the structures of the Kosmos at large (whose self-sense is the Supreme Identity of the Divine Self). The self-system, in other words, switches from the individual ego to the Divine Self or Spirit, which can be described as no-self or Big Self, depending on your preference. But the *exclusive* identification, the narrow "ego," is basically lost.

But if by "ego" you mean that aspect of self-awareness that develops to deal with the conventional world and its sensorimotor reality, then of course that ego remains in existence. The "ego" used in that sense means, not a transitional structure that will be replaced by higher selves until there is the only Self, but rather a functional competence that is part of the enduring structures of the psyche. In that case, the ego is obviously retained in higher development.

I have consistently maintained both of those positions from my first to my most recent book—namely, that the ego as a competency is maintained in higher development, but the ego as an exclusive sense of identity is replaced by higher and wider identities. Both are true. And I am constantly getting into arguments with people who maintain only one of those views and accuse me of maintaining only the other.

Washburn is simply the latest in a line of such critics, who in this case says that I deny that the ego remains in any form in higher development. Since he claims to be reporting the view expressed in *The Atman Project*, here is what I actually said in that book:

> The self must differentiate from the ego, dis-identify with it, transcend it, and then integrate it with the higher and newly-emergent structures. But please remember that the ego remains intact when the self dis-identifies with it—just as the body remained intact when the ego transcended it. Transcendence does not mean deformation. One still possesses an ego—it's just that one's identity is no longer exclusively bound to it. (p. 166)

Washburn summarizes five of what he believes to be the main disagreements between our models. These are particularly the features that Washburn believes my model does not take into account, and thus features that he feels recommend his approach as a better alternative. But if we actually use my overall model, and not just the truncated version that Washburn presents, we find that all of these points immediately collapse, leaving Washburn's position rather untenable.[13]

But there is still one remaining issue, namely, what is the nature of the pre-egoic potential? What is the actual nature of the "Dynamic Ground" that is supposedly "unrestrictedly present" in the infant and then lost in subsequent development? This is the only item on which Washburn's model includes something that mine does not. Thus, if Washburn's model also fails in this particular point, there is nothing left to recommend it as an alternative. It is to this topic we can now turn.

THE ROMANTIC AGENDA

I myself was once an advocate of the Romantic model. In this general view, the infant at birth (and humanity in its dawn state) is the noble savage, fully in touch with a perfectly holistic and unified Ground, "harmoniously one with the whole world." But then through the activity of the analytic and divisive ego, this Ground is historically lost, actually repressed or alienated as a past historical event (as opposed to an involutional event happening now). This historical loss—the loss of a *past actual*—is nonetheless necessary, according to the Romantic view, in order for the ego to develop its own powers of mature independence. And then, in the third great movement (after initial union and subsequent fragmentation), the ego and the Ground are *reunited* in a regenerative homecoming and spiritual marriage, so that the Ground is *recaptured*, but now "on a higher level" or "in a mature form."

Such is the general Romantic view. And, indeed, I began writing both *The Atman Project* and *Up from Eden* in an attempt to validate that view ontogenetically (*Atman Project*) and phylogenetically (*Eden*). I even fancy that I brought some new ideas to this old notion. Although this Romantic model had been eagerly embraced by Jung and the Jungians (especially Edinger and Neumann), and although I strongly agreed with their general formulations, I was also drawn to some of the more daring theorists in psychoanalytic theory (such as Roheim, Ferenczi, and Norman O. Brown), who were in fact quite in line with this Romantic model.

These psychoanalytic theorists allowed me, or so I believed, to give a very precise outline of the specific stages of this loss of primal Ground, or loss of true Self, or loss of very Atman. In ontogenetic development, for example, I postulated the following (pulling all of these various sources together): the infant begins in a state of almost pure adualism, fully in touch with the primal Ground and the true Self (Atman), so that subject and object are one; the self and the "whole world" are united. Then through what I called "primary repression," the subject and object are split, the self and the world (as the Great Mother) are fragmented and alienated from each other, and the world of duality crashes onto the scene, with all the tragedy and terror inherent in that divisive nightmare.

But the developmental damage doesn't stop there. Once the bodyego is split from the world and the Great Mother, the bodyego has two basic but contradictory desires. There is the desire to reunite with the Great Mother and thus recapture that pure oneness and paradisiacal state that it had known before subject and object were brutally split. But in order to reunite with the Great Mother, the bodyego self would have to die to its own separate existence, and this it is terrified of doing. It therefore wants reunion but is also terrified of it, and these conflicting desires drive subsequent development. I called the amalgam of these two drives "the Atman project"—the desire to attain unity (Atman) but the intense fear of it as well, which forces the self to seek substitute gratifications and substitute objects.

(The Atman project is a very real project and a very valid concept, I firmly believe, but the state of unity that is desired is not that of the infant at the mother's breast, but of the self at primordial Emptiness. As we will see, I had wildly "elevated" the nature of the early infantile and prepersonal structure to some sort of transpersonal ground and glory, and so I mistakenly believed that the drive to unity was a drive to recapture that infantile structure, but of course "in a mature form," instead of understanding that the drive to unity is an attempt to recapture something lost in the timeless moment—as I will explain below.)

Once the bodyego has split from the Great Mother or Great Surround, my early Romantic account continued, then because of this primary repression it suffers primary alienation. In the bodyego itself, I suggested, during the first three years of life, this primary alienation drives some very specific events which begin to take place in the actual distribution of emotional-sexual energy, libido, élan vital, or prana (and this is exactly where I directly incorporated the formulations of the more daring psychoanalytic thinkers). Namely, driven by the attempt to regain unity with the world (and the Great Mother), the bodyego organizes the distribution of its libido around various bodily zones where fantasies of this union take place (from the oral zone, with fantasies of uniting with the world through food, to the genital zone, with fantasies of sexually uniting with the world). All of the libidinal organizations are thus simply reduced and restricted versions of a consciousness that was once actually "one with the whole world." I therefore ended one of these early published essays with the conclusion: "God-consciousness is not sublimated sexuality; sexuality is repressed God-consciousness."[14]

That view makes a good deal of developmental sense, but only IF the infantile bodymind is actually in *full* God-consciousness or Ground-consciousness. Because the point, remember, is that this Romantic view depends upon the notion that the infant is immersed in an actual God-consciousness or a *fully present* Ground, which is then literally repressed, sometime during the first or second year of life. *But this view makes no sense whatsoever*, and has no developmental validity, if the pre-egoic structure itself is anything less than God, because it is supposed to be the actual repression of God-consciousness, by the two-year-old, that drives the subsequent developmental scheme. If the "original embedment" of the infantile self is not *fully* in touch with God-consciousness or Ground-consciousness, then this developmental view falls apart altogether.

And it is just that problem that finally undoes the Romantic position, as I quickly found out the more I tried to make that viewpoint work. Jack Crittenden and I had just founded *ReVision Journal*, and, desperate for material, I began serially publishing the early draft of *The Atman Project*, which presented the above scheme, loaded with its Romantic viewpoints and numerous pre/trans fallacies.[15]

But the more I tried to make this Romantic model work—and believe me, I tried very, very hard—the more I realized its central inadequacies and confusions, which I will outline in a moment. I thus furiously reworked the early drafts of both *The Atman Project* and *Up from Eden*—neither had yet been published in book form—to reflect this shift in my thinking, which I also explained at length in "Odyssey."[16] Incidentally, when I wrote "The Pre/Trans Fallacy,"[17] I was in effect cataloging all of the errors that I myself had made in this regard, which is why I seemed to understand them with an all-too-alarming familiarity.

Anyway, let us call my early model "Romantic/Jungian/Wilber-I," and the later model, "Wilber-II."

Now the odd thing about Wilber-I and Wilber-II is that they aren't really all that different. They both move from pre-egoic to egoic to trans-egoic. They both agree on the great domains of prepersonal to personal to transpersonal. They both see development ultimately driven by the attempt to regain Spirit. They both see involution and evolution occurring. That is why both Wilber-I and Wilber-II can handle virtually the same type and amount of available clinical and experimental evidence. The big difference—the crucial difference—is that Romantic/Wilber-I *must* see the infantile pre-egoic structure as being, in some sense, a primal Ground, a perfect wholeness, a direct God-union, a complete immersion in Self, a oneness with the whole world. Since the perfection of enlightenment is a *recontacting* of something present in the infantile structure, then that infantile structure must therefore fully possess that utter Perfection (even if unconscious). Thus, if God is not *fully* present in the infantile structure, the entire scheme collapses.

And here, of course, the Romantic/Wilber-I model runs into a series of fatal difficulties, as is probably obvious. But let's go over it a step at a time: The traditional Romantic view is that the infantile structure is one with the entire Ground or Self, but in an *unconscious* fashion. The self then divides and splits from this Ground, actually represses this Ground, alienates it and loses touch with it. Then, in the third great movement (transegoic), the self and the Ground *reunite*, the Ground is resurrected ("on a higher level," whatever that might actually mean), and a spiritual renewal and regeneration occurs.

(Thus, what we might call *the traditional Romantic view* is that development moves from unconscious Heaven (pre-egoic) to conscious Hell (egoic) to conscious Heaven (transegoic). The self is totally one with the Ground in *both* the first and the third stage, but in the first the union is unconscious, in the third, conscious.)

(The fatal problem with that view is that the second step (the loss of unconscious union) is an absolute impossibility. As the Romantics themselves soon acknowledged, all things are one with Ground; if you actually lost your union with Ground, you would cease to exist. Rather, there are only two options you have with regard to Ground: you can be aware of your union with Ground, or you can be unaware of it. The union itself is always present, but it can be either conscious or unconscious.)

Now, as we saw, according to the traditional Romantic view, the pre-egoic state is one with Ground but in an *unconscious* fashion. But if that is so, then the next step—the move from pre-egoic to egoic—*cannot* therefore be the *loss* of that unconscious union. If that happened, you would cease to exist. You can either be conscious or unconscious of the union with Ground; if you are *already* unconscious of the union, you can't get any lower! The real loss has *already* occurred. The pre-egoic structure or original embedment is *already* fallen, alienated, lost. Involution has priorly occurred. And this the Romantics, very slowly, began to realize, which, of course, undermined their entire project.

The precariousness of their position becomes even more obvious when the standard Romantic notion of "original wholeness" is carefully examined. The infantile structure is supposed to be "one with the whole world in love and bliss," as Norman O. Brown put it. But what is the neonate actually one with? Is the infantile self fully one with the world of poetry, or logic, or economics, or history, or mathematics, or morals and ethics? Of course not, for these have not yet emerged: the alleged "whole world" of the infantile self is a pitifully small slice of reality. The subject and object of the infantile structure are indeed predifferentiated to a large extent (which is simply the oceanic or fusion phase of fulcrum-1), but that fused world excludes and is ignorant of an extraordinary amount of the Kosmos. It certainly is not one with the whole world; it is one with a very small slice of the whole world.

The one-month-old self might come "trailing clouds of glory" (from the rebirth bardo, which I will explain below), but it is still actually immersed and embedded, not in nirvana, but in samsara. It has all the intense seeds of grasping, avoiding, ignoring, hunger, and thirst. The flames of samsaric hell are *already* all around the infantile self, and if this is occasionally a relatively peaceful time, it is the peace of prepersonal ignorance, not transpersonal wisdom. The infantile self is fully immersed in samsara, it just doesn't have enough awareness to register that burning fact. But as the ego develops and gains in consciousness, it will increasingly *realize* its *already* fallen state—realize the fact that it is already living in the fires of samsara.

This shocking realization, this conscious initiation into the fact that the phenomenal world is inherently marked with tears and terror, sin and suffering, trishna and duhkha, is a profound trauma to the self. This *waking-up trauma* begins, in its earliest forms, during the first or second year of life (particularly during fulcrum-2), and that is what has confused the Romantic/Wilber-I theorists: they imagine that at this point the infant is passing from nirvana into samsara, whereas the infant, born in samsara, is simply waking up to that shattering fact.

The ego, now awake to the existential nightmare of its samsaric pain, then has two basic choices in its life course: it can choose those items that favor its continuing growth and evolution of consciousness, or it can choose those items that foster regression in an attempt to blot out consciousness and numb itself to duhkha. If it chooses the former, and quickens this evolutionary growth with appropriate spiritual disciplines, it might even rediscover its own primordial and timeless nature, a primordial nature that was never actually lost in a past period of infancy, but is rather obscured in this very moment by an allegiance to the world of time itself. This is indeed a *rediscovery* and a *remembrance*, not of what was fully present at age one month, but what is fully present in the timeless now—fully present, that is, prior TO involution, not prior IN evolution.

Thus, the real course of manifest historical human development is not from unconscious Heaven to conscious Hell to conscious Heaven, but rather from unconscious Hell to conscious Hell to conscious Heaven. And such was the move from Wilber-I to Wilber-II.

ORIGINAL EMBEDMENT AND THE DYNAMIC GROUND

Washburn in many essential respects echoes a Wilber-I type of model. He uses the same general stages, with the same general terminology, and he generously acknowledges as much—as he puts it, "Wilber (1979) once held a view similar to this but later abandoned it."[18]

At the same time, Washburn has built upon this view and enormously expanded and sophisticated it. He has, after all, based two long books on it. Moreover, Washburn has at least realized some of the profound difficulties with the *traditional* Romantic version, and he has attempted to bypass some of its central and fatal difficulties. But, in my opinion, he is less than successful.

To begin with, Washburn realized early on that if the pre-egoic structure (more specifically, the "original embedment") is one with Ground, then that union with Ground must be *fully conscious in the infant*. Remember, the traditional view was that the original state was a union with the Ground but in an *unconscious* fashion, but Washburn realizes that if that is so, then that original state is *already* fallen, it is already as low as you can go (it is, in fact, not unconscious Heaven but unconscious Hell). So Washburn is forced to maintain that the one-month-old infant is fully open to, and fully conscious of, the unrestricted Dynamic

Ground. There is "the unrestricted power of the Ground within the new-born's body," evidenced in "dynamic plenitude and blissful well-being characteristic of original embedment," marked by "wholeness, fullness, and bliss . . . , undivided, boundless fullness."[19] Washburn acknowledges that the Ground itself *cannot* be lost or the ego would cease to be. So the only item that can actually be *lost* is the consciousness of Ground, and this means that the one-month-old infant must *fully possess* that consciousness of unrestricted Ground, or the entire scheme falls apart.

In short, precisely because it is the *repression* of the consciousness of Ground, starting around age one or two, that drives Washburn's developmental scheme, then if the consciousness of Ground is not fully and *unrestrictedly* present in the infantile self prior to that point, then it's not even there to be repressed, and Washburn's model abruptly collapses (or, as I found out, Wilber-I becomes Wilber-II).

Now a more coherent view of involution/evolution (as found in, say, Plotinus, Asanga, Schelling, Aurobindo, Garab Dorje, the *Lankavatara Sutra*, or, I believe, Wilber-II) would maintain something like this: Spirit manifests as the entire world in a series of increasingly holistic and holarchic spheres, stretching from matter to body to mind to soul to spirit itself. But all of these different dimensions are actually just forms of spirit, in various degrees of self-realization and self-actualization. Thus, there is really spirit-as-matter, spirit-as-prana, spirit-as-mind, spirit-as-soul, and spirit-as-spirit.

Involution (or efflux), this general view continues, is the process whereby these dimensions are manifested as forms of spirit, and *evolution* (or reflux) is the process of recollection and remembrance, moving from spirit-as-matter to a final remembrance of spirit-as-spirit: a recognition of spirit, by spirit, as spirit—the traditional realization of enlightenment.

In this scheme, the infantile self might indeed be trailing clouds of glory (which I will discuss in a moment), but it is primarily adapting to the dimensions of spirit-as-matter and spirit-as-prana (sensuality, emotional-sexual energies, élan vital, diffuse polymorphous life and vital force) as well as the very early forms of spirit-as-mind (images, symbols, protoconcepts). Developmental evolution continues with the further unfolding of the mental dimensions (spirit-as-mind) and then the beginning of the consciously spiritual dimensions (spirit-as-soul), culminating in enlightenment or the direct recognition of spirit-as-spirit, which, transcending all, embraces all.

So the infant is indeed immersed in spirit and is one with Ground—as all things are!—but it is primarily spirit-as-matter and spirit-as-prana, not spirit-as-spirit. (As we will see, not even according to the bardo view is the infantile or neonatal self in touch with spirit-as-spirit!) Thus, in all of these views, the infantile self is not conscious of spirit-as-spirit, or the pure nirvanic estate altogether free of karmic tendencies and desires and hunger and thirst.

But this general view is completely blocked to Washburn (and Wilber-I), because for Washburn the Ground *must be fully conscious and unrestrictedly present* in the one-month-old infantile structure. This forces Washburn into a series of increasingly incoherent stances in an attempt to defend this awkward assertion.

To begin with, Washburn must first separate Ground and spirit. (Since spirit is *not fully manifest* in the infantile structure, which Washburn seems to realize, then *something else* must be fully present in order to drive his scheme, and this something else will be the Dynamic Ground.) Thus, for Washburn, Ground and spirit *are not the same thing*. Ground, he says, can appear as libido, as free psychic energy, and as spirit. I myself will refer to these different organizations of Washburn's Ground with the shorthand phrases Ground-as-prana, Ground-as-psyche, and Ground-as-spirit (Washburn's terminology, for example, is "the power of the Ground as spirit"). Notice that Ground is somehow more than spirit, because it can appear in forms that apparently spirit cannot.

But there is one thing Ground is not: Ground is not the mental ego. Strangely, the Ground can appear as libido, and the Ground can appear as free psyche, and the Ground can appear as all-encompassing spirit, but the Ground is not strong enough to appear as the poor ego. In fact, the ego and the Ground are dramatically separate entities, says Washburn. But in the higher stages of development, Ground somehow appears as spirit (what I am calling Ground-as-spirit) and then Ground-as-spirit and the ego unite, according to Washburn, and thus a *super-entity* (which he never really names or specifies) then emerges: the Ground-as-spirit/one with the ego.

But, says Washburn, this is not a novel state: it is in some sense a *reunion* with the Ground that was directly repressed by the two-year-old. That, of course, is the absolutely crucial point: according to Washburn, the Ground of spiritual realization is essentially the same Ground repressed by the child's ego, which is exactly why Washburn *must* postulate that this Ground is *fully present and conscious* in the infantile structure.

This is where Washburn's very slippery definition of "Ground" becomes crucial. As we saw, Ground can appear as libido, as psyche, and as spirit. Washburn can therefore claim that the child represses the Ground *without ever claiming that the child represses spirit* (because Ground and spirit are not the same). But in order for Washburn's scheme *actually* to work, the Ground that is repressed by the young ego *must* be the Ground-as-spirit, because, Washburn makes clear, the higher union is a union *specifically with Ground-as-spirit*.

But Washburn, apparently realizing that simply will not work, therefore never *explicitly* claims the infantile self is actually in touch with Ground-as-spirit; nor does he ever claim that the young ego represses Ground-as-spirit. In fact, he consistently maintains (in the text and in his tables) that Ground-as-spirit appears *only* in the transegoic stages.

At this point, Washburn's model is starting to look suspiciously like a Wilber-II or evolutionary type of model. But Washburn wants it both ways: he wants to acknowledge that spirit actualizes *only* in the transegoic stages, but he also wants to say that the *same* reality was somehow *fully* present in the infantile structure and was then actually repressed by the ego.

The only way he can do this is to create a notion, "the Dynamic Ground," that has the power of *all three great domains at once* (the libido of the prepersonal, the psychic energy of the personal, and the spirit of the transpersonal), and then he can use the "Ground" in virtually any way he wishes. Thus, when the young ego represses Ground in its form as prana or vital bodily energy, which it certainly might, Washburn will simply claim that the *entire Ground* itself has been repressed, thus *implicitly* claiming a spiritual repression without ever *explicitly* having to say so, which he realizes will not work. Then, when the ego enters the transpersonal domain, Washburn *simply begins calling the Ground by the name "spirit,"* without ever explaining why all of a sudden the Dynamic Ground turns explicitly spiritual—and yet that is, of course, the central problem to be addressed. Instead, in the transpersonal stages Ground is now simply called "the power of the Ground as spirit," which is then *claimed* to be the *same* Ground the infant repressed, whereas in fact (and even according to the actual evidence that Washburn presents), what the infant basically repressed was Ground-as-prana, not Ground-as-spirit.

But Washburn wants it both ways, and therefore, in those rare instances when he actually attempts to define Ground, he must define it in a way that is very nebulous and thus will not challenge his reductionism. Thus, he simply defines the Ground as "physicodynamic processes" (no further explanation is given for that term). Since Washburn loosely identifies Ground with physicodynamism, then he can hide his reductionism and his pre/trans fallacies in this rather nebulous concept, having his pre-egoic spiritual cake and eating it too.

There is, I believe, a fairly straightforward reason that Washburn attempts to identify the entire Dynamic Ground with "physicodynamic" processes, and it relates directly to what I believe is his pre/trans fallacy worldview (ptf-2). Chögyam Trungpa pointed out, in *Shambhala: The Sacred Path of the Warrior*, and Huston Smith confirmed in *Forgotten Truth*, that the great wisdom traditions without exception—from the shamanic to the Vedantic, in the East as well as the West—maintain that reality consists of at least three great realms: earth, human, and sky, correlated with body, mind, and spirit (gross, subtle, and causal), and these are further correlated with the three great states of human consciousness: waking (gross, body), dream (subtle, mind), and deep sleep (causal, spirit).[20]

These are, of course, the three great domains of prepersonal, personal, and transpersonal. *But Washburn refuses to clearly acknowledge these three domains.* Under the burden of his pre/trans collapse, he keeps the ego-mind as one domain, but he then *fuses the gross-body with causal-spirit*: this lump he calls the "Ground," which he then contrasts with the ego-mind. Thus, instead of the three great domains of body, mind, and spirit, he simply has his "two poles" of ego-mind and Ground. And since he has collapsed causal-spirit into gross-body and its vitality, then of course he will refer to the entire Ground as physiological energy or "physicodynamic processes," thus completing his pre/trans plunge. By reducing the Ground of Being to physiology, he can elevate infancy to God.

At this point, Washburn will then accuse my model of not being as simple and as "parsimonious" as his model, which is rather like saying that we will have a much simpler model of the solar system if we just leave out that annoying Jupiter.[21]

Yet it is in the highest stages that Washburn's Romantic/type-I model faces even worse difficulties. According to Washburn, once the ego has necessarily and rather fully repressed the Ground, then it can reunite with the Ground. Since the Dynamic Ground "is originally lost via repression, it can be restored only via regression."[22] More than one critic has puzzled over what that could possibly mean. Does the adult have to regress to preverbal babbling? If not, then what?

Nonetheless, according to Washburn, the ego must regress back to the Ground which was present but repressed in the infantile period, and then these "two poles of the psyche"—namely, Ground and ego—"can be integrated to form a single, perfected, psychic whole."[23] This means, rather oddly, that Ground is now a *subset* of the whole psyche (an incoherent point I will return to below).

But what, according to Washburn, is actually *recontacted*? It is not Ground-as-spirit, since that manifests, he says, only in the transegoic. Since it can't be spirit that is recontacted, Washburn reverts to his catchall concept: the physicodynamic potentials are recontacted: "Primal repression is lifted and physicodynamic potentials are reawakened."[24] That somehow means spirit is now manifest. In any event, it is at this transegoic point that Ground can manifest as spirit.

But this means that a *completely new entity* therefore comes into being with this awakening: namely, the "single, perfected, psychic whole"—the union of ego and Ground. The real conclusion is obvious: *this whole was never repressed or lost, because it never existed before.* It is an emergent, a newly realized entity.

Thus, according to Washburn's own presentation, the infantile self is actually in touch with *neither* Ground-as-spirit *nor* the Ground-and-ego unified state, from which it follows that enlightenment or spiritual awakening is not in any essential fashion a recontacting of something fully or actually present in the infantile structure but subsequently lost. That being the case, Washburn/Wilber-I reverts to Wilber-II.

One of Washburn's central theoretical difficulties, in my opinion, is a failure to understand the difference between differentiation and dissociation. As I tried to show in *Sex, Ecology, Spirituality*, this confusion is a hallmark of the general Romantic view. Development actually proceeds by differentiation-and-integration, a failure of which involves either fusion, on one side (where differentiation fails), or dissociation, on the other (where differentiation goes too far into alienation and fragmentation).

But for Washburn, as for the Romantics, there is basically either fusion or dissociation, with no middle ground of differentiation itself. Washburn says as much. "There is no middle ground. The body ego can either yield to the Great Mother and thereby submit to continued reembedment [fusion] . . . , or it can separate itself from the Great Mother and thereby perpetuate a repression [dissociation]. . . ."[25] What he fails to see, in my opinion, is that the differentiation of self and other is neither a fusion nor a dissociation, but the necessary process of differentiation-and-integration (transcendence-and-inclusion), which is the very process of growth itself.

But once you are committed to seeing every differentiation as a dissociation, then development must be viewed as primarily a dismal downhill slide, because every normal differentiation is going to be interpreted as a horrible dissociation, fragmentation, alienation. The oak is somehow a terrible violation of the acorn.

Human development must then be viewed as doing what no other organic system ever does: in this Romanticized view, each stage grows and develops primarily by brutalizing and crippling its previous stages. (How could that even work? How would natural selection ever select for *that*? Not the occasional repression, but the actual shattering of the entire Ground of Being? Is nature that . . . confused?)

This misunderstanding of differentiation and dissociation is, I believe, exactly why Washburn must maintain that self development involves a *necessary* repression of Ground (unrestrictedly present in babies), and why he must likewise maintain that in order for spiritual awakening to occur, everybody, with virtually no exceptions, must completely regress to those potentials fully present in the one-month-old infant. Without this massive regression, in virtually all cases, there is no enlightenment and no spiritual awakening.

For Wilber-II, various types of repression (or dissociation and pathology) can occur at each of the nine or ten fulcrums of self development, and this certainly includes the first two fulcrums. As I pointed out, what is repressed or dissociated in these early fulcrums, however, is generally spirit-as-prana, not spirit-as-spirit. This repression varies in degree of severity from person to person; in harsh cases, this repression can bring development to a grinding halt. In most cases, however, individuals cope relatively well and development continues until arrest, which also varies from person to person.

Thus, for Washburn/Wilber-I, primal repression of Ground is the way development proceeds *by necessity*, and thus spiritual awakening requires the recapture of something actually and fully present in the infantile structure. Repression is part of the actual mechanism of development. For Wilber-II, repression is something that may or may not occur, but in any event it is not the mechanism of growth, and when it does occur in these early stages, it is a repression essentially of spirit-as-prana, not spirit-as-spirit. But if this repression is moderate to severe, then in the higher stages of growth, regression might have to occur in order to reintegrate these lower potentials. Whether this regression does occur will vary from person to person, and the amount of this regression will vary from person to person, but it is not a wholesale necessity for all cases, and in any event it is not a recontacting of an infantile but repressed spirit-as-spirit.

In short, for Washburn/Wilber-I, profound regression *must* occur in all spiritual development, as a recontacting of a Ground unrestrictedly present in the infantile structure. For Wilber-II, regression *might* occur, usually if necessitated by a recontacting of Ground-as-prana or some earlier-fulcrum lost potentials, dissociations, pathologies, and so on (a regression in service of ego, prior to transcendence of ego).

There are, of course, numerous cases of enlightenment occurring without wholesale infantile regression, which *prima facie* condemns the Washburn model. In the one carefully conducted investigation of the merits of Washburn versus Wilber, L. Eugene Thomas et al. conclude that, of those individuals who had reached transpersonal stages of development, "only about half gave indications of having undergone a regressive transition period. On the basis of this, and other internal evidence, support was found for Wilber's theory."[26]

7

Born Again

STAN GROF AND THE
HOLOTROPIC MIND

*Stanislav Grof is one of the world's greatest living psychologists.
He is certainly a pioneer in every sense of the word, and one
of the most comprehensive psychological thinkers of our era.
Fortunately, Stan and I are in substantial agreement about many
of the central issues in human psychology, the spectrum of consciousness, and the realms of the human unconscious.*

*But we are here, of course, to discuss our differences. In Sex,
Ecology, Spirituality I offer a sustained criticism of Grof's position, highlighting some of what I believe are major weaknesses
in his model. I'll summarize those weaknesses here, and then
generally respond to Stan's criticism of my own work.*

MONOLOGICAL SCIENCE

GROF HAS CONSISTENTLY maintained that "Western science is approaching a paradigm shift of unprecedented proportions."[1] Perhaps so, but the new paradigm and the approaches he discusses are all
monological, which means that they reduce the world to it-language. He
points to quantum and relativity physics, cybernetics, systems theory,
M-fields, chaos and complexity theories, Young's theory of process, and
so on, all of which are unrelentingly monological. They reduce the Kos-

mos to merely Right-Hand terms; they fundamentally embody the *subtle reductionism* that is one of the unfortunate legacies of the Cartesian tradition.

Both "mechanistic" and "systems" sciences are monological. Both "causality" and "chaos" theories are monological. Both "materialism" and "organicism" are monological. Both "deterministic" and "complexity" theories are monological. Both "mechanistic" and "process theory" are monological. No matter what advantages the latter have over the former (and there are many!), they are all, in themselves, flatland approaches.

Grof and the monologically inclined theorists he cites in support of the "new paradigm" are constantly lamenting the fragmentation of the modern and postmodern world, and they emphasize the urgent need for integrative vision. I agree entirely, but this monological "new paradigm" is in fact a symptom of, not a medicine for, the primary fragmentation itself. As such, it is part of the cause, not the cure, of the modern fragmentation.

Thus, for example, when Joanna Macy criticizes *Sex, Ecology, Spirituality* by saying that it doesn't take feedback mechanisms into account and thus does not fully represent systems theory, I believe she misses the central point. Of course I take feedback into account, and explicitly say so; moreover, feedback theory is merely part of the first wave of systems sciences, which have been supplemented with chaos and complexity theories—but all of them are perfectly and equally monological, capable of being fully described in process it-language, which is the defining hallmark of subtle reductionism and the brutal stamp of the colonization of the lifeworld by monological imperialism, which actually promotes the fragmentation it wishes it to heal. To paraphrase Karl Krauss, systems theory is the disease of which it claims to be the cure.

Grof has unfortunately, in my opinion, sunk his philosophical foundations into this monological cement, and this throws his psychological model into several disadvantages.

MONOLOGICAL CONSCIOUSNESS

One of the great discoveries of the postmodern West is that what we previously took to be an unproblematic consciousness reflecting on the world at large ("the mirror of nature") is in fact anchored in a network of nonobvious *intersubjective* structures (including linguistic, ethical, cultural, aesthetic, and syntactic structures). Both subjective consciousness (Upper Left) and the objective world (Right-Hand) arise in large measure due to the differentiating powers and capacities of these intersubjective (Lower-Left) structures, structures that *do not themselves appear as objects or phenomena of immediate awareness*, but rather form the *background* context by virtue of which subjects and objects can appear in the first place (see the Introduction).

For this reason, the discovery of these intersubjective structures was not immediately available to phenomenology in any of its traditional forms, but rather awaited the developments in contextual analysis, structuralism, post-structuralism, linguistics, and semiotics: awaited, that is, the very broad movement from modernism to postmodernism in general.

The simple example I usually give is that of a card game—say, poker. In the poker game, each card follows a specific set of rules, but the actual rules of the game are not written on any of the cards. Thus, if you merely describe each card, no matter how carefully—that is, if you do a pure phenomenology—you will never discover the rules that each card is obeying, you will never discover the "inter-card patterns" (the "intersubjective" patterns) that in fact drive each and every card. Here phenomenology fails miserably, and some form of structuralism alone will disclose these patterns.

This rather extraordinary historical development was summarized by Foucault: "So the problem of language appeared and it was clear that phenomenology was no match for structural analysis in accounting for the effects of meaning that could be produced by a structure of the linguistic type. And quite naturally, with the phenomenological spouse finding herself disqualified by her inability to address language, structuralism became the new bride."[2] And this means "structuralism" in the broadest sense, which included semiology (Saussure), semiotics (Peirce), structuralism per se (Lévi-Strauss, Barthes, Lacan), developmental structuralism (Piaget, aspects of Habermas, Kohlberg, Loevinger), neo-structuralism (Foucault), and post-structuralism (Derrida, Lyotard). Despite their numerous differences, all of them share a movement from the philosophy of the subject monologically accessing a pregiven world, to a dialogical investigation of the intersubjective structures that allow subjects and objects to differentiate and appear in the first place. (In other words, postmodern theorists are united in their insistence that the Upper-Left quadrant [or individual consciousness] and the Right-Hand quadrants [or monological objects] can only be fully understood with reference to the Lower-Left or *intersubjective* domains. As I would also put it, we need an "all-quadrant" approach.)

This was further coupled with an increasing appreciation of the *historicity* of many of these intersubjective and dialogical structures (Nietzsche, Heidegger, Wittgenstein, Dewey, Rorty)—and suddenly we are out of the modern and into the postmodern mood, where, no matter how much these various theorists disagree with each other, they are all united in a firm demonstration that monological consciousness and monological methodology are severely limited models, if not outright distortions, of human experience and reality.

Now the crucial point about these developments is that most of the pioneering psychological theorists of the modern West—including Freud, Jung, Adler, Rank, James, Watson, Titchener, Wundt—were all ensconced in the pre-intersubjective era. That is, they all, without exception, were embedded in a profoundly monological framework. For each of them, a subject reports the phenomena of consciousness, and those phenomenological reports are taken as foundational, even if they eventually lead elsewhere. Thus, whether the technique is introspection (Wundt), free association (Freud), psychedelics (James), active imagination (Jung), or stream of consciousness (James), for each of them the basic adequacy of phenomenology is never profoundly questioned.[3] Each of them dramatically expanded the *content* of acceptable phenomenology, stretching it from typical rational-egoic contents into such areas as primary process, magical cognitions, collective mythic images and archetypes, religious experiences, and so forth; but none of them challenged, or were even clearly aware of, the intersubjective structures allowing this phenomenology to occur in the first place. In short, they all discovered new cards in the phenomenological game, but none spotted the nonphenomenological rules of the game itself.

Most psychological researchers to this day, including Grof, remain largely embedded in this monological consciousness framework, in my opinion, even as they continue to extend the phenomenology of consciousness into nonordinary states (NOSC). In other words, no amount of LSD, or holotropic breathing, or hypnosis, or shamanic experiences, or rituals, or intense bodywork will disclose the moral, cultural, linguistic, and syntactical structures in which and through which those subjective experiences arise. And thus, *you will find none of those crucial intersubjective patterns on any of the maps or cartographies or cosmologies in Grof's model* (nor in any of the traditions he cites in any of his works). These constitutive patterns are all invisible to Grof's mode of investigation, and, I believe, they constitute an area of neglect and inadequacy in his system.

Thus, in Grof's overall model, monological science joins with monological consciousness, and this, I believe, severely limits our understanding of human consciousness in general. It further makes it quite difficult to conceptualize how temporary *states* of consciousness can be converted into enduring *traits* (or structures) of consciousness, because these structures are, in large measure, intersubjectively constructed and will thus appear in no phenomenology of consciousness, including Grof's.

Likewise, the application of Grof's model to larger issues (historical, cultural, sociological, aesthetic) simply reproduces this inadequacy. Thus, for example, when Tarnas uses Grof's model to interpret the rise of modernity (in *The Passion of the Western Mind*), the inadequacies of the model translate themselves directly into the inadequacies in Tarnas's account, which is why, in my opinion, he seems to miss so much that is crucial to the historical emergence of modernity. Tarnas is also strongly committed to a Romantic/Washburn/Wilber-I viewpoint, which further limits his account, in my opinion.

This monological hegemony is regrettable enough, but in my view it further predisposes Grof to what I believe is the central misconception in his model, the nature and importance of the perinatal level.

PERINATAL REDUX

Grof defines the word "perinatal" as follows: "The prefix *peri-* means literally 'around' or 'near,' and *natalis* translates as 'pertaining to delivery.' It suggests events that immediately precede, are associated with, or follow biological birth."[4] In Grof's early psychedelic research, he consistently found that as a typical session unfolded, individuals would in some sense contact successively earlier stages of their own development, moving first from surface abstract or aesthetic patterns, to earlier biographical (and Freudian) material, and eventually to what appeared to be an actual reliving of biological birth. Grof named the spectrum of experiences that seemed organized around the imprints of the actual delivery process "perinatal." Once this perinatal level was contacted, it often acted as a doorway to transpersonal and spiritual experiences.

Further observations suggested that perinatal experiences in general, although not merely a reliving of biological birth, nonetheless organized themselves in four fairly distinct classes that in many important ways

seemed to parallel the clinical stages of childbirth. Grof therefore postulated that "basic perinatal matrices" (BPM) were laid down during the
actual biological delivery. Although not all perinatal experiences can be
reduced to an actual reliving of biological birth, nonetheless these matrices, as deeply imprinted structures in the bodymind, act as formative
patterns in perinatal experiences in general.

"The connection between biological birth and perinatal experiences
is quite deep and specific," says Grof. "This makes it possible to use the
clinical stages of delivery in constructing a conceptual model that helps
us to understand the dynamics of the perinatal level of the unconscious."
The general stages of clinical delivery cement the blueprints of the four
basic perinatal matrices: BPM I, the oceanic or amniotic universe;
BPM II, cosmic engulfment and no exit; BPM III, the death-rebirth struggle; and BPM IV, the death-rebirth experience. These blueprints, stencils,
or matrices "have deep roots in the biological aspects of birth."[5]

Nonetheless, Grof points out that perinatal experiences rarely involve
a simple reliving of the birth trauma. Rather, perinatal experiences tend
to be *the doorway to transpersonal experiences in general*. Thus, Grof
is at pains to point out that "In spite of its close connection to childbirth,
the perinatal process transcends biology and has important psychological, philosophical, and spiritual dimensions. . . . Certain important characteristics of the perinatal process clearly suggest that it is a much
broader phenomenon than reliving of biological birth."[6]

That very well might be true, but nonetheless, right there, I believe,
Grof has begun to lose track of his definitions. He deliberately introduced the term *perinatal* because it pertained specifically to experiences
surrounding the actual biological birth process. But when aspects of
these experiences "clearly suggest that it is a much broader phenomenon
than reliving of biological birth," he explicitly rejects the reduction of
these experiences to biological birth *but keeps the term "perinatal."*

Thus, any time an intense death-rebirth struggle occurs, of any sort,
at any age, under any circumstance, Grof will tend to do a dual analysis,
reflecting his hidden, dual definition of perinatal. He will first claim that
a reliving of the actual birth trauma is the central core of the death-
rebirth phenomenon; then he will disavow reduction to that specific
trauma and open his analysis to all sorts of other levels, factors, and
dimensions. In doing so, he will deny reductionism to biological birth,
but he will keep the term *perinatal* to describe any and all intense experiences of death-rebirth, experiences that he nevertheless continues to in-

sist are anchored to, if not reducible to, blueprints laid down in actual childbirth.

This is typical: "On this [perinatal] level of the unconscious, the issue of death is universal and entirely dominates the picture."[7] So far, this demonstrates that all deep perinatal experiences involve intense life-and-death issues; it does not in the least demonstrate that all life-and-death issues are perinatal. So it is necessary for Grof to move from this broad and general account of perinatal as involving death, to perinatal in the specific sense of being directly related to childbirth. This he does in the next step: "The connection between biological birth and perinatal experiences is quite deep and specific."[8] "Experiential confrontation with death at this depth of self-exploration tends to be intimately interwoven with a variety of phenomena related to the birth process. . . . Subjects often experience themselves as fetuses and can relive various aspects of their biological birth . . . many of the accompanying physiological changes that take place make sense as typical concomitants of birth."[9]

Now Grof might be correct that intense life-and-death issues have at their core a biological birth stencil, but his evidence in no fashion establishes this. Rather, those particular observations stem primarily from intense LSD or holotropic sessions, where individuals might indeed regress to an actual reliving of the clinical delivery process. But on the face of it, those observations do not in any way describe, for example, the transpersonal stages of vipassana meditation as one enters nirvikalpa samadhi (the *necessity* of first experiencing oneself as a fetus is found in none of the traditional texts). Grof is referring to a specific nexus of phenomena that occur under intense LSD sessions, and, occasionally, under other intense forms of physiological stress.

I am not denying Grof's data; it very well might be quite accurate. What I am questioning is the immediate and massive generalization from this very specific and narrow situation, where intense life-and-death issues appear to coalesce around childbirth, to issues of death and rebirth in general, not all of which appear to involve a reliving of clinical delivery.

I will return to that point in a moment. But in the meantime, notice that Grof immediately makes that unwarranted and generalized leap (and he will do so using exactly his hidden, dual definition of perinatal). Thus: "The central element in the complex dynamics of the death-rebirth process seems to be reliving the biological birth trauma." He always adds that the death-rebirth is more than a mere reliving of the birth trauma, but nonetheless the core and *necessary element* is a reliving of biological birth: "Although the entire spectrum of experiences occurring on this level cannot be reduced to a reliving of biological birth, the birth trauma seems to represent an important core of the process. For this reason, I refer to this domain of the unconscious as *perinatal*."[10]

And here exactly we have the hidden dual definition. What actually is "this level of self-exploration"? It is the confrontation with death and rebirth. What is an important *core* of this confrontation—that is, a *necessary* ingredient? The reliving of biological birth, which is why it is called perinatal. But what does the *perinatal level* itself consist of? Any intense existential death-rebirth experiences. But that moves from the first definition (biological birth) to the second (any intense existential crisis in general), and does so in a fashion that is not in the least supported by Grof's evidence or arguments. There is, as he puts it, "the entire spectrum of experiences occurring on this [life-death] level," and there is the "process of biological birth," and his dual definition refers to *both* of them as perinatal.

At this point, Grof's definition of "perinatal" has slipped completely loose from its original mooring and is running indiscriminately through the existential world at large. "Deep experiential encounter with birth and death is typically associated with an existential crisis of extraordinary proportions during which the individual seriously questions the meaning of his or her life and existence in general."[11]

But all that follows from Grof's actually presented evidence is that perinatal experience can be profoundly existential; it does not follow in the least that all existential crises are perinatal. But with that elemental confusion, Grof resorts to his dual definition and anchors all *existential* death-rebirth phenomena squarely in the actual *childbirth* stencils, so much so that he begins referring to any death-rebirth experience as THE death-rebirth experience, and this monolithic death-rebirth blueprint is, of course, biological birth: "The experiences of the death-rebirth process . . . can be . . . derived from certain anatomical, physiological, and biochemical aspects of the corresponding stages of childbirth with which they are associated."[12]

When it is necessary to use his dual definition in order to expand the role of childbirth trauma beyond that warranted by his evidence, Grof will switch from biological birth to "the perinatal level," because, as we have seen, by his dual definition they are now not the same thing at all. This dual definition (childbirth/existential) allows him to implicitly keep his reductionism while explicitly denying it.

Thus, says Grof, the perinatal level of the unconscious is at the intersection between the personal and the transpersonal. But all that actually means is that *an existential death-rebirth lies between personal and transpersonal development.* Grof has not in any fashion demonstrated that a reliving of biological birth is necessary in all or even most cases in order for that development to occur. Intense LSD and holotropic sessions might indeed involve an actual reliving of childbirth; but in attempting to generalize beyond those quite specific situations to existential and transpersonal dimensions in general, Grof has stepped quite beyond the warrant of his evidence.

In fact, it is my own opinion that with this hidden, dual definition of perinatal (it means both existential and childbirth), Grof has confused chronology with ontology. With intense LSD sessions—which formed and still form the core of Grof's model—individuals might regress in a chronological sequence: from present day to early childhood (Freudian) to birth trauma (Rankian), beyond which, once the individual has dropped an exclusive identification with the gross bodymind, properly transpersonal experiences do indeed disclose themselves.

But by confusing this chronology with an actual ontology of dimensions of awareness, Grof must insert the actual biological birth process between the personal and the transpersonal domains, and that is the only fashion in which he can generalize his model beyond the specific and rather narrow conditions in which it was developed. And thus he is forced generally to postulate that a reliving of specific biological birth, in one form or another, is generally necessary for transpersonal development.

At that point Grof's model, I believe, is out of touch with the preponderance of evidence from the meditative and contemplative traditions, from Western depth psychology (including Jungian), and from most of the evidence generated in NOSC research. The issue, to state it rather crudely, is not whether an existential level exists between the personal and the transpersonal domains. Virtually all parties (including me) agree that is usually the case. Rather, the question is, does that existential level necessarily involve, in part, the actual reliving of the clinical birth delivery? Not might it occasionally, but must it as a rule, do so? Grof basically says yes, virtually everybody else says no.

You do not find the *necessity* to relive clinical birth in any of the major spiritual manuals and techniques. It is rarely if ever found in any of the ascetic practices, shamanic techniques, or contemplative yogas. You do not find it in the great classics of the perennial philosophy or in any of the major wisdom tradition texts. Nor do you find it in the vast majority of the Western depth psychologists, including James and Jung and the general Jungian tradition. (You don't even find it in Washburn, who, as a regressivist, might be expected to concur; he does not.)

Huston Smith has given what is still perhaps the definitive critique of Grof's model from the view of the great wisdom traditions. Of the many crucial points Smith makes—and I am in substantial agreement with all of them—especially relevant are the charges that (1) Grof confuses chronological regression with ontological modes of being and consciousness, thus fundamentally misunderstanding their actual origin; (2) this leads Grof to misunderstand the actual role of clinical birth in existential and spiritual domains, since they are "influenced only, not caused" by such; (3) this leads Grof to fail to appreciate that "birth and death are not physical only."[13]

On the other hand, Huston has always acknowledged that the holarchy of basic structures as I have outlined them is in substantial agreement with the perennial traditions as he summarizes them in *Forgotten Truth*. Massive amounts of meditative and phenomenological evidence from the great traditions squarely support this view, which Grof's model does not handle in its present form.

Grof tends to respond to such criticism by saying that all of those wisdom traditions do in fact recognize death-rebirth phenomena, and they all agree that such existential crises are the crucial transition from personal bondage to transpersonal liberation. This is quite true, but Grof goes further and, in the same breath, equates existential death-rebirth with perinatal/birth, which is exactly the equation that is altogether unwarranted by the preponderance of evidence, and an equation that gains currency *only* by his hidden dual definition of perinatal. Grof is assuming exactly that which he is supposed to demonstrate—namely, not that there exists an existential level lying between all personal and transpersonal development (all parties agree that is so), but that the essential core of that existential level is a stencil of clinical childbirth (which virtually nobody but Grof maintains, and for which he has presented no generalized evidence).

Thus, in my opinion, what may be typical in intense LSD and holotropic sessions has been unjustifiably made paradigmatic for all forms of transpersonal development, an extension for which there is no evidential warrant whatsoever. In doing so, this approach devalues and ignores other equally crucial components of the human psyche, most notably the constitutive nature of vast intersubjective networks of moral, cultural, linguistic, and syntactical structures, with the net result that, in my opinion, this remains an extremely important and fruitful, but quite limited, model of overall consciousness and its development.

FULCRUM-0 AND FULCRUM-6

I am not denying the existence of the basic perinatal matrices, nor the possibility that they might play a formative role in certain psychospiritual developments. I will now briefly indicate how I believe Grof's data, shorn of their hidden dual definitions, can find resonance with my own model.

Let me begin with what I call the actual *existential level*. In my model, the basic structure of this level is called "vision-logic"; the self-need is that for "self-actualization"; the moral sense is postconventional; and the self-sense or self-identity is called "centauric" or "existential" (fulcrum-6).

I have consistently, from my first book to my latest, maintained that the vast majority of evidence, culled from hundreds of sources East and West (which I have cited), clearly suggests that an existential level (by whatever name) is the great doorway to the spiritual and transpersonal dimensions. *The existential level is, as it were, the intersection between the personal and the transpersonal* (or, more technically, between the gross-oriented bodymind and the transegoic subtle and causal domains). Accordingly, in order for development to continue beyond the individual and existential level, the self (or consciousness) must break or deconstruct its exclusive identification with the gross bodymind and all its relations.[14]

This is a "death," to be sure, but in my model, as Stan acknowledges, every fulcrum possesses a signature death-rebirth struggle. Each developmental shift in the center of gravity means that the self has ceased identifying with the basic structure of that stage—has actually died to that level, disidentified with that level, transcended that level—and is reborn into the new and deeper and wider sphere of the consciousness of the next wave. Every fulcrum embodies a death to one basic level and a rebirth on the next, so that, making stepping stones of our dead selves, we are finally delivered unto the Deathless.[15]

The specific contour of each death-rebirth transformation depends upon the basic level of the given fulcrum at which it occurs: there is death to the (exclusive) pleroma, death to the uroboros, death to the typhon, death to the persona, death to the ego, death to the centaur, death to the soul (which are modes of self-sense at some of the important basic waves). *Each death is difficult in its own way*; sufficient unto the day is the death thereof.

Nonetheless, the death-rebirth struggle of the centaur/existential level is, in some ways, the most dramatic, simply because, as we noted, it is the great transition from the personal to the transpersonal domains. And, as we also noted, existential death is the deconstruction of the extensive networks of biologically oriented identifications (death to an exclusive identification with the gross-oriented bodymind in general). As such, the death-rebirth struggle of the existential level is profoundly significant and altogether intense.

Accordingly, the real question is, Does this great death-rebirth transition necessarily involve the actual reliving of the clinical delivery? I maintain, contrary to Grof, that in *some* cases this *might* indeed happen, just as Grof recounts, but it is *not necessary*, and, not being necessary, *it cannot be the actual mechanism of the great transition to the transpersonal.*

Recall that, in my own model, biological birth—the actual delivery process—is fulcrum-0. Like all fulcrums, it has that very general 1-2-3 process of fusion/differentiation/integration. These broad subphases of fulcrum-0 are quite similar to Grof's BPMs.[16]

I believe that these fulcrum-0 birth matrices are indeed imprinted on the gross bodymind of the human being. However, exactly how much importance they assume cannot yet be decided, given the evidence presently available. In my opinion, Grof exaggerates the evidence for these imprints and their influence; and, in any event, I believe he steps across the line of actual evidence in generalizing their importance for existential and transpersonal domains. Here is what I believe we can say on the basis of the available evidence:

A general existential level (by whatever name) lies between personal and transpersonal developments. On this, Washburn, Grof, the great traditions, and I all agree. In my model, this is fulcrum-6. This does *not* mean that transpersonal experiences cannot occur prior to fulcrum-6; they can and often do, but only as temporary states of consciousness (NOSC), or as peak experiences, or as part of the "trailing clouds of glory" (as I will explain below). But in order for such *states* to be converted to *traits* (i.e, in order for temporary and exclusive states of consciousness to be converted to enduring and incorporative structures and patterns constantly available to consciousness), the individual will have to grow and develop into them. At some point, if growth continues, he or she will confront the general existential domain, beyond which can be found more enduring transpersonal patterns.

Washburn, Grof, and I also agree that this existential transition is something of a total life/death confrontation (or series of them), often difficult and brutal, but in most cases profoundly transformative.

At that point, our accounts diverge. Both Washburn and Grof see this as (in part) a literal and necessary regression: Washburn, to fulcrum-1; Grof, further back into the intrauterine state of fulcrum-0. I myself maintain that such regression *might* occur, but it is *not* the defining or essential core and doorway to the transpersonal.

Under what circumstances, then, might an actual regression occur? In my overall model, wherever there are developmental malformations at any of the self-fulcrums, there results a "stick-point" or "lesion" in consciousness. These malformations (splitting, alienation, repression, fragmentation, fixation, dissociation, etc.) will, in various ways and degrees, sabotage subsequent development. If these dissociations are severe, higher development cannot easily proceed without recontacting and to some degree reintegrating the dissociated aspects (the "undigested experiences," since one of the self's characteristics is that it is the locus of experiential "metabolism").

Moreover, at the existential level itself, as consciousness begins to deconstruct an exclusive identity with the gross bodymind, it likewise begins to deconstruct the *repression barrier* which instituted much of the dissociation of the various aspects of that gross and vital bodymind, and consequently any particularly severe past repressions/fixations tend especially at this point to jump into awareness (or in other ways act as a regressive magnet that must be negotiated in order for further development to occur). Thus, particularly at the existential level (fulcrum-6), any significant malformations in any of the earlier fulcrums—including fulcrum-0 and fulcrum-1—might resurface to aggressively command attention.[17]

Thus, as I see it, this model can handle the evidence and data of both the Grof and Washburn models, but the reverse is not true. If, in any individual case, actual regression occurs, either to fulcrum-1 (Washburn) or fulcrum-0 (Grof), there is ample room for such phenomena in my model. But if such massive regression does *not* occur in some cases, both of their models fail. Since the total web of cross-cultural evidence indicates that regression and direct recontacting of the infantile state is not a necessary prerequisite for, say, sahaj samadhi, then these models have already failed in that regard.

FRONTAL AND PSYCHIC DEVELOPMENTAL LINES

I will now suggest what I suspect is actually behind Grof's data and his perinatal orientation.

The fact that fulcrum-0 is the "beginning of the line" in terms of this life does not mean it is the beginning of the line for consciousness itself. I believe we must hold open the possibility that, prior to fulcrum-0, there are the entire bardo (and past-life) realms. I extensively outlined this possibility in *The Atman Project*—in fact, I devoted the entire last chapter to it.

As I point out in that chapter, prior to conception in the gross body-mind, consciousness has traversed the causal Dharmakaya and then the subtle Sambhogakaya, and then finally takes gross form with conception in the womb (where it then begins fulcrum-0). This is why, since *The Atman Project*, I have always used Wordsworth's "Not in entire forget-fulness . . . But trailing clouds of glory do we come" to describe this situation. This is also why I have never denied that transpersonal experiences of various sorts are available during the pre-egoic period; I have simply denied that they are due to any pre-egoic structures.

In the Tibetan Buddhist model (which I represented in *The Atman Project*), the individual psyche or consciousness is composed of two distinct essences or drops (*tigle*). That is, in the heart center of every human, there is the empty essence (*tigle*) of consciousness, divided into two layers or two drops: (1) the "lifetime indestructible drop," which develops during a particular lifetime, but perishes upon biological death, and (2), within or interior to the lifetime indestructible drop, the "eternal indestructible drop," which lasts until Buddhahood and thus transmigrates from life to life until radical Enlightenment. This interior drop is, in my terminology, the psychic/subtle being—which I also deliberately refer to as the "soul," since that, too, lasts until actual spiritual resurrection in the causal/nondual Divine Domain of pure Emptiness. (This, as we will see, is also quite similar to Aurobindo's distinction between the frontal consciousness, which develops in this lifetime, and the deeper/psychic being, which transmigrates.)[18]

In general, for this Tibetan/Aurobindo/Wilber-II model, the highest level of stable evolution reached in any given life permeates the eternal indestructible drop and thus is carried, not usually as specific memories but as a mood of adaptation, to the next life. As I explained it in *The Atman Project*, the more evolved the soul is, the less involved it is (i.e., the less it forgets its higher source and suchness), and this continues until radical Enlightenment, whereupon the soul is completely subsumed or superseded (negated and preserved) in prior Unborn Spirit or radical Emptiness, which is simply the luminous transparency of this and every moment.

In *The Atman Project*, I describe the prior bardo domains through which this soul-drop travels on its way to rebirth in the gross bodymind (i.e., the *involutionary* journey from causal to subtle to gross bodymind), where it then ends up in the prenatal state. In other words, this prenatal state is then the beginning of fulcrum-o, or the *beginning of frontal consciousness development and evolution* (the beginning of the lifetime indestructible drop), a development or evolution which occurs through the nine or ten basic structures of (frontal) consciousness and their associated self-fulcrums.

Several points might be noted in regard to this "two-source" (frontal/soul) Tibetan/Aurobindo/Wilber-II model.

1. As frontal consciousness development gets under way, the psychic/soul witnessing capacity is progressively forgotten. In *The Atman Project*, I specifically describe this as an *amnesis*, a forgetting, in a section called "Amnesia and the In Between" (the bardo is the "in between" state, in between death and rebirth).

2. The traditions vary on how long it takes, in infancy, for these "trailing clouds of glory" of the psychic/soul witnessing to fade. Teachers I have talked to (and various texts themselves) suggest that it seems to vary from a few weeks to a few years, depending primarily on the "strength" of the transmigrating soul-drop.

3. Any veridical memories of the prenatal and perinatal and early infancy period, should they prove valid—and I have Stan's data in mind here—would have to be carried by this psychic/soul consciousness, and *not* by any structures or consciousness in the *frontal* personality, since those structures and their neuronal supports (myelin sheaths) are very poorly developed. In my model, this is the proposed explanation for the subjective carrier of Grof's perinatal memories, should evidence continue to support their existence.[19]

4. This also means, once again, that any transpersonal occasions during the pre-egoic period are *not* due to any of the pre-egoic frontal structures themselves, but rather to the deeper psychic/soul being, which is increasingly forgotten (amnesia) as frontal development gets under way. Thus, contacting the psychic/soul level is not a recapture of any pre-egoic or infantile structures in the frontal line (which actually obscure that consciousness). In other words, the transpersonal psychic/soul of

the *pre-egoic period* is not in any fashion a *pre-egoic structure* laid down or developed during the pre-egoic or infantile period itself.

5. When frontal consciousness development itself passes the existential level (fulcrum-6) and reaches the actual psychic level (fulcrum-7), the psychic/soul dimension begins to enter frontal awareness.

6. For just that reason, this is precisely where a reliving of the birth trauma *might* occur, since that perinatal awareness/memory is carried, not by the ego, which did not exist at the time, but by the psychic/soul, which now emerges in frontal consciousness.

7. This reliving of the birth trauma is therefore not in any way *necessary* for spiritual growth and development; what is crucial here is simply the emergence of the psychic level into frontal awareness, and this *may or may not* involve a flashback of its entry into the gross domain.

8. In any event, this psychic/soul witness, whether trailing clouds of glory in the prenatal and perinatal state or emerging at stage 7 of frontal development, is not the ultimate or in any way the highest seat of consciousness, but is already a samsarically bound and transmigrating being. In no case, then, does it have anything to do with radical Enlightenment: it is precisely what has to be deconstructed (negated and preserved) in order for Enlightenment to shine forth.

Thus, in Wilber-I, I imagined that any transpersonal experiences of prenatal to early childhood were due to the fact that the pre-egoic structures *were themselves* transpersonal in their *actual structure*. This was the pre/trans fallacy. In Wilber-II, I maintain that any transpersonal experiences of infancy are *not* due to pre-egoic frontal structures, but (1) to these trailing clouds of glory of the psychic/soul drop; (2) to the continual cycle of waking/dream/sleep *states*, which plunges each self through the gross/subtle/causal domains every twenty-four hours (not to mention the microgenetic involutional cycle occurring every second, for which, see the last chapter in *The Atman Project*); and (3) temporary peak experiences. [See *Integral Psychology*, chapter 11, for a full discussion of this topic.]

The pre/trans fallacy results when any genuinely transegoic structure or state—including the psychic/soul consciousness, wherever it appears—is identified or confused with structures that are pre-egoic (such as emotional-vitality, polymorphous perversity, free libido distribution, infantile adualism, and so on)—which is, of course, the Romantic/Washburn/Wilber-I "mistake." In other words, the transpersonal states that appear in the pre-egoic period are not due to any pre-egoic structures.

Moreover, the pre/trans fallacy fully applies to the events in both the frontal consciousness and in the psychic/soul line. The reason, I believe, that Grof and others have sometimes found that the pre/trans fallacy is "not quite right" is that, in my opinion, they confuse these two lines of development. In other words, what is *genuinely* "trans" in one line (the psychic/soul) appears during the *pre* period of the other line (the frontal line). If we keep these two lines distinct, and realize that the pre/trans fallacy *applies to each of the lines individually*, then these confusions, I believe, will almost instantly clear up.

For example, we have already seen how the pre/trans fallacy applies to the frontal development or frontal *evolution* (i.e., pre-egoic frontal structures ought not be confused with transegoic frontal structures; to do so results either in reductionism or elevationism). *But precisely the same pre/trans principle is fully operative in the involutionary arc as well*—and the pre and the trans should not be confused in that sequence either.

In fact, the *Tibetan Book of the Dead* gives one basic and profound reason that the soul falls away from the Clear Light Emptiness and thus ends up in lower and lower states (causal to subtle to gross): namely, the soul-drop confuses the lower or pre states with the higher or trans states, and under this pre/trans confusion, the soul-drop actually *chooses the lower, thinking it is the higher*! A bad case of elevationism is exactly the mechanism that lands it in samsara! This is an excellent description of the pre/trans fallacy operating in the bardo realms and the involutionary movement, just as it operates in the evolutionary as well (although headed, of course, in the "opposite" direction).

I have always described the pre/trans fallacy as a confusing of involution per se with something that happens in evolution, and this is simply another way of saying, Don't confuse these evolutionary and involutionary lines, because the crisscrossing of those lines usually leads to a pre/trans confusion of one sort or another.

Finally, this is why I have always maintained that regressive therapies, such as rebirthing and breathwork, enter the transpersonal from the "back door." This does not mean I am somehow putting them down. I am not; I am simply describing the unarguable *chronological sequence* of certain of these experiences. When Stan describes a typical LSD session as moving from present-day concerns, to past biological events and Freudian concerns, then to Rankian childbirth trauma (which is then often the doorway to the transpersonal), there is no mistaking that chronological order: it is unarguably regressive (which is why I call that door to the transpersonal the "back door").

But what is being contacted in these regressive therapies is not *essentially* the biological birth ordeal, but the psychic/soul consciousness *present at that ordeal*. And, most important of all, that psychic/soul consciousness can *just as easily be contacted without the regression*; and in fact, in almost all forms of consciousness disciplines, it is most definitely contacted *without the regression*. After all, the psychic/soul consciousness is simply the same consciousness that emerges at stage 7, after the existential crisis (of stage 6) is negotiated. As the psychic/soul being comes to the fore, it might indeed recall its biological birth, but usually it does not, and it certainly *is not necessary* to do so for further growth, because it has already handled the crucial existential life-death crisis of fulcrum-6. And in any event, this psychic/soul being is destined itself only to pass, superseded by the unborn Spirit of the causal and nondual occasions.

Stan's dual definition of perinatal, I believe we can now see, hinges on a confusion between the psychic/soul consciousness present at fulcrum-0, and the actual stencils of that childbirth fulcrum. Fulcrum-0 is the *beginning* of the pre-egoic realms, but the *end* of the bardo realms, and this intersection—the intersection toward the *beginning* of frontal *evolution* and toward the *end* of psychic/soul *involution*—generates the strange dual experiences that Stan has named perinatal.

But because he does not distinguish carefully enough between these two lines (evolution and involution), the result is that, in my opinion, he sometimes uncritically *identifies* them at their cross-section (biological birth = the gateway to the transpersonal). He then understandably denies reductionism, even though the identification itself is in fact very reductionistic (and simply not true). But if we keep these two lines separate, not only does the pre/trans fallacy still guide our path in both of them, Stan's data immediately opens itself to a more benevolent match with the world's great wisdom traditions, not to mention with my own model and the large amounts of evidence supporting it. As it is now, there are vast amounts of clinical, experimental, phenomenological, intersubjective, meditative, and psychotherapeutic evidence and data (from perennial to postmodern sources) that Grof's model, by itself, fails to take into account.[20]

Nevertheless, I would like to end on the same note with which I began: in terms of the overall "big picture" of the spectrum of consciousness and the realms of the human unconscious, there is an extraordinary amount of overlap and agreement between Washburn, Grof, and myself. I prefer to think in terms of those many similarities, even as we continue to hash out the details.

8

Integral Feminism

SEX AND GENDER ON THE
MORAL AND SPIRITUAL PATH

Does Spirit manifest as male and female? Is there God and God-
dess? Do men and women therefore have different, if comple-
mentary, types of spirituality? At what point, if any, do we cease
to be male and female and start being human? Has feminism
outlived its usefulness? Or does it simply need a more integral
approach?

A FEMINIST PERSPECTIVE

WHAT WOULD A TRULY integral feminism look like? An approach
to feminism that is actually "all-level, all-quadrant"? In this
chapter we will explore exactly that theme, after first addressing a few
common misconceptions that are hindering the emergence of a more
integral view.[1]

Carol Gilligan

We can start with some of the typical misunderstandings of Carol Gilligan's work and the notion of hierarchy. I believe that many feminist
writers rather badly misunderstand the nature of hierarchy, which leads
them to misconstrue both my model and Carol Gilligan's, which is a
deeply hierarchical model.

Gilligan found that men and women both move through three broad hierarchical stages of moral development, but that men tend to progress through these stages based more on judgments of rights and justice, whereas women tend to negotiate these hierarchical stages based on judgments of care and responsibility. Thus, Kohlberg's mistake was *not* the broad hierarchical stage conception itself (which Gilligan accepts),[2] but the belief that, *within* those stages, male ranking represented a higher stage than female linking, which is simply not true. (This is the confusing of permeable with prepersonal, a fallacy we most definitely want to avoid.) But notice: each successive stage of female judgment is indeed superior in its capacity to express and manifest care. Each female stage is hierarchically ranked, but within each stage, judgments occur by linking and connection. So the same vertical, hierarchical, developmental ranking of stages occurs in both men and women, but men progress through these stages while making judgments of rights and justice, women making judgments of care and responsibility.

I have summarized the large amount of research in this area by saying that both men and women exist as agency-in-communion (as do all holons), but men tend to *translate* with an emphasis on *agency*, women with an emphasis on *communion*. But both of them *transform* through the same broad, gender-neutral, holarchical stages of consciousness unfolding.

Thus, for Gilligan, women move through three general stages: selfishness to care to universal care (which she also calls selfish to conventional ethical to postconventional metaethical). These are the three broad stages of preconventional, conventional, and postconventional, which I have also termed *egocentric, sociocentric,* and *worldcentric* (and, in my model, the worldcentric or global stage is the platform and the gateway to higher spiritual domains). For Gilligan, each of those successive stages is *higher* and *more valuable* precisely because, as I would word it, the woman can extend the *circle of care* to more and more people (just as when men move through those same stages, they extend the *circle of justice* to more and more people, from egocentric to ethnocentric to worldcentric modes).

Gilligan has suggested that "these two distinct moral orientations . . . can be further integrated in a hierarchical moral stage beyond the formal operational level."[3]

Note also: besides being hierarchical, Gilligan's model is linear, in the sense meant by developmentalists. That is, her three (or four) major stages unfold in a linear fashion that cannot be reversed or bypassed, because each stage depends upon certain competences provided by the previous stages (you cannot get to universal care without the previous stage of care, for example). The first two things to note about Gilligan's model, then, is that it is *linear* and *hierarchical* for *both* men and women.[4]

All of this unfortunately tends to be ignored or overlooked by many feminists, who somehow imagine that Gilligan was saying women are altogether free of that nasty "ranking." I believe this is typical of a certain feminist approach that tends to ignore and deny any sort of female ranking hierarchy, under the performative contradiction of web-only models. By focusing essentially on heterarchy in women's experience, advocates of this approach ignore and devalue the important aspects of women's experience that are also hierarchical, which, I believe, badly distorts this entire approach, and makes it virtually impossible to give a coherent account of female development at all.

In other words, these linking-only models are deeply involved in what I call pathological heterarchy: not a communion but a fusion, not a linking but a meltdown, not a connecting but an indissociation—an incapacity to rank values at all, which actually devalues all values, a pathology that one feminist (observing "process queens" at work) called "the bland leading the bland."

The typical pathological form of male agency is "power over," or brutal dominance and rigid autonomy. The male does not want to be a *part* of anything else (communion), he wants only to be the *whole* himself (alienated agency): he fears relationship and values only autonomy. This is not male agency, but a pathology of male agency. Likewise, the typical pathological form of female communion is fusion: the female fears autonomy and disappears into relationship, often destroying her own identity in the process. She does not want to be a *whole* (with its own agency), but merely a *part* of something else (exaggerated communion). This is not normal female heterarchy or mutual equivalence, but pathological heterarchy or meltdown: all ranking is out, linking alone reigns.

And it is, alas, pathological heterarchy that drives too many of these "web-only" and "permeable" models of alleged female development. More accurate, I believe, is a model that acknowledges and honors both hierarchy and heterarchy in both male and female, and thus can account for both development and pathology in each sex. And one thing is certain: we do not overcome pathological masculinity with pathological femininity.[5]

The Permeable Self

Many feminists agree with the extensive research that suggests that men tend to emphasize agency (or the autonomous self) and women communion (or "connection" and the "permeable" self). However, I believe that because many feminists devalue and marginalize hierarchical integration in females, they do not often present a coherent explanation of the development of the permeable self. My approach does so, or at least attempts to do so, in the following way:

We saw that men and women both develop through the same gender-neutral basic structures or expanding spheres of consciousness, but men tend to develop through these expanding spheres with an emphasis on agency, rights, justice, and autonomy, whereas women tend to develop through the same holarchical spheres based more on communion, responsibility, relationship, care, and connection.[6]

Thus, in my model, the "permeable" self of women develops through the same general stages of egocentric, sociocentric, worldcentric, and spiritual domains as the male, but with a different emphasis ("in a different voice"), a different set of priorities, a different mood, and a rather different set of spiritual disciplines.

Accordingly, for the female, there is egocentric permeable (selfish), sociocentric permeable (care), worldcentric permeable (universal care), and spiritual permeable (universal union), precisely as the male negotiates those same general spheres with a somewhat more agentic emphasis (agentic egocentric, agentic sociocentric, and so on). The same basic stages—preconventional to conventional to postconventional to post-postconventional—are operative in both, but in a different voice.

Thus, it is absolutely not the case, as some critics have suggested, that in my model the prepersonal stages are simply equated with "permeable" boundaries, thus intrinsically devaluing the female orientation.[7] Rather, there is prepersonal permeable, personal permeable, and transpersonal permeable. Thus, in overall development, the female self becomes permeable to deeper and wider spheres of consciousness, right up to and including a permeability to Spirit or Ground—the same basic spheres through which the male develops with a more agentic orientation. Neither gender orientation is in any fashion privileged or made paradigmatic.

INTEGRAL FEMINISM: ALL-LEVEL, ALL-QUADRANT

There are today at least a dozen major schools of feminism (liberal, socialist, spiritual, eco, womanist, radical, anarchist, lesbian, Marxist, cultural, constructivist, power), and about the only thing they all agree on is that females exist (actually, at least two of the schools deny that). There simply is no consensus view on "the" voice of women, despite the claim of some feminists to be speaking for such.

Rather, I believe that what we need is a much more integral approach, an approach that, in acknowledging the truly different perspectives of a dozen or so different feminist schools, might actually find a scheme that would be more accommodating to each of them. This more integral approach is indeed part of what *Sex, Ecology, Spirituality* attempts to develop, at least in rough and outline form. SES is volume 1 of the Kosmos trilogy; in the forthcoming volume 2 (tentatively entitled *Sex, God, and Gender: The Ecology of Men and Women*), I expand and fill in the details of this general model of sex and gender.

The idea, I believe, is to bring an "all-quadrant, all-level" approach to sex and gender issues—an integral feminism. This approach, in my opinion, gives us a chance to bring together a dozen different schools of feminism, which, ironically, have heretofore resisted being linked, integrated, and connected. For example, each of the different theories of sex and gender (orthodox as well as feminist) has tended to focus on only one quadrant (and usually only one level in one quadrant), with an attempt to make it paradigmatic and exclusionary. I'll go around the four quadrants and give examples from each, and then suggest how their crucial insights, when freed of their hegemonic claims, might be honored and incorporated in a more integral embrace.

Upper Right (Behavioral)

These are the objective aspects of individual holons, which, in the case of human beings, include biological and hormonal factors, such as the effects of testosterone, oxytocin, and estrogen on individual human behavior. These factors, most researchers agree, *influence* (but do not strictly *cause*) sometimes quite different behavioral patterns in the sexes (sexual profligacy in the male being a typical example).

The *radical feminists* have particularly embraced the notion that there are dramatic, biologically based differences between the sexes, as have their strange bedfellows, the sociobiologists. For radical feminists, this is sometimes portrayed as: estrogen is the Goddess, testosterone is the Devil. (There is more than a grain of truth to that, alas; but on balance, both hormonal dispositions have their own appropriate and equally important work to do.) Both the radical feminists and the sociobiologists are onto some important (if limited) aspects of the biological basis of some very significant differences in the sexes. This approach also forms an important part of the increasingly influential school of evolutionary psychology.

These Upper-Right factors also include the macrobiological constants that researchers also agree are present universally and cross-culturally. For example, women give birth and lactate, while men have an average advantage in physical strength and mobility. Both second- and third-wave feminists, as well as orthodox researchers, agree on the existence and importance of most of these factors (they are crucial, for example, in explaining the statistically different roles of men and women in the productive and private spheres, once oppression fails as a causal category).

As I would summarize all of their conclusions, there is a *biological basis* for males to tend toward agency, women toward communion, and these tendencies are the product of perhaps several million years of natural selection, which is why we find them *cross-culturally*—there is nothing "androcentric" about these sex differences, as many radical feminists have made quite clear. However, the actual value attached to these sex differences does indeed *vary from culture to culture* (on this, see the next section.)

Lower Left (Cultural)

The reason that these biological factors are *tendencies*, not *causes*, is that whatever biological factors are present, they nonetheless are taken up and reworked by powerful cultural factors, which can in many cases increase, neutralize, or reverse the biological tendencies.

Most researchers refer to these *biological* differences as *sex*, and the *cultural* differences as *gender*. Likewise, researchers usually refer to the biological sexes as *male* and *female*, and the cultural differences as *masculine* and *feminine*.

There are, in my opinion, two errors that are constantly being made in the study of sex and gender. The first (common with conservatives) is to assume that all gender issues are totally determined by sex differences (so that biology is destiny). The second (common with liberals) is that all sexual differences are merely culturally constructed (so that biology can be ignored). Both of these stances are distorted, I believe, and almost always seem driven by ideology.

What we want to do instead, it seems to me, is to acknowledge and honor the moments of truth in both those positions: biologically constant sex differences (such as the fact that women give birth and lactate, males have an average advantage in physical strength) are taken up and reworked, often in dramatic ways, by cultural factors and influences.

In this regard, I have particularly focused on the role of *worldviews* in the formation of gender. These worldviews (archaic, magic, mythic, mental, existential, etc.) are, recall, part of the intersubjective cultural patterns *within which* individual subjects and objects arise. As such, they play a decisive role in helping to *select which factors from the male and female value spheres will in fact be honored in any given society.*[8] The point is that women and men co-create (sometimes intentionally, sometimes unintentionally) the intersubjective patterns within which their own subjects and objects will be manifest and recognized, and these cultural patterns are sometimes decisive in sex and gender issues as well.

The *constructivist feminists* and the *cultural feminists* have furthered to a great degree our understanding of the important role of this Lower-Left quadrant, and their voices are very much needed in the choir. Unfortunately, they sometimes go beyond the warrant of their own evidence and claim that this quadrant is the only important quadrant in existence, which not only lands them in performative self-contradictions, but also distorts the equally important voices of the other quadrants (and the other schools of feminism). What then happens is that the *influence* of those other quadrants, since they are not fully acknowledged on their own terms, must be ascribed to *oppression*, because the constructivists can figure out no other way that they got there. Thus, for example, biological differences in function must be ascribed to male imposition of ideology. Giving birth and lactating are somehow a male plot of the patriarchy, since all differences are culturally constructed.

That approach, of course, *defines* women as primarily molded by an Other (precisely the definition these feminists say they wish to overcome). And it defines males as essentially oppressors of one sort or another—"All men are rapists" being the most typical example, which is simply outrageous. All men are not rapists; as everybody knows, all men are horse thieves.

But we can ignore those differences of emphasis for the moment, and simply note that all of these important Lower-Left approaches are united in the affirmation of the strong and crucial role played by intersubjective cultural factors in the unfolding of sex and gender.

Lower Right (Social)

Nonetheless, worldviews are not disembodied structures, hanging in idealistic midair. That is, all worldviews—indeed, all cultural factors in general—are strongly anchored in the material components of the society—such as the forces of production, modes of technology, architectural structures, economic base, geopolitical locations, and so forth, all of which I refer to as "social." In other words, all cultural factors have social correlates (all four quadrants have correlates in all the others, and this applies to the cultural and social as well). The social system and cultural worldviews are intimately interwoven, and this, of course, directly relates to gender issues.

In particular, there is now almost overwhelming evidence that, as I would put it, *worldviews follow the base*, not in any strong Marxist or deterministic fashion, but in the general sense that the techno-economic base sets certain broad limits within which worldviews tend to unfold. For example, agrarian (plow) societies place the means of production (the heavy animal-drawn plow) almost exclusively in male hands, and the accompanying worldviews are thus intensely androcentric. There are other factors involved, of course; I am simply pointing out that the techno-economic base is one of the crucial factors.

Thus, with regard to sex and gender issues, the discussion at this point turns to an analysis of *the types of gender roles available to men and women at each of the five or six major stages of techno-economic development in the formation of the human species.* These stages include foraging (scavenging, hunting, gathering), early and late horticultural, early and late agrarian, early and late industrial, and early informational.

These stages, of course, like all evolutionary stages, are asymmetrical and irreversible: steam engines never precede plows. Time's arrow, as always, sinks its claws into the thermodynamics of the material domain, and any theories of social and techno-economic development that ignore these irreversible and "linear" processes are severely deficient, as Prigogine and Jantsch and Laszlo keep reminding us. These social systems are, as I said, interactive with corresponding cultural worldviews, precisely because all four quadrants are mutually interactive. (The five broad technological stages correlate respectively with archaic, magic, mythic, mental, and existential worldviews.)

What we find, with this more integral approach, is that the techno-economic base has a profound influence in *selecting those factors from the male and female value spheres that will be evolutionarily advantageous for a given society.*

For example, horse and herding societies place a premium on physical strength and mobility, which selects for the male value sphere in the public and productive domain (indeed, 97 percent of such societies are strongly patriarchal, with oppression playing no explanatory *causal* role). Likewise, horticultural societies, whose primary force of production is the digging stick or hoe, place a premium on the female work force, because pregnant women can easily handle a hoe with no serious side effects (indeed, 80 percent of the foodstuffs in all horticultural societies are produced by women). Not surprisingly, one-third of these societies have female-only deities (so that wherever you find the Great Mother religions, you find a horticultural base, with only one or two maritime exceptions).[9]

The *Marxist feminists* and the *social feminists* have contributed much to our understanding of the importance of this Lower-Right quadrant for an overall view. Likewise, one of my favorite writers, Janet Chafetz, has contributed a social systems–oriented analysis that is brilliant and thorough. And the *ecofeminists* have emphasized the role of Gaia as the ultimate social system.[10]

All of those factors—behavioral, cultural, and social (at each of their developmental waves)—will have a strong hand in determining how individual men and women experience their own embodiment, engenderment, and gender status. Which brings us to the Upper-Left quadrant.

Upper Left (Intentional)

The Upper-Left quadrant is, recall, the interior of the individual, the site of consciousness itself, which is composed of (at least) the self-system and the developmental streams as they all unfold through preconventional, conventional, postconventional, and post-postconventional waves of the overall spectrum.

Within this spectrum of consciousness, it is important to examine both the horizontal dimension—that of *translation*—and the vertical dimension—that of *transformation*. Translation is a process of agency-in-communion, or the relational exchange between any holon and its interwoven environs. Transformation is the shift to a higher or deeper domain altogether (a different level of agency-in-communion).

Where agency and communion operate horizontally on every level, Eros and Agape operate between levels, as it were. Eros is ascending or evolving transformation, Agape is descending or involving transformation (which I will explain in a moment). The important point is simply that both the horizontal or translative dimension and the vertical or transformative dimension need to be taken into account.

If we do so, with regard to sex and gender differences, I believe we will find the following: Men *translate* with an emphasis on agency, women with an emphasis on communion. And men *transform* with an emphasis on Eros, women with an emphasis on Agape.

This is where the Gilligan/Tannen approach becomes an important (if limited) part of the overall picture, and where the extensive research on male agency and female communion needs to be taken into account. But it is not enough simply to contrast male and female in the *translative* dimension (agency/separation versus communion/relationship), because men and women tend to *transform* with a different emphasis as well— namely, Eros/ascending versus Agape/descending.

This tends to confuse people, because they imagine it means that men only ascend and women only descend, which is not the case at all. Rather, it means that, in any stage of vertical growth and development, men and women tend to face in different directions when they negotiate these stages, and these directions are not explainable merely in terms of agency and communion, but of ascending and descending *orientations in the nested holarchy of their own being*. Eros tends to reach up, as it were, and assault the heavens, whereas Agape tends to reach down and embrace the earth. Eros is more transcendental, Agape more immanent (and each has its own agency and communion, which refer to horizontal, not vertical, orientations).

These are not airy abstractions but a rather good summary of much of the cross-cultural research on modes of transformative (or developmental) orientation in men and women. Thus, to give only one brief example, Phil Zimbardo, in his widely acclaimed psychology series on public television, summarizes the cross-cultural differences in the behavioral patterns already demonstrated in young boys and girls—differences that show up in everything from eating habits to types of friendships to styles of play: "Girls have roots, boys have wings."

Roots and wings. Agape and Eros. It is this vertical dimension of depth that needs to be added to the horizontal dimension of agency and communion in order to take into account the multidimensional differences in the native styles of men and women.

Thus, in my view, men and women develop through the same gender-neutral basic structures (the same basic waves in the spectrum of consciousness), but they tend to do so with somewhat different values and styles in both the translative and transformative domains: men tend toward agency and Eros, women toward communion and Agape. (Of course, any specific individual will show a unique proportion of those four factors, and all four factors are decisively present in men and women alike. These are simple tendencies and average probabilities, not causal determinants!)

Nonetheless, and most significantly, these simple sex-class probabilities allow us immediately to stop interpreting females as being deficient males, or the more recent trend of trying to interpret males as being deficient females. Neither the male nor female disposition is itself higher or lower, or deeper or wider, on the nested holarchy of basic waves of consciousness unfolding.

Moreover, this approach prevents the more recent attempts, by various spiritual feminists, to remove female spirituality from any sort of transformational requirements at all. This attempt simply paints women as the "permeable" (communion) self, which is fine, but it then rather straightforwardly equates this permeable self with a spiritual self and an ecological self, thus effectively denying the demand for any hierarchical transformation in women. This unfortunately ignores not only Gilligan's female hierarchy but all others as well, which effectively aborts any sort of transformation in women at all.

What that flatland approach fails to take into account is that the permeable self (or the self-in-connection) itself undergoes growth, development, and transformation. The permeable self holarchically unfolds and transforms through the same expanding spheres of consciousness that the male agentic self must also negotiate in its own fashion (thus, for the female: egocentric permeable, sociocentric permeable, worldcentric permeable, spiritual permeable). The permeable self is not, in itself, a spiritual self at all—only its highest or deepest reaches are. In fact, the lower stages of the permeable self (the prepersonal stages) are just as egocentric, narcissistic, and altogether unpleasant as the shallower stages of the male agentic self. Both of them are equally locked into the orbit of their own endless self-regard, which is, by any definition, the antithesis of all things spiritual.

And as for the permeable self and its alleged regard for ecological connections, it is often quite the opposite. The lower stages of the permeable self (like the lower stages of the agentic self) are altogether prepersonal, preconventional, and egocentric in their stance—which is precisely the stance that is the prime contributor to ecological despoliation in general. Simple communion or permeability will, in itself, do nothing to alleviate this: it simply extends its own narcissism, spreads its own egocentricity, permeably shares its own disease.

Communion is the interwoven, weblike relationship of all of the elements in a given domain, but Agape is the capacity to embrace deeper domains altogether. When we understand that communion and Agape are not simply the same thing, then it becomes obvious that merely possessing a permeable self is not, as these feminists imagine, enough to bring moral light and salvation into the wretched world of male agency. Rather, the shallower and egocentric stages of the permeable self, along with the shallower and egocentric stages of the agentic self, are the twin faces of evil in this world, and one of those smiling faces has female written all over it.

FEMALE SPIRITUALITY

(It is precisely the two basic native differences in the male and female value spheres (males tending toward agency and Eros, females toward communion and Agape) that, when they unfold through the basic waves of consciousness, under the influence of different worldviews and different stages of techno-economic development, generate the various modes of gender that have historically been observed in men and women.)

This "all-quadrant, all-level" approach gives us a chance, I believe, to bring together an enormous number of very important, indeed crucial, factors in the discussion of sex and gender. Thus, the gender-neutral basic waves play themselves out differently for men and women, dependent on factors in all four quadrants, from hormonal differences to worldviews to modes of production to translative/transformative differences. Since all four quadrants intimately interact, none of those factors can be overlooked in a genuinely comprehensive theory of sex and gender.

And this relates directly, I believe, to spiritual development as well. Volume 2 of the Kosmos trilogy is a sustained look at the different types of spiritual development—in many cases, decisively different from male patterns—that certain highly original women saints, shamans, and yogis have pioneered over the centuries. (These female practices generally involve an intense mode, not merely of *translative* communion and permeability, but of *transformative* Agape (incarnational, body-centered, immanent, descended, involutional, and profoundly *embodied mysticism*). They offer a stunning contrast to the more traditionally ascending, transcendental, agentic, and Eros-driven modes of spirituality typical of males.)

But these more female-oriented spiritual practices are still practices in profound *transformation*, not mere translation. As such, these women mystics offer a stinging criticism of the merely "permeable" self theories that find permeability in itself to be spiritual (as if communion and Agape were simply the same).

In other words, in order to manifest a genuine spiritual consciousness, women have just as much hard work to do as the men. As we noted, "permeable" and "spiritual" are not even remotely the same thing. Rather, only the deepest stages of the permeable self are genuinely spiritual ("spirit-as-spirit"), and these deeper developments require intense and sustained spiritual practice. But where the men need to transform their agentic selves, the women need to transform their permeable selves (from selfish to care to universal care to spiritual recognition). These are the same expanding waves of consciousness (egocentric to sociocentric to worldcentric to authentic spiritual), but negotiated with different styles.

What too many "permeable self" theorists actually mean is, "I am a woman, and by virtue of my permeable self, I am already more spiritual than men." What the genuine female mystics demonstrate, on the contrary, is that for women actually to transform their permeable selves, and not merely translate differently, requires an enormous amount of intense and profound work (just as it does in the men). These extraordinary women mystics say to their sisters, in effect: "Fine, you have a relational, embodied, permeable self. But within those givens, here is what you still must do—with intensity and fire and unrelenting dedication—in order to actually transform that self and render it fully transparent to the Depths of the Divine."

Indeed, some of the transformative practices of these remarkable women—which almost always involve wrenching bodily ordeals as they bring Spirit down and into the bodily being via descending or incarnational Agape and its unrelenting compassion—are so intense that they even make for difficult reading; in any event, they are not for the fainthearted, and they put to shame the "wonderful permeable self" assumptions of merely translative female spirituality. These extraordinary women practitioners are blazing beacons of what a woman actually has to do if she is genuinely to transform in depth, and not merely claim a superiority based on translative permeability.

At the same time, we simply cannot forget that both men and women have decisive access to both agency and communion, as well as to Eros and Agape. That they might inherently tend to emphasize one or the other does not mean that they are different species altogether. This is why, I believe, we need constantly to keep our eye on both the profound similarities as well as the intricate differences between men and women, and resist the urge to sink our discussion in an ideological fervor to promote one at the expense of the other.

MALE AND FEMALE MORAL DEPTH

Which brings us to our last and somewhat delicate area, that of actual moral development itself. Many radical feminists and ecofeminists constantly claim, explicitly or implicitly, that the general female mode is in some profound sense more moral or ethical than the male mode. But actual feminist research itself demonstrates something quite different—and much more fascinating.

Radical feminists and ecofeminists emphasize, quite correctly it seems to me, that women do indeed tend to stress embodied personal relationship (the "connected self"). And this very fact, it seems, makes it rather difficult for women to develop to Gilligan's third and highest stage of female moral development—that is, from the stage Gilligan calls "conventional ethical" to what she calls "postconventional metaethical" (she also calls this moving from care to universal care).

(In other words, precisely because women tend to remain attached to personal and conventional relationships, they find it harder to reach the postconventional and universal stages *in their own female development* (based on their own relational terms, not on male agentic terms).) Thus, even if we use the Jane Loevinger test originally developed using solely women, more men reach the higher stages. Men, being less personally attached to sociocentric relationships, find it easier to take a universal and postconventional "big picture" view, and thus more men make it into the universal, postconventional moral stages than do women (even when the women are judged by their own scales and values).

On balance, male and female moral development tend to display an interesting split. Just as, in IQ tests, more males score both lower and higher than females (most of the really dumb, and really brilliant, are male), so men score both lower and higher than women in most scales of generalized moral development. Again, women seem to gravitate to personal, embedded, conventional relationships, and thus they have a harder time moving from *conventional communion* (care) to *postconventional communion* (universal care, Gilligan's "postconventional metaethical").

Men, on the other hand, due to their predominantly agentic outlook, tend to gravitate *to either side of that conventional divide*: more of them reach the postconventional worldcentric stage of universal embrace, but more of them also remain at the preconventional and egocentric mode. For every Abraham Lincoln and Mahatma Gandhi, there is a Charles Manson and Son of Sam. Historically, this has made men both truly stunning moral and spiritual beacons, as well as the most viciously evil animals, without exception, to walk the face of the earth.

But the point, once again, is that simply possessing female communion, as opposed to male agency, is not enough to make you spiritual or moral. In fact, it might slow your growth into universal and global domains (spiritual as well as moral), and it might actually cripple anything resembling a genuine global ecological stance (which calls into question one of the central tenets of ecofeminism, namely, the native superiority of the female when it comes to the global biosphere).

But the central conclusion, in all cases, is that the communion self needs just as much work as the agentic self, sometimes more, in order to move from egocentric selfish, to sociocentric care, to worldcentric universal care, there to stand open to the radiance of the Divine. Women, just like men, face years, and often decades, of blood, sweat, tears, and toil, in order to claim their birthright.

9

How Straight Is the Spiritual Path?

THE RELATION OF PSYCHOLOGICAL
AND SPIRITUAL GROWTH

Does psychological growth have to be completed before genuine spiritual growth can occur? What is the relation of psychotherapy and meditation? Are there actually stages of spiritual development? If there are stages of spiritual growth, are they the same for everybody? How can these stages be ascertained? Is there a direction to Spirit's unfolding? Does it really matter?

DAVID BOHM, JENNY WADE, AND THE HOLONOMIC PARADIGM

JENNY WADE'S *Changes of Mind: A Holonomic Theory of the Evolution of Consciousness* is an account of the evolution of consciousness according to what she calls a "holonomic paradigm." This is an enormously competent book with much to recommend it. It gives a fine overview of transpersonal developmental psychology, drawing on sources both ancient and modern, and it is grounded in much data and information from numerous researchers. The core of the book is a transpersonal developmental stage model of consciousness, consisting of nine basic stages (quite compatible with the nine basic waves and fulcrums of development). Around this stage model Wade adds a "two-source" theory of consciousness (also quite compatible with a frontal/soul model), and

David Bohm's implicate/explicate notions. My only reservations about the book are that it doesn't clearly distinguish between levels and lines (which is easily remedied), and it attempts to use David Bohm's purely monological notion of an implicate order to explain the richness of dialogical and translogical realms. But the central message of the book is quite clear: consciousness evolution is at the core of any truly integral psychology.

Transpersonal Developmental Psychology

In chapter 6 I mentioned that, in my own theoretical work, I had moved from a Romantic/Wilber-I to a Wilber-II model because of what I believe are certain recalcitrant difficulties in the Jungian and retro-Romantic orientations. And, as I indicated, Wilber-II was first presented in *The Atman Project*—a model with seventeen general stages, from birth to enlightenment (stages that are variations on matter, body, mind, soul, and spirit); it also specifically included the bardo stages of preconception, prenatal, and postlife states (the frontal/soul or evolution/involution lines).[1] In that and subsequent books, I usually simplified these seventeen waves to nine or so (although the seventeen are still necessary for the overall model, and even those can be further subdivided). But these simplified nine waves (and the corresponding self-fulcrums) are the ones that I emphasize, for example, in *Transformations of Consciousness* and *A Brief History of Everything*.

These nine stages are quite similar to the nine stages that Wade presents in her model, and her rigorous defense of these basic waves points up the truly imposing amount of evidence in support of such a model.[2] What I especially appreciate about her treatment of the first six or seven stages (the conventional stages, from prepersonal to personal) is the wealth of data she brings to the model.[3] This is exactly the type of detailed work that needs to be done, and for the most part, I found this part of the book thorough, accurate, and compelling. Wade has an exceptional gift for assembling innumerable details into a coherent presentation, and this is especially obvious in these sections of the book.

Among other things, this part of Wade's presentation highlights once again the central importance of the stage model in transpersonal studies, and points up why a developmental model is so crucial to the field. It also, by implication, demonstrates how impoverished the alternatives are. This is a superb contribution on Wade's part, and it will have, I believe, a lasting impact on the field. As we will see in a moment, a developmental model needs to be supplemented in several important areas, but it certainly seems that its basic features will be central to any truly comprehensive model of consciousness.

Wade also adopts the "two-source" thesis (a deeper psychic being and the frontal development). Although this is essentially the Aurobindo/Vajrayana concept, she brings a wealth of research data to the task, and this, too, is a very useful part of the book. I particularly liked the phenomenological approach to prenatal and neonatal experiences, and her graphs of the psychic awareness "behind" or "alongside" the frontal. This is another fine contribution, and adds yet further support to the frontal/soul model.

Levels and Lines

In addition to these superb contributions, there are a few minor weaknesses in the book, I believe. In keeping with the reflections on the history of my own work, I might introduce these "mistakes"—or what I believe are mistakes, anyway—by saying that I understand them fairly well because, once again, I made most of them myself.

Almost as soon as I had published the Atman Project/Wilber-II model, I realized that it needed to be refined in a very specific direction. The seventeen basic waves (or basic colors in the spectrum of consciousness) were still generally valid, but that model did not fully *differentiate the various lines of development through each of those waves* (nor did that model carefully distinguish between, for example, enduring structures and transitional structures).

Thus, less than one year after I published Wilber-II, I published its refinement, which we might as well call Wilber-III. Wilber-II and Wilber-III still share the same basic stages, but Wilber-III explicitly distinguishes *the different developmental streams that unfold through those basic waves*. These different developmental lines include affective, cognitive, moral, interpersonal, object-relations, self-identity, and so on, *each of which develops in a relatively independent fashion through the general levels or basic waves of consciousness*. There is no single, monolithic line that governs all of these developments (as I will further explain below).

I also distinguished between the enduring and the transitional features of each of those developmental sequences; outlined six major characteristics of the self-system navigating the basic waves in its own development (resulting in the corresponding "self-fulcrums"); and emphasized even more the importance of temporary *altered states* and *peak experiences* in addition to the more directional and structural frontal unfolding (although, as usual, in order for these temporary states to become enduring traits, they must be converted to permanent structures via development).

(That is the model (Wilber-III) that I have consistently presented since its first publication (1981), and that I generally summarize as "self, waves, streams, and states.")[4] It was becoming fairly obvious by that time that a monolithic "one line" developmental spectrum would not do justice to the evidence. On the other hand, using waves, streams, and states, one could follow both the "linear" or purely developmental and hierarchical aspects of consciousness unfolding *and* the many nonlinear, amorphous, holographically interwoven aspects as well.

Thus, it was somewhat disappointing to see Wade follow mostly a "levels" model and not enough of a "levels and lines" model. Among other things, the Wade/Wilber-II model does tend toward a unilinear development, which is why I abandoned it (or rather, refined it into Wilber-III).[5]

Let me give a specific example. Wade observes the following: "An individual's noetic [consciousness] growth is not uniform across all social domains. Thus a person may operate at one stage in one social milieu and at a higher or lower one in another setting." I believe that is quite true, and a Wade/Wilber-II model can easily handle that fact; individuals simply fluctuate up or down the basic levels of consciousness in different settings, depending on, for example, social triggers.

But what the Wade/Wilber-II model cannot handle is the fact that a person in the *same* setting has components of his or her consciousness each existing at a different level. In the *same* social domain, and in a *single* transaction, a person can, for example, be at a very high cognitive level of development (e.g., formop), while *simultaneously* being at a low level of moral development (e.g., stage 2), with an unconscious fixation at an even earlier affective stage (some facet of the self dissociated at, say, stage 1).

The Wade/Wilber-II model fails in accounting for those facts—because it fails, in general, to distinguish carefully enough between levels and lines (and further, to account for just what is preserved, and what is negated, in evolution).[6] These distinctions are just the minimum, I believe, that we need to account for development in general and nonlinear developments in particular. [Subsequent discussions with Jenny indicate that she is comfortable with a "waves, streams, and states" type of model, and she hopes to bring out a second edition of *Changes of Mind* that will reflect her specific thoughts on these issues.]

The Implicate Order

Wade's use of David Bohm's notions of an implicate/explicate order is the least satisfactory part of the book, in my opinion. The central difficulty with Bohm's theory is that, based on physics, it is purely monological. (Physics only adequately covers the lowest levels in the Upper-Right quadrant, and trying to make it "foundational" for all other quadrants is the essence of reductionism.) But Bohm makes the attempt to extend this purely monological conception into dialogical and translogical realms, at which point the monological approach, appropriate in its own domain, becomes distortingly reductionistic.

(The results are unfortunate. Reality is forced into a two-level hierarchy, the explicate and the implicate. Models based on this explicate/implicate notion then tend to identify the explicate order with the world of separate things and events, Newtonian physics, ordinary time and space, separate selves, and so on, and the implicate order is identified with unity, wholeness, a holographic reality, a spiritual unity, a timeless ground of being, and so forth. This is a simple two-tier monological model, which allows only physics and spirit.) A more acceptable holarchy might include, as we have seen: matter, body, mind, soul, and spirit. But the explicate/implicate notion forces any theorist who adopts it to basically acknowledge only matter and spirit, with nothing much in between. Poor biology, psychology, and theology are all therefore going to feel the monological hammer come crashing down to crack their skulls—they are all forced into the monological scheme.

Bohm himself tended to realize the inadequate nature of his position, and for a while he went through an awkward period of adding implicate levels. There was the implicate level, and then along with that there was a super-implicate level, then at one point, a super-super-implicate level. And all of this was claiming to be based on empirical findings in physics!

I published (1982b) a strong criticism of Bohm's position, which has never been answered by him or any of his followers. It was a heady time, and Marilyn Ferguson's *Brain/Mind Bulletin* had just awarded its fourth Annual Greatest Breakthrough of the Century Award to Bohm and Pribram for the holographic paradigm. I was editor-in-chief of *ReVision* at the time, and we pulled together dozens of essays on this new paradigm, which we published, appropriately enough, as *The Holographic Paradigm*. It was the editor of the book, yet in the awkward position of being the only strongly dissenting voice. Nobody wanted to hear criticisms of the new paradigm; everybody thought me an altogether rude fellow.

(In my critique, I pointed out that, according to the Great Holarchy theorists, what is explicate at one level is implicate at the next (that is, what is explicitly whole at one level is an enfolded and implicit part of the next), and thus you can construct an explicate/implicate relation *at each of the levels in the Great Holarchy,* which preserves the moment of Bohm's truth but without the necessity to engage in reductionism.) I also pointed out what seemed to be the many self-contradictions that resulted from Bohm's constant attempt to qualify that which he maintained was unqualifiable.[7] Until this critique is answered, I believe we must consider Bohm's theory to be suspect. And, anyway, over the last decade and a half it has generally fallen into disrepute (and it has little support from most physicists).

I was therefore surprised to see Wade attempt to inject transpersonal theory into this monological model. But it is indeed this implicate/explicate notion—the "holonomic paradigm"—with which Wade wishes to ground her transpersonal developmental model, and unfortunately this infects it with Bohm's reductionism and monological flatland approach, or so it seems to me.

I realize that Wade is in some ways simply using Bohm's ideas as a metaphor for the interconnectedness of all events. But I believe that whatever usefulness might be gained by claiming support from physics for a "mystically interwoven world" is actually outweighed by the fact that the "support" is purely monological and thus profoundly reductionistic. (Not to mention based on interpretations of physics that most physicists reject; but even if they didn't, the "support" is still monological, claiming that the holons in the Upper-Right quadrant are the "really real" holons upon which all theory must be grounded: and there is the monological nightmare.)

But why even worry about this? So what if physics is monological? So what if systems sciences, complexity theory, chaos theory, autopoiesis, and so on are all monological, Right-Hand theories? Can't they be a welcomed part of any integral approach? Absolutely. The problem is, as they are usually presented, they are not used *in addition* to Left-Hand interior transformations of consciousness but *instead of* those interior transformations—at which point they hurt, not help, the actual evolution of consciousness.

Let us assume that the nine or ten basic waves of consciousness development exist, just as outlined by Jenny. Any truly new and integral paradigm would then say something like this: The world is a unified whole, a great interwoven system of mutually interpenetrating events. Even modern physics and systems theories agree. But in order to fully realize this great Unity, individuals must grow and evolve their own consciousness to the degree that they can actually embrace this Unity in their own being—where they can fully realize it as an awakened reality and not merely as a concept or idea. Research has consistently suggested that this growth and evolution occurs through at least nine basic waves of consciousness unfolding. What is therefore required, by the new paradigm, is not a new monological description of the Right-Hand world, but the understanding that individuals need to actually grow and develop through all nine waves of their own interior potentials. We do not need merely a more accurate map of the unified Kosmos; we need ways for the mapmaker to grow and evolve through at least nine major waves of his or her own consciousness, thereupon to stand open to a direct and authentic Unity with the Kosmos. We do not need more maps; we need ways to change the mapmaker. We need new forms of *practice,* not just new forms of *theory.* And simply *thinking* about the world in holistic terms does little to transform and move the thinker through those nine waves toward a genuine Unity. *Theoria* just isn't enough; *praxis* is required.

As it is now, most "new paradigm" approaches are completely silent about the *interior stages* of growth and practice required for any genuinely integral paradigm. They simply present a unified systems theory of the Right-Hand world, a theory that itself can be learned and memorized without the slightest interior growth and Left-Hand development. *Right-Hand theories can be learned without Left-Hand transformation*—and there, in a nutshell, is the problem with most of the "new paradigms" based merely on "holistic thinking" instead of interior stages of growth.

Of course, an integral paradigm would include all of the above—it would be all-level, all quadrant. And I know that Jenny Wade is generally of the same opinion. But the danger of attempting to ground an integral theory in monological, Right-Hand models (from physics to ecological sciences to systems theory to chaos and complexity theory) is that it downplays, and in many cases even neglects, the necessity for Left-Hand growth. It is not just about finding a new objective model of the world, it is about how to transform subjects, that constitutes a truly integral approach.

Jenny Wade is a natural-born developmentalist, with a keen eye and a sure grasp of many developmental issues, and I believe she can be a very important voice in the field of transpersonal developmental theory. But I urge her to be careful about the use of Bohm's monological notions. A theorist of such talent is rare in any field, and I believe Wade will have many further contributions to make.

ARE THERE STAGES OF SPIRITUAL DEVELOPMENT?

Are there really universal and invariant stages of spiritual development for everybody? What is the relation of spiritual and psychological development? Does a person have to complete psychological development before genuine spiritual development can occur?

My overall view on "stages" is exactly as Rothberg summarizes it: "Development doesn't somehow proceed in some simple way through a series of a few comprehensive stages which unify all aspects of growth. . . . The [different] developmental lines may be in tension with each other at times, and some of them do not show evidence, Wilber believes, of coherent stages. . . . There might be a high level of development cognitively, a medium level interpersonally or morally, and a low level emotionally. These disparities of development seem especially conditioned by general cultural values and styles."[8]

As we have briefly seen, in my overall model (Wilber-III), there are the basic waves of consciousness (the spectrum of consciousness), as a type of central skeletal frame, but through those basic waves there move at least a dozen different developmental streams. These developmental lines include affective, moral, interpersonal, spatiotemporal, death-seizure, object-relations, cognition, self-identity, self-needs, worldview, psychosexual, conative, aesthetic, intimacy, creativity, altruism, various specific talents (musical, sports, dance, artistic), and so forth. These are relatively independent ("quasi-independent") lines of development, loosely held together by, of course, the self-system.[9]

The immediate question then becomes: Is spirituality itself a separate developmental line? Or is spirituality simply the highest level(s)—the deepest or highest reaches—of the other lines?

In other words, the meaning of the word "spiritual" becomes crucial in this discussion, because all of the arguments in this area tend to reduce to two different definitions of that word. There are those who define "spiritual" as a *separate developmental line* (in which case spiritual development is alongside or parallel to psychological and emotional and interpersonal development). And there are those who define "spiritual" as the *highest reaches* of all of those lines (in which case spiritual development can only occur *after* psychological development is mostly completed).

I believe that both of those stances are correct, but in each case we must indicate exactly what we mean by "spiritual." If, for example, we define "spiritual" specifically as transmental, then clearly the transmental cannot stably emerge until the mental has in some rudimentary sense been solidified. Likewise, if we define "spiritual" as transverbal, or as transegoic, or as specifically transpersonal, then the spiritual domain cannot stably emerge until there is a verbal, mental, egoic self to transcend in the first place.

On the other hand, if we define spirituality as a separate developmental line, then clearly it can develop alongside, or behind, or parallel with developments in the other lines, affective, interpersonal, moral, and so on.

Take several examples: in the affective line, we have preconventional affect (e.g., narcissistic rage), conventional affect (feelings of belongingness), postconventional affect (global concern, universal love), and post-postconventional affect (ananda, transcendental love-bliss). In the moral line, we have preconventional morals (what I wish is what is right), conventional morals (my country right or wrong), postconventional morals (universal social contract), and post-postconventional morals (bodhisattvic vows). In the cognitive line, we have preconventional cognition (sensorimotor, preoperational), conventional cognition (concrete schemas, rule/role), postconventional cognition (formal rational to post-formal vision-logic), and post-postconventional cognition (prajna, gnosis, savikalpa, nirvikalpa, post-postformal).

Now, in the first definition, spirituality is the highest or post-postconventional level of each of those lines. In the second definition, spirituality would be a separate line alongside those, most likely with its own unfolding forms. Since this topic is obviously crucial to this particular discussion, it bears looking at a little more closely. Let's set aside the meaning of "spirituality" for the moment, and focus on "levels and lines" in general. We will then return to the definition of "spiritual" and attempt closure. (At that point, I will also discuss altered states and peak experiences and their relation to spirituality.)

Streams and Waves

My general thesis is this: an overall spectrum of consciousness through which more than a dozen different developmental lines proceed, each of which may have a different architecture, dynamic, structure, and function—"quasi-independent" of each other—but all loosely held together by the self-system. This thesis was implicit in *The Atman Project* (1980) but then made very explicit, as I said, a year later, with the full-fledged emergence of what we are calling Wilber-III.

But at that time, there was very little evidence for such a conjecture. The term "developmental line" had been suggested by Anna Freud (which is where I got it), but her use was very narrow and restricted. Indeed, the dominant developmental paradigm was Piagetian, which saw virtually all developmental lines subsumed in one dominant domain, that of logico-mathematical cognitive development.

In the intervening fifteen years, several types of theory and research have made a general Wilber-III ("levels and lines") thesis much more plausible, and I will here simply mention a few of the more significant and influential.

Howard Gardner's *Frames of Mind*, published in 1983, was instrumental in highlighting the need to "loosen" the Piagetian scheme without abandoning its enduring strengths. Piaget himself had already opened the door: "Piaget conceded that formal thought did not necessarily obtain across all domains [logico-cognitive development was not the sole axis of development], but in fact might be found only in those lines of practice where an individual worked steadily. Here was a tacit recognition of a plurality of domains [plurality of developmental lines] in which humans can be competent, as well as acknowledgment of the possibility that the processes or products involved in one domain might not be identical to those that figure in others."[10]

Gardner points out that today "There is increasing evidence to suggest that [development] is better thought of as composed of a variety of domains [developmental lines], including not only logical-mathematical thought [the Piagetian line, and the line that is still typically but narrowly called "cognitive"] and linguistic knowledge [e.g., Chomsky], but also . . . visual-spatial thinking, bodily-kinesthetic activity, musical knowledge, and even various forms of social understanding [including moral and interpersonal competence]."[11]

Gardner and his colleagues have intensively investigated early development in several of these quasi-independent lines (what he calls "domains"), including language, symbolic play, music, number, drawing, block building, and bodily expression or dance. "Our effort has been to provide a portrait of . . . development in each of these several domains, but even more, to *establish what commonalities might obtain across different [domains]*."[12]

The crucial point, in other words, besides tracing the different development *lines*, is to see if they share any similar *levels* of development (or commonalities across domains). The conclusion of their empirical research, a conclusion I strongly share, is this: "Much of what happens within each symbol system [developmental line] proves peculiar to that symbol system. . . . Part of the story of symbol development is an account of the ordinal scales in each of these particular domains—what we have elsewhere labeled the 'streams' of symbolization [the developmental lines]. Yet there are *definite parallels across development in particular domains*."[13]

What Gardner and his associates found was that the different developmental lines each progressed through what Gardner calls "waves," to indicate the flowing and fluid nature of these stages. He and his associates found four invariant waves in each of the domains (narrative, music, dance, drawing, symbolic play, etc.), and another two or three waves that appear invariant but require further research. Gardner summarizes all of these waves as being *preconventional, conventional*, and *postconventional*. (Add post-postconventional, and we are in full accord!)

According to Gardner's research, these waves are universal, invariant, and based on deep biological (and probably psychological/cultural) constants. "The waves of symbolization are obligatory. The child has no choice but to use them, and to do so in the order in which they emerge."[14]

In other words, both the *streams* (different developmental lines) and the *waves* (the stage-like sequence common to all the streams) show features that are largely universal, even though their specifics often vary. "We have been equipped by our biological heritage with mechanisms—here termed streams and waves of symbolization—for making preliminary sense of these symbol systems. It is our speculation that those streams and waves arise in rather similar ways in human beings around the world. . . ."[15]

At the same time, different cultures would emphasize different lines or streams, although all of those would still navigate the same stage-like waves. Thus, "Symbolic development does not consist of a single strand. Rather, it comes in multiple lines that reflect the particular domains that cultures may stress at various phases of development. The waves [preconventional, conventional, postconventional—and, we add, post-postconventional] *are brought to bear in each domain*, but the importance of each wave, and the time at which it makes its maximum impact, will depend upon the particular symbolic domain in question."[16]

Finally, and this deserves emphasis, Gardner points out that this approach (combining both lines and levels, or streams and waves) "may offer hope for reconciling an increasingly severe split in developmental psychology. We have come to think of Piaget, on the one hand, as focusing on the most general aspects of development and presupposing that there is one pivotal domain, that of logical-rational thought. Chomsky (and others influenced by the 'modularity hypothesis') have been cast as embracing the contrasting view that development occurs differently in each of a number of domains (if development occurs at all). Our waves suggest that certain general wavelike psychological processes may occur across domains but that the particular way in which they are realized may well reflect the nature and the structure of particular domains. Were this theory to help reconcile two seemingly conflicting structuralist approaches, it would be a desirable theoretical outcome indeed."[17]

A Spiritual Line?

Thus, in my view, the common axis (of which precon, con, postcon, and post-postcon are all measures) is simply *consciousness* as such—the basic waves themselves, the Great Holarchy of Being, the spectrum of consciousness (which I usually present as nine or ten basic levels of consciousness, which can also be simply summarized as precon to con to postcon to post-postcon). These are the universal waves through which the dozen or so developmental lines quasi-independently proceed. The levels of the spectrum constitute the waves of developmental unfolding; the various lines are the different streams that move through those waves; and the self-system is that which attempts to juggle and balance those quasi-independent streams with their cascading waves of development.

To return to "spirituality." In the first definition, spirituality is simply the post-postconventional levels of any of the lines. In the second definition, spirituality is itself a separate line with its own unfolding. I believe both of those are completely acceptable usages, as long as we specify exactly what we mean, because they obviously are referring to rather different phenomena.)

Let us start with spirituality as a separate line. I believe we can do this, but nonetheless we are immediately faced with several difficulties. To begin with, how can we define "spiritual" in a way that does *not* use only the terms of higher, transpersonal, transmental levels? You see, if we define "spiritual" using any of those "trans" or "post" terms—transverbal, transmental, transconventional, postformal, transegoic—then we revert to the other model (where spirituality exists only in the higher domains, and thus can develop only *after* the lower domains). Nor can we define "spirituality" using only the terms of *other* developmental lines (affective, moral, interpersonal, cognitive, etc.). (In order to make spirituality a separate line of development, we cannot define spirituality as emotional openness, or as love, or as moral compassion, or as affective bliss, or as cognitive intuition and insight, and so on (for all of those already have their own developmental lines).)

Defining the "spiritual line," you see, becomes extremely tricky, and most people who maintain that spiritual development is parallel to psychological and other lines do so only by not defining "spiritual" in any specific sense at all.

Those difficulties are the main reasons that, in the past, I have sometimes (but by no means always)[18] kept a studied silence about a separate "spiritual line" alongside the others. I have instead usually confined my discussion specifically to more definable lines such as cognition, affect, motivation, self-sense, moral response, self-needs, worldviews, and so on. This has led to the understandable (but incorrect) view that I think spirituality only exists in the "higher" levels. Although I often refer to those higher domains as "spiritual" (or "authentically spiritual"), I have never maintained that spirituality is simply absent in the lower levels (since, in fact, all levels are levels of Spirit!). Not only are altered states or spiritual peak experiences available at virtually any stage of development (see below), but we can also look to a spiritual line itself.

(Thus, I have often referred to magical religion, mythic religion, rational religion, psychic religion (shamans/yogis), subtle religion (saints), causal religion (sages), and nondual religion (siddhas), each of which is a level or wave of the spiritual line or stream—in other words, the developmental line of spirituality as it spans the entire spectrum of consciousness.)

The real difficulty, as I see it, is not in identifying or characterizing a developmental line that we might call "spiritual." It is getting almost anybody else to agree with what we call "spiritual." The term is virtually useless for any sort of coherent discussion, let alone model. (And remember, to define a spiritual line of development, we must use terms neither from the higher transpersonal levels, nor from other developmental lines, or else we are dealing with an amalgam of other lines and levels, not a genuinely separate spiritual line itself.)

So I will simply state my own preference. I will follow Paul Tillich in defining the spiritual line as that line of development in which the subject holds its *ultimate concern.* That is, the spiritual line of development is the developmental line of ultimate concern, regardless of its content. And, like almost all other developmental lines, the line of ultimate concern will itself unfold through the same general expanding spheres of consciousness, from preconventional concern (egocentric), to conventional concern (sociocentric), to postconventional concern (worldcentric), to post-postconventional concern (bodhisattvic). Or again, in more detail, using the terms of the associated worldviews: archaic concern to magic concern to mythic concern to mental concern to psychic concern to subtle concern to causal concern.[19]

Fowler's work in this area is a beginning, of course, and I have gratefully made use of his pioneering efforts. Fowler's six stages do not reach much beyond vision-logic/psychic, but up to that point they are an almost perfect match.[20] Moreover, Fowler deserves much credit for the truly pioneering nature of his research and his sophisticated evidence for the early to intermediate levels of the stages of the spiritual line of development.

Spiritual Level and Spiritual Line

Thus, so far we have two very different uses of the term "spiritual," both of which I believe are acceptable, as long as we carefully specify which we mean. In the first, it is a level; in the second, a line.

In the first, "spiritual" generally means *the post-postconventional waves of any of the developmental lines.* Thus, post-postconventional cognition (e.g., savikalpa and nirvikalpa samadhi, gnosis, jnana) is spoken of as "spiritual cognition," whereas concrete schemas and conventional rules generally are not. Likewise, post-postconventional affect (e.g., transcendental love-bliss) is spoken of as spiritual, whereas preconventional narcissistic rage is not. The post-postconventional modes of self-identity (soul, Self) are spoken of as spiritual, whereas the conventional ego is not, and so on.

In that usage, the "further reaches" of human nature—the post-post-conventional stages of any of the developmental lines, including cognition, affect, morals, and self-sense—are generally referred to as "spiritual" or "authentically spiritual" or similar terms. And in each of those lines, research to date strongly indicates that the developmental sequence is generally from precon to con to postcon to post-postcon, either in a "strong" or "soft" sense, but present nonetheless. Thus, in this sense, spiritual developments (post-postconventional developments) cannot stably emerge until the precon, con, and postcon waves have been, at least to a significant degree, secured.

In the second major use, "spiritual" means a *separate developmental line itself*, and thus spiritual developments can occur alongside (or parallel to) developments in the other lines, cognitive, affective, moral, interpersonal, psychological, and so on. But it is incumbent on those who use this meaning to specify *exactly what characteristics* they mean by the "spiritual line," because they can use neither the characteristics that define other lines (love, awareness, morality, etc.), nor can they use simply the highest reaches of the other lines (that is the first usage).

Fowler, for example, has on occasion been criticized because his working definition of "faith" is sometimes indistinguishable from "morality" (which is why the Kohlberg test and the Fowler test show an extremely high correlation of results, so much so that some researchers claim they are measuring the same thing). But whatever we decide, you can see the delicate and tricky nature of defining a separate spiritual line.

When I use spiritual as a separate line, I have defined it as the line of ultimate concern. This clearly differentiates it from morality (one's ultimate concern might be for food), from interpersonal development (ultimate concern is sometimes nonpersonal), and from self-development (ultimate concern is not necessarily subject-oriented). But this is simply my own working specification, and it by no means rules out any other legitimate definitions.[21]

So those are the two usages (a separate stream and the highest waves of any stream), and as I said, I believe both of those uses are acceptable, but we must be extremely careful to specify exactly what we mean. Most of the arguments about the relation of "psychology" and "spirituality"—or psychotherapy and meditation—arise only because those terms are not clearly specified.

We will return to this general topic in the next chapter, and give several more examples (at that point, I will also discuss altered states or

peak experiences). In the meantime, let us simply keep these two different uses of "spiritual" firmly in mind.

Spiritual Stages

We can now return to our original question: Are there actually stages of
spiritual unfolding?

According to the first usage, the spiritual is simply the higher reaches
of any of the lines, and so with that usage spirituality is definitely a
stage-like phenomenon. The post-postconventional stages of any line
emerge only after the earlier stages are generally consolidated.

The question then becomes, if we view spirituality as a separate line,
are there also stages there?

I believe that almost any separate spiritual line that might be postulated will be, in some respects, a developmental holarchy. I believe it will
show important stage-like aspects because each wave will unavoidably
build upon previous competences, while adding new and defining features that replace the narrower and shallower orientations.

Thus, for example, in order to move from preconventional spirituality
(archaic, magic, egocentric) to conventional spirituality (mythic-membership), it is *necessary* to learn to take the role of other. Care and concern simply cannot expand from the self to the group without that
growth, and there is no corresponding unfolding of a deeper spiritual
concern without it. (Cf. "The waves of symbolization are obligatory.
The child has no choice but to use them, and to do so in the order in
which they emerge.")

That is an example of why the general stage conception is so important, and why I believe it is crucial in the spiritual line as well. It does
not tell the whole story by any means (we still have to discuss altered
states), but it seems to be a very important part of the story. Moreover,
no alternative account that completely leaves out the stage aspect has
yet been credibly advanced (I keep hearing alternative metaphors like a
flower unfolding, but flowers unfold in stages).

Thus, although many details need to be refined, the stage conception
itself continues to match the great preponderance of available evidence.
In Alexander and Langer's thoughtful book, *Higher Stages of Human
Development*, the editors present a rather comprehensive overview of
the models of development that acknowledge higher or deeper domains
than the typical egoic state, and of the twelve major models that are
presented, the editors point out that most of them acknowledge hierar-

chical stages (including Carol Gilligan, Daniel Levinson, Robert Kegan, Michael Commons, and Charles Alexander). This is the baby that we must not toss with the bathwater. And given the American climate of hostility to "stages" (and anything "higher" than the ego), it is a baby whose life we must carefully defend.

Greater Depth, Less Span

This brings us to a rather delicate issue. One study showed that only 1–2 percent of the population reach the autonomous stage on Loevinger's scale, which is her next-to-highest stage, and less than 0.5 percent reach the highest or integrated stage (those two stages correspond to middle and late centauric). Similar studies have shown that less than 4 percent reach Kohlberg's stage 6; Fowler found less than 1 percent reached his highest stage; and so on. Let us simply accept, for argument's sake, that those are generally true statistics.

The question then becomes: Does this mean that people have to pass through those stages (autonomous, integrated, centauric, postconventional) *in order to make genuine spiritual progress?*

Once again, you see, it depends upon the meaning of "spiritual." If we define spirituality as postformal and post-postconventional, the answer is yes, definitely. But if we define spiritual as being a separate line of development, the answer is no, definitely not. In that case, spiritual development is occurring alongside or behind or parallel to those other lines of development, and thus it may race ahead of, or lag behind, those other lines.

But that simply pushes the question back: If we view spirituality as a separate line, does stable postconventional spiritual development then depend upon passing from its own preconventional wave to its conventional wave to its postconventional wave? And I believe the answer, backed by the preponderance of evidence, is most definitely yes.

Either way, then, we arrive at a similar conclusion: Whether spirituality is the highest wave or a separate stream, the same general waves still have eventually to be negotiated—precon to con to postcon to postpostcon (or, generally, gross to subtle to causal).

To say the same thing using other terms, the spiritual line itself moves from a *prepersonal* wave (archaic, food, safety, preconventional concern) to a *personal* wave (from belongingness and conventional concern to postconventional/global concern) to a *transpersonal* wave (post-postconventional, subtle, causal, bodhisattvic concern). In short, the spiritual stream runs through subconscious to conscious to superconscious waves, by whatever name.

Nonetheless, this is not a rigid clunk and grind view. There are, as always, regressions, spirals, and temporary leaps forward, in all sorts of fluid and flowing ways. And the self, as usual, can be "all over the place." (Moreover—and this is perhaps the most important item—an individual at virtually any stage of development can have an *altered state* or *peak experience* of psychic, subtle, causal, or nondual realms. Many people define "genuine spirituality" in terms of such peak experiences (in fact, that is probably the third most common meaning of "spirituality"). I fully acknowledge that meaning; the only reason I am not stressing it here is that in order for temporary altered states to become stable traits, they must be converted into permanent realizations (or permanently available structures in consciousness), and that demands development. Thus, the altered-states view of spirituality eventually connects to one of the two developmental definitions (level or line), although all three are important components of an integral view, I believe.) [See *Integral Psychology* for a comprehensive statement of this model and its relation to levels, lines, and states of spirituality, as well as childhood spirituality.]

But the developmental aspects of spirituality are truly significant, for example, because you simply *cannot* get from preconventional concern to conventional concern without learning to take the role of other. And you *cannot* get from conventional concern to postconventional or global concern without learning to establish perspectivism. In that sense, spiritual development most definitely progresses through these broad and general waves in a stage-like fashion. The spiritual stream runs through the same general waves as any other skill acquisition, if it is to be a stable adaptation and not merely a peak experience or a temporary state.

At the same time, those developments are occurring quasi-independently from the other developmental lines, so that one's spiritual development (as a separate stream) may forge ahead of, or it may lag behind, one's development in psychological, affective, interpersonal, artistic, object-relations, defense mechanisms, and other lines.

(If we focus now specifically on the spiritual stream—and given the fact that late postconventional *anything* is very rare (1–2 percent or so)—does that mean that even less than 1 percent of the general population will actually develop to the *post-postconventional* or transpersonal wave of spirituality (psychic, subtle, causal)? In my opinion, yes. (This is no real surprise, in that evolution produces greater depth, less span.)

In fact, I would even say that not much more than 1 percent of the *meditating* population develops stably to the post-postconventional levels of the spiritual line (or any other line, for that matter). But this, of course, is a matter for empirical research (see below).

Discriminating Wisdom

This is a particularly delicate issue for spiritual teachers of any persuasion. A large number of individuals who come to, say, a meditation retreat, might be at a preconventional level of moral, self, and interpersonal development. They might make strides in the spiritual line of concern or in the cognitive line of insight, only to see those insights gobbled up by the low center of gravity operating in the rest of the psyche. Spiritual teachers constantly find themselves having to cater to these lowest common denominator trends, where, no matter how much development one might accomplish in the spiritual line, it is not enough to pull the other lines along with it, and might itself be merely dragged down.

At the same time, we all know of spiritual teachers who have glimpsed very high stages of spiritual and/or cognitive development, while their moral, affective, defense, object-relations, and interpersonal lines are very poorly developed—often with disastrous consequences. Moreover, the great traditions themselves often emphasize the spiritual line alone (particularly in its ascending mode), and thus they sorely neglect the interpersonal, affective, and psychological lines, so that they remain, as it were, the last place to look for help in these areas.

My suggestion for an "all-level, all-quadrant" approach is a suggestion for a more integral orientation, drawing on the strengths of the various approaches (psychological to interpersonal to spiritual to social) in an attempt to fill in the gaps left by each alone. I am by no means alone in this call; but it is disappointing to see the widespread resistance to a more integral and balanced approach.

Another difficulty for spiritual teachers in America is that, as Jack Engler noted, a disproportionately large number of people who are drawn to transpersonal spirituality are often at a preconventional level of self development. This means that much of what American teachers have to do is actually engage in supportive psychotherapy, not transformative and transpersonal spirituality. Needless to say, these teachers will rarely see stages of development of anything.

As I earlier suggested, for the post-postconventional stages of spiritual awareness, I would say that, in any given meditation retreat—and speaking very generally—less than 1 percent will actually reach a profound satori or rigpa cognition (stable causal or nondual access). I have been in retreats of several hundred dedicated and long-term practitioners where only two people strongly accessed rigpa and had it fully confirmed. Two people is not exactly a huge pool from which to draw data, and yet it is only from such a pool that the full dimensions of the stage conception will stand forth. (We will return to this research and its implications in the next chapter.)

The Poor Self

(It might be appropriate to mention why I have consistently placed the self-system (or the self) at the center of all of the various streams and waves, levels and lines, structures and stages and states. Namely, the self is the balancing act of the psyche. It has to balance—as best it can—virtually every other aspect of the psychic system (indeed, balance the four quadrants in general as they impinge on the individual).

Some critics have implied that I conceptualize transpersonal development around cognitive structures, and this is not quite right. The basic structures are, as I said, simply the Great Holarchy of Being, and that certainly has a cognitive aspect. *But the self is where the action is.* And if we are to speak generally of "overall development" or "development on the whole," it would be driven, in my view, not by a Piagetian cognitive motor (which is a type of cognitive dissonance that attempts to overcome discord by developing toward formal equilibration, where it can come to rest), but rather by something like "self-dissonance," in which the self juggles the various developmental lines, and is pushed (by Eros) and pulled (by Agape) until it comes to rest in Emptiness. That is not the end of the story, but the beginning of post-Enlightenment unfolding, as the sage enters the marketplace with open hands.

To take it a step at a time. The self has to juggle (and navigate) whatever basic levels of consciousness are present, and whatever developmental lines are present, and all the various states of consciousness, heterarchic competences, and discrete talents: all of those, juggled by the self. And development "on the whole" is driven by the tension within (and beyond) that juggling act. Some developmental lines have omega points, and thus are pulled; some are more causal, and thus are pushed; some are spiral, and run in circles; some are mandalic, and unfold from within. But the self—the poor lonely self—has to juggle them all, to the degree it can. And it is a calculus of those pushes and pulls and spirals and swirls that constitutes the overall developmental unfolding. The stage conception is an important part—but just a part—of the overall story.

(Does this *overall self* follow an invariant sequence of stages? Not at all, precisely because it is an amalgam, a juggling act, a mixture, of whatever developmental levels and lines are occurring. There are specific aspects of self-identity in a narrow sense (such as ego development) that research has shown follow a stagelike unfolding, which I will explain in an endnote.[22] But those are simply aspects of the overall self—they constitute one line among many, not one line that dominates all—and thus, once again, the self-system is all over the place. And its sole job, so to speak, is to get over itself.)

Is This Trip Really Necessary?

Some people, I believe, are put off by the notion that rationality (and vision-logic) might somehow be a *necessary* prerequisite for higher or transpersonal development. And these folks especially do not trust this notion when it comes from egghead theorists. Does the transpersonal really "integrate" the rational, and if so, what about nontechnological cultures that do not seem to access rationality? Do we deny them spirituality?[23]

Developmental psychologists (such as Kegan) and philosophers (such as Habermas) tend to use "rational" in a very broad and general fashion, which sometimes confuses people. The simple capacity to *take the perspective of another person*, for example, is a rational capacity. You must be able mentally to step out of your own perspective, cognitively picture the way the world looks to the other person, and then place yourself in the other's shoes, as it were—all extremely complicated cognitive capacities, and all referred to as "rational" in the very general sense.

Thus, as I explain in SES, rational in this broad sense means, among other things, the capacity for perspectivism, for sustained introspection, and for imagining "as-if" and "what-if" possibilities. Rationality, to put it simply, is the sustained capacity for cognitive *pluralism* and *perspectivism*.

Some theorists have claimed that "rationality" (as used by Piaget or Habermas) might actually be, in effect, Eurocentric, and that its "lack" in other cultures might reflect Western biases. But, as Alexander et al. point out, several researchers "have convincingly argued that formal operational capacities are evident within nontechnological societies when tasks appropriate to the culture are employed."[24] Rationality doesn't mean you have to be Aristotle; it means you can take perspectives. This is why Habermas maintains that even in foraging societies, formal operations were available to a significant number of men and women. You are operating within reason when you operate within perspective. You don't have to be doing calculus.

Likewise, vision-logic does not mean that you have to be Hegel or Whitehead. Rationality means perspective; vision-logic means integrating or coordinating different perspectives. Even in the earliest foraging tribes, it is quite likely that a chieftain would have to take multiple perspectives in order to coordinate them: vision-logic. The Western forms of reason and vision-logic are just that: Western forms, but the deep capacities themselves are not.

But you can't coordinate perspectives if you can't take perspective in the first place; and you can't take perspective if you can't take the role of other. And there, once again, is the limited but crucial role of the stage conception.

And yes, I most definitely believe that *postconventional* spirituality depends upon the capacity to coordinate different perspectives. I do not believe, for example, that the bodhisattva vow can operate fully without it—without, that is, vision-logic. I believe it is the gateway through which stable psychic, subtle, causal, and nondual stages of spirituality must pass, and upon which they rest. Indeed, by definition, the bodhisattva vow rests upon vision-logic, because if you have ever vowed to liberate all perspectives, you have operated with vision-logic.

Nevertheless, you certainly can have spiritual development without perspectival reason and without integral-aperspectival vision-logic, for the simple reason that the spiritual line is a quasi-independent line of development (not to mention temporary states). The spiritual line goes right down to the archaic, sensorimotor level, where one's religion—one's ultimate concern—is food. And the spiritual line will continue through the early prerational realms (magical, egocentric). With the capacity to take the role of other, the spiritual line will begin to expand its ultimate concern from the self to the group and its beliefs (mythic-membership). From there it will learn to take a more universal perspective (mythic-rational, rational), where its ultimate concern will begin to include the welfare of a global humanity, regardless of race, gender, creed. That awareness will flower into a global vision-logic, with its concern for *all sentient beings as such*, and that will be the platform of the transpersonal spiritual stages themselves, which take as their foundation the liberation of the consciousness of all sentient beings without exception.

Thus, you can have all sorts of spirituality without "integrating reason." But you cannot have a global spirituality, a bodhisattvic spirituality, a post-postconventional spirituality, an authentically transpersonal spirituality, unless the perspectives of all sentient beings are taken into account and fully honored. Unless, that is, you integrate the deep capacities of reason and vision-logic, and then proceed from there.

Anybody can say they are being "spiritual"—and they are, because everybody has some type and level of concern. Let us therefore see their actual conception, in thought and action, and see how many perspectives it is in fact concerned with, and how many perspectives it actually takes into account, and how many perspectives it attempts to integrate, and thus let us see how deep and how wide runs that bodhisattva vow to refuse rest until all perspectives whatsoever are liberated into their own primordial nature.

10

The Effects of Meditation

SPEEDING UP THE ASCENT TO GOD
AND THE DESCENT OF THE GODDESS

What is the relation of meditation and psychotherapy? Does meditation alter the course of psychological development? If there are stages of spiritual growth, can they be accelerated? What exactly does meditation do, anyway?

VEDIC PSYCHOLOGY AND TRANSCENDENTAL MEDITATION

CHARLES ALEXANDER has been an important voice in transpersonal developmental psychology for many years, beginning with his doctoral dissertation at Harvard (1982) on ego development and personality changes in prison inmates practicing Transcendental Meditation (TM).* I have always appreciated his work, and I especially appreciate the wealth of research and empirical findings he always brings to the task. Instead of merely talking about a "new paradigm," he and his colleagues have been actually gathering data, collecting evidence, and proposing injunctions (such as meditation) to engage the higher levels of development, without which mere talk about the new paradigm is rather useless.

---

*With great sadness I must report that Skip Alexander recently died. He was one of those few "beloved by all"; his loss is truly tragic.

Moreover, unlike most of the meditation teachers in this country, Alexander and his colleagues have been taking standard tests of the various developmental lines (including Loevinger's ego development, Kohlberg's moral development, tests of capacity for intimacy, altruism, and so on) and applying them to populations of meditators, with extremely significant and telling results. The importance of this line of research is simply incalculable.[1]

In "Growth of Higher Stages of Consciousness: Maharishi's Vedic Psychology of Human Development," Alexander et al. present their model for the overall stages of consciousness development. They note that "Although independently drawn from a wide range of Eastern and Western traditions, Wilber's model, in particular, bears certain similarities to our own."[2]

It is within that broad range of agreement that I would like to proceed, but focusing mostly on some of the details of disagreement. But I will end, as usual, with a reaffirmation of our many commonalities.

STATES, STAGES, AND STRUCTURES

One of the central difficulties in their overall model, I believe, is a confusion of temporary states, enduring structures, and transitional stages.

Their model is explicitly based on the Vedic (more properly, the Vedantic) notion of the five koshas or five sheaths: matter, prana/desire, lower or concrete mind, higher mind or intellect, and transcendental intuition, beyond which is the ahamkara (root of the separate-self sense, the ultimate contraction in awareness), and then the pure Self (the causal), and finally, the ultimate Nondual (Brahman-Atman). That is, of course, yet another version of the traditional Great Holarchy of Being and Consciousness—the spectrum of basic structures of consciousness—and obviously I am in substantial agreement with that basic spectrum.[3] They maintain that these basic levels are universal and invariant, and that, as they emerge, they remain in existence and are hierarchically integrated in subsequent development.

In fact, the overall thesis of Alexander et al. is exactly that suggested in *The Atman Project*, namely, that development moves hierarchically from physical and sensorimotor to cosmic and ultimate consciousness, with each stage differentiating-and-integrating its predecessors: "According to our life-span model, during growth from the sensorimotor period to cosmic consciousness, progressively deeper levels of [consciousness] are differentiated, but each continues to operate at its own characteristic level of refinement, while being hierarchically reorganized within an increasingly integrated whole."[4]

But then they make what I believe are two unfortunate theoretical moves: they attempt to turn those *levels* of consciousness into the major developmental *lines* as well (they try to derive all of their important streams from their waves), and then, following on that, they further confuse various *transitional* states and stages with those *enduring* hierarchical levels.

The first difficulty is that they take their developmental levels (level 1: sensorimotor; level 2: prana-desire; level 3: representational mind; level 4: abstract mind; level 5: transcendental intuition; level 6: self or ego; level 7: pure Self) and attempt to turn them into the important developmental *lines* as well, so that anything not found in their levels does not show up as a line. Obviously, music is not a particular level of consciousness; neither is ethics, nor aesthetics, nor dance, nor object relations, nor needs, nor worldviews, and so on. Those are all lines, not levels, and therefore, if you try to make your levels serve also as the major lines, then you will be forced to ignore all of those real lines—which is exactly what Alexander et al. do.[5]

I quite agree with Alexander et al. when they state that "all knowledge in the domains of cognitive, social, and moral development is a function of the depth of unfoldment of consciousness awareness," but in fact their model actually has no domains that are moral and social (or musical, or dance, or artistic, etc.), because their domains are nothing but a horizontal unfolding of their vertical basic levels. This is why their diagram, which summarizes their model, has nothing listed on it that corresponds to moral, interpersonal, artistic, worldview, musical, dance, and so forth.

Moreover, this confusion extends then into a confusion between the *enduring* basic structures or levels of consciousness—which indeed are hierarchically integrated as the authors indicate—and the various *transitional* structures that develop around those basic levels, and which are not so much integrated as replaced. In other words, Alexander et al. confuse transitional with enduring, and this renders their account of development occasionally incoherent.

For example, when the authors state, "Thus, even in cosmic consciousness, sensory perception may remain, though witnessed from the level of the Self," that is certainly true—basic structures essentially remain (though subsumed). But you do not, and cannot, at the level of the

Self, have equal access to the moral structures of stage 1: those are long gone, so thoroughly differentiated and integrated that they are basically lost in any sort of original form. You absolutely do not have access to those at the level of cosmic consciousness! And since the authors' model is predicated on hierarchic inclusion alone, it fails in these particular areas.

In short, I believe that, apart from the many profound and important aspects of the model presented by Alexander et al., they unfortunately attempt to make their levels of consciousness serve also as the major lines of development, and this redundancy distorts both, forcing them as well to confuse enduring and transitional structures.[6]

Subject Permanence

Let us look now to the self that is navigating the basic levels of consciousness.

"[We] propose that the primary mechanism of development is the spontaneous shifting of the locus of conscious awareness to progressively deeper inherent levels of mind."[7] This "locus of conscious awareness" that shifts from level to level is, in my view, the self (or self-system), the locus of proximate self-identity. This is the pure Self (or consciousness as such) *identified with a particular and limited level of its own manifestation.* As the authors put it, and I concur: "The unbounded Self, in projecting itself through the currently available structure of the mind [level of consciousness], becomes embedded in or restricted by the limits of that structure and hence assumes the status of a 'bounded I,' or self."[8]

They also call this bounded self the "the stationing of awareness," a phrase that is particularly appropriate. In my model, this is the stationing of proximate self-identity, the actual stations of the self-sense, the stages of the I on its way to the I-I or pure Witness. In that developmental unfolding, the pure Witness is stably reached at the causal level, and the authors refer to the *stable attainment* of this pure Witnessing as "subject permanence." In their view (and I agree), just as the acquisition of *object permanence* (the ability to uninterruptedly follow objects) marks the great transition from the prerepresentational realm (sensorimotor/gross) to the representational realm (mental/subtle), so the acquisition of stable Witnessing or *subject permanence* marks the great transition from the representational to the postrepresentational (causal) realm. (And please, no Buddhist bickering: this Self permanence is simply unbroken mindfulness, which discloses all objects to be selfless—Self permanence is no-self awareness.))

This "subject permanence" is a constant state of witnessing carried unbroken through waking, dream, and deep sleep states, a constancy which, I entirely agree, is prerequisite and mandatory to full realization of nondual Suchness (and a constancy which is unmistakable, self-referential, postrepresentational, nondual, self-validating, self-existing, and self-liberating). [See *One Taste* for examples of this.]

To return to the "bounded I" or the proximate self-sense, the authors also refer to it as "the dominant locus of functional awareness." The central dynamic of their model is the identifying of the unbounded Self with a particular level of consciousness (which generates a "bounded self"), followed by the subsequent disidentifying with that level (and identifying with the next deeper/higher level), until the pure Self reawakens as Itself. As they put it, "In this view, the ultimate status of the knower is always pure consciousness. However, in the process of experience, awareness becomes localized as the individual [self] and identified with (i.e., unable to distance or distinguish itself clearly from) the processes of the current dominant level of [consciousness]."[9]

Now that is quite similar to the dynamic set forth in detail in *The Atman Project*, and before proceeding any further, it might help to briefly review that dynamic.

THE FORM OF DEVELOPMENT

Chapter 10 of *The Atman Project* begins, "This chapter—the most important in the book—will be short and succinct, because I would like its major points, simple in themselves, to stand alone. For what has so amazed me, as I surveyed the overall stages of development, is that although the content of each developmental growth is quite different, the *form* is essentially similar. The form of development, the form of transformation—this is constant, as far as I can tell, from the womb to God."

I outlined this form in a few paragraphs, which I will reprint for convenience. Here is the rest of the chapter:

At each stage, a higher-order structure—more complex and *therefore* more unified—*emerges* through a differentiation of the preceding, lower-order level. This higher-order structure is introduced to consciousness, and eventually (it can occur almost instantaneously or it can take a fairly prolonged time), the self *identifies* with that emergent structure. For example, when the body emerged from its pleromatic fusion with the material world, consciousness became, for the first time, a bodyself: which means, *identified with the body*. The self was then no longer *bound* to the pleromatic fusion, but it *was* bound to the body. As language emerged in consciousness, the self began to shift from a solely biological bodyself to a syntaxical ego—the self eventually identified itself with language, and operated *as* a syntaxical self. It was then no longer bound exclusively to the body, but it *was* bound to the mental-ego. Likewise, in advanced evolution, the deity-Archetype emerges, is introduced to consciousness (in the subtle realm), the self then identifies with and as that Deity, and operates from that identification. The self is then no longer exclusively bound to the ego, but it *is* bound to its own Archetype. The point is that as each higher-order structure emerges, the self eventually identifies with that structure—which is normal, natural, appropriate.

As evolution proceeds, however, each level in turn is differentiated *from* the self, or "peeled off," so to speak. The self, that is, eventually *dis-identifies* with its present structure so as to *identify* with the next higher-order emergent structure. More precisely (and this is a very important technical point), we say that the self detaches itself from its *exclusive* identification with that lower structure. It doesn't throw that structure away, it simply no longer exclusively identifies with it [i.e., basic/enduring vs. transitional/exclusivity]. The point is that because the self is differentiated from the lower structure, it *transcends* that structure (without obliterating it), and can thus *operate* on that lower structure using the tools of the newly emergent structure.

Thus, when the bodyego was differentiated from the material environment, it could operate on the environment using the tools of the body itself (such as the muscles). As the ego-mind was then differentiated from the body, it could operate on the body and world with *its* tools (concepts, syntax, etc.). As the subtle self was differentiated from the ego-mind, it could operate on the mind, body, and world using its structures (psi, siddhi), and so on.

Thus, at each point in growth or development, we find: (1) a higher-order structure emerges in consciousness; (2) the self identifies its being with that higher structure; (3) the next higher-order structure eventually emerges; (4) the self dis-identifies with the lower structure and shifts its essential identity [proximate identity] to the higher structure; (5) consciousness thereby transcends the lower structure; (6) and becomes capable of operating on that lower structure from the higher-order level; (7) such that all preceding levels can then be integrated in consciousness, and ultimately as Consciousness. We noted that each successively higher-order structure is more complex, more organized, and more unified—and evolution continues until there is only Unity, ultimate in all directions, whereupon the force of evolution is exhausted, and there is perfect release in Radiance as the entire World Flux.

Every time one remembers a higher-order deep structure, the lower-order structure is subsumed within it. That is, at each point in evolution, what is the *whole* of one level becomes merely a *part* of the higher-order whole of the next level [i.e., holon]. We saw, for example, that the body is, during the earlier stages of growth, the *whole* of the self sense—that is the bodyego. As the mind emerges and develops, however, the sense of identity shifts to the mind, and the body becomes merely one aspect, one part, of the total self. Similarly, as the subtle level emerges, the mind and body—which together *had* constituted the whole of the self-system—become merely aspects or parts of the new and more encompassing self [i.e., in each shift, the proximate self becomes distal, merely part of the new overall self].

In precisely the same way, we can say that at each point in evolution or remembrance [anamnesis], a *mode* of self becomes merely a *component* of a higher-order self (e.g., the body was *the* mode of the self before the mind emerged, whereupon it becomes merely a component of self). This can be put in several different ways, each of which tells us something important about development, evolution, and transcendence: (1) what is *whole* becomes *part*; (2) what is *identification* becomes *detachment*; (3) what is *context* becomes *content* (i.e., the context of cognition/experience of one level becomes simply a content of experience of the next); (4) what is *ground* becomes *figure* (which releases higher-order ground); (5) what is *subjective* becomes *objective* (until both of these terms become meaningless); (6) what is *condition* becomes *element* (e.g., the mind, which is the a priori condition of conventional experience, becomes merely an a posteriori element of experience in the higher-order realms; as it was put in *The Spectrum of Consciousness*, one is then looking at these structures, and therefore is not using them as something with which to look at, and thus distort, the world).

Each of those points is, in effect, a definition of *transcendence*. Yet each is also a definition of a stage of *development*. It follows that the two are essentially identical, and evolution, as has been said, is actually "self-realization through self-transcendence."

The point is that development and transcendence are two different words for the very same process. "Transcendence" has often been thought of as something odd, strange, occult, or even psychotic—whereas in fact there is nothing special about it all. The infant learning to differentiate his body from the environment is simply *transcending* the pleromatic world; the child learning mental language is simply *transcending* the world AND the simple body; the person in subtle meditation is simply transcending the world AND the body AND the mind. The soul in causal meditation is transcending the world AND the body AND the mind AND the subtle realm. The form of each growth is essentially the same, and it is the form of transcendence, the form of development: it traces a gentle curve from subconsciousness through self-consciousness to superconsciousness, remembering more and more, transcending more and more, integrating more and more, unifying more and more, until there is only that Unity which was always already the case the from start, and which remained both the alpha and omega of the soul's journey through time.

The Embedded Self

After presenting that summary of the form of development, I then outlined five different types of unconscious processes that occur in the wake of development itself. I called these the ground-unconscious, the archaic-unconscious, the submergent-unconscious, the embedded-unconscious, and the emergent-unconscious. I personally believe this is one of the most important contributions of that book, but here I will focus on only one: the embedded-unconscious, because it bears directly on the present discussion.

The essential point is that, as the self identifies with each basic level or wave of consciousness, the self is thoroughly *embedded* in those structures, fused with those structures, so much so that they cannot be seen or experienced as an object. The actual subjective structures of the self, at that stage, are unconscious: they are the embedded-unconscious. They are part of the seer, and thus cannot themselves be seen—not at that level, anyway. At the next stage, the self will *dis-embed* from those structures (disidentify with them, detach, differentiate, transcend), and then identify with the next higher level, which will then constitute the embedded-self, whose structures the self cannot see as an object, and thus whose structures constitute the embedded-unconscious at that stage.[10] Development is a constant process of embedding and disembedding, identifying with and then transcending. (And we are controlled by everything we have not transcended.)

Shortly after *The Atman Project* was published, Robert Kegan, now senior lecturer at the Harvard Graduate School of Education and the Massachusetts School of Professional Psychology, published a truly wonderful book, *The Evolving Self*. In it, he outlined five major stages of the evolving self—incorporative (pleromatic), impulsive (typhonic), imperial (magical), interpersonal (mythic-membership), institutional/formal (mental-egoic), and interindividual/postformal (relational, vision-logic, centauric). Although he recognized no post-postconventional or transpersonal stages, the match up to that point was almost perfect.

But what I appreciated most about *The Evolving Self* was the way that Kegan took the concept of embeddedness (a concept that he developed independently, based on the work of Schachtel and Piaget, who also influenced me) and made it a central pillar of development. As he brilliantly summarizes it, "We have begun to see not only how the subject-object balance can be spoken of as the deep structure in meaning-evolution, but also that there is something regular about the process of evolution itself. (Growth always involves a process of differentiation, of emergence from embeddedness, thus creating out of the former subject a new object to be taken by the new subjectivity.) This movement involves what Piaget calls 'decentration,' the loss of an old center, and what we might call 'recentration,' the recovery of a new center."[11]

Thus, in Kegan's overall model, "The subject is always embedded within and identified with the organizing principles (the cognitive structures) [for me, the more general basic structures], whereas the object is that which gets organized. A new stage arises when the subjective pole undergoes differentiation through the de-embedding of the self from the organizing structures. Standing outside of these structures, the self can systematically organize them and render them as objects. However, it can do so only through a higher level of organizing structures within which it in turn becomes embedded."[12]

The similarities are striking, almost identical (at least in this regard). *The Atman Project* was published in 1980, *The Evolving Self* in 1982, and thus we arrived at these conceptions independently, which I take as my great good fortune, in that disagreeing with Kegan is not a good sign for your model. We have each been asked about the other's model, and I regret that I did not have access to Kegan's extensive formulations when I was doing *The Atman Project*. For Kegan's part, he reports that people are always pointing out the similarities of his general model with

Eastern models and with mine. Thus, in his latest book, *In Over Our Heads* (which I highly recommend),[13] Kegan points out that "What we take as subject and object are not necessarily fixed for us. They are not permanent. They can change. (In fact, transforming our epistemologies, making what was subject into object so that we can 'have it' rather than 'be had' by it—this is the most powerful way I know to conceptualize the growth of the mind. [Indeed!] It is a way of conceptualizing the growth of the mind that is as faithful to the self-psychology of the West as to the 'wisdom literature' of the East.)"[14] With Kegan, you become a ditto-head. He graciously adds that "For those interested in an integration of Eastern philosophy with [this] perspective more generally, see the work of Ken Wilber: *The Atman Project, Up from Eden*, and especially, 'The Spectrum of Development' in *Transformations of Consciousness.*"[15] Thus, Kegan and I have been theoretically crossing paths for fifteen years, and it is a pleasure to finally have the chance to acknowledge how important his work has been and continues to be.

My major disagreement, of course, is that Kegan might wish to consider even more seriously the genuinely post-postconventional or transpersonal waves of growth. *The same principles apply, the same form of development is operative*, and his entire scheme can easily be continued from self-consciousness into superconsciousness, at which point one's entire bodymind becomes object—as Dogen Zenji summarized Enlightenment, "Bodymind dropped!" That is, exclusive identity with the bodymind drops; the entire bodymind becomes object of the True Self; you relate to your entire bodymind in exactly the same way you relate to clouds floating through a clear autumn sky. The entire bodymind floats in transparent Emptiness, in the radical I-I that is one's Original Face: all subjects have been transcended, all deaths have been died, all selves disembedded, and there stands instead the radiant Self that is the Kosmos at large, released into its own true nature, self-liberated in its own condition, self-seen in its own recognition—the Self of all that was, and all that is, and all that ever will be.

The Self-System

We can return now to Alexander et al. and pick up their story of consciousness development. For Alexander et al., "We suggest that [development] occurs through the very process of spontaneously shifting the dominant locus of awareness [proximate self-identity] to progressively deeper levels of mind [levels of consciousness]. . . . In our view, the shifting of awareness to function actively from each deeper level underlies the differentiation of this new mental structure from the prior levels of mind. Further, when awareness shifts from the cognitive structure in which it was previously 'embedded,' it becomes capable of hierarchically integrating and controlling all cognitive processes occurring at the prior level. . . . Thus, the deep motive of development may be seen as the progressive rediscovery ["remembrance" or anamnesis] by the Self of its own inner nature as the basis for increasing perspective on and mastery over the subjective and objective world."[16] At each of these stages of recollection, what is whole becomes part of a larger whole, so that, as they put it, each "takes on the status of a subsystem within, rather than executor of, mental life."

All of that is virtually identical to *The Atman Project*, and as far as it goes, I am obviously in complete agreement. But again, the full usefulness of this view is blocked to Alexander et al. because of what I believe is their confusion of level and line, as well as of enduring and transitional. (In other words, I believe that they have a certain amount of difficulty refining what amounts to a Wilber-II type of model into a Wilber-III type of conception.)

This becomes especially obvious, I believe, if we look at what they call the four higher stages of growth (which they term transcendental consciousness, cosmic consciousness, refined cosmic consciousness, and unity consciousness), because two of those are actually enduring basic structures that remain in subsequent development, and two are merely transitional stages, lost in subsequent development. The enduring structures are the causal Self and the nondual Brahman-Atman. The *temporary state* of tasting the causal is transcendental consciousness, usually evoked in meditation. As this transcendental consciousness becomes *constant* and *unbroken* through the waking, dreaming, and deep sleep state, the authors call that cosmic consciousness: it is the permanent realization of the Self, the Witness (subject permanence). Thus transcendental consciousness—the *temporary* taste of the Self—is lost as such (it is negated; it is transitional); but the causal Self disclosed in cosmic consciousness is the enduring Atman (the causal realm).

With refined cosmic consciousness, the Self begins to break down the final and subtle dualism between the subject and object. This *transitional* stage (of refined cosmic consciousness) is completed when the Self is subsumed (negated and preserved, differentiated and integrated) in pure Nonduality as Such (Brahman-Atman), a permanent and unbroken realization that persists in the midst of all manifestation, now recognized as forms of its own involvement.)[17]

Thus, more carefully distinguishing enduring and transitional, as well as level and line, would allow Alexander et al. to move to a more balanced and comprehensive model, a model that includes waves, streams, and states (which I have called Wilber-III), but a model that, by whatever name, attempts to come to terms with these more subtle and interesting facets of transpersonal development.

MEDITATION AND DEVELOPMENT

The role of meditation in human development is an extremely large and complicated topic, consisting of at least the following issues, about which I will make a few quick and general comments:

The effect of meditation on the psychological unconscious

In *The Atman Project*, I pointed out that the effect of meditation on the unconscious depends on what you mean by "the unconscious." I then outlined the five types of the unconscious that I mentioned above (ground, archaic, submergent, embedded, emergent), and I gave examples of how meditation affects each of those differently. Interested readers can consult that discussion, but in general, we might note the following:

(Meditation sooner or later begins to *dislodge the embedded-self* and the embedded-unconscious. By assuming a witnessing stance of mindfulness, one's subjective structures start to become objective, and thus one begins to disidentify or detach from one's present level of development (the embedded-self is loosened and dislodged from its given subjective attachment; the embedded-unconscious is de-embedded).[18] Precisely because this embedded-unconscious houses the *repressing* structures of the psyche, then when this repressing structure is deconstructed (or profoundly relaxed and loosened), two different things tend to happen, sometimes simultaneously: the lower or submergent unconscious (the "shadow") comes rushing up, and the higher or emergent consciousness (the superconscient and supramental) comes rushing down.)

Not only does this confuse meditators, it has completely confused many theorists, who cannot decide whether meditation is the door to the Devil or to God—that is, whether meditation is catatonic withdrawal (Dr. Franz Alexander's characterization of Zen), or perhaps regression to oceanic adualism (Freud's response to Romain Rolland), or, in general, a deautomatization or move down the mental hierarchy to lower and less differentiated (and more infantile and primitive) states. Or is it rather a contacting of our deeper Self, our true Nature, the God within, the angels and the archetypes of our highest possibilities?

I am saying it is both. But this depends on a precise understanding of the nature of the submergent-unconscious, the emergent-unconscious, and the embedded-unconscious which lies between them. By seeing that the embedded-self is the filtering screen that hides both the lower/submergent and the higher/emergent, we can see that the disembedding that generally occurs with intense meditation sets both of those realms free to roam. Which leads directly to the next issue.

The effect of meditation on human development

What is the effect of meditation on the overall growth and development of the human being? Aurobindo gave a pioneering and now classic formulation: "The spiritual evolution obeys the logic of a successive unfolding; it can take a new decisive main step only when the previous main step has been sufficiently conquered: even if certain minor stages can be swallowed up or leaped over by a rapid and brusque ascension, the consciousness has to turn back to assure itself that the ground passed over is securely annexed to the new condition; a greater or concentrated speed [which is indeed possible] does not eliminate the steps themselves or the necessity of their successive surmounting." (Aurobindo's point is that meditation (or spiritual practice in general) can accelerate—but not alter the form or sequence—of this developmental unfolding.)

As profound as Aurobindo's point is, let us refine it. That is, let us move from that type-II model to a type-III model, and ask instead: given that there are at least a dozen different lines of development, then (1) how does the development in one line affect the development in the others, and (2) what is the effect of meditation on each of those lines?

The relation of the various lines of development

The various quasi-independent lines of development include the following: moral development, self-identity or proximate-self development (generally called "ego development"), visual-spatial thinking, logico-mathematical thought, linguistic-narrative knowledge, cognitive development, worldviews, interpersonal capacity, psychosexual, conative and motivational drives, intimacy, spiritual development (ultimate concern), self-needs, altruism, creativity, affective development, level of typical defense mechanisms, mode of spacetime (spatiotemporal architecture), form of death-seizure, epistemic mode, various specific talents (musical, artistic, bodily-kinesthetic, sports, dance), and object relations—among others.

Based on research to date, it appears that these various developmental lines often stand in a relation of *"necessary but not sufficient."* From what we can tell so far, physiological development is necessary but not sufficient for cognitive development, which is necessary but not sufficient for interpersonal (and self) development, which is necessary but not sufficient for moral development. Research to date has repeatedly confirmed those relationships.

But all of those lines reach right down to the archaic level, so none of them are stacked rigidly on top of each other. They are not sitting on top of each other like so many bricks, but rather occur alongside each other like columns in a building. But there is one proviso: due to the specific nature of their interrelations, *some of the columns can never be taller than others*, a fact we have determined to be so empirically, and that we understand theoretically as a "necessary but not sufficient" relation (some lines are serving as necessary contexts for others).

Thus, even though these lines are occurring alongside each other, the "necessary but not sufficient" nature of their relationship means that ethical development cannot race ahead of interpersonal development, which cannot race ahead of cognitive development, which itself rests on certain physiological maturational schedules (all juggled, of course, by the self).

Conversely, the "necessary" part *can* race ahead of the "sufficient" part. For example, a person can be at very high level of cognition and yet still be at stage 1 moral development. We all know people who are very smart and yet quite immoral; but highly moral people are also highly cognitively developed: cognitive is necessary but not sufficient for moral.

The reason for this seems to be that, although the basic ladder of awareness can develop quite rapidly, the self's willingness to actually climb that ladder might not. You can *think* from a higher level (that's fairly easy) without actually *living from* that level (which requires moral courage). You can talk the talk but not walk the walk.

Thus, the ladder of basic structures can develop quite ahead of the self's willingness to actually climb those rungs. The self and its "center of gravity"—which is always where the action is—can remain quite low, even debased, while talking a mighty fine talk. (This applies as well, of course, to "spiritual development"—a "peak experience" is one thing; a stable adaptation, quite another.)[19]

The self will have to undergo a disembedding from the lower level—a death to the lower level—and a rebirth on the next higher level, in order to actually live from that higher and wider wave of awareness, an authentic living which will then be directly reflected in its actual moral stance, interpersonal relations, affective mode, and so forth. In order to live from a higher level, the self has to actually die to its embeddedness in a lower level, and it is much easier to chat about the higher level than to actually die to the lower. . . .

The specific details of these "necessary but not sufficient" relationships between the quasi-independent developmental lines will, for the most part, yield to direct empirical and phenomenological investigation. There are several hundred graduate-level research projects waiting to be undertaken.

The effect of meditation on any given line of development

We have seen that the various lines of development often stand in a necessary but not sufficient relation. Let us now ask, what might be the effect of meditation on each of the two dozen or so developmental lines?

That is a question that will also yield to direct empirical and phenomenological investigation—a hundred more graduate theses await, and it is a field that is virtually wide open. So far, much of the work in this area has been done by Alexander and his associates, yet another reason that I find their contributions so significant; and Daniel P. Brown, a coauthor of *Transformations of Consciousness*.

The protocol is relatively simple: administer the various tests (Loevinger scale of ego development, Kohlberg test of moral development, standard tests of altruism, defense mechanisms, empathy, interpersonal competence, creativity, physical coordination, T-scope, etc.) to groups of individuals at various stages of meditative competence. Graph the results (or otherwise analyze).

On the basis of research to date, I believe we already have enough data to answer: *Meditation can profoundly accelerate the unfolding of a given line of development, but it does not significantly alter the sequence or the form of the basic stages in that developmental line. Streams flow faster, but through the same waves.*

Meditation, for example, can accelerate moral development (gauged by the Kohlberg test), but under no circumstances has it been shown to bypass any of those stages. Meditation might help you move from stage

1 to stage 2 to stage 3 more quickly, but it will not allow you to skip stage 2. (Likewise, LSD might rattle your world, open you to higher possibilities, reintegrate past actuals, revive various traumas, heal various fractures; but it will not allow you to permanently bypass stage 2 in your moral development.)

Theoretically, of course, this makes perfect sense: stage 3, even though it basically replaces stage 2, is nonetheless built upon certain competences and skills developed in stage 2. An acorn cannot get to an oak by skipping the seedling stage.

Alexander's work has been instrumental in gathering a great deal of research data that rather unequivocally supports this conclusion, and I urge those interested to consult his published accounts. In the meantime, his overall research conclusion is that meditation will "accelerate development of consciousness markedly without altering its basic form or sequence."[20]

Conclusions

(Whatever else meditation does, and it does many things, it eventually begins to loosen the embedded-unconscious; it begins to deconstruct the embedded-self (the nexus of identifications that constitute the proximate self-sense at any given wave of its development). As the embedded-unconscious begins to loosen, the self's hold on *all* of the various developmental lines begins to loosen; *all of the developmental lines are put into play.*

The self-system, recall, is that which juggles and balances all of the different developmental lines, and attempts to give some sort of coherence to the psyche. As the self's present level of identity begins to loosen—as the embedded-unconscious shakes loose—the self begins to disembed from that level, disidentify with that level, and this sets everything in play; the various development lines are all set loose to some degree.

For example, in the developmental line of defense mechanisms, there might be a (usually temporary) regression to earlier, more primitive, less differentiated defenses; but if these are negotiated, and meditation progresses, there is often a substantial growth in the level of defenses employed, moving along the developmental hierarchy which itself runs from: psychotic defenses (delusional projection, distortion, hallucinatory wish fulfillment, projective identification), to borderline defenses (projection, splitting, selfobject fusion), to neurotic defenses (displacement, isolation/intellectualization, repression, reaction formation), to mature-ego defenses (suppression, sublimation)—and from there into the transpersonal defense mechanisms characteristic of the psychic, subtle, and causal realms (which I outlined in *Transformations of Consciousness*). This, too, is open to a variety of direct empirical and phenomenological investigations.

Thus, as the self disembeds and disidentifies with a given level, and the various lines are all put into play, there might indeed be temporary regression in any of the lines (including defenses, moral response, visual-spatial perceptions, and so on), but the net effect, on the long haul, is that the natural tendency of the psyche to grow (that is, Eros), and the natural tendency of the higher levels to emerge and descend (that is, Agape), are all more intensely engaged.

Empirical and phenomenological tests of each of the developmental lines, administered longitudinally to various groups of meditators, will yield significant empirical data on precisely these crucial issues. What we will likely find, as we have thus far, is that meditation *accelerates but does not alter the sequence or form of these various lines.* Temporary regression in any of the lines is quite possible at any point due to the *continual disembedding that is the essence of meditation.* But the overall net effect is an intensification of Eros (the Ascent to God) and Agape (the descent of the Goddess). The self finds its own higher and deeper engagements accelerated by the meditative stance, which is most profoundly nothing but an opening to one's own deepest possibilities.)

PSYCHOTHERAPY AND MEDITATION: AN INTEGRAL THERAPY

The relation of meditation and psychotherapy is obviously an intricate and complicated topic, with dozens of difficult and obscure factors all entering into a series of complex equations we have not yet begun to decipher.

(Nonetheless, the transpersonal field has moved beyond its initial and introductory statements in this area—such as, "Meditation increases capacity for witnessing and equanimity, and thus can facilitate the 'evenly hovering attention' requisite for analysis." Or "Meditation relaxes the repression barrier and thus can facilitate regression in service of the ego." Or "Meditation allows deep reparation of narcissistic wounds, thus speeding the formation of a cohesive self." Or "Meditation encourages a mental spaciousness that lessens the defensive stance." All of those might be true enough in a general and introductory fashion, but we now have enough data, evidence, and advanced theoretical models to start to decipher those equations with a little more precision.)

I believe that, as research and theory continue to become more sophisticated, we will very soon be able to proceed in something like this fashion:

A DSM-IV diagnosis would be accompanied by a "psychograph" of the levels of each of the major developmental lines in the client, including the vertical level (not just horizontal type)[21] of self development (i.e., the level of "ego development"), level of basic pathology,[22] level of object relations, level of major defense mechanism(s), predominant self-needs, moral stage, spiritual development, and so on. Of course, once again, these are fluid waves of development and not rigidly discrete levels, but they are very useful for a general orientation on the evolution of consciousness through its many domains.

Based on that psychograph, an *integral therapy* could then be suggested. This integral therapy will itself depend on continued research into *the effects of various transformative practices on each of the major developmental lines.*

Thus, for example, what is the effect of, say, hatha yoga on the developmental line of object relations? What is the effect of vipassana meditation on proximate self-sense (or "ego development")? What is the effect of concentrative-type meditation on defense mechanisms?

The various transformative practices include (moving up the spectrum): physical or gross body practices (hatha yoga, diet, nutritional supplements, weight training, aerobic exercise; "physical" also includes the effects of pharmacological agents, no matter what level they actually elicit); affective psychotherapy (emotional catharsis therapy); bioenergetics ("prana" therapy); psychoanalytic and various uncovering therapies; hypnotherapy; script, role, and cognitive therapy; existential therapy; kundalini yoga; deity yoga; nada and shabd yoga; tsogyal and spontaneous luminosity; vipassana, causal inquiry, witnessing meditation; shikantaza, trekchod; sahaj and bhava samadhi. (That is simply a very brief sampling of some of the transformative practices addressing the various levels of the spectrum of consciousness; the list is by no means complete.)

The research agenda is then very simple to state: clinically determine the effect of each of those transformative practices on each of the major developmental lines.

Then, based on the psychograph of the client, and the knowledge of the effect of various transformative practices on each developmental line, an integral therapy could be prescribed that would be the most likely to (1) renormalize the bodymind of the individual seeking help; (2) engage postformal development if desired.

To give a few crude examples:

- A client with borderline pathology, impulsive ego, preconventional morality, and splitting defense mechanism might be offered: structure building therapy, bibliotherapy, weight training, nutritional supplements, pharmacological agents (as required), verbalization and narrative training, and short sessions of a concentration-type meditation (not awareness-training meditation, which tends to dismantle subjective structure, which the borderline does not yet adequately possess).
- A client with anxiety neurosis, phobic elements, conventional morality, repression and displacement defense mechanisms, belongingness needs, and persona self-sense might be offered: uncovering psychotherapy, bioenergetics, script analysis, jogging or biking (or some other individual sport), desensitization, dream analysis/therapy, and vipassana meditation.
- A client with existential depression, postconventional morality, suppression and sublimation defense mechanisms, self-actualization needs, and a centauric self-sense might be offered: existential analysis, dream therapy, a team sport (e.g., volleyball, basketball), bibliotherapy, t'ai chi chuan (or prana circulating therapy), community service, and kundalini yoga.
- A client who has been practicing Zen meditation for several years, but suffers life-goal apathy and depression, deadening of affect, postconventional morality, postformal cognition, self-transcendence needs, and psychic self-sense might be offered: uncovering therapy, combination weight training and jogging, tantric deity-yoga (visualization meditation), tonglen (compassion training), and community service.

Those are obviously simplistic examples, but I think the point of an integral therapy is clear enough.[23] I would simply like to repeat that those types of integral recommendations will rest on actual clinical evidence and research into the effects of various transformative practices on the major developmental streams. We are simply following the evolution of consciousness through its pluridimensional domains, looking for ways to help facilitate that evolution, and for ways to help unblock it whenever it gets "stuck." This will allow us to determine, not only which practices are indicated for specific occasions, but just as important, which are contraindicated (I gave the example of intense awareness training being contraindicated with borderline syndromes; I believe we will find numerous and very specific indications and contraindications as the research data accumulates).

As it is now, each transpersonal therapist in effect follows that protocol in an intuitive, hit-and-miss fashion. I believe the field is now ready and capable of moving to an entirely new level in this regard.

PSYCHOLOGY AND SPIRITUALITY

We are now in a position to address the issue at the crux of the "psychology and spirituality" debate: Is psychological development necessary for spiritual development?

We begin by unpacking those terms. What we loosely call "psychological" development is actually an amalgam of several different developmental lines, including the line of self-identity or proximate-self development (generally called "ego development"), the line of defense mechanisms (which usually follow the line of self development, but may be split off and operate at earlier and more primitive levels), the line of interpersonal development (the capacity for role taking and self-other interaction), and the line of affect (disposition, feeling-awareness). All of those are quasi-independent lines, and although they generally develop as a "bundle" (held together by the self-sense), nonetheless disjunctures and tensions between them can and often do occur. (And, as we saw, meditation in general can be expected to accelerate but not alter the sequence or form of each of those lines.)

"Spirituality" is likewise a loose and vague term. As we have seen, some people use it to refer mostly to the (higher stages of any of the developmental lines,) and some people use it to refer to a separate spiritual line itself. Let us start with the former. In this sense, "spiritual" means the specifically post-postconventional, transpersonal, supramental stages of any of the developmental lines: transpersonal affect (bliss), transpersonal consciousness (the superconscient), transpersonal self (both the psychic/subtle soul and the causal Self or Witness), transpersonal interpersonal (compassion), transpersonal cognition (prajna, jnana, gnosis), and transpersonal states (nirvikalpa, nirvana, nirodh).

(In that common usage, "psychological" tends to mean "mental and personal," and "spiritual" tends to mean "supramental and transpersonal.)" Or, to say essentially the same thing, in that quite common usage, "psychological" means the precon, con, and postcon levels of any of the lines, and "spiritual" means the post-postcon levels in any of the lines. Thus, for example, the conventional ego is generally considered to be in the realm of the personal/psychological, and the transpersonal soul is in the realm of the spiritual. The preconventional affect of rage is in the realm of psychology, the post-postconventional affect of transcendental love is in the realm of the spiritual, and so on. I am not saying those are the only definitions of "psychological" and "spiritual," simply that they are two of the most common, and since they do refer to legitimate realities (precon, con, postcon, and post-postcon waves), let us use those to start the discussion.

(Using those specific definitions, then *in any particular developmental stream,* psychological development must generally be completed before spiritual development can begin.) As much research has confirmed, for actual developmental lines there exists something like precon, then con, then postcon, then post-postcon waves, because each successive wave builds upon certain necessary competences provided by its predecessors (just as you must have letters, then words, then sentences, then paragraphs). And to the extent that we define psychology as letters/words/sentences, and we define spirituality as the all-encompassing paragraphs, then we must complete psychology before spirituality can begin.

(This has given rise to the commonly accepted view that personal development must be generally completed before transpersonal development can begin in any stable fashion. This is the general "you have to be somebody before you can be nobody" view, the general Aurobindo view ("a logic of successive unfolding"), and the view of the Wilber-II type of models, all of which have been (derogatorily) summarized as the "linear" or "ladder" view.)[4]

As far as it goes, I believe that view is quite correct. But, as we will see, the problem is that it leaves out several other, equally important facets of spirituality and development. Thus, opponents of that ladder view have pointed out that spirituality is nowhere near that linear. These opponents generally have one of two alternative models in mind: spiritu-

ality involves altered states (which can happen at any time), or spirituality is a separate line *alongside* the others (not something occurring *after*
the others). In these alternative conceptions, psychology and spirituality
occur together, not one after the other.

But what both the proponents and the opponents of the ladder view
tend to miss, in my opinion, is a third option, which I have been calling
Wilber-III, and which, I believe, effectively includes both of those views.

Thus, even if, for the moment, we use the common meaning of psychology and spirituality—namely, as the personal waves and the post-
personal (or transpersonal) waves in any of the lines, respectively—the
fact is that these lines develop in a relatively independent fashion, and
thus a person can be at a very high (or "spiritual") level in some lines
and a low or medium (or "psychological") level in others. Thus, although in any one line, psychological development must be generally
completed before spiritual development can begin, *overall development
shows no such requirements at all,* so that numerous psychological and
spiritual developments are occurring simultaneously at almost every
point.

Say there are ten developmental lines (affective, cognitive, moral, interpersonal, and so on). Say that a person is at a preconventional wave
in lines 1 and 5; a conventional wave in lines 3 and 8; a postconventional
wave in lines 4 and 9; and a post-postconventional wave in lines 2, 6,
and 10. Using the common definitions, this person is at a psychological
(or personal) level in six lines and a spiritual (or transpersonal) level in
four lines. Obviously, psychological development does *not* have to be
completed before spiritual development can begin. And yet, in each of
the lines, that *does* have to happen. By adopting a type-III model, we
can easily understand, or so it seems to me, exactly why both of those
views are correct (the ladder view of spirituality after psychology, *and*
the simultaneous view of spirituality concurrent with psychology). Both
of those views are correct, and both have substantial evidence supporting them, and only a type-III model, I believe, can integrate those findings.

Let us also look at the other two common meanings of "spiritual"
(altered states and separate line); they, too, can be accommodated in a
III-type model. As for spirituality being a separate line itself, which unfolds *alongside* the other lines (beginning as early as fulcrum-0 or ful-
crum-1, like many other developmental lines), then it is quite true that,
in this case, psychological development does not have to be completed
before spiritual development (since they are occurring alongside each

other). But note: the spiritual line itself—to the extent it is a genuine line—unfolds in its own waves of precon, con, postcon, and post-postcon, and thus the early stages in that line need to be completed before the higher stages can stably unfold (as, e.g., Fowler's research demonstrated).[25]

In that sense, the early personal/psychological stages of the spiritual line need to be completed before the higher/transpersonal stages of the spiritual line can unfold—and thus proponents of this view are right back to a ladder model of spiritual development, which, as we saw, is completely valid *as far as it goes*. It just leaves out altered states (see below) and it leaves out all the other developmental streams, each of which can be at a "psychological" or "spiritual" wave in their own unfolding, so that overall development itself follows no ladder sequence at all.

As for altered states, we have seen that a spiritual peak experience (of the psychic, subtle, causal, or nondual realms) can occur at virtually any level or stage of development. As such, a "spiritual" influx can occur at any psychological stage. Thus, there is no "ladder" sequence here, either. But, as we also noted, for altered states to become permanent traits, they must enter the stream of stable development, at which point altered states become a developmental stream themselves, and accordingly "spirituality" reverts to one of the previous two definitions (highest levels in any stream, a separate stream itself).

Summary

We have seen that the relation of "spirituality" and "psychology" depends in large part upon how we define those terms. Using some of the most common definitions—where psychology means personal (precon, con, and postcon) and spirituality means transpersonal (post-postcon)—then in any single developmental line, the psychological must be generally completed before spiritual development can stably begin. Likewise, if spirituality is considered its own developmental line, the personal stages in that line (precon, con, and postcon) need to be generally completed before the transpersonal (or post-postcon) stages can stably unfold. Thus, even if we define spirituality as its own separate line, that line or stream still unfolds through the same basic waves as the other streams (from precon to con to postcon to post-postcon), so that it is still quite true that, in any given stream, "You have to be con before you can be postcon." And it is still as true as ever that, in any given stream, we do not want to confuse preconventional and postconventional simply because both are nonconventional.

From the evidence we have seen thus far, we might expect that meditation would accelerate—but not alter—that sequence of spiritual unfolding, in both male and female modes.[26] Thus, whether we use "spiritual" to mean the highest waves of any of the streams, or whether we use it to mean a separate stream itself, it appears that meditation helps to accelerate, but not otherwise alter, the unfolding of those streams.

Altered states can occur at any stage, but in order for them to become permanent realizations, they will have to enter the stream of development and thus follow its currents as well, and thus altered states eventually fall into one of the two previous definitions.

Nonetheless, even though in any given line the psychological generally has to be completed before the spiritual can begin, because the lines themselves develop in a relatively independent manner, a person can be at numerous psychological waves in some lines and numerous spiritual waves in others—*psychological development most definitely does not have to be completed before spiritual development can occur*. Sometimes psychological issues will predominate, sometimes spiritual issues will come to the fore, and always they will interpenetrate and mutually influence each other, from the earliest to the highest stages. (Even if someone is stably at the "spiritual" or post-postcon waves in all streams, much of the conventional or "psychological" waves still remain as basic waves and functional capacities in awareness, mutually interacting with the spiritual realms.) As usual, overall development follows no set sequence at all, and each individual's journey through the spectrum of consciousness is a multifaceted, flowing, fluid affair of waves, streams, states, and realms.

Thus, all three common uses of "spiritual" find room in a type-III model. Spirituality as the highest levels, spirituality as a separate line, and spirituality as an altered state or religious experience all fit comfortably in an integral view, or so it seems to me. And all three of those uses of "spiritual" are valid, in my opinion, but it is important to specify which is meant before suggestions on the relation of psychology and spirituality are offered.)

ON THE PHYSIOLOGY OF MEDITATION

(Since the physiological and cognitive lines are the two earliest strands in the "necessary but not sufficient" sequence (which I gave above), this means that they are the most fundamental lines, the foundational lines, upon which all the others tend to rest, at least according to most research to date. (They are, it seems, the Right- and Left-Hand foundations of the entire sequence; the physiological is the foundation of the Upper-Right quadrant; the cognitive, of the Upper-Left).

This, too, is an important area of empirical investigation to which the TM researchers (particularly Wallace, Orme-Johnson, and Dillbeck) have significantly contributed; namely, the physiological correlates of meditative states and stages.

Recall that it was Wallace's 1970 landmark publication in *Science* ("The Physiological Effects of Transcendental Meditation") that shocked the scientific world into recognizing that *something real* was happening in meditation. Of course, empirical scientists recognize *only* the Right-Hand (or empirical) aspects of any holon anyway, but since all holons do indeed possess those aspects, then meditation ought to clearly register in that empirical and physiological domain. It does, Wallace proved it, and that dramatically exploded the dogma that meditation was ineffectual fantasy. This opened an enormous number of doors for further scientific-empirical research, of which the TM movement has remained in the forefront.

As we will see in the next chapter, an integral approach to consciousness would attempt to simultaneously track events in an all-level, all-quadrant fashion, and that would certainly include the physiological correlates of consciousness states. But such an all-level, all-quadrant approach also bears directly on *spiritual practice* itself. As I suggested in chapter 9, what we especially need at this point is not just an integral *theory* of the Kosmos, but an *integral practice* that can help us effectively actualize that integral potential in all of us.

INTEGRAL PRACTICE

The fact that the physiological (or "material") and the cognitive (or "mental") are two of the most fundamental lines in the human being ("matter" and "consciousness," Right and Left) means that a truly integral spiritual practice would, at the very least, put an equal emphasis on both body and mind at each and every stage of general evolution, gross bodymind to subtle bodymind to causal bodymind.

As straightforward as that conclusion might sound now, it is historically a rather radical idea, as Michael Murphy knows. Drawing on the pioneering insights of Aurobindo, but extending them in many profound and significant ways, Murphy has been arguing for many years that what is sorely needed is a truly *integral practice*. His masterwork, *The Future of the Body*, is devoted to just that topic. Charles Tart noted that "The only way to adequately describe this book is to state that it is the most important work on the relationship between mind and body ever written."

(But by "mind" and "body" Murphy does not mean the standard and rather narrow notions of material flesh and immaterial soul. He rather means the entire sweep of the Upper-Left quadrant ("mind" or consciousness in the broadest sense) and the entire sweep of the Upper-Right quadrant ("body" in the broadest sense).) And his point is: you cannot actually have one without the other at any level of human development, and therefore we ought to *consciously engage both*, equally, intensely, fully. This integral engagement then acts as an accelerator of evolution from the gross bodymind to the subtle bodymind to the causal bodymind, each stage of which embraces and radiantly transfigures its predecessors, uniting the ascending current of evolution with the descending current of involution, transforming the self, the body, and the world in the process.

(Murphy is also fully aware of the importance, in overall practice, of integrating not just the Upper Left and Upper Right, but also the Lower Left and Lower Right—intentional, behavioral, cultural, and social— that is, an "all-level, all-quadrant" approach to integral practice. Thus, in his latest book, <u>*The Life We Are Given,*</u> coauthored with his friend George Leonard, the authors develop a program of balanced practice set in the context of family and community and service, which they call Integral Transformative Practice.)

Mike and I have often discussed the "three waves" that the human potential movement itself has gone through in the last several decades. The first wave was the introduction, in the '60s, of the initial human potential movement. Although a varied beast, it tended to focus on the quick fix, the peak experience, the weekend workshop, the satori-in-seven-days seminar. It was a wild explosion, marvelous and frightening, wonderful and warped, glorious and grotesque. It was centered at Esalen Institute, cofounded by Mike and his friend Richard Price.

(Within a decade or so, the goal of a "peak experience" started to give way to the goal of a "plateau experience," and the second wave of the human potential movement began.) The limitations of the quick fix started to become all too apparent; useful as it was for an initial wakeup, the results tended to fade rapidly, sometimes leaving the individual in even worse shape than before. In any event, it soon became obvious that to engage in genuine transformation requires time, effort, work, and sustained intentionality—in a word, practice. People began to take up actual transformative practices: perhaps Zen, or yoga, or sustained psychotherapy, or prolonged body work, or extended dream work, or physical/sports/body training, and so on. The five-day fix gave way to the five-year engagement.

But even those forms of commendable practice had a limitation: they usually exercised only one faculty of the human organism—perhaps awareness, or dreams, or physical skill, or insight training, or emotional openness—while neglecting the others. That is, these approaches generally emphasized one line of development and followed it through its various levels—they grabbed one stream and surfed its waves—only to find, at the conclusion of that otherwise commendable practice, that the other lines of development were still rather immature, undeveloped, poorly evolved, or even withered, but now with the added difficulty: the person was burdened with a very unbalanced constitution. The poor self, which has to juggle all the various developmental lines, often found itself saddled with one giant and a dozen pygmies. And the more its particular practice genuinely *advanced*, the *worse* the situation got, which totally confused everybody.

(Thus, the second wave of specific practice gave way to the third wave of integral practice. Once again the field transcended and included, negated and preserved, as it went through its own three waves of learning)

(In other words, the field itself evolved from its initial sensory-dominated explosiveness ("lose your mind and come to your senses!") to its second wave of concrete practice, all of which were necessary for its third wave, just now starting, of universal/integral practice—its own precon, con, and postcon waves.)

And, it might be noted, Michael Murphy was instrumental in all three waves. It has been Murphy who, working quietly and often behind the scenes, has prepared much of the ground in which each of those three waves could unfold. Michael Murphy very well might be the most significant spiritual pioneer of our generation, if for no other reason than the extraordinary spaces that he created in which others could transform as well.

The third wave of integral practice is in its infancy, but, like all infants, growing at a dizzying speed. Indicative of the trend is the book *What Really Matters: Searching for Wisdom in America*, by former *New*

York Times reporter Tony Schwartz. I think if Tony had the book to do over, there are a few small points he might change, but the book remains a fine compendium of the best of the transformative technologies now available. And the overall conclusion of the book is unmistakable: integral practice is now the most viable mode of human transformation.

To catch the crest of the third wave: has there ever been a more exciting surfing adventure in consciousness?

11

Heading toward Omega?

WHERE EXACTLY IS THE
GROUND OF BEING?

Where are we to locate Spirit? What are we actually allowed to acknowledge as Sacred? Where exactly is the Ground of Being? In infancy? In the matriarchy? In enlightenment? In Gaia? At some far-off but perhaps rapidly approaching Omega Point? Where is this ultimate Divine?

In this and the next chapter we address this most crucial of all questions.

WHERE IS THE SACRED ACTUALLY LOCATED?

MAX PLANCK IS CREDITED with first pointing out that old paradigms die only when the believers in old paradigms die. Because paradigms are self-confirming, there is no type of data that can dislodge the paradigm from within, and so new evidence or better arguments rarely dissuade believers. And thus, as I have often paraphrased Planck, the knowledge quest proceeds funeral by funeral.

On this, everybody agrees, and it is simply a matter of being honest about whose funeral you await.

Gus diZerega and Richard Smoley published a review of *Sex, Ecology, Spirituality* that is most interesting, and in many ways strikes me as something of a "paradigm clash," irresolvable with evidence. They begin by questioning my interpretation of Aristotle as being one of the West's archetypal Ascenders. They point out that Aristotle spent so much time categorizing the Many that he couldn't have been much of an Ascender. True, Aristotle spent most of his time in this-worldly study, and much of the West's science, for example, finds roots in Aristotle. I don't contest that. But in that section of the book I am discussing where various theorists located *ultimate reality*. And Arthur Lovejoy's extremely perceptive point was that, for Aristotle, ultimate reality (God) was not to be found anywhere in this world. Aristotle's God, rather, is entirely otherworldly; his God neither creates nor is substantially immanent in any manifest domain (things strive to reach God as final cause, but they never succeed).

Thus, to the utterly fundamental question, *Where is the real and final and ultimate reality?*, Aristotle would say: Not anywhere on this earth. And thus, when you look to the extraordinarily important notion of where final reality lies—and therefore, what is to be viewed as *profoundly sacred*—Aristotle is, in every way, otherworldly and ascending. Lovejoy makes that fascinating point—a point which had profound historical ramifications—and that is what I was reporting.

Lovejoy's concomitant point is that if we then look at Plato (who also in the conventional mentality is viewed as the real "otherworldly" philosopher, as opposed to the "this-worldly" orientation of Aristotle), we again find that things are actually reversed on this deepest of levels. Of course Plato had an enormously powerful otherworldly component to his philosophy; but as Lovejoy points out (and I quote this directly in the book): "But the most notable—and the less noted—fact about [Plato's] historic influence is that he did *not* merely give to European otherworldliness its characteristic form and phraseology and dialectic, but that he also gave the characteristic form and phraseology and dialectic to precisely the contrary tendency—to a peculiarly *exuberant kind of this-worldliness.*" For example, Plato in the *Timaeus* describes the actual manifestation of this world from the ultimate reality, so that this very earth he calls "a visible, sensible God." This is the strand that would give rise to the Neoplatonic emphasis on sacred manifestation, which would easily see this earth and this world as sacred to the core, something for which Aristotle—and his immense influence—had no room at all.

Now *that's* fascinating, it seems to me, and quite true, and it much more clearly sets the record straight on just where *ultimate reality* could be found in these two most influential thinkers—and thus, just what could, or could not, *be viewed as sacred*. This, of course, upsets a common ecophilosopher and neopagan prejudice, which views a strawman Plato as being nothing but a fountain of Western hatred of this world. And it further goes to show why Plato, not Aristotle, could *actually* be (and was in fact historically) the father of so much of the West's this-worldly pantheism, neopaganism, and naturalism. All of this seems to be ignored by diZerega and Smoley, unfortunately.

They then attempt a similar questioning of my treatment of Emerson, although they do not in any fashion demonstrate that I misunderstood or misrepresented Emerson.[1] My interpretation of Emerson is so mainstream, so widely accepted, so uncontroversial, that you can even find it in standard college texts.[2] I stayed right down the middle of the interpretive road on such giants as Emerson and Plotinus, simply because, in claiming to integrate their views, I could not afford to be charged with integrating a "far-out" or contested interpretation, and thus I intentionally adopted a very safe, widely-accepted stance.[3] This balanced interpretation upset what I believe are the rather narrow, neopagan interpretations of diZerega and Smoley, and "paradigm clash" circled hauntingly in the background. Smoley's most recent book (with Kinney) continues to misrepresent my work as phase-II only (ignoring phases III and IV); but Gus diZerega's work on ecology and economic theory is really quite impressive, and I find myself in much agreement with his recent work (we are planning a few joint ventures).

POINTS OF LIGHT

1. I have often described Roger Walsh as one of the guiding lights of transpersonal studies, and I am always glad to have the opportunity to repeat my deep appreciation for his work (and our friendship). I have a similar estimate of his partner, Frances Vaughan, and their combined voices are a strong beacon for the entire field.

Roger wrote a superb summary of some of the central themes of *Sex, Ecology, Spirituality*, which has been published in several journals.[4] Given that his essay, in its various forms, has now been read by approximately three times the number of people who have read SES itself, you will understand that I am altogether relieved that it is fair, accurate, and informative.

2. Another superb summary of SES is by Kaisa Puhakka, "Restoring Connectedness in the Kosmos: A Healing Tale of a Deeper Order,"

which appeared in *The Humanistic Psychologist* (Fall 1996). It was truly gratifying to see the summaries by Walsh and Puhakka. You don't look for reviewers to necessarily agree with you, but simply to show that they have to some degree understood you. And I must say, these are two pieces that especially seemed to genuinely understand *Sex, Ecology, Spirituality*, and I can recommend them very highly on that count alone.

3. A sign that the transpersonal orientation is starting to have a major impact on conventional and mainstream psychology is the recent publication, by Basic Books, of the *Textbook of Transpersonal Psychiatry and Psychology*, edited by Bruce Scotton, M.D., Allan B. Chinen, M.D., and John Battista, M.D. This is an excellent collection of articles and essays touching on almost every aspect of the transpersonal orientation, and it deserves the widest possible readership.

At the same time, this is simply the most recent in a line of superb anthologies on adult and postformal development, beginning perhaps with *Beyond Formal Operations*, edited by Michael L. Commons, Francis A. Richards, and Cheryl Armon. This was (and still is) a pioneering work, appearing in 1984, and excellent in every respect. I will mention several other important anthologies in an endnote.[5]

All of these works are a clear indication that the fields of psychiatry and psychology are increasingly ready to move beyond their postconventional to their own post-postconventional wave of awareness, a healthy sign by any standard.

4. Bryan Wittine's review of *Sex, Ecology, Spirituality* in *The Journal of Transpersonal Psychology* (1995, 27[2]) is thoughtful, balanced, and perceptive. But within a broad range of agreement, he had several criticisms. One was that I presented a rigidly stratified view of development with clear-cut levels. This, of course, is not the case (see chapters 9 and 10), but I understand how a reviewer could get that impression from my short summary in SES.

Wittine's second criticism concerned my treatment of Jung and the archetypes. Again, I can understand how Bryan might get some of his impressions from the short summary I gave in SES. The problem is that Jung (and his followers) had at least three different uses of "archetype," and I believe that there are insuperable difficulties with all of them.

The first and most common use is *archaic image*. This was Jung's earliest formulation, and it is still the most prevalent and most widely used (for example, by the mythopoetic movement, the men's movement, and folk psychology). These collectively inherited archaic images, Jung believed, were a phylogenetic heritage, "the instinct's perception of itself." Jung believed that a particularly rich fund of these archetypes could be found in the world's mythologies (which led Jung's early critics to accuse him of "mythomania"). These archaic mythic images were nonrational, and because of this, Jung felt they were a direct source of spiritual awareness, which is exactly what he had in mind when he stated that "mysticism is experience of the archetypes."

In that usage, Jung is most definitely guilty of the pre/trans fallacy. He simply does not differentiate with sufficient clarity between prerational and transrational occasions, and thus he tends to elevate prerational infantilisms to spiritual glory, for no other reason than that they are not rational. This use of "archetype," because it is still the most common and most widely associated with Jung's name, is the use I have criticized the most. In this usage, the archetypes are found in the earlier stages of evolution, phylogenetic and ontogenetic. I have pointed out that those archaic image "archetypes" should therefore really be called "prototypes," because they are prerational, magic, and mythic forms, not subtle, transrational, and post-postconventional forms (which is the way they are used in the perennial philosophy, from Plotinus to Garab Dorje to Asanga and Vasubandhu).[6]

Jung's second use of archetype was much broader; it simply referred to archetypes as collectively inherited "forms devoid of content." In *The Atman Project* I quote him saying exactly that, and I point out that if that is our definition of archetype, then all of the deep structures of each level of the spectrum of consciousness (except the formless) can be called *archetypal*, and that is fine with me. But then that has absolutely nothing to do with archaic images, does it?

That use of archetype (as deep structures devoid of content) is one of the uses that Wittine wishes to rehabilitate. "My understanding is that archetypes are innate structural predispositions that are definable only in terms of ordering principles, never in terms of specific content." Wittine says I ignore this use, which, as we just saw, is not the case. I simply point out that that definition is massively at variance with Jung's first and most common usage. If Wittine wishes to follow that definition, that is completely acceptable, but a great deal of clarity is required in order to differentiate it from the first use and avoid pre/trans fallacies. I myself have not found the Jungian literature useful in this regard.

The third use of archetype by Jung and his followers is more in line with the perennial philosophy, which sees archetypes as *the first forms in involution*. The entire manifest world arises out of the Formless (or causal Abyss), and the first forms to do so are the forms upon which all others will rest—they are "arche-forms" or archetypes. Thus, in this use, the archetypes are the highest Forms of our own possibilities, the deepest Forms of our own potentials—but also the last barriers to the Formless and Nondual.

As the first (and earliest) forms in involution or manifestation (or movement away from causal Source), the archetypes are the last (and highest) forms in evolution or return to Source. As the Forms right on the edge of the Formless, they are the first forms the soul embraces as it contracts in the face of infinity and hides its own true nature; but they are also, for just that reason, the highest beacons on the way back to the Formless, and the final barrier to be deconstructed on the edge of a radiant infinity.[7]

(And note: because these archetypes are the first forms in *early involution*, they are almost the exact opposite of archaic images, which are some of the first forms that arise in *early evolution*—yet another reason that confusing them has caused such theoretical problems.)[8]

Jung and the Jungians *occasionally* use archetype in this high fashion, but even then it tends to be a rather anemic discussion. I believe Hameed Ali has brutally but accurately summarized the situation: "Jung got very close to [high archetypal] essence and its various manifestations but stayed on the level of imagination. So he fell short of realizing [archetypal] essence and living it, and his psychology remained a mental construct not directly connected with the presence of essence."[9]

Thus, we have three different uses of "archetype" by Jung and the Jungians, and all of them, I believe, are problematic. The archaic images exist, but they have little if anything to do with post-postconventional development. Archetypes as deep structures devoid of content is an acceptable usage, but it is almost totally at variance with the first use (e.g., formal operational has a deep structure and is "archetypal" in that sense, but you do not find formop in archaic images), and the Jungian development of this use I have found rather limited. Finally, archetype as "high archetype" or forms of the subtle (the first forms in involution, the last forms in evolution) is also acceptable, but here I find the Jungian use, as does Hameed Ali, to be anemic (see below).

And in all three of those uses, the Jungian archetype is still profoundly monological (see note 3 to chapter 7). For all of these reasons, I have increasingly found the Jungian approach, pioneering as it was, to be less than fruitful for third-wave transpersonal studies. Of course, any individual can make exemplary exercise of the Jungian path, using its strengths to transcend its limitations. Bryan Wittine is such a one, and there are many others. But the Jungian light is one we must use with much caution, I now believe.

5. In the late seventies, the system known as Psychosynthesis, developed by Roberto Assagioli, became a fairly popular and widespread spiritual psychology and therapy. Assagioli was an extraordinary pioneer in the transpersonal field, weaving the best of many important psychological and spiritual traditions together into a powerful approach to inner growth. Among many other contributions, he was one of the first to call for an integration of "depth psychology" with what he called "height psychology," and to combine "psychoanalysis" with "psychosynthesis."

Nonetheless, for various reasons, Psychosynthesis as a major force declined in influence.[10] I had always wondered if there would arise another fairly popular yet well-rounded approach to psychology and therapy, uniting both depth and height psychology, and in the past several years, it appears that there has: the Diamond Approach, originated by Hameed Ali.

I will reserve a long discussion of this approach for an endnote.[11] Here I will simply say that, in my opinion, the Diamond Approach is a superb combination of some of the best of modern Western psychology with ancient (and spiritual) wisdom. It is one type of a more integral approach, uniting Ascending and Descending, spiritual and psychological, into an effective form of inner work.

As is always the case with these more public and popular movements, much hinges on the actual personalities of those drawn to the approach. Psychosynthesis floundered in part because, although it was a fairly well-rounded theory, its emphasis on disidentification meant that in practice it attracted a large number of dissociative types, inmates who in some cases took over the hospital. The Diamond Approach thus far seems to be running smoothly, and it has earned recognition from many quarters, including my hard-to-impress friends Larry Spiro and Tony Schwartz. We will simply have to wait and see what forces surface as this generally well-rounded approach grows into a large organization with much influence: whom it will attract, what fate awaits it, what forces are unleashed as it moves into the culture at large.

In the meantime, the fact that such a therapeutic/growth system can gain a strong and respected foothold in the culture—this, too, a sign of the post-postconventional waves that are very slowly but very surely washing upon our collective shores.

The Idealist Dream

A few reviewers categorized *Sex, Ecology, Spirituality* as being primarily an Idealist treatise. I can understand why that might seem to be the case (especially for reviewers, who don't often have a great deal of time to spend with a book, not to mention an 800-page book). Nonetheless, although I have some profound sympathies with the Idealist project, I am not a member of that camp in any strict sense. In SES I express great appreciation for the Idealists—especially Schelling—because they were some of the first to attempt to articulate a modern form of spirituality— that is, a transpersonal philosophy that would take into account the worldview of modernity, including development and evolution, which is basically something that no spiritual view had done prior to that time (and which traditional spiritual approaches still often neglect). Evolution as "Spirit-in-action" is simply one of many Idealist tenets that I have happily adopted.

But I outline two severe inadequacies that prevent the typical Idealist approach from finally working: it has no injunctions or paradigms or yoga; and it tends to equate vision-logic with spirit. These are crucial points, because they indicate what I believe to be the only viable way out of the Idealist impasse.

Lacking injunctions means lacking a genuine methodology to reproduce transpersonal knowledge. The great Idealist philosophers—indeed, many great "spiritual" philosophers, including Spinoza, Schelling, Fichte, Hegel, Nietzsche, Schopenhauer, Whitehead, James—almost certainly had a variety of profound "peak experiences" or glimpses into the transpersonal (or post-postconventional) waves of awareness.

But a peak experience is not a reproducible mode of knowledge acquisition. The peak experience must give way to the plateau experience, which must give way to permanent adaptation, before the knowledge of that level of development becomes verifiable (confirmable/rejectable) and thus can actually enter the stream of valid knowledge.

In other words, to have any genuine cognitive status, these temporary *states* of consciousness must be converted into stable and enduring *traits* or structures of consciousness. And this, by any other name, is the role and function of yoga—a sustained practice, injunction, exemplar, or paradigm which acts as the foundation of all genuine transpersonal knowledge. None of the philosophers that I just listed had a stable transpersonal practice, exemplar, or paradigm, and thus all of their views soon degenerated into metaphysics (where "metaphysics" means a system of thought without experiential proof).

But if a genuine yoga (transpersonal injunction and practice) is fully engaged, and if consciousness grows and evolves and gains in strength—precisely through the ongoing flow of developmental structuration—it will increasingly remain "awake" under all possible states. In the advanced waves of spiritual practice, the self will remain fully conscious in waking, dream, and deep sleep ("subject permanence"), and thus it will eventually recognize *that which remains the same under all possible changes of state*. In other words, it will recognize the changeless, the timeless, the spaceless—it will recognize, or re-cognize, its own Original Face, its own primordial nature, the ever-present Emptiness in which and through which all states arise, remain a bit, and pass. God-consciousness has become, not a changing state, but an enduring trait. Moreover, this is not merely a philosophical thought, but a direct and reproducible cognition. [See *One Taste* for further discussion of this theme.]

Thus, as sympathetic as I am with all of those philosophers, I cannot finally be counted among their ranks. What the postmodern West is struggling to evolve, I believe, is a postempirical, postidealist yoga. Since Kant, we have been forced to acknowledge, not that metaphysics is meaningless, but that metaphysics without direct experience is meaningless. And direct *transpersonal experience* relies on genuine transpersonal practices, paradigms, injunctions, and exemplars, which disclose the domains of post-postconventional experience that alone can ground a verifiable spiritual knowledge, thus fulfilling the Idealist promise precisely by transcending its limited agenda.

AN INTEGRAL THEORY OF CONSCIOUSNESS

The first step toward a genuine theory of consciousness, I believe, is the realization that consciousness is not located in the organism. Rather, consciousness is a four-quadrant affair, and it exists, if it exists at all, distributed across all four quadrants, anchored equally in each.[12]

There has recently been something of an explosion of interest in the development of a "science of consciousness." The major approaches in this recent surge of interest include the following:

1. *Cognitive science,* which tends to view consciousness as anchored in functional schemas of the brain/mind, either in a simple representational fashion (such as Jackendoff's "computational mind") or in the more complex emergent/connectionist models, which view consciousness as an emergent of hierarchically integrated networks. The emergent/connectionist is perhaps the dominant model of cognitive science at this point, and is nicely summarized in Alwyn Scott's *Stairway to the Mind,* the "stairway" being the hierarchy of emergents summating in consciousness.

2. *Introspectionism* maintains that consciousness is best understood in first-person accounts—the inspection and interpretation of immediate awareness and lived experience—and not in third-person or objectivist accounts, no matter how "scientific" they might appear. This includes introspective psychology, existentialism, phenomenology.

3. *Neuropsychology* views consciousness as anchored in neural systems, neurotransmitters, and organic brain mechanisms. Unlike cognitive science, which is often based on computer science and is consequently vague about how consciousness is actually related to organic brain structures, neuropsychology is a more biologically based approach. Anchored in neuroscience more than computer science, it views consciousness as intrinsically residing in organic neural systems of sufficient complexity.

4. *Individual psychotherapy* uses introspective and interpretive psychology to treat distressing symptoms and emotional problems; it thus tends to view consciousness as primarily anchored in an individual organism's adaptive capacities.

5. *Social psychology* views consciousness as embedded in networks of cultural meaning, or, alternatively, as being largely a byproduct of the social system itself. This includes approaches as varied as ecological, Marxist, constructivist, and cultural hermeneutic.

6. *Clinical psychiatry* focuses on the relation of psychopathology, behavioral patterns, and psychopharmacology; it increasingly views consciousness in neurophysiological terms: consciousness resides in the neuronal system.

7. *Developmental psychology* views consciousness not as a single entity but as a developmentally unfolding process with a substantially different architecture at each of its stages of growth.

In its more avant-garde forms, this approach includes higher stages of exceptional development and well-being, and the study of gifted, extraordinary, and supranormal capacities, viewed as higher developmental potentials latent in all humans. This includes higher stages of cognitive, affective, somatic, moral, and spiritual development.

8. *Psychosomatic medicine* views consciousness as strongly and intrinsically interactive with organic bodily processes, evidenced in such fields as psychoneuroimmunology and biofeedback. In its more avant-garde forms, this approach includes consciousness and miraculous healing, the effects of prayer on remarkable recoveries, light/sound and healing, spontaneous remission, and so on. It also includes any of the approaches that investigate the effects of intentionality on healing, from art therapy to visualization to psychotherapy and meditation.

9. *Nonordinary states of consciousness*, from dreams to psychedelics, constitute a field of study that, its advocates believe, is crucial to a grasp of consciousness in general. Although some of the effects of psychedelics—to take a controversial example—are undoubtedly due to "toxic side-effects," the consensus of opinion in this area of research is that they also act as a "nonspecific amplifier of experience," and thus they can be instrumental in disclosing and amplifying aspects of consciousness that might otherwise go unstudied.

10. *Eastern and contemplative traditions* maintain that ordinary consciousness is but a narrow and restricted version of deeper or higher modes of awareness, and that specific injunctions (yoga, meditation) are necessary to evoke these higher and exceptional potentials.

11. What might be called the *quantum consciousness* approaches view consciousness as being intrinsically capable of interacting with, and altering, the physical world, generally through quantum interactions, both in the human body at the intracellular level (e.g., microtubules), and in the material world at large (psi). This approach also includes the many and various attempts to plug consciousness into the physical world according to various avant-garde physical theories (bootstrapping, hyperspace, strings).

12. *Subtle energies* research has postulated, and in some cases apparently confirmed, that there exist subtler types of bioenergies

beyond the four recognized forces of physics (strong and weak nuclear, electromagnetic, gravitational), and that these subtler energies play an intrinsic role in consciousness and its activity. Known in the traditions by such terms as prana, ki, and chi—and held to be responsible for the effectiveness of acupuncture, to give only one example—these energies are often held to be the "missing link" between intentional mind and physical body. For the Great Chain theorists, both East and West, this bioenergy acts as a two-way conveyor belt, transferring the impact of matter to the mind and imposing the intentionality of the mind on matter.

13. *Evolutionary psychology* and its close relative sociobiology see behavior and consciousness in functional terms as expressions of evolutionary pressures. From this perspective, consciousness and its various forms arise because of, and are to be understood in terms of, the evolutionary advantage they confer.

You might guess that I will maintain that all of those approaches are equally important for an integral view of consciousness, and that is true enough. An "all-level, all-quadrant" approach finds important truths in each of them, and in very specific ways. But it is not simply that we have a given phenomenon called "consciousness" and that these various approaches are each giving us a different view of the beast. Rather, consciousness actually exists distributed across all four quadrants with all of their various levels and dimensions. There is no one quadrant (and certainly no one level) to which we can point and say, There is consciousness. Consciousness is in no way localized in that fashion, in my opinion.

It is true that the Upper-Left quadrant is the locus of consciousness as it appears in an individual, but that's the point: as it appears in an individual. Yet consciousness on the whole is anchored in, and distributed across, all of the quadrants—intentional, behavioral, cultural, and social. If you "erase" any quadrant, they all disappear, because each is intrinsically necessary for the existence of the others.

Thus, it is quite true that consciousness is anchored in the physical brain (as maintained by theories 1, 3, 6, 8). But consciousness is also and equally anchored in interior intentionality (as maintained by theories 2, 4, 7, 10, 11), an intentionality that cannot be explained in physicalist or empiricist terms nor disclosed by their methods.

By the same token, neither can consciousness be finally located in the individual (whether of the Upper Left or Upper Right or both together), because consciousness is also fully anchored in cultural meaning (the intersubjective chains of cultural signifieds), without which there is simply no individuated consciousness at all. Without this background of cultural practices and meanings, my individual intentions do not and cannot even develop, as the occasional cases of "wolf boy" demonstrate. In precisely the same way that there is no private language, there is no strictly individual consciousness. You cannot generate meaning in a vacuum, nor can you generate it with a physical brain alone, but only in an intersubjective circle of mutual recognition. Physical brains raised in the wild ("wolf boy") generate neither personal autonomy nor linguistic competence, from which it plainly follows, the physical brain per se is not the autonomous seat of consciousness.

Likewise, consciousness is also embedded in, and distributed across, the material social systems in which it finds itself. Not just chains of cultural signifieds, but chains of social signifiers, determine the specific contours of any particular manifestation of consciousness, and without the material conditions of the social system, both individuated consciousness and personal integrity fail to emerge.

(In short, if you take away any of those quadrants—intentional, behavioral, cultural, or social—you will destroy any manifest consciousness. And that means, very simply, that consciousness is located solely in none of those domains.) Consciousness is not located merely in the physical brain, nor in the physical organism, nor in the ecological system, nor in the cultural context, nor does it emerge from any of those domains. Rather, it is anchored in, and distributed across, all of those domains with all of their available levels.[13]

Thus, the methodologies that purport to give us a "theory of consciousness," but which investigate only one quadrant (not to mention only one level in one quadrant) are clearly not giving us an adequate account of consciousness at all. Rather, I believe that an "all-quadrant, all-level" approach holds the only chance of an authentic theory of consciousness, if such indeed exists.

HOLONIC ECOLOGY

Michael Zimmerman's essay, "A Transpersonal Diagnosis of the Ecological Crisis," is a thoughtful review of *Sex, Ecology, Spirituality*. As usual, I am in substantial and widespread agreement with much of Zimmerman's presentation, and I am glad to again have the opportunity to publicly express appreciation for the clarity, care, and brilliance he always brings to the task at hand. I cannot speak too highly of his expositions of Heidegger (*Eclipse of the Self* and *Heidegger's Confrontation with Modernity*), as well as his own *Contesting Earth's Future*.

Zimmerman's main point is that, whether one agrees with all the minor details in SES, it constitutes a genuinely transpersonal approach to ecophilosophy, an approach that simultaneously challenges most of the standard ecophilosophies (including deep ecology and ecofeminism). Zimmerman particularly focuses on one of the central tenets in SES—namely, that the biosphere is a part of the noosphere, and not vice versa—and points out that such a tenet strongly undercuts most ecophilosophies while simultaneously offering a genuinely transpersonal alternative (which SES refers to as *holonic ecology*).

Within that broad agreement, Zimmerman raises a handful of criticisms. He particularly believes that my treatment in SES of the actual schools of ecophilosophy is short and sometimes overgeneralized. This is true; but volume 2 is devoted to a full discussion, with all the appropriate differences and distinctions, of the major schools of this broad and varied movement (including the work of W. Fox, Naess, Swimme, Berry, Warren, Eckersley, Merchant, Spretnak, Bookchin, et al.). Zimmerman knows, from personal correspondence, that I have relied on his wonderful *Contesting Earth's Future* as a superb source, and that in many ways I am in substantial and widespread agreement with the important views he advances therein.

Zimmerman nonetheless maintains that my treatment of the ecophilosophers in SES is occasionally distorted and that I have not been fair to the deeper aspects of ecophilosophy. I disagree, and I think volume 2 will bear this out amply.

Zimmerman gives as an example of my alleged misrepresentation the work of Arne Naess, whose philosophy Zimmerman maintains is compatible with the great Nondual traditions of Mahayana Buddhism and Advaita Vedanta (which Naess also claims). But this "similarity" or "compatibility," I believe, is true in only the most superficial sense. In volume 2 I present an in-depth analysis of Naess's Ecosophy T, and find it lacking in many respects when compared with the great Nondual traditions. Even Naess himself, when attempting to present the similarities, fails to account for even the simplest and most crucial issues—for example, the notion of unity-in-multiplicity, a hallmark of Nondual realization. Naess fumbles in the worst of ways: "The widening and deepening of the individual selves *somehow* never makes them into one 'mass'. . . . How to work this out in a fairly precise way I do not know" (his italics).[14] I point out the same problems for representatives of each of the major ecophilosophies, and thus their "compatibility" with the Nondual traditions likewise is exposed as largely superficial. Not one of them, for example, even mentions "subject permanence," which the Nondual traditions recommend as an important prerequisite of nondual awareness (see chap. 10).

Thus, the generalizations I make in SES about ecofeminism, deep ecology, and the general ecophilosophies, far from being "distorted" or "lumped together," are based on a deep level of analysis which reveals that most of them are caught in flatland orientations, and the detailed analysis of volume 2 supports that conclusion. These are not wild generalizations, but the summary of a series of very specific and detailed analyses. (Holonic ecology is presented as an alternative that embraces the spirit of the ecological movements but in a more full-spectrum fashion.)

Zimmerman, in what seems to be a rare nod to political correctness for its own sake, implies that all "big pictures" command totalizing agendas that inherently marginalize social differences. Since SES is a big picture, couldn't it be marginalizing?

Some "totalizing" schemes are indeed marginalizing; others offer dramatically different incentives. My "big picture" explicitly does the following: it simply says, here are some areas of research and theory and evidence that perhaps you should look at. I am not trying to cram all differences into monological uniformitarianism. I thoroughly condemn that approach. Rather, my "big picture" is simply an explicit offer to take a larger view of things, a view that invites researchers to stop any marginalization that they might otherwise be involved with. It's open-ended; it is not a "foregone conclusion" nor a conceptual straightjacket.

There is nothing inherently alienating in open-ended big pictures. And, in fact, it is increasingly becoming obvious that those critics, such as Lyotard or Rorty, who rail against metanarratives and big pictures, do so only under severe performative contradictions. Ask them why big pictures are not desirable or even possible, and they will give you a very big picture of why big pictures don't work. This performative contradiction has been pointed out by theorists from Charles Taylor to Quentin Skinner to Gellner to Habermas. Karl-Otto Apel is simply the most recent theorist to point out that "Rorty himself confirms this structure by the validity claims raised by each one of his own verdicts against all universal validity claims of philosophy. He thus ends up with the novel rhetorical figure of constantly committing a *performative self-contradiction.*"[15]

Human beings, it seems, are bound to create big pictures of one sort or another. Therefore, choose your big pictures with care. I simply think an all-level, all-quadrant approach is one of the better alternatives.

SHAKING THE SPIRITUAL TREE

Robert McDermott, in his essay "The Need for Dialogue in the Wake of Ken Wilber's *Sex, Ecology, Spirituality*," raises the issue of whether polemical discourse is ever appropriate for academic and especially spiritual dialogue. He ends up rather strongly condemning polemic, his major point being that it isn't "spiritual." But I believe that this reflects an impoverished and narrow view of spirit—what it is, and where it is located.

McDermott asks if we would ever hear polemic from the great spiritual philosophers, such as Aurobindo or James or Plotinus. The answer, of course, is yes. In fact, the vast majority of spiritual philosophers have engaged at one time or another in intense polemical discourse—Plato, Hegel, Kierkegaard, Nietzsche, Fichte, Schopenhauer, Schelling, Augustine, Origen, Plotinus, to name a very few. They do so, I believe, precisely because they understand the difference between what Chögyam Trungpa Rinpoche called "compassion" and "idiot compassion." This is perhaps the hardest lesson to learn in politically correct America, where idiot compassion—the abdication of discriminating wisdom and the loss of the moral fiber to voice it—is too often equated with "spirituality."

I think, on the contrary, that we admire these spiritual philosophers because idiot compassion was foreign to them, because they all had the moral courage to speak out in the most acerbic of terms when necessary, to make the hard calls and make them loud and clear. People too often imagine that "choiceless awareness" means making no judgments at all. But that itself is a judging activity. Rather, "choiceless awareness" means that both judging and no judging are allowed to arise, appropriate to circumstances. I think this is why so many great spiritual philosophers engaged in such incredibly *intense* polemic, Plotinus being a quite typical example. Plotinus so aggressively attacked the astrologers that Dante felt it necessary to consign the entire lot of them to the eighth ring of hell, and Plotinus unrelentingly tore into the Gnostics as having "no right to even speak of the Divine."

I used to think that if somebody engaged in that type of forceful polemic, they couldn't be very enlightened. I see now it is exactly the opposite. We tend to believe genuine spirituality should avoid all that, whereas in fact it quite often engages it passionately as a manifestation of its capacity to judge depth (i.e., its capacity for discriminating wisdom). Plotinus's acerbic and occasionally sarcastic attack on the astrologers and gnostics is paradigmatic: they were a politically powerful and unpleasant lot, and it took courage to claim they had no right to even speak of the Divine. If McDermott is sincere about his pronouncements, then he would have been there to publicly condemn Plotinus, no doubt; but the point is that right or wrong Plotinus stood up to be counted, and it is a service to us that he did so in no uncertain terms. Moreover, Plotinus is not saying one thing in public and another in private; you know exactly where he stands.

The question is thus not whether these great spiritual philosophers engaged in polemic, for they did; the question is why. When such sages engage in intense polemic, I suppose we sometimes get nothing but their lingering neurosis; but we often get the full force of the overall judgment of their entire being, a shout from the heart in a sharp scream. It takes no effort at all to act out the former; it takes courage to stand up and voice the latter, and this is what I have come to admire in all the sages and philosophers I mentioned who have left us the full force of their summary judgments.

Contrary to McDermott's misplaced pronouncements, such polemic comes not from this, but from the other, side of equanimity. One Taste is the ground of intense judgments, not their abdication. These are not lunatics blathering prejudices; more like what the Tibetans would call the wrathful aspect of enlightened awareness.

McDermott tells us that he used to publicly and passionately voice his own judgments of qualitative distinctions and discriminating wisdom, but that he quit doing so in order to become a better administrator. I accept his choice. But I think it would be unfortunate for everybody in the spiritual field to adopt that same stance and abdicate the public voicing of their discriminating wisdom.[16]

There are many who see all too clearly the sad shape our field is in. They talk about it often in private. They tell me about it all the time. They are truly alarmed by the reactionary, prerational, and regressive fog thickly creeping over the entire field. Yet most of them are not willing to stand up and be counted, precisely because the countercultural police await, poised and ready to sanctimoniously damn them. A little less administrative juggling, and a little more discriminating wisdom backed with occasional polemic, is exactly what the entire field could use, in my opinion. I, at any rate, can no longer sit by and smile numbly as depth takes a vacation. And in a more honest process, where our public pronouncements actually match our private statements, we just might find that spiritual awareness includes, not excludes, the fiercest of judgments.

OMEGA POINT

A few reviewers assumed that I believed we were heading for an ultimate Omega point, a final point in manifest time where spirit realizes itself as spirit and we all go up in light. It is true that, in individuals, spirit can awaken as spirit ("spirit-as-spirit," traditional enlightenment). And it is true that this is in some important ways a *developmental* or *evolutionary* process. That is, certain developments clear the way for this timeless realization: both humans and rocks are equally spirit, but only humans can consciously realize that fact, and between the rock and the human lies evolution.

This is behind the Buddhist prayer of thanks "for this precious human body"—only in a human body can enlightenment be attained. Not gods, not animals, not demons, not angels: only with this human body can I awaken to the empty Ground that is equally present in all other sentient beings. This, too, is Aurobindo's and Murphy's emphasis on *The Future of the Body*, the precious human body. And that human body is, among many other things, the product of evolution.

And *that* means that Spirit has evolved the vehicle for its own self-realization. Because Spirit is involved with and as this world, this world evolves with and as Spirit, to the point that Spirit superconsciously realizes its own Original Face. The possibility of that realization is a product of Spirit's own evolutionary unfolding, and in that sense, this realization has a very strong developmental aspect.

But it is not the whole story. Evolution occurs in the world of time and space and form, whereas Spirit's primordial nature is finally timeless and Formless, prior to the world of evolution but not other to it. We do not find Spirit or Emptiness by reaching some evolutionary Omega point in time, but rather by stepping off the cycle of time and evolution altogether (or ceasing to contract into it).

In other words, a certain amount of evolution is required before you can step off of evolution, out of time, and into the timeless itself—into that shocking re-cognition of your own True Self, the Self that was prior to the Big Bang, prior to the temporal world altogether, eternally shining in this and every moment, untouched by the ravages of time and the motion sickness of space: your own primordial awareness is not the Omega point of the show but the Emptiness of the show, radiant in all directions, full beyond what time or space could ever do for it, yet embracing all time and all space for no other reason than that Eternity is in love with the productions of time and Infinity those of space.

Once you learn to count, you don't have to count to a million to get the point. Once you profoundly recognize Emptiness, you don't have to watch its endless displays in order to awaken. Emptiness is fully present at every point of evolution; it is not merely the end point of evolution. The game is undone in that primal Glance, and all that remains is the radiance itself, perfectly obvious in the singing of a robin, early on a bright spring dawn.

In the next chapter, we will follow the great Nondual traditions into this timeless, ever-present awareness, which is said to be nothing less than the actual location of Spirit itself.

12

Waves, Streams, States, and Self

A SUMMARY OF MY
PSYCHOLOGICAL MODEL
(OR, OUTLINE OF AN
INTEGRAL PSYCHOLOGY)

Abstract: Although far from unanimous, there seems to be a general consensus that neither mind nor brain can be reduced without remainder to the other. This essay argues that indeed both mind and brain need to be included in a nonreductionistic way in any genuinely integral theory of consciousness. In order to facilitate such integration, this essay presents the results of an extensive cross-cultural literature search on the "mind" side of the equation, suggesting that the mental phenomena that need to be considered in any integral theory include developmental levels or waves of consciousness, developmental lines or streams of consciousness, states of consciousness, and the self (or self-system). A "master template" of these various phenomena, culled from over one hundred psychological systems East and West, is presented. It is suggested that this master template represents a general summary of the "mind" side of the brain-mind integration. The essay concludes with reflections on the "hard problem," or how the mind-side can be integrated with the brain-side to generate a more integral theory of consciousness.

This essay also ends up being a fairly comprehensive sum-

mary of my own psychological model, or an outline of an integral psychology.

INTRODUCTION

T HE AMOUNT OF THEORY and research now being devoted to the study of consciousness is rather amazing, given its history of neglect in the previous decades. As encouraging as this research is, I believe that certain important items are still missing from the general discussion of the role and nature of consciousness. In this essay, I would therefore like to outline what I believe is a more integral model of consciousness, not to condemn the other approaches but to suggest ways in which their important contributions can be further enriched by a consideration of these neglected areas.

This is a follow-up to a previous essay ("An Integral Theory of Consciousness," Wilber, 1997).[1] Since this is also a summary of evidence and arguments developed elsewhere, I will rarely quote other authorities in this presentation; works of mine that I reference in this article do so extensively, and interested readers can follow up with those references. (I realize that failing to include the original references in this article—several thousand of them—is reader-unfriendly, but the added length would be prohibitive. I have compromised and added a few representative references in each of the fields.)

Much of today's research into consciousness focuses on those aspects that have some sort of obvious anchoring in the physical brain, including the fields of neurophysiology, biological psychiatry, and neuroscience. While there seems to be an uneasy consensus that consciousness (or the mind) cannot be fully reduced to physical systems (or the brain), there is as yet no widespread agreement as to their exact relation ("the hard problem"). This essay begins by attempting to provide a compendium of those aspects from the "mind" side of the equation that need to be brought to the integrative table.

Integral Psychology (Wilber, 2000b) compared and contrasted over one hundred developmental psychologists—West and East, ancient and modern—and from this comparison a "master template" was created of the full range of human consciousness, using each system to fill in any gaps left by the others. This master template, although a simple heuristic device and not a reading of the "way things are," suggests a "full-spectrum catalog" of the types and modes of consciousness available to men and women. This catalog might therefore prove useful as we seek a "brain-mind" theory that does justice to both sides of the equation—the brain and the mind—because what follows can reasonably be expected to cover much of the "mind" aspects that should be included, along with the "brain" aspects derived from neuroscience, in order to arrive at any sort of sturdy and comprehensive model of consciousness.

After outlining this "full-spectrum" catalog of mind, I will suggest my own model for fitting mind with brain, culture, and social systems. In other words, I will summarize one version of a more comprehensive or integral theory of consciousness, which combines the full-spectrum mind catalog (or master template) with current neuroscience, brain research, and cultural and social factors, all of which seem to play a crucial role in consciousness.

To begin with the full-spectrum catalog of mind states: The conclusion of the cross-cultural comparison presented in *Integral Psychology* is that there are at least five main components of human psychology that need to be included in any comprehensive theory: developmental *levels* of consciousness, developmental *lines* of consciousness, normal and altered *states* of consciousness, the *self* or self-system, and what I call the four *quadrants* (which include culture and worldviews, neurophysiology and cognitive science, and social systems). To take them in order.

Levels or Waves

Not all components of the psyche show development, but many of them do, and those developmental aspects or stages need to be taken into account. They are not the whole story of the psyche, but they are an important part. We live in an evolutionary universe, and those currents of evolution appear to operate in the human mind as well.

There is abundant evidence that some aspects of cognition, morals, psychosexuality, needs, object relations, motor skills, and language acquisition proceed in developmental stages, much as an acorn unfolds into an oak through a series of process phases (Alexander and Langer, 1990; Loevinger, 1976; Wilber, 2000b). These stages or levels of development are not the rigid, linear, rungs-in-a-ladder phenomenon portrayed by their critics, but rather appear to be fluid, flowing, overlapping waves (Beck and Cowan, 1996).

(I use all three terms—structures, levels, and waves—to describe these developmental milestones. "Structure" indicates that each stage has a holistic pattern that blends all of its elements into a structured whole. "Level" means that these patterns tend to unfold in a relational sequence, with each senior wave transcending but including its juniors (just as cells transcend but include molecules, which transcend but include atoms, which transcend but include quarks). And "wave" indicates that these levels nonetheless are fluid and flowing affairs; the senior dimensions do not sit on top of the junior dimensions like rungs in a ladder, but rather embrace and enfold them (just as cells embrace molecules, which embrace atoms). These developmental stages appear to be concentric spheres of increasing embrace, inclusion, and holistic capacity.)

In the human psyche, what exactly is the nature of these levels? Basically, they are *levels of consciousness*, which appear to span an entire spectrum from subconscious to self-conscious to superconscious (Murphy, 1992; Wade, 1996; Wilber et al., 1986; Wilber, 2000b).[2] This overall spectrum of consciousness is well known to the world's major wisdom traditions, where one version of it appears as the Great Chain of Being, which is said to range from matter to body to mind to soul to spirit (Smith, 1976). The "Great Chain" is perhaps a misnomer. It is not a linear chain but a series of enfolded spheres: it is said that spirit transcends but includes soul, which transcends but includes mind, which transcends but includes body, which transcends but includes matter. Accordingly, this is more accurately called the "Great Nest of Being." Some modern thinkers accept the existence of matter, body, and mind, but reject soul and spirit. They therefore prefer to think of the levels of consciousness as proceeding from, for example, preconventional to conventional to postconventional. My essential points can be made using any of these levels, but because we will also be discussing spiritual or "superconscious" states, let us for the moment simply assume that the overall spectrum of consciousness does indeed range from prepersonal to personal to transpersonal (Murphy, 1992; Walsh, 1999).[3]

Based on various types of cross-cultural evidence, many scholars have suggested that we can divide this overall spectrum of consciousness into seven colors or bands or waves (as with the seven chakras); others suggest around twelve (as with Aurobindo and Plotinus); some suggest even more (as in many of the well-known contemplative texts. See Wilber, 2000b, for over one hundred models of the levels of consciousness, taken from premodern, modern, and postmodern sources). In many ways this seems somewhat like a rainbow: we can legitimately divide and subdivide the colors of a rainbow in any number of ways.

I often use nine or ten *basic levels* or waves of consciousness (which are variations on the simple matter, body, mind, soul, spirit), since evidence suggests that these basic waves are largely universal or generally similar in deep features wherever they appear (e.g., the human mind, wherever it appears, has a capacity to form images, symbols, and concepts. The contents of those images and symbols vary from culture to culture, but the capacity itself appears to be universal [Arieti, 1967; Beck et al., 1996; Berry et al., 1992; Gardiner et al., 1998; Shaffer, 1994; Sroufe et al., 1992]). This general stance is well stated by Berry et al. (1992), summarizing the existing research: "*Cross-cultural Psychology* is a comprehensive overview of cross-cultural studies in a number of substantive areas—psychological development, social behavior, personality, cognition, and perception—and covers theory and applications to acculturation, ethnic and minority groups, work, communication, health, and national development. Cast within an ecological and cultural framework, it views the development and display of human behavior as the outcome of both ecological and sociopolitical influences, and it adopts a 'universalistic' position with respect to the range of similarities and differences in human behavior across cultures: basic psychological processes are assumed to be species-wide, shared human characteristics, but culture plays variations on these underlying similarities" (which will be investigated below as the "four quadrants").[4]

Nonetheless, all of these various codifications of the developmental levels appear to be simply different snapshots taken from various angles, using different cameras, of the great rainbow of consciousness, and they all seem useful in their own ways. They are simple categorizations provided by humans; but each of them, if carefully backed by evidence, can provide important ingredients of a more integral model.

That these levels, nests, or waves are arranged along a great rainbow or spectrum does not mean that a person actually moves through these waves in a merely linear or sequential fashion, clunking along from body, then to mind, then to soul, then to spirit. Those are simply some of the basic levels of consciousness that are potentially available. But an individual possesses many different capacities, intelligences, and functions, each of which can unfold through the developmental levels at a different rate—which brings us to the notion of various independent modules in the human psyche, which I also call lines or streams.

LINES OR STREAMS

Evidence suggests that through the developmental levels or *waves* of consciousness move various developmental lines or *streams* (such as

cognition, morals, affects, needs, sexuality, motivation, and self-identity)
[Gardner, 1983; Loevinger, 1976; Wilber, 2000b, 2002b]). It further
appears that, in any given person, some of these lines can be highly
developed, some poorly (or even pathologically) developed, and some
not developed at all. Overall development, in short, is a very uneven
affair!

The reason seems to be that the numerous developmental lines are to
some degree *independent modules*, and these modules can and do develop in relatively independent ways (but not totally independently).[5]
Each of these modules probably evolved in response to a series of specific
tasks (e.g., cognition of the external world, needs and desires in different
environments, linguistic communication, sexual release mechanisms,
and so on). There is an enormous amount of theory and research on
modularity (both pro and con), although it is generally accepted in the
psychological literature.[6]

According to this body of research, a person can be at a relatively
high level of development in some lines (such as cognition), medium in
others (such as morals), and low in still others (such as spirituality).
Thus, *there is nothing linear about overall development*. It is a wildly
individual and idiosyncratic affair (even though many of the developmental lines themselves unfold sequentially).

The most common criticism of my model is that it is linear, a view I
have not held for twenty years. But what about spirituality itself? Does
it necessarily unfold in stages? My answer, again, is absolutely not. But
before we see why, let's discuss states of consciousness.

STATES OF CONSCIOUSNESS

Several states of consciousness are quite familiar. For example, waking,
dreaming, and deep sleep. Those are some of the "normal" or "ordinary" states. Some of the "altered" or "nonordinary" states appear to
include peak experiences, religious experiences, drug states, holotropic
states, and meditative or contemplative states) (Goleman, 1988; Grof,
1998; Tart 1972). (Evidence strongly suggests that a person at virtually
any *stage* or level of development can have an altered *state* or peak
experience—including a spiritual experience) (Wilber, 1983, 2000b).
Thus, the idea that spiritual experiences are available only at the higher
stages of development is incorrect. States themselves rarely show development, and their occurrence is often random; yet they seem to be some
of the most profound experiences human beings ever encounter. Clearly,

those important aspects of spirituality that involve altered states do not follow any sort of linear, sequential, or stage-like unfolding.

What types of higher states are there? Considerable cross-cultural comparisons (Forman, 1990, 1998a; Murphy, 1992; Smart, 1984; Smith, 1976; Walsh, 1999; Wilber, 2000b), taken as a whole, suggests that there are at least four higher or transpersonal states of consciousness, which I call *psychic, subtle, causal,* and *nondual.* (As we will see in a moment, when these *temporary* states become *permanent* traits, these transitory states are converted into permanent structures of consciousness, and I call those permanent structures, levels, or waves by the same four names.)

Briefly, the psychic state is a type of *nature mysticism* (where individuals report a phenomenological experience of being one with the entire natural-sensory world; e.g., Thoreau, Whitman. It is called "psychic," not because paranormal events occur—although evidence suggests that they sometimes do—but because it seems to be increasingly understood that what appeared to be a merely physical world is actually a psychophysical world, with conscious, psychic, or noetic capacities being an intrinsic part of the fabric of the universe, and this often results in an actual phenomenological experience of oneness with the natural world [Fox, 1990]). The subtle state is a type of *deity mysticism* (where individuals report an experience of being one with the *source* or *ground* of the sensory-natural world; e.g. Saint Teresa of Ávila, Hildegard of Bingen). The causal state is a type of *formless mysticism* (where individuals experience cessation, or immersion in unmanifest, formless consciousness; e.g., *The Cloud of Unknowing*, Patanjali, pseudo-Dionysus; see Forman, 1990). And the nondual is a type of *integral mysticism* (which is experienced as the union of the manifest and the unmanifest, or the union of Form and Emptiness; e.g., Lady Tsogyal, Sri Ramana Maharshi, Hui Neng [Forman, 1998b]).

As I have suggested in *Integral Psychology* (Wilber, 2000b), these apparently are all variations on the natural states of waking, dreaming, and deep sleep—which seems to be why a person at virtually any stage of development can experience any of these nonordinary states (because everybody, even an infant, wakes, dreams, and sleeps). However, in order for these *temporary* states to become *permanent* traits or structures, they must enter the stream of development (see below). Of course, for most people, the dream and deep sleep states are experienced as being less real than the waking state; but with prolonged meditative practice, it is said that these states can be entered with full awareness and an expansion of consciousness, whereupon they yield their higher secrets (Deutsche, 1969; Gyatso, 1986; Walsh, 1999).

In many of the wisdom traditions, the three great normal *states* (of waking, dreaming, and deep sleep) are said to correspond to the three great *bodies* or *realms* of being (gross, subtle, and causal). In both Vedanta and Vajrayana, for example, the bodies are said to be the energy support of the corresponding mind or state of consciousness (i.e., every mental mode has a bodily mode, thus preserving a bodymind union at all levels). The gross body is the body in which we experience the waking state; the subtle body is the body in which we experience the dream state (and also certain meditative states, such as savikalpa samadhi, and the bardo state, or the dream-like state which is said to exist in between rebirths); and the causal body is the body in which we experience the deep dreamless state (and nirvikalpa samadhi and the formless state) (Deutsche, 1969; Gyatso, 1986).

The point is that, according to these traditions, each state of consciousness has a corresponding body that is "made" of various types of gross, subtle, and very subtle energy (or "wind"), and these bodies or energies "support" the corresponding mind or consciousness states. In a sense, we can speak of the gross bodymind, the subtle bodymind, and the causal bodymind (using "mind" in the very broadest sense as "awareness" or "consciousness").[7] The important point, which I will provisionally accept for this "master template," is simply that *each state of consciousness is supported by a corresponding body*, so that consciousness is never merely disembodied.[8]

THE RELATION OF STRUCTURES AND STATES

One way of looking at the evidence thus far is to say, as a heuristic device, that *states* of consciousness (with their correlative bodies or realms) contain various *structures* of consciousness. For example, the waking state can contain the preoperational structure, the concrete operational structure, the formal operational structure, and so on. In Vedanta, these structures or levels of consciousness are known as the koshas (or sheaths).

For Vedanta, the *three* major bodies/states support *five* major structures. The subtle body, experienced in the dream state (and the bardo realm, savikalpa samadhi, etc.), is said to support three major koshas or consciousness structures—the prana-maya-kosha (élan vital), the mano-maya-kosha (conventional mind), and the vijnana-maya-kosha (higher and illumined mind). The gross body/waking state supports the anna-maya-kosha (the sheath made of food, or the physical mind), and the causal body/formless state supports the ananda-maya-kosha (the sheath or consciousness structure made of bliss, or the transcendent mind).

Both Vedanta and Vajrayana maintain that, for example, each night when you dream (when you are in the subtle body), you have access to at least three major structures (you can experience sexual élan vital [prana-maya-kosha], mental images and symbols [mano-maya-kosha], and higher or archetypal mind [vijnana-maya-kosha]—i.e., the dream state can *contain* all three of those levels/structures), but you do not experience the gross body, the sensorimotor realm, or the gross physical world—those are not directly present. In the dream you are phenomenologically existing in a subtle body experiencing the (three) consciousness structures supported by that subtle body and contained in that state.

In short, any given broad *state* of consciousness (such as waking or dreaming) can contain several different *structures* (or levels) of consciousness. These structures, levels, or waves, as earlier suggested, span the entire spectrum and include many of those structure-stages that have been extensively studied by Western developmental psychologists, such as the structure-stages of moral, cognitive, and ego development (e.g., Cook-Greuter, 1990; Gilligan, 1990; Graves, 1970; Kegan, 1982; Kohlberg, 1981; Loevinger, 1976; Piaget, 1977; Wade, 1996). When, for example, Spiral Dynamics (a psychological model developed by Beck and Cowan [1996], based on the research of Clare Graves) speaks of the red meme, the blue meme, the orange meme, and so on, those are structures (levels) of consciousness.

Why are all these seemingly trivial distinctions important? One reason is that recognizing the difference between states of consciousness and structures of consciousness allows us to understand how a person at any structure or stage of development can nevertheless have a profound peak experience of higher and transpersonal states—for the simple reason that everybody wakes, dreams, and sleeps (and thus they have access to these higher states and realms of subtle and causal consciousness, no matter how "low" their general stage or level of development might be). However, the ways in which individuals *experience* and *interpret* these higher states and realms will depend largely on the level (or structure) of their own development. We will return to this important point in a moment.

PHENOMENAL STATES

Finally, and following this simple heuristic, within the major structures of consciousness there appear to be various *phenomenal states* (joy, happiness, sadness, desire, etc.). In short, one way of conceptualizing these events is to say that within broad states of consciousness there are structures of consciousness, within which there are phenomenal states.[9]

Notice that neither states of consciousness nor structures of consciousness are directly experienced by individuals.[10] Rather, individuals directly experience specific phenomenal states. Structures of consciousness, on the other hand, are *deduced* from watching the behavior of numerous subjects. The *rules* and *patterns* that are followed by various types of cognitive, linguistic, moral (etc.) behaviors are then abstracted. These rules, patterns, or structures appear to be very real, but they are not directly perceived by the subject (just as the rules of grammar are rarely perceived in an explicit form by native-language speakers, even though they are following them).

This is why structures of consciousness are almost never spotted by phenomenology, which inspects the present ongoing stream of consciousness and thus only finds phenomenal states. This appears to be a significant limitation of virtually all forms of phenomenology. That is, phenomenology usually focuses on phenomenal states and thus fails to spot the existence of structures of consciousness. Thus, if you introspect the phenomenal states of body and mind, you will never see something that announces itself as a "stage-4 moral thought" (Kohlberg); nor will you find something called "the conformist stage" (Loevinger); nor will you spot "the relativistic stage" (Graves). The only way you spot those *intersubjective structures* is to watch populations of subjects interact, and then look for regularities in behavior that suggest they are following intersubjective patterns, rules, or structures. This suggests that phenomenology is a useful, if limited, aspect of a more integral methodology.[11]

DEVELOPMENTAL ASPECTS OF SPIRITUALITY

It appears that all *structures* of consciousness generally unfold in a developmental or stage-like sequence, and, as virtually all developmentalists agree, *true stages cannot be skipped* (Combs, 1995; Cook-Greuter, 1990; Gilligan, 1990; Kegan, 1982; Loevinger, 1976; Wade, 1996). For example, in the cognitive line, there is sensorimotor, preoperational, concrete operational, formal operational, vision-logic, and so on. (Researchers are unanimous that none of those stages can be skipped, because each incorporates its predecessor in its own makeup (in the same way that cells contain molecules, which contain atoms, and you cannot go from atoms to cells and skip molecules).)

(No true stages in any developmental line can be skipped, nor can higher stages in that line be "peak-experienced." A person at preoperational cannot have a peak experience of formal operational. A person at Kohlberg's moral-stage 1 cannot have a peak experience of moral-stage 5. A person at Graves's animistic stage cannot have a peak experience of the integrated stage, and so on. (Not only are those stages in some ways learned behaviors, they are incorporative, cumulative, and enveloping, all of which preclude skipping.)

But the three great *states* (waking, dreaming, sleeping) represent *general realms* of being and knowing that can be accessed at virtually any stage in virtually any line—for the simple reason that individuals wake, dream, and sleep, even in the prenatal period (Wilber, 2000b, 2002b). Thus, gross, subtle, and causal *states* of consciousness are available at virtually any structure/stage of development.

However, the ways in which these altered states will (and can) be *experienced* depend predominantly on the *structures* (stages) of consciousness that have developed in the individual (Wilber, 1983, 2000b). As we will see, individuals at, for example, the magic, mythic, and rational stages can all have a peak experience of a subtle realm, but how that subtle realm is experienced and interpreted depends in large measure on the structures of consciousness that are available to unpack the experience.

(Technical point: the lower reaches of the subtle I call the "psychic"; and the union of causal emptiness with all form I call "nondual." This gives us the four major transpersonal states that I mentioned [psychic, subtle, causal, and nondual]; but they are all variations on the normal states available to virtually all individuals, which is why they are generally available at almost any stage of development. See *Integral Psychology* [Wilber, 2000b] for a full discussion of this theme.)

Evidence suggests that, under conditions generally of prolonged contemplative practice, a person can convert these *temporary* states into *permanent* traits or structures, which means that they have access to these great realms on a more or less *continuous* and *conscious* basis (Shankara, 1970; Aurobindo, 1990; Walsh, 1999). In the case of the subtle realm, for example, this means that a person will generally begin to lucid-dream (which is analogous to savikalpa samadhi, or stable meditation on subtle forms) (LaBerge, 1985); and with reference to the causal, when a person stably reaches that wave, he or she will remain tacitly conscious even during deep dreamless sleep (a condition known as permanent turiya, constant consciousness, subject permanence, or unbroken witnessing, which is analogous to nirvikalpa samadhi, or stable meditation as the formless) (Alexander and Langer, 1990). Pushing through even that level, the causal formless finds union with the entire world of form, a realization known as nondual (sahaja, turiyatita, bhava) (Alexander and Langer, 1990; Wilber, 1999a).

In each of those cases, those great realms (psychic, subtle, causal, nondual) are no longer experienced merely as *states*, but have instead become permanently available patterns or structures of consciousness—which is why, when they become a permanent competence, I then call them the psychic level (or structure or wave), the subtle level, the causal level, and the nondual. The use of those four terms (psychic, subtle, causal, and nondual) to cover *both* structures and states has led some critics to assume that I was confusing structures and states, but this is not the case.[12]

The important question then becomes: do those four *states*, as they become permanent *structures*, show stage-like unfolding? Are they then actually *levels* of consciousness? In many ways, the answer appears to be yes (again, not as rigid rungs but as fluid and flowing waves). For example, a person who reaches *stable* (permanent) causal witnessing will automatically experience lucid dreaming (because stable causal witnessing means that one witnesses *everything* that arises, which includes the subtle and dream states), but not vice versa (i.e., somebody who reaches stable subtle awareness does not necessarily reach pure causal witnessing)—in other words, this is a stage sequence (i.e., the causal is a higher level than the subtle—e.g., the ananda-maya-kosha is a higher level than the vijnana-maya-kosha, or the overmind is a higher level than the intuitive mind, and so on—exactly as maintained by the great wisdom traditions [Smith, 1976; Walsh 1999]).

This is why Aurobindo says, of these higher, transpersonal levels/ structures: "The spiritual evolution obeys the logic of a successive unfolding; it can take a new decisive main step only when the previous main step has been sufficiently conquered: even if certain minor stages can be swallowed up or leaped over by a rapid and brusque ascension, the consciousness has to turn back to assure itself that the ground passed over is securely annexed to the new condition; a greater or concentrated speed [which is indeed possible] does not eliminate the steps themselves or the necessity of their successive surmounting" (Aurobindo, 1990, II, 26). His overall writing makes it clear that he does not mean that in a rigid ladder fashion, but more as was suggested: a series of subtler and subtler waves of consciousness unfolding, with much fluid and flowing overlap, and the possibility of nonlinear altered states always available. But for those states to become structures, "they obey the logic of a successive unfolding," as all true stages do. The world's contemplative literature, taken as a whole, is quite clear on these points, and in this regard we justifiably speak of these transpersonal structures as showing some stage-like and level-like characteristics.[13]

Again, that is *not* the entire story of spirituality. In a moment I will suggest that spirituality is commonly given at least four different definitions (the highest levels of any of the lines, a separate line, an altered state, a particular attitude), and a comprehensive or integral theory of spirituality ought charitably to include all four of them. Thus, the developmental aspects we just discussed do not cover the entire story of spirituality, although they appear to be an important part of it.

To give a specific example: If we focus on the cognitive line of development, we would have these general levels or waves in the overall spectrum of cognition: sensorimotor, preoperational, concrete operational, formal operational, vision-logic, psychic, subtle, causal, and nondual. Those nine general *levels* or *structures* Aurobindo respectively calls sensory/vital, lower mind, concrete mind, logical mind, higher mind, illumined mind, intuitive mind, overmind, and supermind, stretching along a single rainbow from the densest to the finest to the ground of them all.

The respective *worldviews* of those nine general structures of consciousness can be described as: archaic, magic, mythic, rational, aperspectival, psychic (yogic), subtle (saintly), causal (sagely), and nondual (siddha) (Adi Da, 1977; Gebser, 1985; Wilber 1996a, 1996b, 2000b, 2002b).

Those are *levels* of consciousness or *structures* (stages), during whose *permanent* unfolding, no stages can be readily skipped; but at virtually *any* of those stages, a person can have a peak experience of psychic, subtle, casual, or nondual *states*. Overall or *integral development* is thus a continuous process of converting temporary states into permanent traits or structures, and in that integral development, no structures or levels can be bypassed, or the development is not, by definition, integral.

UNEVEN DEVELOPMENT

This does not prevent all sorts of spirals, regressions, temporary leaps forward via peak experiences, and so-on. Notice, for example, that somebody at the psychic *level* can peak experience the causal *state*, but cannot stably access that realm because their *permanent* development has not yet reached the causal as a stage (or a permanent acquisition or structure). In order for that to happen, they must traverse the subtle realm (converting it into an objective stage) before they can *stably* maintain the witnessing position of the causal (turiya), because the permanent witness is, by definition, continuously aware of all that arises, and that means that if the subtle arises, it is witnessed—which means the subtle has become a permanently available pattern or structure in consciousness. Thus, stages in integral development, as elsewhere, cannot be skipped (they do not have to be perfected or mastered to the nth degree, but they do have to be established as a general competence. Somebody who cannot witness the subtle state cannot, by definition, be the causal witness—hence, the stage-like nature of these higher structures as they become *permanent* acquisitions.) See Addendum A.

(Still, what usually happens is that because these three great realms and states (waking/gross, dream/subtle, and formless/causal) are constantly available to human beings, and because as *states* they can be practiced to some degree independently of each other (and might even develop independently to some degree [Wilber, 2000b]), many individuals can and do evidence a great deal of competence in some of these states/realms (such as meditative formlessness in the causal realm), yet are poorly or even pathologically developed in others (such as the frontal or gross personality, interpersonal development, psychosexual development, moral development, and so on). The "stone Buddha" phenomenon—where a person can stay in extraordinary states of formless absorption for extended periods—and yet be poorly developed, or even pathologically developed, in other lines and realms, is an extremely common phenomenon, and it happens largely because integral development has not been engaged, let alone completed. Likewise, many spiritual teachers show a good deal of proficiency in subtle states, but little in causal or gross, with quite unbalanced results—for them and their followers.

In short, what usually happens is that development is partial or fractured, and this fractured development is taken as the paradigm of natural and normal spiritual development, and then students and teachers alike are asked to repeat the fracture as evidence of their spiritual progress.

The fact that these three great realms/states can be engaged separately; the fact that many contemporary writers equate spirituality predominantly with altered and nonordinary states (which is often called without irony the fourth wave of transpersonal theory); the fact that lines in general can develop unevenly (so that a person can be at a high level of development in some lines and low or pathological in others)—and that this happens more often than not—have all conspired to obscure those important aspects of spiritual development that do indeed show some stage-like phenomena. My point is that *all* of these aspects of spirituality (four of which I mentioned and will elucidate below) need to be acknowledged and included in any comprehensive theory of spirituality—and in any genuinely integral spiritual practice.[14]

A Grid of Religious Experiences

(If we combine the idea of *levels* of development with *states* of consciousness, and we realize that a person at virtually any level or stage of development can have a peak experience or an altered state, we get a rather remarkable grid of many of the various types of spiritual and nonordinary experiences.)

(For example, let us use Jean Gebser's (1985) terms for some of the lower-to-intermediate levels of consciousness: archaic, magic, mythic, rational, and aperspectival (there are higher, transpersonal structures, as we have seen, but these will do for now).[15] To those five levels, let us add the four states of psychic, subtle, causal, and nondual. The point is that a person at any of those five structures can peak-experience any of those four states, and that gives us a grid of twenty types of spiritual, transpersonal, or nonordinary experiences (Wilber, 1983, 2000b).)

As suggested earlier, the reason this grid occurs is that the way in which individuals *interpret* an altered state depends in part upon their general level of development. For example, individuals at the mythic level might peak-experience a psychic state, but they generally interpret that psychic peak experience in the terms of their mythic structure. Likewise, there is a magic experience of a subtle state, a mythic experience of a subtle state, a rational experience of a subtle state; and so on with causal and nondual.[16] Putting these altogether gives us a phenomenological grid of the many types of altered, nonordinary, and religious experiences available to men and women. For more details on this grid, see *A Sociable God* and *Integral Psychology*.[17]

THE SELF

So far we have explored states, waves, and streams. We might look now at the "self" (or self-system or self-sense), and although there are many ways to depict it, one of the most useful is to view the self as that which attempts to integrate or balance all of the components of the psyche (i.e., the self attempts to integrate the various states, waves, and streams that are present in the individual) (Wilber et al., 1986; Wilber 1996c, 2000b, 2002b).

A striking item about the levels, lines, and states is that in themselves they appear to be devoid of an inherent self-sense, and therefore the self can *identify* with any of them (as suggested by ancient theorists from Plotinus to Buddha). That is, one of the primary characteristics of the self seems to be its capacity to *identify* with the basic structures or levels of consciousness, and every time it does so, according to this view, it generates a specific type of self-identity, with specific needs and drives. The self thus appears to be a functional system (which includes such capacities as identification, will, defense, and tension regulation [Wilber et al., 1986]), and it also undergoes its own type of development through a series of stages or waves (as investigated by, e.g., Loevinger, 1976; Kegan, 1982; Cook-Greuter, 1990). The main difference between the self-stages and the other stages is that the self has the job of balancing and coordinating all of them.

This balancing act, this drive to integrate the various components of the psyche, appears to be a crucial feature of the self. Psychopathology, for example, cannot easily be understood without it (Blanck and Blanck, 1974, 1979; Kohut, 1971, 1977). The basic structures of consciousness do not themselves get sick or "broken." They either emerge or they don't, and when they do, they are generally well functioning (barring organic brain damage). For example, when concrete operational thinking (conop) emerges in a child, it emerges more or less intact—but what the child does with those structures is something else indeed, and that specifically involves the child's self-sense. For the child can take any of the contents of the conop mind and repress them, alienate them, project them, retroflect them, or deploy any number of other defensive mechanisms (Vaillant, 1993). This a disease, not of conop, but of the self.

(Here is a more extreme example: a psychotic might be, among other things, temporarily plugging into a subtle realm and hence begin dream-like hallucinations. The subtle realm is not malfunctioning, it is working just fine; but the self cannot *integrate* these realms with the gross/frontal structures, and therefore it suffers a severe pathology. The pathology is not in the subtle, it is in the self-system and its failed capacity to integrate.)

Most psychopathology (on the interior domains) seems to involve some sort of failure in the self's capacity of differentiation and integration—a failure that occurs during what can be called a *fulcrum* of self-development (Blanck and Blanck, 1974, 1979; Kegan, 1982; Wilber et al., 1986; Wilber, 2000b).[18] A fulcrum occurs each time the self encounters a new level of consciousness. The self must first *identify* with that new level (embed at that level, be in fusion with that level); it eventually *disidentifies* with (or transcends) that level so as to move to a yet higher wave; then it ideally *integrates* the previous wave with the higher wave.

A miscarriage at any of those points in the particular fulcrum (failed identification, failed differentiation, failed integration) will generate a pathology; and the type of the pathology depends upon *both* the level of consciousness that the fulcrum occurs and the phase within the fulcrum that the miscarriage occurs (Wilber et al., 1986). If we have nine general levels or waves of consciousness (each of which has a corresponding fulcrum that occurs when the self identifies with that level), and each fulcrum has these three basic subphases (fusion, transcendence, integration), then that gives us a typology of around twenty-seven major self pathologies (which range from psychotic to borderline to neurotic to existential to transpersonal). Far from being a mere abstract typology, there are abundant examples of each of these types (Rowan, 1998; Walsh and Vaughan, 1993; Wilber et al., 1986; Wilber, 2000b).[19]

Again, none of this is a rigid, linear type of classification. The various waves and fulcrums overlap to a great extent; different pathologies and treatment modalities also overlap considerably; and the scheme itself is a simple generalization. But it does go a long way toward developing a more comprehensive overview of both pathology and treatment, and as such it seems to constitute an important part of any genuinely integral psychology.

The fluid nature of all of these events highlights the fact that the self-system is perhaps best thought of, not as a monolithic entity, but as the *center of gravity* of the various levels, lines, and states, all orbiting around the integrating tendency of the self-system (Wilber, 2000b,

2002b). When any aspects of the psyche become cut off from this self-organizing activity, they (as it were) reach escape velocity and spin out of orbit, becoming dissociated, fragmented, alienated pockets of the psyche. Therapy, on the interior domains, thus generally involves a re-contacting, befriending, reintegrating, and "reentry" of the dissociated elements back into the orbit of conscious inclusion and embrace.

FOUR MEANINGS OF "SPIRITUAL"

If we focus for a moment on states, levels, lines, and self, we will find that they appear to underlie four of the most common definitions of "spirituality."

In *Integral Psychology*, I suggest that there are at least four widely used definitions of spirituality, each of which contains an important but partial truth, and all of which need to be included in any balanced account: (1) spirituality involves peak experiences or altered states, which can occur at almost any stage and any age; (2) spirituality involves the highest levels in any of the lines; (3) spirituality is a separate developmental line itself; (4) spirituality is an attitude (such as openness, trust, or love) that the self may or may not have at any stage.[20]

We have already discussed some of the important ingredients of those usages. We have particularly examined the idea of spirituality as involving peak experiences or altered states (#1). Here is a quick review of the other three.

Often, when people refer to something as "spiritual," they explicitly or implicitly mean the highest levels in any of the developmental lines. For example, in the cognitive line, we usually think of transrational awareness as spiritual, but we don't often think of mere rationality or logic as spiritual. In other words, the highest levels of cognition are often viewed as spiritual, but the low and medium levels less so. Likewise with affects or emotions: the higher or transpersonal affects, such as love and compassion, are usually deemed spiritual, but the lower affects, such as hate and anger, are not. Likewise with Maslow's needs hierarchy: the lower needs, such as self-protection, are not often thought of as spiritual, but the highest needs, such as self-transcendence, are.

This is a legitimate usage, in my opinion, because it reflects some of the significant developmental aspects of spirituality (namely, the more evolved a person is in any given line, the more that line seems to take on spiritual qualities). This is not the only aspect of spirituality—we have already seen that states are very important, and we will see two other aspects below—but it is a factor that needs to be considered in any comprehensive or integral account of spirituality.

(The third common usage sees spirituality as a separate developmental line itself. James Fowler's stages of faith is a well-known and well-respected example (Fowler, 1981). The world's contemplative literature is full of meticulously described stages of contemplative development (again, not as a series of rigid rungs in a ladder but as flowing waves of subtler and subtler meditative experiences, often culminating in causal formlessness, and then the breakthrough into permanent nondual consciousness [Brown, 1977; Goleman, 1988]). In this very common usage, the spiritual line begins in infancy (or even before, in the bardo and prenatal states), and eventually unfolds into wider and deeper spheres of consciousness until the great liberation of enlightenment. This is yet another important view of spirituality that any comprehensive or integral theory might want to take into account.)

Viewing spirituality as a relatively independent line also explains the commonly acknowledged fact that somebody might be highly developed in the spiritual line and yet poorly—or even pathologically—developed in other lines, such as interpersonal or psychosexual, often with unfortunate results.[21]

(The fourth usage is that spirituality is essentially an attitude or trait that the self may or may not possess at any stage of growth, and this attitude—perhaps loving-kindness, inner peace, charity, or goodness—is what most marks spirituality. In this usage, you could have, for example, a spiritual or unspiritual magic wave, a spiritual or unspiritual mythic wave, a spiritual or unspiritual rational wave, and so on, depending on whether the self had integrated that wave in a healthy or unhealthy fashion. This, too, is a common and important usage, and any integral account of spirituality would surely want to take it into consideration.)[22]

Two general claims: One, those four major definitions are indeed common definitions of "spirituality." They are not the only uses, but they are some of the most prevalent. And two, those four common uses arise because of the actual existence of states, levels, lines, and self, respectively. People seem to intuitively or natively grasp the existence of states, levels, lines, and self, and thus when it comes to spirituality, they often translate their spiritual intuitions in terms of those available dimensions, which gives rise to those oft-used definitions.

(Those definitions of spirituality are not mutually incompatible. They actually fit together in something of seamless whole, as I try to suggest in *Integral Psychology*. We can already see, for example, that any model that coherently includes states, levels, lines, and self can automatically give a general account of those four aspects of spirituality. But in order to see how this would specifically work, we need one more item: the four quadrants. (The four quadrants are not to be confused with the four uses of spirituality; the number four in this case is coincidental.) But the four quadrants are crucial, I believe, in seeing how the many uses of spirituality can in fact be brought together into a more mutual accord.)

QUADRANTS

Most people find the four quadrants a little difficult to grasp at first, then very simple to use. The quadrants refer to the fact that anything can be looked at from four perspectives, so to speak: we can look at something from the inside or from the outside, and in the singular or the plural. For example, my own consciousness in this moment. I can look at it from the inside, in which case I see all my various feelings, hopes, fears, sensations, and perceptions that I might have in any given moment. This is the first-person or phenomenal view, described in "I" language. But consciousness can also be looked at in an objective, "scientific" fashion, in which case I might conclude that my consciousness is the product of objective brain mechanisms and neurophysiological systems. This is the third-person or objective view, described in "it" language. Those are the inside and the outside views of my own consciousness.

But my consciousness or self does not exist in a vacuum; it exists in a community of other selves. So in addition to a *singular* view of consciousness, we can look at how consciousness exists in the *plural* (as part of a group, a community, a collective). And just as we can look at the inside and the outside of the individual, we can look at the inside and the outside of the collective. We can try to understand any group of people from the inside, in a sympathetic resonance of mutual understanding; or we can try to look at them from the outside, in a detached and objective manner (both views can be useful, as long as we honor each).

On the inside of the collective, we see all of the various shared worldviews (archaic, magic, mythic, rational, etc.), ethics, customs, values, and intersubjective structures held in common by those in the collective (whether that be family, peers, corporation, organization, tribe, town, nation, globe). The insides of the collective are described in "we" language and include all of those intersubjective items that you might experience if you were truly a member of that culture. From the outside, we see all of the objective structures and social institutions of the collective, such as the physical buildings, the infrastructures, the techno-economic base (foraging, horticultural, agrarian, industrial, informational), the quantitative aspects of the society (the birth and death rates, the monetary exchanges, the objective data), modes of communication (written words, telegraph, telephone, internet), and so on. Those are all "its" or patterns of interobjective social systems.

So we have four major perspectives (the inside and the outside of the singular and the plural): I, it, we, and its. Since the objective dimensions (the outside of the individual and the outside of the collective) are both described in third-person it-language, we can reduce the four quadrants to just three: I, we, and it. Or first-person, second-person, and third-person accounts.[23] Or art, morals, and science. Or the beautiful, the good, and the true.

The major point is that each of the levels, lines, and states of consciousness has these four quadrants (or simply the three major dimensions of I, we, and it) (Wilber, 1996d, 2000b, 2000c, 2002b).[24] This model therefore explicitly integrates first-, second-, and third-person accounts of consciousness at each of the levels, lines, and states. This gives what I believe is a more comprehensive and integral model of consciousness. This "all-quadrants, all-levels, all-lines, all-states" model is sometimes referred to simply as "all-quadrant, all-level," or AQAL for short. I have explored this model at length in several books, such as *Sex, Ecology, Spirituality*; *A Brief History of Everything*; and *Integral Psychology*. If we systematically investigate the implications of this AQAL model, we might also find that it opens up the possibility of a more integral approach to education, politics, business, art, feminism, ecology, and so on (see, e.g., Crittenden, forthcoming; Wilber, 2000d).

It should be emphasized that this article has dealt almost exclusively with only one quadrant, namely, the interior of the individual (which is called the "Upper-Left quadrant"). But in other works I have dealt extensively with the other quadrants, and my point is certainly that all of the quadrants need to be included in any balanced account of consciousness. We will return to the quadrants below, and suggest how an AQAL formulation can contribute to a solution to the "hard problem."

THE RELIGIOUS GRID, REVISITED

To see why the four quadrants are important for understanding even individual psychology, we can return to our "religious grid" as an example. We earlier discussed only the Upper-Left quadrant factors (the interior of the individual), which is fine for the phenomenology of spiritual experiences. But for an integral account, we need also to include the other quadrants.

The Upper-Right quadrant (the exterior of the individual): During any spiritual, religious, or nonordinary state of consciousness, what are the neurophysiological and brain-state correlates? These might be investigated by PET scans, EEG patterns, physiological markers, and so on. Conversely, what are the effects of various types of physiological and pharmacological agents on consciousness? An enormous amount of this type of research has already been done, of course, and it continues at an increasing pace. Consciousness is clearly linked in complex ways to objective biological and neurophysiological systems, and continued research on these correlations is surely an important agenda. This type of consciousness research—anchored in the brain side of the brain-mind connection—is now one of the most prevalent in conventional consciousness studies, and I wholeheartedly support it as providing some crucial pieces of the overall puzzle.

Nobody, however, has successfully demonstrated that consciousness can be reduced without remainder to those objective systems; and it is patently obvious that phenomenologically it cannot. Unfortunately, the tendency of the third-person approaches to consciousness is to try to make the Upper-Right quadrant the only quadrant worth considering and thus reduce all consciousness to objective "its" in the individual body/brain—but those cover only one-fourth of the story, so to speak.

Still, this is an incredibly important part of the story. This quadrant, in fact, is the home of the increasingly dominant schools of psychology and consciousness studies that I mentioned in the introduction (cognitive science, evolutionary psychology, systems theory applied to brain states, neuroscience, biological psychiatry, etc.). This quadrant provides the "brain" side of the equation that needs to be correlated with the "mind" side (represented by, for example, the master template or full-spectrum cartography of waves, streams, and states summarized in this article).[25] And my further point is that those are just two of the quadrants that need to be brought to the integral table.

The Lower-Left quadrant (the interior of the collective): How do different intersubjective, ethical, linguistic, and cultural contexts mold consciousness and altered states? The postmodernists and constructivists have demonstrated,—correctly, I believe—the crucial role played by background cultural and intersubjective contexts in fashioning individual consciousness (Wilber, 1998, 2000c). But many postmodernists have pushed this insight to absurd extremes, maintaining the self-contradictory stance that cultural contexts *create* all states. Instead of trying to reduce consciousness to "it"-language, they try to reduce all consciousness to "we"-language. All realities, including those of objective science, are said to be merely cultural constructions. To the contrary, research clearly indicates that there are numerous quasi-universal aspects to many human realities, including many altered states (e.g., all healthy humans show similar brainwave patterns in REM sleep and in deep dreamless sleep). Nonetheless, these patterns are indeed given some of their contents and are significantly molded by the cultural context, which therefore forms an important part of a more integral analysis (Wilber, 1998, 2000b, 2000c, 2002a). (For the nature of intersubjectivity itself, and the reasons that it cannot be reduced to the exchange of linguistic signifiers, see note 23.)

Lower-Right quadrant (the exterior of the collective): How do various techno-economic modes, institutions, economic circumstances, ecological networks, and social systems affect consciousness and altered states? The profoundly important influence of objective social systems on consciousness has been investigated by a wide variety of approaches, including ecology, geopolitics, ecofeminism, neo-Marxism, dynamical systems theory, and chaos and complexity theories (e.g., Capra, 1997; Diamond, 1990; Lenski, 1995). All of them tend to see the world ultimately as a holistic system of interwoven "its." This, too, is an important part of an integral model. Unfortunately, many of these theorists (just like specialists in the other quadrants) have attempted to reduce consciousness to just this quadrant—to reduce consciousness to digital bits in a systems network, a strand in the objective Web of Life, or a holistic pattern of flatland "its," thus perfectly gutting the I and the we dimensions. Surely a more integral approach would include all of the quadrants—I, we, it, and its—without trying to reduce any of them merely to the others.[26]

Of course, the foregoing analysis applies not only to states but also to levels, lines, and self: all of them need to be situated in the four quadrants (intentional, behavioral, cultural, and social) for a more integral understanding, resulting in an "all-quadrants, all-levels, all-lines, all-states" panoptic.)

A RESEARCH SUGGESTION

I have tried to suggest that many of the levels, lines, and states in the various quadrants are, in principle, capable of being investigated via a type of "simultracking" (Wilber, "An Integral Theory of Consciousness," in CW7). The specific research agenda is spelled out in that essay, but the point is simple enough: in addition to the extensive research that is now being done *separately* on the various levels, lines, and states in the various quadrants, the time is now ripe to (1) begin detailed correlations of these events with each other; and thus (2) move toward a more integral theory, not only of consciousness, but of the Kosmos at large; a theory that (3) would begin to show us the how and why of the *intrinsic* connections between all things in existence.[27] This would truly be a "theory of everything," at least in outline, even if all of the details remain beyond our grasp.

In short, whether or not one agrees with my particular version of an integral model of consciousness, I believe the evidence is now quite substantial that any comprehensive model would want to at least consider taking into account quadrants, waves, streams, states, and self. This fledgling field of integral studies holds great promise, I believe, as an important part of a comprehensive and balanced view of consciousness and Kosmos.

ADDENDUM A: STAGES OF SPIRITUAL UNFOLDING?

This chapter has suggested that there are at least four different, commonly used definitions of "spirituality" (i.e., spirituality involves altered states, the highest levels in any of the lines, a separate line itself, a quality of the self at any given level), and that each of them appears to reflect an important phenomenon in consciousness (i.e., states, levels, lines, and self). In recent years there has been an intense, sometimes acrimonious debate about whether or not spirituality involves stages, some claiming that it definitely does, others responding that it definitely does not, with each side often adding ad hominen explanations of the other side's motives.)

(A more integral view of spirituality recognizes that both sides are correct. Some aspects of spirituality clearly show stages, and some aspects do not. In the four aspects listed above, the first and the last do not involve stages. The second and the third do.)

We can examine a few of these developmental aspects of spirituality by using Robert Forman's excellent article, "What Does Mysticism Have to Teach Us about Consciousness?" (1998b). (Forman begins by highlighting three particularly important and apparently universal types of mystical consciousness, which he calls the "pure consciousness event" (PCE), which is a state of formless consciousness with no thoughts, objects, or perceptions; the "dual mystical state" (DMS), where formless consciousness is present (usually as a type of witnessing awareness) simultaneously with forms and objects of thought and perception (but the subject-object duality is still in place, hence "dualistic" mystical state); and the "unitive mystical state" (UMS), where subject and object are one or nondual.)

In my scheme, the PCE is a causal (formless) *state* of consciousness; since, as Forman points out, it is always a temporary state, it cannot become a permanent structure (if it did, it would become a type of irreversible nirodh, or permanent formless cessation). The DMS, on the other hand, generally begins as a *state* of consciousness but can increasingly become a more or less permanent *structure* of causal witnessing (i.e., the causal state has become a causal structure). Likewise, the UMS often begins as a temporary nondual *state* but also increasingly can become a permanent nondual structure or wave. I agree entirely with Forman that those are three very real and quasi-universal mystical events; I am also in substantial agreement with his conclusions about what these events mean for consciousness studies, which is why they are part of the "full-spectrum cartography" or "master template" presented in *Integral Psychology* (and summarized above).

(Forman points out—correctly, I believe—that these three events are often temporary (in which case they are what I call *states*), but the last two can become more or less permanent acquisitions (in which case I call them *structures*, even if some of them are "formless" or "structureless"; structure or level or wave simply signifies constancy).) As Forman says, "Their discriminating feature is a deep shift in epistemological structure: the experienced relationship between the self and one's perceptual objects changes profoundly. In many people this new structure becomes permanent" (186).

The question then becomes, do these three events unfold in a stage-like sequence? Forman cautiously replies, "Usually." "These long-term shifts in epistemological structure often take the form of two quantum leaps in experience [namely, the shift from PCE to DMS, and then from DMS to UMS]; typically they develop sequentially" (186). Forman then adds, "I say typically because sometimes one may skip or not attain a particular stage. Ken Wilber claims sequence. William Barnard, however, disputes this claim of sequence" (186). After several mutually fruitful discussions on this topic, Forman realizes that my position is actually more complex. As we have seen, there are temporary peak experiences of higher realms available at virtually every stage, and thus, for example, even if one is permanently at the DMS, one can still temporarily peak-experience the UMS. This makes it very hard to spot any sort of sequentiality, because structure-stages (which are sequential) and states (which are not) can and do exist simultaneously. Thus, for these higher events, I maintain that there are both sequential and nonsequential spiritual phenomena (of the four aspects of spirituality outlined above, aspects #1 and #4 are not stage-like, aspects #2 and #3 are), and those who claim only one or the other do not appear to have a very integral model.

My further claim is simply this: in the *permanent* acquisition of these higher competences, certain prerequisites must be met. For example, using Forman's useful categories, in order for the DMS state to be a permanent acquisition, one must have some sort of access to the PCE, because the DMS is a combination of the experience of pure consciousness alongside waking objects and thoughts. Of necessity, there is some sort of stage sequencing, however brief (i.e., one can attain PCE without attaining DMS, but not vice versa). Likewise with the UMS, in which the final barrier between pure causal consciousness and the world of form is transcended (either temporarily as a nondual state or permanently as a nondual wave). In order for that to happen, consciousness must relinquish all attachments to any particular objects, while the objects are still present (i.e., DMS), or else the hidden attachment will prevent true unity. Thus, the DMS must be passed through, however briefly, in order for a permanent acquisition of constant unitive consciousness. That is, one can attain the DMS without attaining UMS, but not vice versa: we therefore have a stage sequence with reference to permanent acquisition.

(For further discussion of these themes, see *Integral Psychology*; also, with reference to the Vedantic/TM model of the seven states of consciousness, which Forman's work is partially inspired by, see chapter 10 above, "The Effects of Meditation.")

One final comment about the UMS (unitive mystical state) and nature mysticism. These two items are often confused, but they are actually quite distinct. Here, from *Integral Psychology*, is an endnote dealing with this topic (note 14 for chap. 7), using James Mark Baldwin's notion of "unity consciousness" as a beginning point:

> Baldwin's "unity consciousness" is a gross-realm unity or nature mysticism (psychic level). It does not recognize archetypal mysticism, subtle consciousness, lucid dreaming, or savikalpa samadhi (all forms of deity or subtle-level mysticism); nor does it recognize formless consciousness (causal), and therefore it does not reach the pure nondual (which is a union of form and emptiness). Union with nature, when it does not recognize the formless state of cessation, is always psychic-level, gross cosmic consciousness, or nature mysticism (not nondual or integral mysticism). Nonetheless, it is a genuine and profound transpersonal experience.
>
> One of the easiest ways to tell if a "unity experience" is gross realm (nature mysticism), subtle realm (deity mysticism), causal realm (formless mysticism), or genuine nondual consciousness (union of the form in all realms with the pure formless) is to note the nature of consciousness in dreaming and deep sleep. If the writer talks of a unity experience while awake, that is usually gross-realm nature mysticism. If that unity consciousness *continues into the dream state*—so that the writer talks of lucid dreaming, union with interior luminosities as well as gross exterior nature—that is usually subtle-realm deity mysticism. If that consciousness *continues into the deep sleep state*—so that the writer realizes a Self that is *fully present in all three states* of waking, dreaming, and deep sleep—that is usually causal-realm formless mysticism (turiya). If that formless Self is then discovered to be one with the form in all realms—gross to subtle to causal—that is pure nondual consciousness (turiyatita).

Many nature mystics, ecopsychologists, and neopagans take the gross-realm, waking-state unity with nature to be the highest unity available, but that is basically the first of four major samadhis or mystical unions. The "deep self" of ecopsychology is thus not to be confused with the True Self of Zen, Ati of Dzogchen, Brahman-Atman of Vedanta, etc. These distinctions also help us situate philosophers like Heidegger and Foucault, both of whom talked of mystical-like unions with nature. Those were often profound and authentic experiences of gross-realm unity (Nirmanakaya), but again, those should not be confused with Zen or Vedanta, for the latter push through to causal formlessness (Dharmakaya, nirvikalpa samadhi, jnana samadhi, etc.), and then into pure nondual unity (Svabhavikakaya, turiyatita) with any and all realms, gross to subtle to causal. Many writers confuse Nirmanakaya with Svabhavikakaya, which ignores the major realms of interior development that lie between the two (e.g., Sambhogakaya and Dharmakaya).

ADDENDUM B: THE HARD PROBLEM

The "all-quadrant, all-level" (AQAL) model presented in this chapter, because it includes the transpersonal and nondual waves, also has—or claims to have—an answer to the "hard problem" of consciousness (the problem of how we can get subjective experience out of an allegedly objective, material, nonexperiential world).

The wisdom traditions generally make a distinction between relative truth and absolute truth (the former referring to relative truths in the conventional, dualistic world, and the latter referring to the realization of the absolute or nondual world, a realization known as satori, moksha, metanoia, liberation, etc.) (Deutsch, 1969; Gyatso, 1986; Smith, 1993). An integral model would include both truths. It would suggest that, from the *relative* perspective, all existing entities have four quadrants, including an interior and an exterior, and thus "subjective experience" and "objective matter/energy" arise correlatively from the very start.[28] From the *absolute* perspective, an integral model suggests that the final answer to this problem is actually discovered only with satori, or the personal awakening to the nondual itself. The reason that the hard problem remains hard is the same reason that absolute truth cannot be stated in relative words: the nondual can only be known by a change of consciousness, not a change of words or maps or theories.

The hard problem ultimately revolves around the actual relation of subject and object, and that relation is said to yield its final truth only with satori (as maintained by philosophers of the nondual traditions, from Plotinus to Lady Tsogyal to Meister Eckhart [Alexander, 1990; Forman, 1998b; Murphy, 1992; Rowan, 1993; Smith, 1993; Walsh, 1999; Wilber, 1996c, 2002b]). We could say that what is "seen" in satori is that subject and object are nondual, but those are only words, and when stated thus, the absolute or nondual generates only paradoxes, antinomies, contradictions. According to this view, the nondual "answer" to the hard problem can only be seen from the nondual state or level of consciousness itself, which generally takes years of contemplative discipline, and therefore is not an "answer" that can be found in a textbook or journal—and thus it will remain the hard problem for those who do not transform their own consciousness. In short, the ultimate, absolute, or nondual solution to the hard problem is found only with satori.

On the relative plane—which involves the types of truths that can be stated in words and checked with conventional logic and facts—the relative solution to the relation of subject and object is best captured, I believe, by a specific type of panpsychism, which can be found in various forms in Leibniz, Whitehead, Russell, Charles Hartshorne, David Ray Griffin, David Chalmers, and others, although I believe it must be clearly modified from a monological and dialogical to a quadratic formulation, as suggested in detail in *Integral Psychology* (especially note 15 for chap. 14).

With regard to such a (relatively true) panpsychism, David Chalmers, in a particularly illuminating discussion (1997), reaches several important conclusions:

1. "One is forced to the conclusion that no reductive explanation of consciousness can be given" (44). That is, consciousness (or experience or proto-experience—or as I technically prefer it, interiority) is an intrinsic, given component of the Kosmos, and it cannot be completely derived from, or reduced to, something else. In my view, this is because every holon has an interior and exterior (in both singular and plural). Thus, only an integral model that includes consciousness as fundamental will likely succeed.

2. "Perhaps the best path to such an integrated view is offered by the Russellian picture on which (proto)experiential properties constitute the intrinsic nature of physical reality. Such a picture is most naturally associated with some form of panpsychism. The resulting integration may be panpsychism's greatest theoretical benefit" (42). As I would put it, the general idea is simply that physics (and natural science) discloses only the objective, exterior, or extrinsic features of holons, whose interior or intrinsic features are subjective and experiential (or proto-experiential). In other words, all holons have a Left- and Right-Hand dimension.

3. Once that interior/exterior problem is handled (with a modified panpsychism, which suggests that all holons have an interior and exterior), we face a second problem. "The second is the problem of how fundamental experiential or proto-experiential properties at the microscopic level somehow together *constitute* the sort of complex, unified experience that we possess. (This is a version of what Seager calls the 'combination problem.') Such constitution is almost certainly required if our own experiences are not to be epiphenomenal, but it is not at all obvious how it should work: would not these tiny experiences instead add up to a jagged mess? . . . *If* [the combination problem] can be avoided, then I think [this modified panpsychism] is clearly the single most attractive way to make sense of the place of experience in the natural order" (29). Chalmers echoes Thomas Nagel in saying that the combination problem is central to the hard problem. As Chalmers says, "This leaves the combination problem, which is surely the hardest" (43).

But, as I try to show in *Integral Psychology* (especially note 15 for chap. 14), the combination problem is actually something that has been successfully handled (on the relative plane) for quite some time by developmental psychology and Whiteheadian process philosophy. In essence, with each wave of development, the subject of one stage becomes an object of the next (as Robert Kegan would put it), so that each stage is a prehensive unification of all of its predecessors. In Whitehead's famous dictum, "The many become one and are increased by one." This process, when viewed from the interior, gives us, in healthy development, a cohesive and unified self-sense (reaching from sensation to perception to impulse to image to symbol . . . and so on up the waves of the Great Nest, where each wave *transcends and includes*—or moves beyond but embraces—its predecessors, thus gathering together into one the many subunits that precede it; thus each healthy wave successfully solves the combination problem). This same process, when viewed from the exterior, appears as, for example: many atoms become one molecule, many molecules become one cell, many cells become one organism, and so on.

On both the interior and the exterior, the result is not a "jagged mess" because each unit in those series is actually a *holon*—a whole that is a part of other wholes. As I try to show in *Sex, Ecology, Spirituality* and *A Brief History of Everything,* both the interiors and the exteriors of the Kosmos are composed of holons (that is, all holons have an interior and exterior, in singular and plural); and thus the "combination problem" is actually an inherent feature of holons in all domains. All four quadrants are composed of whole/parts or holons, all the way up, all the way down, and because each holon is already a whole/part, each holon is an existing solution to the combination problem. Far from being rare or anomalous, holons are the fundamental ingredients of reality in all domains, and thus the combination problem is not so much a problem as it is an essential feature of the universe.)

(Assuming that the combination problem can be thus solved, the way is open for a holonic model of the Kosmos ("all-quadrants, all-levels"), a subset of which is an integral theory of consciousness.) Of course, what I have presented here and in other writings is only the briefest skeleton of such a model, but I believe that these preliminary speculations are encouraging enough to pursue the project more rigorously.

(Finally, let me return to the original point. The hard problem can perhaps best be solved on the relative plane with a holonic or integral model. But that is still just a conceptual tool on the relative plane. You can completely learn or memorize the holonic model, and yet you still experience your consciousness as residing "in here," on this side of your face, and the world as existing "out there," dualistically. That dualism is ultimately overcome, not with any model, no matter how "nondualistic" it calls itself, but only with satori, which is a direct and radical realization (or change in level of consciousness), and that transformation cannot be delivered by any model, but only by prolonged spiritual practice. As the traditions say, you must have the actual experience to see exactly what is revealed, just as you must actually see a sunset to know what is involved (cf. *Eye to Eye*, Wilber, 1996c). But the mystics are rather unanimous: the hard problem is finally (dis)solved only with enlightenment, or the permanent realization of the nondual wave. For a discussion of this theme, see especially chapters 3 and 11 above (particularly note 13), and the revised "An Integral Theory of Consciousness," found in CW7.)

ADDENDUM C: THE DEATH OF PSYCHOLOGY AND THE BIRTH OF THE INTEGRAL

In 1983, I stopped referring to myself as a "transpersonal" psychologist or philosopher.[29] I began instead to think of the work that I was doing as "integrative" or "integral." I therefore began writing a textbook of integral psychology called *System, Self, and Structure*, a two-volume work that, for various reasons, has never been published. In 2000, however, I brought out a one-volume, simplified outline of integral psychology called, appropriately enough, *Integral Psychology: Consciousness, Spirit, Psychology, Therapy*. The chapter presented above is a summary of that book, and hence a summary of my present psychological model.

But it is true that integral psychology fits none of the existing four forces (behavioristic, psychoanalytic, humanistic, or transpersonal). The claim of integral psychology is that it "transcends and includes" those four forces, but that claim is exactly what the four forces all sharply dispute. In any event, my own opinion is that integral psychology is not a transpersonal psychology; it appears to be more encompassing than anything that today calls itself transpersonal. Nor do I believe that transpersonal can or will become truly integral; all of its main factions are rooted in models that seem demonstrably less than integral. I believe that the field of transpersonal psychology in this country has become a rather specialized field, confined largely (but not totally) to the Bay Area, and that as such it is a very important but restricted endeavor. Some critics have said that it has become a California fad, like hot tubs and psychedelics, but I think that is too harsh. I do believe, however, that it has narrowed its focus, on the one hand, and loosened its quality standards, on the other, and thus it has ceased to speak to all but a relatively small group. Because of this, it has continually failed to achieve recognition by the American Psychological Association, and it is now all but impossible to get funding for transpersonal research or to be taken seriously by anyone but the converted. The relative lack of substantial research has increasingly moved it into mere ideology, or opinions divorced from any credible evidence.

My hope is that integral psychology, in moving outside of transpersonal psychology and building more bridges to the conventional world, will provide a complementary approach to move consciousness studies forward, while maintaining a respectful and mutually beneficial dialogue with the four forces. I have long supported all four forces of psychology, and I will continue to do so.[30]

Some critics have called integral psychology a fifth force, but I don't think that is a useful way to proceed (and it can also become an unfortunate game: okay, then I have the sixth force . . .). Besides, I believe the four forces of psychology are slowly dying, and being the fifth force of that death march is perhaps not desirable. Psychology as we have known it, I believe, is basically dead. In its place will be more integral approaches.

Put differently, my belief is that psychology as a discipline—referring

to any of the four traditional major forces (behavioristic, psychoanalytic, humanistic/existential, and transpersonal)—is slowly decaying and
will never again, in any of its four major forms, be a dominant influence
in culture or academia.)

(At this point in Western history (basically, an amalgam of traditional,
modern, and postmodern currents)—and specifically at this time in
America (circa 2000)—we are going through a period of an intense
flatland cascade, a combination of rampant scientific materialism (the
orange meme) and the "nothing but surfaces" of the extreme postmodernists (the green meme): in short, interiors are out, *exteriors are all*;
there is no depth, only surfaces as far as the eye can see. This puts an
intense selection pressure *against* any sort of psychology that emphasizes
solely or mostly the *interiors* (psychoanalytic, humanistic/existential,
and transpersonal).)

(This is compounded by numerous specific social factors, such as the
medical/insurance and "managed care" industry supporting only brief
psychotherapy and pharmacological interventions. Again, the interior
psychologies are selected against in this negative cultural current.) The
only acceptable orthodox approaches to psychology are increasingly the
Right-Hand approaches, including biological psychiatry, behavioral
modification, cognitive therapy (and remember, "cognition" is defined
as "cognition of objects or its," and thus cognitive therapy is not so
much an interior exploration of depths but simply a manipulation of the
sentences one uses to objectively describe oneself; cognitive therapy in
general works with "adjusting your premises" so that they match scientific, objective, Right-Hand evidence)—and, finally, an increasing, almost epidemic, reliance on the use of medication (Prozac, Xanax, Paxil,
etc.), all of which focus almost exclusively on Right-Hand interventions.
(See, for example, the superb *Of Two Minds*, by Tanya Luhrmann; the
"two minds" are, of course, the Upper-Left and Upper-Right approaches
to psychology, and Luhrmann leaves no doubt as to which is winning
the survival race; if I may be allowed a pun, interiors are out, exteriors
are in.) Silly things like trying to find out *why* you behave in such a
fashion, or trying to find out the *meaning* of your existence, or the *values*
that constitute the good life, are not covered by insurance policies, and
so, in this culture, they basically do not exist. Three of the four forces
(psychoanalytic, humanistic/existential, and transpersonal) are thus,
once again, selected against; a negative cultural pressure is moving them
to extinction and in some ways has already succeeded, (so that these

major forces are one jot away from dinosaur status. (This is not necessarily a bad thing, as we will see.)

The old behaviorism (one of the four forces) has survived, precisely
because it is focused almost exclusively on exterior behavior, but also
because it has morphed into more sophisticated forms, two of which
are now dominant: cognitive science and evolutionary psychology. It is
important to note that both of these endeavors are quintessentially exterior or Right-Hand approaches. *Cognitive science* focuses on the Upper-
Right quadrant—the exteriors of individuals—and studies those holons
in an objective, scientific, empirical fashion: human consciousness is
viewed as the result of neurophysiological mechanisms, organic systems,
and brain neural networks that summate in individual awareness. Psychopathology is viewed as a pathology of these organic pathways, and
cure involves fixing these organic pathways (usually with medication,
sometimes with behavioral modification). All of this is conducted in
third-person it-language.

Evolutionary psychology focuses on the objective organism (Upper
Right) and how its *interaction* with the objective environment (Lower
Right) has resulted, via variation and natural selection, in certain behaviors of the individual organism, most of which originated to serve survival (which is defined, as LR truths always are, as functional fit). Thus,
you tend to behave in the way that you do (e.g., males are profligate sex
fiends, females are nesting homebodies) because a million years of natural selection has left you with these genes. (I am not contesting the truths
of evolutionary psychology; I am pointing out that they are Right-Hand
only.)

In both of those dominant forms of present-day psychology, there is
no introspection to speak of, no searching the interiors, the within, the
deep, the Left-Hand quadrants. There are only objective "its" scurrying
about in objective systems, networks, and the empirical web of life: no
within, no interiors, no depth. And thus, once again, the three major
forces of interior psychology (psychoanalytic, humanistic/existential,
and transpersonal) are left to slowly wither, which slowly they are.

In my opinion, the only interior psychologies that will survive this
new sociocultural selection pressure are those that adapt by recognizing
an "all-quadrant, all-level" framework, for only that framework (or
something equally integral) can embrace *both* the Right- and Left-Hand
realities. Thus the Left-Hand or interior psychologies can securely hook
themselves to the tested truths of cognitive science and evolutionary psychology without succumbing to the reductionism that says there are only

Right-Hand realities. That is, the only psychologies that will survive will be those that plug themselves into an AQAL formulation, which fully concedes the biological, objective, empirical, and cognitive components of consciousness, but *only* as set in the four quadrants. This *integral* approach concedes the relative truths of the dominant Right-Hand psychologies but simultaneously paints a much broader and more encompassing picture of consciousness and Kosmos.

The integral approach is thus constantly on hand to point out all of the correlations of the exterior events in brain and body (the Upper-Right quadrant studied by cognitive science and evolutionary psychology) with the interior events in mind and consciousness (the Upper-Left quadrant studied by interior psychologies), and to further show how all of them are inescapably anchored in cultural and social realities as well (the Lower-Left and Lower-Right quadrants)—with none of those quadrants being reducible to the others. As an extraordinary number of scholars have pointed out, the arguments against reductionism are simply overwhelming; an AQAL formulation therefore stands as a constant reminder that we can in fact fully honor the truths in all four quadrants without trying to reduce any of them to the others. As the severe limitations of the merely objectivistic, exterior, Right-Hand approaches become clear to individual researchers (as they almost always eventually do), an integral framework thus stands available to help them make the leap to a more comprehensive approach.

If the only psychologies that will survive are psychologies that are plugged into an "all-quadrant, all-level" framework (which includes behavioral, intentional, cultural, and social dimensions, all of which stretch from matter to body to mind to spirit)—such a psychology is not really psychology as we have known it. That is, a four-quadrant psychology is no longer psychology (which is why integral psychology is not actually a fifth force, although many people will continue to call it such). Rather, integral psychology is an inherent feature of a Kosmology, and its practice is a movement of the Kosmos itself. This is why I believe the four forces will continue to wither, and their places will increasingly be taken by various forms of integral psychology that adapt to this new cultural selection pressure (or Eros) by recognizing niches of reality as yet unoccupied (namely, an AQAL space), into which they can evolve with the assurance of survival by adapting to yet higher and wider dimensions of reality. The integral claim is that because an AQAL formulation is more adequate to reality, evolution into a consciously AQAL space has inherent survival value. Correlatively, less adequate and comprehensive approaches will increasingly face extinction pressures.

This might well leave the four forces as historical dinosaurs.[31] At the same time—and this is the claim of integral psychology that the other psychologies dispute—any truly integral psychology will "transcend and include" all of the important truths of the four forces. Nothing is lost, all is retained; even dinosaurs live on in today's birds. The test of any integral psychology is to what degree it can accept and *coherently* integrate the valid research and data from the various schools of psychology—not just the four major forces, but developmental psychology, evolutionary psychology, cognitive sciences, phenomenological/hermeneutic approaches, and so on. Of course, this is a daunting challenge, perhaps forever unreachable; but as of today we know too much to ever settle for less.

13

Always Already

THE BRILLIANT CLARITY OF
EVER-PRESENT AWARENESS

*Where are we to locate Spirit? What are we actually allowed to
acknowledge as Sacred? Where exactly is the Ground of Being?
Where is this ultimate Divine?*

THE GREAT SEARCH

THE REALIZATION OF the Nondual traditions is uncompromising:
there is only Spirit, there is only God, there is only Emptiness in all
its radiant wonder. All the good and all the evil, the very best and the
very worst, the upright and the degenerate—each and all are radically
perfect manifestations of Spirit precisely as they are. There is nothing
but God, nothing but the Goddess, nothing but Spirit in all directions,
and not a grain of sand, not a speck of dust, is more or less Spirit than
any other.

This realization undoes the Great Search that is the heart of the separate-self sense. The separate-self is, at bottom, simply a sensation of
seeking. When you feel yourself right now, you will basically feel a tiny
interior tension or contraction—a sensation of grasping, desiring, wishing, wanting, avoiding, resisting—it is a sensation of effort, a sensation
of seeking.

In its highest form, this sensation of seeking takes on the form of the

Great Search for Spirit. We wish to get from our unenlightened state (of sin or delusion or duality) to an enlightened or more spiritual state. We wish to get from where Spirit is not, to where Spirit is.

But there is no place where Spirit is not. Every single location in the entire Kosmos is equally and fully Spirit. Seeking of any sort, movement of any sort, attainment of any sort: all profoundly useless. The Great Search simply reinforces the mistaken assumption that there is some place that Spirit is not, and that I need to get from a space that is lacking to a space that is full. But there is no space lacking, and there is no space more full. There is only Spirit.

The Great Search for Spirit is simply that impulse, the final impulse, which prevents the present realization of Spirit, and it does so for a simple reason: the Great Search presumes the loss of God. The Great Search reinforces the mistaken belief that God is not present, and thus totally obscures the reality of God's ever-present Presence. The Great Search, which pretends to love God, is in fact the very mechanism of pushing God away; the mechanism of promising to find tomorrow that which exists only in the timeless now; the mechanism of watching the future so fervently that the present always passes it by—very quickly— and God's smiling face with it.

The Great Search is the loveless contraction hidden in the heart of the separate-self sense, a contraction that drives the intense yearning for a tomorrow in which salvation will finally arrive, but during which time, thank God, I can continue to be myself. The greater the Great Search, the more I can deny God. The greater the Great Search, the more I can feel my own sensation of seeking, which defines the contours of my self. The Great Search is the great enemy of what is.

Should we then simply cease the Great Search? Definitely, if we could. But the effort to stop the Great Search is itself more of the Great Search. The very first step presumes and reinforces the seeking sensation. There is actually nothing the self-contraction can do to stop the Great Search, because the self-contraction and the Great Search are two names for the same thing.

If Spirit cannot be found as a future product of the Great Search, then there is only one alternative: Spirit must be fully, totally, completely present right now—AND you must be fully, totally, completely aware of it right now. It will not do to say that Spirit is present but I don't realize it. That would require the Great Search; that would demand that I seek a tomorrow in which I could realize that Spirit is fully present, but such seeking misses the present in the very first step. To keep seeking would be to keep missing. No, the realization itself, the awareness itself: this, too, must somehow be fully and completely present right now. If it is not, then all we have left is the Great Search, doomed to presume that which it wishes to overcome.

There must be something about our *present* awareness that contains the entire truth. Somehow, no matter what your state, you are immersed fully in everything you need for perfect enlightenment. You are somehow looking right at the answer. One hundred percent of Spirit is in your perception right now. Not 20 percent, not 50 percent, not 99 percent, but literally 100 percent of Spirit is in your awareness right now—and the trick, as it were, is to recognize this ever-present state of affairs, and not to engineer a future state in which Spirit will announce itself.

And this simple recognition of an *already present* Spirit is the task, as it were, of the great Nondual traditions.

To Meet the Kosmos

Many people have stern objections to "mysticism" or "transcendental-ism" of any sort, because they think it somehow denies this world, or hates this earth, or despises the body and the senses and its vital life, and so on. While that may be true of certain dissociated (or merely Ascend-ing) approaches, it is certainly not the core understanding of the great Nondual mystics, from Plotinus and Eckhart in the West to Nagarjuna and Lady Tsogyal in the East.

Rather, these sages universally maintain that absolute reality and the relative world are "not-two" (which is the meaning of "nondual"), much as a mirror and its reflections are not separate, or an ocean is one with its many waves. So the "other world" of Spirit and "this world" of separate phenomena are deeply and profoundly "not-two," and this nonduality is a direct and immediate realization which occurs in certain meditative states—in other words, seen with the eye of contemplation—although it then becomes a very simple, very ordinary perception, whether you are meditating or not. Every single thing you perceive is the radiance of Spirit itself, so much so that Spirit is not seen apart from that thing: the robin sings, and just that is it, nothing else. This becomes your constant realization, through all changes of state, very naturally, just so. And this releases you from the basic insanity of hiding from the Real.

But why is it, then, that we ordinarily don't have that perception?

All the great Nondual wisdom traditions have given a fairly similar answer to that question. We don't see that Spirit is fully and completely present right here, right now, because our awareness is clouded with some form of *avoidance*. We do not want to be choicelessly aware of the present; rather, we want to run away from it, or run after it, or we want to change it, alter it, hate it, love it, loathe it, or in some way agitate to get ourselves into, or out of, it. We will do anything except come to rest in the pure Presence of the present. We will not rest with pure Presence; we want to be elsewhere, quickly. The Great Search is the game, in its endless forms.

In nondual meditation or contemplation, the agitation of the separate-self sense profoundly relaxes, and the self uncoils in the vast expanse of all space. At that point, it becomes obvious that you are not "in here" looking at the world "out there," because that duality has simply collapsed into pure Presence and spontaneous luminosity.

This realization may take many forms. A simple one is something like this: You might be looking at a mountain, and you have relaxed into the effortlessness of your own present awareness, and then suddenly the mountain is all, you are nothing. Your separate-self sense is suddenly and totally gone, and there is simply everything that is arising moment to moment. You are perfectly aware, perfectly conscious, everything seems completely normal, except you are nowhere to be found. You are not on this side of your face looking at the mountain out there; you simply are the mountain, you are the sky, you are the clouds, you are everything that is arising moment to moment, very simply, very clearly, just so.

We know all the fancy names for this state, from unity consciousness to sahaj samadhi. But it really is the simplest and most obvious state you will ever realize. Moreover, once you glimpse that state—what the Buddhists call One Taste (because you and the entire universe are one taste or one experience)—it becomes obvious that you are not entering this state, but rather, it is a state that, in some profound and mysterious way, has been your primordial condition from time immemorial. You have, in fact, never left this state for a second.

This is why Zen calls it the Gateless Gate: on this side of that realization, it looks like you have to do something to enter that state—it looks like you need to pass through a gate. But when you do so, and you turn around and look back, there is no gate whatsoever, and never has been. You have never left this state in the first place, so obviously you can't enter it. The gateless gate! "Every form is Emptiness just as it is," means that all things, including you and me, are always already on the other side of the gateless gate.

But if that is so, then why even do spiritual practice? Isn't that just another form of the Great Search? Yes, actually, spiritual practice is a form of the Great Search, and as such, it is destined to fail. But that is exactly the point. You and I are already convinced that there are things that we need to do in order to realize Spirit. We feel that there are places that Spirit is not (namely, in me), and we are going to correct this state of affairs. Thus, we are already committed to the Great Search, and so nondual meditation makes use of that fact and engages us in the Great Search in a particular and somewhat sneaky fashion (which Zen calls "selling water by the river").

William Blake said that "a fool who persists in his folly will become wise." So nondual meditation simply speeds up the folly. If you really think you lack Spirit, then try this folly: try to become Spirit, try to discover Spirit, try to contact Spirit, try to reach Spirit: meditate and meditate and meditate in order to get Spirit!

But of course, you see, you cannot really do this. You cannot reach Spirit any more than you can reach your feet. You always already are Spirit, you are not going to reach it in any sort of temporal thrashing around. But if this is not obvious, then try it. <u>Nondual meditation is a serious effort to do the impossible, until you become utterly exhausted of the Great Search, sit down completely worn out, and notice your feet</u>.

It's not that these nondual traditions deny higher states; they don't. They have many, many practices that help individuals reach specific states of postformal consciousness. These include states of transcendental bliss, love, and compassion; of heightened cognition and extrasensory perception; of Deity consciousness and contemplative prayer. But they maintain that those altered states—which have a beginning and an end in time—ultimately have nothing to do with the timeless. The real aim is the stateless, not a perpetual fascination with changes of state. And that stateless condition is the true nature of this and every conceivable state of consciousness, so any state you have will do just fine. <u>Change of state is not the ultimate point; recognizing the Changeless is the point, recognizing primordial Emptiness is the point</u>, recognizing unqualifiable Godhead is the point, recognizing pure Spirit is the point, and if you are breathing and vaguely awake, that state of consciousness will do just fine.

Nonetheless, traditionally, in order to demonstrate your sincerity, you must complete a good number of preliminary practices, including a mastery of various states of meditative consciousness, summating in a stable post-postconventional adaptation, all of which is well and good. But none of those states of consciousness are held to be final or ultimate or privileged. And changing states is not the goal at all. Rather, it is precisely by entering and leaving these various meditative states that you begin to understand that *none* of them constitute enlightenment. All of them have a beginning in time, and thus none of them are the timeless. The point is to realize that change of state is *not* the point, and *that* realization can occur in *any* state of consciousness whatsoever.

EVER-PRESENT AWARENESS

This primordial recognition of One Taste—not the creation but the recognition of the fact that you and the Kosmos are One Spirit, One Taste, One Gesture—is the great gift of the Nondual traditions. And in simplified form, this recognition goes like this:

(What follows are various "pointing out" instructions, direct pointers to mind's essential nature or intrinsic Spirit. Traditionally this involves a great deal of intentional repetition. If you read this material in the normal manner, you might find the repetitions tedious and perhaps irritating. If you would like the rest of this particular section to work for you, please read it in a slow and leisurely manner, letting the words and the repetitions sink in. You can also use these sections as material for meditation, using no more than one or two paragraphs—or even one or two sentences—for each session.)

We begin with the realization that the pure Self or transpersonal Witness is an *ever-present* consciousness, even when we doubt its existence. You are right now aware of, say, this book, the room, a window, the sky, the clouds. . . . You can sit back and simply notice that you are aware of all those objects floating by. Clouds float through the sky, thoughts float through the mind, and when you notice them, you are effortlessly aware of them. There is a simple, effortless, spontaneous witnessing of whatever happens to be present.

In that simple witnessing awareness, you might notice: I am aware of my body, and therefore I am not just my body. I am aware of my mind, and therefore I am not just my mind. I am aware of my self, and therefore I am not just that self. Rather, I seem somehow to be the Witness of my body, my mind, my self.

This is truly fascinating. I can see my thoughts, so I am not those thoughts. I am aware of bodily sensations, so I am not those sensations. I am aware of my emotions, so I am not merely those emotions. I am somehow the Witness of all of that!

But what is this Witness itself? Who or What is it that witnesses all of these objects, that watches the clouds float by, and thoughts float by, and objects float by? Who or What is this true Seer, this pure Witness, which is at the very core of what I am?

That simple witnessing awareness, the traditions maintain, is Spirit itself, is the enlightened mind itself, is Buddha-nature itself, is God itself, *in its entirety.*

Thus, according to the traditions, getting in touch with Spirit or God or the enlightened mind is not something difficult to achieve. It is your own simple witnessing awareness in exactly this moment. If you see this book, you already have that awareness—all of it—right now.

A very famous text from Dzogchen or Maha-Ati Buddhism (one of the very greatest of the Nondual traditions) puts it like this: "At times it happens that some meditators say that it is difficult to recognize the nature of the mind"—in Dzogchen, "the nature of the mind" means primordial Purity or radical Emptiness—it means nondual Spirit by whatever name. The point is that this "nature of the mind" is *ever-present witnessing awareness*, and some meditators, the text says, find this hard to believe. They imagine it is difficult or even impossible to recognize this ever-present awareness, and that they have to work very hard and meditate very long in order to attain this enlightened mind— whereas it is simply their own ever-present witnessing awareness, fully functioning right now.

The text continues: "Some male or female practitioners believe it to be impossible to recognize the nature of mind. They become depressed with tears streaming down their cheeks. There is no reason at all to become sad. It is not at all impossible to recognize. Rest directly in that which thinks that it is impossible to recognize the nature of the mind, and that is exactly it."

As for this ever-present witnessing awareness being hard to contact: "There are some meditators who don't let their mind rest in itself [simple present awareness], as they should. Instead they let it watch outwardly or search inwardly. You will neither see nor find [Spirit] by watching outwardly or searching inwardly. There is no reason whatsoever to watch outwardly or search inwardly. Let go directly into this mind that is watching outwardly or searching inwardly, and that is exactly it."[1]

We are aware of this room; just that is it, just that awareness is ever-present Spirit. We are aware of the clouds floating by in the sky; just that is it, just that awareness is ever-present Spirit. We are aware of

thoughts floating by in the mind; just that is it, just that awareness is
ever-present Spirit. We are aware of pain, turmoil, terror, fear; just that
is it.)

In other words, the ultimate reality is not something seen, but rather
the ever-present Seer. Things that are seen come and go, are happy or
sad, pleasant or painful—but the Seer is none of those things, and it does
not come and go. The Witness does not waver, does not wobble, does
not enter that stream of time. The Witness is not an object, not a thing
seen, but the ever-present Seer of all things, the simple Witness that is
the I of Spirit, the center of the cyclone, the opening that is God, the
clearing that is pure Emptiness.

There is never a time that you do not have access to this Witnessing
awareness. At every single moment, there is a spontaneous awareness of
whatever happens to be present—and that simple, spontaneous, effortless awareness is ever-present Spirit itself. Even if you think you don't
see it, that very awareness is it. And thus, the ultimate state of consciousness—intrinsic Spirit itself—*is not hard to reach but impossible to avoid.*

And just that is the great and guarded secret of the Nondual schools.

It does not matter what objects or contents are present; whatever
arises is fine. People sometimes have a hard time understanding Spirit
because they try to see it as an object of awareness or an object of comprehension. But the ultimate reality is not anything seen, it is the Seer.
Spirit is not an object; it is radical, ever-present Subject, and thus it is
not something that is going to jump out in front of you like a rock, an
image, an idea, a light, a feeling, an insight, a luminous cloud, an intense
vision, or a sensation of great bliss. Those are all nice, but they are all
objects, which is what Spirit is not.

Thus, as you rest in the Witness, you won't see anything in particular.
The true Seer is nothing that can be seen, so you simply begin by disidentifying with any and all objects:

I am aware of sensations in my body; those are objects, I am not
those. I am aware of thoughts in my mind; those are objects, I am not
those. I am aware of my self in this moment, but that is just another
object, and I am not that.

Sights float by in nature, thoughts float by in the mind, feelings float
by in the body, and I am none of those. I am not an object. I am the pure
Witness of all those objects. I am Consciousness as such.

And so, as you rest in the pure Witness, you won't see anything in
particular—whatever you see is fine. Rather, as you rest in the radical
subject or Witness, as you stop identifying with objects, you will simply

begin to notice a sense of vast Freedom. This Freedom is not something you will see; it is something you are. When you are the Witness of thoughts, you are not bound by thoughts. When you are the Witness of feelings, you are not bound by feelings. In place of your contracted self there is simply a vast sense of Openness and Release. As an object, you are bound; as the Witness, you are Free.

We will not see this Freedom, we will rest in it. A vast ocean of infinite ease.

And so we rest in this state of the pure and simple Witness, the true Seer, which is vast Emptiness and pure Freedom, and we allow whatever is seen to arise as it wishes. Spirit is in the Free and Empty Seer, not in the limited, bound, mortal, and finite objects that parade by in the world of time. And so we rest in this vast Emptiness and Freedom, in which all things arise.

We do not reach or contact this pure Witnessing awareness. It is not possible to contact that which we have never lost. Rather, we rest in this easy, clear, ever-present awareness by simply noticing what is *already* happening. We already see the sky. We already hear the birds singing. We already feel the cool breeze. The simple Witness is already present, already functioning, already the case. That is why we do not contact or bring this Witness into being, but simply notice that it is always already present, as the simple and spontaneous awareness of whatever is happening in this moment.

We also notice that this simple, ever-present Witness is completely effortless. It takes no effort whatsoever to hear sounds, to see sights, to feel the cool breeze: it is already happening, and we easily rest in that effortless witnessing. We do not follow those objects, nor avoid them. Precisely because Spirit is the ever-present Seer, and not any limited thing that is seen, we can allow all seen things to come and go exactly as they please. "The perfect person employs the mind as a mirror," says Chuang Tzu. "It neither grasps nor rejects; it receives, but does not keep." The mirror effortlessly receives its reflections, just as you effortlessly see the sky right now, and just as the Witness effortlessly allows all objects whatsoever to arise. All things come and go in the effortless mirror-mind that is the simple Witness.

When I rest as the pure and simple Witness, I notice that I am not caught in the world of time. The Witness exists only in the timeless present. Yet again, this is not a state that is difficult to achieve but impossible to avoid. The Witness sees only the timeless present because only the timeless present is actually real. When I think of the past, those past thoughts exist right now, in this present. When I think of the future, those future thoughts exist right now, in this present. Past and future thoughts both arise right now, in simple ever-present awareness.

And when the past actually occurred, it occurred right now. When the future actually occurs, it will occur right now. There is only right now, there is only this ever-present present: that is all I ever directly know. Thus, the timeless present is not hard to contact but impossible to avoid, and this becomes obvious when I rest as the pure and simple Witness, and watch the past and future float by in simple ever-present awareness.

That is why when we rest as the ever-present Witness, we are not in time. Resting in simple witnessing awareness, I notice that time floats by in front of me, or through me, like clouds float through the sky. And that is exactly why I can be aware of time; in my simple Presentness, in my I AMness as pure and simple Witness of the Kosmos, I am timeless.

Thus, as I right now rest in this simple, ever-present Witness, I am face to face with Spirit. I am with God today, and always, in this simple, ever-present, witnessing state. Eckhart said that "God is closer to me than I am to myself," because both God and I are one in the ever-present Witness, which is the nature of intrinsic Spirit itself, which is exactly what I am in the state of my I AMness. I am not this, I am not that; I rest as pure open Spirit. When I am not an object, I am God. (And every I in the entire Kosmos can say that truthfully.)

I am not entering this state of the ever-present Witness, which is Spirit itself. I cannot *enter* this state, precisely because it is ever-present. I cannot *start* Witnessing; I can only notice that this simple Witnessing is *already* occurring. This state never has a beginning in time precisely because it is indeed ever-present. You can neither run from it nor toward it; you *are* it, always. This is exactly why Buddhas have *never* entered this state, and sentient beings have *never* left it.

When I rest in the simple, clear, ever-present Witness, I am resting in the great Unborn, I am resting in intrinsic Spirit, I am resting in primordial Emptiness, I am resting in infinite Freedom. I cannot be seen, I have no qualities at all. I am not this, I am not that. I am not an object. I am neither light nor dark; neither large nor small; neither here nor there; I have no color, no location, no space and no time; I am an utter Emptiness, another word for infinite Freedom, unbounded to infinity. I am the opening or clearing in which the entire manifest world arises right now, but I do not arise in it—it arises in me, in this vast Emptiness and Freedom that I am.

Things that are seen are pleasant or painful, happy or sad, joyous or fearful, healthy or sick—but the Seer of those things is neither happy nor sad, neither joyous nor fearful, neither healthy nor sick, but simply Free. As pure and simple Witness I am free of all objects, free of all subjects, free of all time and free of all space; free of birth and free of death, and free of all things in between. I am simply Free.

When I rest as the timeless Witness, the Great Search is undone. The Great Search is the enemy of the ever-present Spirit, a brutal lie in the face of a gentle infinity. The Great Search is the search for an ultimate experience, a fabulous vision, a paradise of pleasure, an unendingly good time, a powerful insight—a search for God, a search for Goddess, a search for Spirit—but Spirit is not an object. Spirit cannot be grasped or reached or sought or seen: it is the ever-present Seer. To search for the Seer is to miss the point. To search forever is to miss the point forever. How could you possibly search for that which is right now aware of this page? YOU ARE THAT! You cannot go out looking for that which is the Looker.

When I am not an object, I am God. When I seek an object, I cease to be God, and that catastrophe can never be corrected by more searching for more objects.

Rather, I can only rest as the Witness, which is already free of objects, free of time, free of suffering, and free of searching. When I am not an object, I am Spirit. When I rest as the free and formless Witness, I am with God right now, in this timeless and endless moment. I taste infinity and am drenched with fullness, precisely because I no longer seek, but simply rest as what I am.

Before Abraham was, I am. Before the Big Bang was, I am. After the universe dissolves, I am. In all things great and small, I am. And yet I can never be heard, felt, known, or seen; I AM is the ever-present Seer.

Precisely because the ultimate reality is not anything seen but rather the Seer, it doesn't matter in the least what is seen in any moment. Whether you see peace or turmoil, whether you see equanimity or agitation, whether you see bliss or terror, whether you see happiness or sadness, matters not at all: it is not those states but the Seer of those states that is *already* Free.

Changing states is thus beside the point; acknowledging the ever-present Seer is the point. Even in the midst of the Great Search and even in the worst of my self-contracting ways, I have immediate and direct access to the ever-present Witness. I do not have to try to bring this simple awareness into existence. I do not have to enter this state. It involves no

It is not the object se mountain that is god or ultimate reality... it is the pure awareness of it that is

effort at all. I simply notice that there is already an awareness of the sky. I simply notice that there is already an awareness of the clouds. I simply notice that the ever-present Witness is already fully functioning: it is not hard to reach but impossible to avoid. I am always already in the lap of this ever-present awareness, the radical Emptiness in which all manifestation is presently arising.

When I rest in the pure and simple Witness, I notice that this awareness is not an experience. It is aware of experiences, it is not itself an experience. Experiences come and go. They have a beginning in time, they stay a bit, and they pass. But they all arise in the simple opening or clearing that is the vast expanse of what I am. The clouds float by in this vast expanse, and thoughts float by in this vast expanse, and experiences float by in this vast expanse. They all come, and they all go. But the vast expanse itself, this Free and Empty Seer, this spacious opening or clearing in which all things arise, does not itself come and go, or even move at all.

Thus, when I rest in the pure and simple Witness, I am no longer caught up in the search for experiences, whether of the flesh or of the mind or of the spirit. Experiences—whether high or low, sacred or profane, joyous or nightmarish—simply come and go like endless waves on the ocean of what I am. As I rest in the pure and simple Witness, I am no longer moved to follow the bliss and the torture of experiential displays. Experiences float across my Original Face like clouds floating across the clear autumn sky, and there is room in me for all.

When I rest in the pure and simple Witness, I will even begin to notice that the Witness itself is not a separate thing or entity, set apart from what it witnesses. All things arise within the Witness, so much so that the Witness itself disappears into all things.

And thus, resting in simple, clear, ever-present awareness, I notice that there is no inside and no outside. There is no subject and no object. Things and events are still fully present and clearly arising—the clouds float by, the birds still sing, the cool breeze still blows—but there is no separate self recoiling from them. Events simply arise as they are, without the constant and agitated reference to a contracted self or subject. Events arise as they are, and they arise in the great freedom of not being defined by a little I looking at them. They arise with Spirit, as Spirit, in the opening or clearing that I am; they do not arise to be seen and perceptually tortured by an ego.

In my contracted mode, I am "in here," on this side of my face, looking at the world "out there," on the "objective" side. I exist on this side

1. ✳✱ can go in either direction
2. "self" screen removed

of my face, and <u>my entire life is an attempt to save face, to save this self-contraction, to save this sensation of grasping and seeking, a sensation that sets me apart from the world out there</u>, a world I will then desire or loathe, move toward or recoil from, grasp or avoid, love or hate. The <u>inside and the outside are in perpetual struggle</u>, all varieties of hope or fear: the drama of saving face.

We say, "To lose face is to die of embarrassment," and that is deeply true: we do not want to lose face! We do not want to die! We do not want to cease the sensation of the separate-self! But that primal fear of losing face is actually the root of our deepest agony, because saving face—<u>saving an identity with the bodymind—is the very mechanism of suffering</u>, the very mechanism of tearing the Kosmos into an inside versus an outside, a brutal fracture that I experience as pain.

But when I rest in simple, clear, ever-present awareness, I lose face. Inside and outside completely disappear. It happens just like this:

As I drop all objects—I am not this, not that—and I rest in the pure and simple Witness, all objects arise easily in my visual field, all objects arise in the space of the Witness. I am simply an opening or clearing in which all things arise. I notice that all things arise in me, arise in this opening or clearing that I am. The clouds are floating by in this vast opening that I am. The sun is shining in this vast opening that I am. The sky exists in this vast opening that I am; the sky is in me. I can taste the sky, it's closer to me than my own skin. The clouds are on the inside of me; <u>I am seeing them from within. When all things arise in me, I am simply all things. The universe is One Taste, and I am That.</u>

<u>And so, when I rest as the Witness, all things arise in me, so much so that I am all things. There is no subject and object because I do not see the clouds, I am the clouds. There is no subject and object</u> because I do not feel the cool breeze, I am the cool breeze. There is no subject and object because I do not hear the thunder clapping, I am the thunder clapping.

I am no longer on this side of my face looking at the world out there; I simply am the world. I am not in here. I have lost face—and discovered my Original Face, the Kosmos itself. The bird sings, and I am that. The sun rises, and I am that. The moon shines, and I am that, in simple, ever-present awareness.

<u>When I rest in simple, clear, ever-present awareness, every object is its own subject. Every event "sees itself," as it were, because I am now that event seeing itself. I am not looking at the rainbow; I am the rainbow, which sees itself. I am not staring at the tree; I am the tree, which</u>

sees itself. The entire manifest world continues to arise, just as it is, except that all subjects and all objects have disappeared. The mountain is still the mountain, but it is not an *object* being looked at, and I am not a separate *subject* staring at it. Both I and the mountain arise in simple, ever-present awareness, and we are both set free in that clearing, we are both liberated in that nondual space, we are both enlightened in the opening that is ever-present awareness. That opening is free of the set-apart violence called subject and object, in here versus out there, self against other, me against the world. I have utterly lost face, and discovered God, in simple ever-present awareness.

When you are the Witness of all objects, and all objects arise in you, then you stand in utter Freedom, in the vast expanse of all space. In this simple One Taste, the wind does not blow on you, it blows within you. The sun does not shine on you, it radiates from deep within your very being. When it rains, you are weeping. You can drink the Pacific Ocean in a single gulp, and swallow the universe whole. Supernovas are born and die all within your heart, and galaxies swirl endlessly where you thought your head was, and it is all as simple as the sound of a robin singing on a crystal clear dawn.

Every time I *recognize* or *acknowledge* the ever-present Witness, I have broken the Great Search and undone the separate self. And that is the ultimate, secret, nondual practice, the practice of no-practice, the practice of *simple acknowledgment*, the practice of remembrance and recognition, founded timelessly and eternally on the fact that there is only Spirit, a Spirit that is not hard to find but impossible to avoid.

Spirit is the only thing that has *never* been absent. It is the *only* constant in your changing experience. You have known this for a billion years, literally. And you might as well acknowledge it. "If you understand this, then rest in that which understands, and just that is Spirit. If you do not understand this, then rest in that which does not understand, and just that is Spirit." For eternally and eternally and always eternally, there is only Spirit, the Witness of this and every moment, even unto the ends of the world.

THE EYE OF SPIRIT

When I rest in simple, clear, ever-present awareness, I am resting in intrinsic Spirit; I am in fact nothing other than witnessing Spirit itself. I do not become Spirit; I simply recognize the Spirit that I always already am. When I rest in simple, clear, ever-present awareness, I am the Witness of the World. I am the eye of Spirit. I see the world as God sees it. I see the world as the Goddess sees it. I see the world as Spirit sees it: every object an object of Beauty, every thing and event a gesture of the Great Perfection, every process a ripple in the pond of my own eternal Being, so much so that I do not stand apart as a separate witness, but find the witness is one taste with all that arises within it. The entire Kosmos arises in the eye of Spirit, in the I of Spirit, in my own intrinsic awareness, this simple ever-present state, and I am simply that.

From the ground of simple, ever-present awareness, one's entire bodymind will resurrect. When you rest in primordial awareness, that awareness begins to saturate your being, and from the stream of consciousness a new destiny is resurrected. When the Great Search is undone, and the separate-self sense has been crucified; when the continuity of witnessing has stabilized in your own case; when ever-present awareness is your constant ground—then your entire bodymind will regenerate, resurrect, and reorganize itself around intrinsic Spirit, and you will arise, as from the dead, to a new destiny and a new duty in consciousness.

You will cease to exist as separate self (with all the damage that does to the bodymind), and you will exist instead as vehicle of Spirit (with the bodymind now free to function in its highest potential, undistorted and untortured by the brutalities of the self-contraction). From the ground of ever-present awareness, you will arise embodying any of the enlightened qualities of the Buddhas and Bodhisattvas—"one whose being (sattva) is ever-present awareness (bodhi)."

The Buddhist names are not important; the enlightened qualities they represent are. The point is simply that, once you have stably recognized simple, ever-present awareness—once the Great Search and the self-contraction have been robbed of separative life and returned to God, returned to their ground in ever-present awareness—then you will arise, from the ground of ever-present awareness, and you will embody any of the highest possibilities of that ground. You will be vehicle of the Spirit that you are. That ever-present ground will live through you, as you, in a variety of superordinary forms.

Perhaps you will arise as Samantabhadra, whose ever-present awareness takes the form of a vast equality consciousness: you will realize that the ever-present awareness that is fully present in you is the *same awareness* that is fully present in all sentient beings without exception—one and the same, single and only—one heart, one mind, one soul that breathes and beats and pulses through all sentient beings as such—and your very countenance will remind all beings of that simple fact, remind them that there is only Spirit, remind them that nothing is closer to God than anything else, for there is only God, there is only Goddess.

Perhaps you will arise as Avalokiteshvara, whose ever-present awareness takes the form of gentle compassion. In the brilliant clarity of ever-present awareness, all sentient beings arise as equal forms of intrinsic Spirit or pure Emptiness, and thus all beings are treated as the sons and daughters of the Spirit that they are. You will have no choice but to live this compassion with a delicate dedication, so that your very smile will warm the hearts of those who suffer, and they will look to you for a promise that they, too, can be liberated into the vast expanse of their own primordial awareness, and you will never turn away.

Perhaps you will arise as Prajnaparamita, the mother of the Buddhas, whose ever-present awareness takes the form of a vast spaciousness, the womb of the great Unborn, in which the entire Kosmos exists. For in deepest truth, it is exactly from the ground of your own simple, clear, ever-present awareness that all beings are born; and it is to the ground of your simple, clear, ever-present awareness that all beings will return. Resting in the brilliant clarity of ever-present awareness, you watch the worlds arise, and all the Buddhas arise, and all sentient beings as such arise. And to you they will all return. And you will smile, and receive, in this vast expanse of everlasting wisdom, and it will all begin again, and yet again, and always yet again, in the womb of your ever-present state.

Perhaps you will arise as Manjushri, whose ever-present awareness takes the form of luminous intelligence. Although all beings are equally intrinsic Spirit, some beings do not easily acknowledge this ever-present Suchness, and thus discriminating wisdom will brilliantly arise from the ground of equality consciousness. You will instinctively see what is true and what is false, and thus you will bring clarity to everything you touch. And if the self-contraction does not listen to your gentler voice, your ever-present awareness will manifest in its wrathful form, which is said to be none other than the dreaded Yamantaka, Subduer of the Lord of Death.

And so perhaps you will arise as Yamantaka, fierce protector of ever-present awareness and samurai warrior of intrinsic Spirit. Precisely those items that pretend to block ever-present awareness must be quickly cut through, which is why ever-present awareness arises in its many wrathful forms. You will simply be moved, from the ground of equality consciousness, to expose the false and the shallow and the less-than-ever-present. It is time for the sword, not the smile, but always the sword of discriminating wisdom, which ruthlessly cuts all obstacles in the ground of the all-encompassing.

 Perhaps you will arise as Bhaishajyaguru, whose ever-present awareness takes the form of a healing radiance. From the brilliant clarity of ever-present awareness, you will be moved to remind the sick and the sad and those in pain that although the pain is real, it is not what they are. With a simple touch or smile, contracted souls will relax into the vast expanse of intrinsic awareness, and disease will lose all meaning in the radiance of that release. And you will never tire, for ever-present awareness is effortless in its functioning, and so you will constantly remind all beings of who and what they really are, on the other side of fear, in the radical love and unflinching acceptance that is the mirror-mind of ever-present awareness.

 Perhaps you will arise as Maitreya, whose ever-present awareness takes the form of a promise that, even into the endless future, ever-present awareness will still be simply present. From the brilliant clarity of primordial awareness, you will vow to be with all beings, even unto an eternity of futures, because even those futures will arise in simple present awareness, the same present awareness that now sees just exactly this.

Those are simply a few of the potentials of ever-present awareness. The Buddhist names don't matter; any will do. They are simply a few of the forms of your own resurrection. They are a few of the possibilities that might animate you after the death of the Great Search. They are a few of the ways the world looks to the ever-present eye of Spirit, the ever-present I of Spirit. They are what you see, right now, when you see the world as God sees it, from the groundless ground of simple ever-present awareness.

AND IT IS ALL UNDONE

Perhaps you will arise as any or all of those forms of ever-present awareness. But then, it doesn't really matter. When you rest in the brilliant clarity of ever-present awareness, you are not Buddha or Bodhisattva, you are not this or that, you are not here or there. When you rest in simple, ever-present awareness, you are the great Unborn, free of all qualities whatsoever. Aware of color, you are colorless. Aware of time, you are timeless. Aware of form, you are formless. In the vast expanse of primordial Emptiness, you are forever invisible to this world.

It is simply that, as embodied being, you also arise in the world of form that is your own manifestation. And the intrinsic potentials of the enlightened mind (the intrinsic potentials of your ever-present awareness)—such as equanimity, discriminating wisdom, mirrorlike wisdom, ground consciousness, and all-accomplishing awareness—various of these potentials combine with the native dispositions and particular talents of your own individual bodymind. And thus, when the separate self dies into the vast expanse of its own ever-present awareness, you will arise animated by any or all of those various enlightened potentials. You are then motivated, not by the Great Search, but by the Great Compassion of these potentials, some of which are gentle, some of which are truly wrathful, but all of which are simply the possibilities of your own ever-present state.

And thus, resting in simple, clear, ever-present awareness, you will arise with the qualities and virtues of your own highest potentials—perhaps compassion, perhaps discriminating wisdom, perhaps cognitive insight, perhaps healing presence, perhaps wrathful reminder, perhaps artistic accomplishment, perhaps athletic skill, perhaps great educator, or perhaps something utterly simple, maybe being the best flower gardener on the block. (In other words, any of the developmental lines released into their own primordial state, released into their own post-postconventional condition.)[2] When the bodymind is released from the brutalities inflicted by the self-contraction, it naturally gravitates to its own highest estate, manifested in the great potentials of the enlightened mind, the great potentials of simple, ever-present awareness.

Thus, as you rest in simple, ever-present awareness, you are the great Unborn; but as you are born—as you arise from ever-present awareness—you will manifest certain qualities, qualities inherent in intrinsic Spirit, and qualities colored by the dispositions of your own bodymind and its particular talents.

And whatever the form of your own resurrection, you will arise, driven not by the Great Search, but by your own Great Duty, your limitless Dharma, the manifestation of your own highest potentials, and the world will begin to change, because of you. And you will never flinch, and you will never fail in that great Duty, and you will never turn away, because simple, ever-present awareness will be with you now and forever, even unto the ends of the worlds, because now and forever and endlessly forever, there is only Spirit, only intrinsic awareness, only the simple awareness of just this, and nothing more.

But that entire journey to what is begins at the beginningless beginning: we begin by simply recognizing that which is always already the case. ("If you understand this, then rest in that which understands, and just that is exactly Spirit. If you do not understand this, then rest in that which does not understand, and just that is exactly Spirit.") (We allow this recognition of ever-present awareness to arise—gently, randomly, spontaneously, through the day and into the night. This simple, ever-present awareness is not hard to attain but impossible to avoid, and we simply notice that.) *Awareness of awareness!*

We do this gently, randomly, and spontaneously, through the day and into the night. Soon enough, through all three states of waking, dreaming, and sleeping, this recognition will grow of its own accord and by its own intrinsic power, outshining the obstacles that pretend to hide its nature, until this simple, ever-present awareness announces itself in an unbroken continuity through all changes of state, through all changes of space and time, whereupon space and time lose all meaning whatsoever, exposed for what they are, the shining veils of the radiant Emptiness that you alone now are—and you will swoon into that Beauty, and die into that Truth, and dissolve into that Goodness, and there will be no one left to testify to terror, no one left to take tears seriously, no one left to engineer unease, no one left to deny the Divine, which only alone is, and only alone ever was, and only alone will ever be.

And somewhere on a cold crystal night the moon will shine on a silently waiting Earth, just to remind those left behind that it is all a game. The lunar light will set dreams afire in their sleeping hearts, and a yearning to awaken will stir in the depths of that restless night, and you will be pulled, yet again, to respond to those most plaintive prayers, and you will find yourself right here, right now, wondering what it all really means—until that flash of recognition runs across your face and it is all undone. You then will arise as the moon itself, and sing those dreams in your very own heart; and you will arise as the Earth itself, and glorify all of its blessed inhabitants; and you will arise as the Sun itself, radiant to infinity and much too obvious to see; and in that One Taste of primordial purity, with no beginning and no end, with no entrance and no exit, with no birth and no death, it all comes radically to be; and the sound of a singing waterfall, somewhere in the distance, is all that is left to tell this tale, late on that crystal cold night, bathed so beautifully in that lunar light, just so, and again, just so.

When the great Zen master Fa-ch'ang was dying, a squirrel screeched out on the roof. "It's just this," he said, "and nothing more."

Notes

Introduction

1. See K. Wilber, *Quantum Questions: Mystical Writings of the World's Great Physicists* (Boston: Shambhala Publications, 1985).

2. "Integral" and "integral studies" have sometimes been associated with Sri Aurobindo, his student Haridas Chaudhuri, and the California Institute of Integral Studies (founded by Chaudhuri and others), so perhaps a few words on each of those is in order.

   As the following pages will make clear, Aurobindo has been and continues to be an influence on my work. In fact, in chapter 6 we will see that he was instrumental in my moving from what I call a "Romantic/wilber-1" model to an "Aurobindo/wilber-2" model. Nonetheless, I eventually refined that model into "wilber-3" and "wilber-4," as I will explain in chapters 9, 10, and 11. Those chapters therefore constitute my critique of Aurobindo (and Chaudhuri).

   The essence of the critique is that both Aurobindo and Chaudhuri were pioneers in individual integral yoga and practice. This yoga especially focused on integrating the Ascending and Descending currents in the human being, thus embracing the entire spectrum of consciousness in both a transcendental/ascending and immanent/descending fashion. "Ascent and descent are then two inseparable aspects of the movement of integral yoga; they are the systole and diastole of integral self-discipline" (Chaudhuri, 1965, p. 41).

   I fully agree. But that approach is really just the beginning of a much more integral view (which I will explain in later chapters as wilber-3 and wilber-4). A truly integral yoga needs to take a much fuller account of the Western contributions to psychology, psychotherapy, and personal transformation (wilber-3), and it needs most especially to be set in the context of the four quadrants and their historical unfolding (wilber-4). Thus, my criticism of Aurobindo and Chaudhuri is a refinement, not a repudiation; but it is a refinement without which their systems are, I believe, limited and partial. This will become clear, I trust, in the succeeding chapters. [See *Integral Psychology* for a full elaboration of these themes.]

   The California Institute of Integral Studies is one of the few institutions of higher learning that will allow students to pursue a more integral orientation, including East/West studies. Nonetheless, it has also recently become, in my opinion, a source of much teaching that is quite anti-evolutionary, anti-Aurobindo, anti-Chaudhuri, and frankly regressive. I can no longer without qualifications recommend this institution to students. At the same time, it is the home of some gifted teachers, and students simply need to be cautious and selective in their courses. The same caution is due, I believe, the Naropa University in Boulder, Colorado. But with that proviso, these are two institutions where, with a little help from a sympathetic advisor, a student might be able to put together an integral program, even though the general atmosphere might resist it. Other noteworthy institutions include the Institute for Transpersonal Psychology, in Palo Alto, and JFK University, in Orinda, California. (For a complete listing of schools offering transpersonal courses and programs, see *The Common Boundary Education Guide*, obtainable from Common Boundary, 5272 River Rd., Suite 650, Bethesda, MD 20816. Also the guide from the Association for Transpersonal Psychology, 345 California St., Palo Alto, CA 94306. Those interested in meditation research might contact the Meditation Research Network, Institute of Noetic Sciences, 475 Gate 5 Road, Sausalito, CA 94965.)

At the same time, as the following chapters will make clear, the integral approach is now widely recognized (if not widely pursued) in many of the nation's higher centers of learning, from Harvard to West Georgia State, from Berkeley to the University of Connecticut, from Stanford to Norwich, from Vermont to Arizona State. A sympathetic advisor at almost any university nowadays can make a course in integral studies a genuine possibility.

3. With extreme constructivism, the individual subject (the I) is dissolved into intersubjective linguistic signifiers, loudly announced in the celebrated death of the subject, the death of the author, the death of man. Language itself replaces the individual self as the real subject of discourse (i.e., you are not talking, language alone is talking through you), and thus you and I are simply along for the irrelevant ride: the I is deconstructed into nothing but the linguistic We, and the death of the subject haunts the halls of the postmodern vacuum.

Not only are all I's (with their truthfulness) dissolved into a linguistic We, all its (with their objective truths) are likewise evaporated in the game of arbitrary construction. Gone is truth and gone is truthfulness, and in their place reigns a cultural construction driven only by power, by ideology, by gender, by this centrism or that centrism, by ugly motives of ugly people all lined up in a row.

And yet by the very fact of setting forth their theories they are actually doing something that their theories categorically state is impossible (namely, present what they feel is a power-free and ideology-free theory). The I and the it, which are both denied real existence in the face of the almighty constructing We, in fact reassert themselves as internal contradictions. And only by admitting the rejected domains can the partial truths of constructivism be taken up and worked into a larger, more open, more integral view.

4. It is very illuminating to contrast the cultural constructivists—who reduce everything to a dynamic collective We (Lower Left)—with the systems theorists, who reduce everything to a dynamic collective It (Lower Right). This is, in other words, another version of *interior* holism versus *exterior* holism.

Thus, for cultural constructivism (or interior holism), truth is primarily a *co-*

herence theory of truth, or intersubjective mesh and cultural meaning, because there are no objective its to anchor any correspondence theories of truth. The cultural alone is real, the We alone is real, and thus all truth and truthfulness are reduced to cultural interests and arbitrary constructions, which themselves exist only because they have a measure of coherence: the cultural alone is real, and all other "truths" are derivative to the great constructing We. No "I's" and no "its" need apply for membership in this culture club—they are barred from entry at the door.

For systems theory (or external holism), truth is found in functional fit, or interobjective mesh: the social alone is the primary reality. What both interior and exterior holism have in common is that they anchor their truth claims in the collective—one cultural (Lower Left), the other social (Lower Right). Since they are both "holistic," you might think they would be happy partners in the cause, but in fact they fairly despise each other, because the former is the epitome of subjectivism, the latter, of objectivism—the big system We versus the big system It.

Thus, you will never hear a systems theorist say that all systems are merely constructed, or arbitrary, or exist only as an ideology of gender, power, racism, and so on. No, systems theorists are by and large dedicated scientists, monological to a great degree, and they believe their systems are actually there, actually existing, largely independent of the terms used to describe them: real scientists study real systems in the real world! None of this "arbitrary constructivism," thank you very much. Exterior holists are realists in almost every sense.

But, of course, the interior holists—the cultural constructivists—don't believe in any independent or realistic "its" at all—whether dynamic, process, interwoven, systems or otherwise—because all "its" and all "I's" are culturally constructed products of the linguistic We. They therefore believe that the "systems" of the systems scientists are just arbitrary fabrications of a Eurocentric rationality driven by its attempt to gain power, a power that finds its ultimate expression in grand narratives and totalizing agendas such as systems theory, agendas that are driven by the worst sort of marginalizing, hegemonic, oppressive, and brutalizing aggression, all dressed up in the name of a knowledge that is in fact nothing but thinly disguised power.

Interior and exterior holism: both of them, ironically, partially true but thus ultimately quite nonholistic—and therefore constantly at each other's throats. And in each case the denied and oppressed quadrants wonderfully reassert themselves, upsetting the imperialists from within as massive self-contradictions, exploding their narrowness in a wider and more open vision, calling to us all in the name of a more integral embrace.

Chapter 1: The Spectrum of Consciousness

1. The Vedanta system (and its distant cousin, the Vajrayana) contains an exquisite overall model of the structures and states of consciousness, which I would explain more technically as follows:

The five sheaths are sheaths of consciousness or "mind" in the very broadest sense—physical consciousness, emotional consciousness, conceptual consciousness, intuitive consciousness, bliss consciousness. These are what I refer to as the *basic structures* of consciousness, the (upper) Left-Hand dimensions and levels of the human psyche.

But Vedanta realized that there is no mind without body, no consciousness without its support. Thus, each mind is supported by a body—the gross body (supporting the lowest mind), the subtle body (supporting the three "middle" minds), and the causal body (supporting the highest or unmanifest mind). These bodies are simply the "material" support of the "conscious" process—they are, in other words, the Right-Hand dimensions of the human psyche. (In Vajrayana, and Tantra in general, the three minds are supported by three "winds" or energy currents, also referred to as gross, subtle, and very subtle.)

Thus, we can quite accurately represent the Vedanta/Vajrayana view by speaking of the gross bodymind, the subtle bodymind, and the causal bodymind, covering the spectrum in both the Left- and Right-Hand domains, with the important proviso: God is always two-handed (i.e., these domains are inseparable, gross mind always occurring with gross body, subtle mind with subtle body, and so on).

Further, according to Vedanta/Vajrayana, these *basic structures*—the levels of the bodymind, gross to subtle to causal, which are permanent sheaths or levels available to human beings—are correlated with temporary consciousness (not permanent *structures*, but temporary *states*) in this fashion: the gross bodymind is experienced most typically in the waking state, the subtle bodymind in the dream state, and the causal bodymind in the deep dreamless state (the unmanifest). What is important here is that structures and states are not simply the same thing (a failure to grasp this elemental distinction has hobbled many transpersonal theories).

In various meditative *states*, the higher levels of the bodymind are brought into awareness, first as temporary states, and then eventually as permanent structures. The final result of this converting of states into traits is moksha, or radical liberation—a radical freedom from all manifestation, as all manifestation. In other words, the radical recognition of that Spirit which is both the goal and the ground of all states and all structures (turiya, the "fourth" beyond the gross, subtle, and causal bodyminds—in other words, the Emptiness and Suchness of the entire display, which is not a change of state but the stateless condition of all states).

This is an extraordinary model of human consciousness, easily the most comprehensive in all of the traditions (incorporating structures, states, and levels of both body/Right and mind/Left). What it lacks, in my opinion, are the developmental details (an approach specialized in by the modern West). With a more Western/developmental sensitivity, we can add an understanding of the developmental *lines* associated with each of those basic *levels*. The result of that synthesis would be a genuinely East-West overview. I present such a model in chapters 6 through 10, and discuss why I believe these additions are necessary to fill out the Vedanta/Vajrayana model.

Finally, what the Vedanta/Vajrayana model lacks—indeed, what the perennial philosophy in general lacks—is an understanding of how the Lower Left (cultural) and Lower Right (social) profoundly influence, and often govern, the individual consciousness and behavior which they otherwise understand so well (Upper Left and Upper Right). The Great Chain, for example, looks different—*is* different—in the magical, mythical, and mental worldspaces. This is yet another way of saying that integral studies must be not just "all-level" but "all-level, all-quadrant." The studies of Gebser (LL) and Marx (LR), for example, make no sense to a traditional Great Chain theorist, and, indeed, find no room in the traditional view, a view that, to just that extent, is woefully inadequate.

2. Stephen Jay Gould is the one theorist that almost everybody quotes when they wish to deny that hierarchy exists in nature. Gould is a staple of antihierarchical, flatland, heterarchical theorists, even though Gould himself has thoroughly abandoned the antihierarchical stance. In fact, Gould now quite avidly embraces hierarchy, both in nature and in our explanatory principles.

In a recent issue of *Sciences* (July/August 1995), Gould states that "Our stories about sequential stages seem to follow one of two modes: either as increments of progress (simple to complex) or as steps in refinement (inchoate to differentiated). The model for the first is addition; for the second, differentiation.

"I had always viewed the primal stories of addition and differentiation as our literary biases imposed upon nature's greater richness. But here nature . . . seems to be telling us that she acquiesces in these alternative readings of her fundamental sequences" (p. 36).

Hierarchical stages, in other words, are quite real, and not simply our anthropocentric creations. Gould is very explicit: "I freely confess my own strong preference . . . for a model that views selection as operating at several levels of a genealogical hierarchy including genes, organisms, local populations, and species. . . . Nature is organized as a hierarchy. . . . Entities at each level of the hierarchy can act as biological 'individuals,' and Darwin's process of selection can therefore occur at all levels . . ." (*New York Review of Books*, Nov. 19, 1992, p. 47).

I totally agree. In fact, in SES (note 49 for chapter 2) I outline the view that the "unit of selection" is in fact any holon in the overall holarchy, which is essentially Gould's view (as he says, "Selection can therefore occur at all levels"). Moreover, according to Gould, each level is ranked according to its *inclusiveness*: "Entities [exist] in a sequence of levels with unique explanatory principles emerging at each more inclusive plateau. This hierarchical perspective must take seriously the principle that phenomena of one level cannot automatically be extrapolated to work in the same way as others" (NYRB, Mar. 3, 1983). This is why, he adds, that emergent properties are real properties of organisms: "Organisms clearly have emergent properties, since their features . . . are products of complex and nonadditive interactions" (NYRB, Nov. 19, 1992, p. 47).

Thus, for Gould—as for virtually all of the great biological theoreticians, from Francisco Varela to Ernst Mayr—nature is hierarchically ordered; the units of Darwinian evolution are hierarchically ordered; and biology's explanatory principles are hierarchically ordered. Isn't it time the antihierarchy folks stopped using Gould to support their untenable position?

3. This is not to say that infancy and childhood can have no types of spiritual experiences. I have never maintained that view. Rather, as I pointed out in *Up from Eden*, even the infant experiences waking (gross), dreaming (subtle), and deep sleep (causal) states, and goes through this entire cycle every twenty-four hours. Further, as I suggested in *The Atman Project*, the infant might indeed come "trailing clouds of glory" from the intermediate bardo realms (via the psychic or deeper being). All of these are indeed temporary transpersonal states, but they are *not* enduring transpersonal structures, which only unfold in the course of ontogenetic (frontal) development. Thus, any of the transpersonal states in infancy are not due to *pre-egoic structures*. All of these points are elaborated in detail in chapters 7, 9, and 10.

Chapter 3: Eye to Eye

1. When philosophy, or intellectual awareness in general, is highly focused on its own source (i.e., witnessing subjectivity, the pure self), then such philosophy can indeed begin to shade into jnana yoga, the yoga of using the mind to transcend the mind. By deeply, profoundly, uninterruptedly inquiring into the Witness of all knowledge, this specific type of philosophical inquiry opens onto contemplative awareness: the mind itself subsides in the vast expanse of primordial awareness, and philosophia gives way to contemplatio.

Rare is the philosopher who uses the mind to transcend the mind. Jnana yoga is quite common in the East, but it only occasionally makes its appearance in the West, although when it does, it is sometimes quite profound (if sporadic). In SES I identified this as "Western Vedanta," and pointed out a few of its practitioners, including Augustine, Descartes, Fichte, Schelling, Hegel, Husserl, Sartre.

Thus, the heart of integral philosophy, as I conceive it, is primarily a *mental activity* of coordinating, elucidating, and conceptually integrating all of the various modes of knowing and being, so that, even if integral philosophy itself does not *deliver* the higher modes, it fully *acknowledges* them, and then allows and invites philosophia to open itself to the practices and modes of contemplatio. Integral philosophy is also, by virtue of its comprehensiveness, a powerful *critical theory*, critical of all less encompassing approaches—in philosophy, psychology, religion, social theory, and politics.

And, finally, it is a *theoria* that is inseparable from *praxis*, on all levels, in all quadrants.

Chapter 4: Integral Art and Literary Theory: Part 1

1. For an outline of integral semiotics, see chapter 5, note 12.
2. Quoted in Passmore, *Serious art*, p. 16.

3. Quoted ibid.
4. G. Bataille, *Visions of Excess*, p. 174.
5. Ibid., p. 174.
6. Quoted in ibid., p. xi.
7. J. Culler, *On Deconstruction*, p. 215. My italics.
8. Ibid., p. 123. My italics.
9. J. Habermas, *The Philosophical Discourse of Modernity*, p. 197.
10. Wimsatt and Beardsley, The Intentional Fallacy, in W. K. Wimsatt, 1966.
11. Passmore, *Serious Art*, p. 34.

Chapter 5: Integral Art and Literary Theory: Part 2

1. Quoted in M. Schapiro, *Theory and Philosophy of Art*, p. 154.
2. Quoted ibid., pp. 135–36.
3. Quoted ibid., chaps 5 and 6. Schapiro deals with the question: to which of the several paintings of shoes Heidegger and Gauguin are referring; since Heidegger says his point can be made with any of the various paintings, my general conclusion is unaffected by the final outcome of this issue. Gauguin has given two extremely moving accounts of this story; I have combined them for fullness of detail.

   Meyer Schapiro's many books are a wonderful source of material (including *Late Antique, Early Christian and Mediaeval Art*; *Romanesque Art*; *Modern Art*; and *Theory and Philosophy of Art: Style, Artist, and Society*), and I highly recommend them.

   Incidentally, when I claim that all four quadrants evolve, this includes the claim that *art itself evolves*. I am constantly challenged on this point. A few people understandably feel that if, for example, Picasso was doing primitivist themes, how could this be *development* with any sort of *directionality*? Or if this is directional, isn't it going backwards? How could art be following the twenty tenets that SES claimed to be operative in all domains? Further, you might like modern, I might like African, she might like postmodern, and so on; what kind of arrogance says one of these is "more evolved"? (The standard postmodern horror of qualitative distinctions—which, of course, is itself a massive qualitative distinction: its stance is *better* than the alternatives!)

   As usual with evolutionary themes, the topic only comes into focus if we back up a sufficiently far distance, so as to let truly long-range trends come into clear focus. Centering on particular artistic styles and contents, although useful and interesting itself, is usually worthless in spotting Eros.

   So let's look to the few art historians who have actually investigated the historical unfolding of artistic fundamentals at a sufficiently deep level (the deep structures of the aesthetic dimension). Meyer Schapiro's book *Theory and Philosophy of Art* is such an approach. Schapiro is a very rare bird: a famous artist himself, he is also a first-rate philosopher and a gifted writer. Richard Wollheim (Mill Professor of Philosophy at Berkeley) summarizes one of the central conclusions of Schapiro's research, which, says Wollheim, "is surely among the fundamental writings of art history":

In the beginning, our ancestors made figurative images of the animals they hunted. In doing so, they paid no attention to the surface on which the images were inscribed. Then they did, and, when they did, found uses for the ground, either representational or to enhance the image. But they paid no attention to the fact that, as surfaces do in nature, the ground had its bounds. Then they did, and, when they did, distinguished between the horizontal and vertical edges, and found distinctive uses for each, but they paid no attention to the fact that the ground with its edges could be looked at various ways up. Then they did, and, when they did, settled for the one way as the right way up, and started to find uses for orientation. And so on [including the further emergence of perspective within the orientation . . .].

Step by step, and not without regression, intentional or accidental, a medium was developed out of the natural materials as each aspect was explicitly recognized. . . . (*London Review of Books*, June 22, 1995)

In other words, we are looking at the unfolding or emergence of worldspaces, each of which transcends and includes the fundamental and learned elements of the previous worldspace (or else it would not and could not itself emerge: the more significant rests on the more fundamental, because it actually incorporates it internally).

And, as Wollheim and Schapiro both make quite clear, the same is true in the artistic and aesthetic dimension itself on a broad scale. "They paid no attention" means "they did not see," precisely because "what they did not see" simply was not in their worldspace: it had not yet emerged, it literally did not yet exist. "And when they did" means, "And then they could" or "and then they could see it," precisely because it had now emerged, it now existed in the new worldspace, it had now come into being: it had now developed or emerged or evolved, building upon its predecessors precisely by incorporating and then transcending them.

As Habermas is fond of saying, learning cannot not occur. And learning occurred in the aesthetic dimension just as it does everywhere else. Schapiro gives a superb summary of the extremely fundamental elements of aesthetic perception as they were historically learned, selected, and passed on (i.e., evolution). And all of this development is missed if you focus on the surface style, content, theme, and so on.

Thus, even when Picasso "regresses" to primitivism, he is using techniques and perspectives that were not present in the original primitives; he has transcended and included those fundamentals even as he tries to hide his own advanced techniques in the crudeness of his simple lines. This is enough to confuse most art critics (who don't see the evolution), but not Schapiro. Perhaps because he himself is a gifted painter and knows all the tricks, he can see ever so clearly the profound developmental progression even in Picasso's wonderful wanderings.

And thus, put bluntly, the aesthetic dimension develops and unfolds/enfolds, just like holons everywhere else in the Kosmos. I would simply add that each of these aesthetic unfoldings has correlates in the other quadrants. A new aesthetic perception will go with a new mode of production, a new sense of self (with new motivations), a new cultural worldview (with new intersubjective values), a new set of behavioral patterns, and so on.

But the aesthetic dimension I have a particular fondness for; it reminds us of the Beauty of each and every stage of Spirit's self-actualization; it leaves a clearly marked trail of beauty to beauty to beauty, shining from the radiant void, inviting each of us to fall in love all over again with the entire majesty of the radiant display, and reminds us always that Beauty is not just a pretty surface but a profoundly deep manner and mode of knowing: Beauty is the direct apprehension of the Depth of the Divine, and as that Depth unfolds, so does that wondrous Beauty.

The history of that unfolding is the history of art and the aesthetic in its many dimensions. And that history ends for any individual when the depth goes to infinity, the beauty goes to Godhead, the I itself dissolves in I-I, agency issues in purest Emptiness—which is the ultimate Depth of the Divine and the ultimate Beauty of Spirit, this vast and infinite Freedom whose It is Dharma, whose We is Sangha, and whose I is Buddha: the True, and the Good, and the Beautiful.

4. D. Hoy, *The Critical Circle*, p. 9.
5. Quoted in Passmore, p. 27.
6. Quoted ibid.
7. Hoy, pp. 164–65.
8. Ibid., p. 69.
9. Quoted in C. Benfey, Native American, *The New Republic*, Oct. 9, 1995, p. 38.
10. In other words, the three strands of all valid knowledge accumulation (injunction, apprehension, confirmation; or exemplar, evidence, justification; or paradigm, data, fallibilism) are most definitely at work in the hermeneutic endeavor, just as they are at work in empirical science and contemplative endeavors.

Incidentally, the interpretation of art symbols has much in common with the interpretation of dreams, and I definitely intend this integral hermeneutics to cover both (as part of an integral semiotics in general).

In chapter 5 of *Transformations of Consciousness*, I outline a theory of dream interpretation that suggests that any given dream symbol might in fact be a carrier of meaning from virtually any level of the spectrum of consciousness, and often the same symbol can *simultaneously* carry numerous multilevel meanings. I suggested that the easiest way to interpret such dreams is to start at the lower levels and work one's way up (physical meaning to emotional meaning to mental meaning to existential meaning to spiritual meaning), using each expanding context to shed new light and new meaning on the dream symbol (each meaning is particularly valid if it "clicks" or elicits the "aha" response, or is otherwise charged and vivid).

The same, of course, is true of art (and symbols in general). The spectrum of consciousness is at work in both the maker (as part of the conscious or unconscious intentionality of the primal holon) and the viewer (any level of the spectrum might be elicited in a particular viewer response). The identical art symbol (e.g., the pair of shoes) can be read on any number of levels of the spectrum—in both artist and viewer alike—and all of those multilevel interpretations might be valid (just as with the dream symbol—or any symbol, for that matter).

Part of integral hermeneutics is the actual determination, as far as possible, of *those levels that can legitimately be invoked for a justifiable interpretation in any given case.* For example, which levels of the spectrum of consciousness are actually operative in the making of any particular piece of art (consciously or unconsciously)? Which levels are most commonly invoked in most viewers (consciously or unconsciously)? Is this evocation intentional or not on the part of the maker? And so on.

The example of Van Gogh's shoes indicated how important the higher levels of the spectrum can be in valid interpretation. As I have been maintaining throughout this volume, the admission of the entire spectrum of consciousness would alter every discipline it touches, and art is no exception.

11. Hoy, pp. 69, 76.
12. We can now do a quick four-quadrant summary of the various theories of art interpretation, which is also a summary of the four facets present in every holon, including the art holon.

The actual material artwork itself (the material painting, book, public display, performed music) is the Upper-Right quadrant. The theories that focus on this artwork holon are particularly the formalist theories: the relation between the elements in the material, signifying artwork—the actual *form* of the artwork holon as it exists in public space.

That artwork is, in part, the expression of the original intention of the artist or maker, and that original intention—the primal holon—is the Upper-Left quadrant. This quadrant is the site of the spectrum of consciousness as it manifests in any individual, which means that there is actually a spectrum of intentionality available to all of us (including, of course, the artist or maker). Any or all of these levels of consciousness and intentionality might have a hand in the formation of the primal holon (the original intent of the artist that eventually finds expression in the public, material artwork). Theories of interpretation that focus on the primal holon include the expressivist and intentionality theories, which seek to reconstruct and recover the original intent of the maker (the primal holon); and also certain symptomatic theories, when they seek to disclose, decode, and interpret any individual unconscious intentionality. (And, we add, *the entire spectrum of consciousness* provides the most complete context against which to discern these overall intentionalities, conscious or unconscious, in artist and viewer alike.)

But neither the primal holon nor the artwork holon exists as an isolated and self-regarding element. They are both set in wider and deeper cultural and social contexts. The intersubjective cultural background in which the primal holon arises is the Lower-Left quadrant. This is the vast pool of collective signifieds and worldviews, within which, and upon which, individual meaning floats like a cork on water, governing which interpretations are and can be made. Theories that focus on this historically embedded cultural background include the theories of reception and response and viewer response, as well as those symptomatic theories that focus on the cultural construction of meaning.

In addition to this intersubjective cultural background, the primal and artwork holons exist in a vast interobjective social system, the Lower-Right quadrant. This is the sum total of the material, structural, institutional, and techno-economic systems—and the vast pool of collective signifiers—that govern the materialities of communication and the social action system in general. It includes everything from forces of production to geopolitical locations, from modes of information transfer to social class distinctions, from income distribution to structures of linguistic signifiers—all of which considerably impact the artist and artwork. Theories of interpretation that focus on the Lower-Right quadrant include Marxist, social feminist, imperialist, ecologist—in short, the symptomatic theories insofar as they focus on the wider currents in the social system.

The point, of course, is that *integral hermeneutics*—integral art and literary theory, and integral semiotics in general—explicitly includes all of those quadrants, *and all of the levels in each of them*: all-quadrant, all-level. And it does so, not as an eclecticism, but as a coherent explication of the very structures of holons.

Finally, a brief word about an *integral theory of semiotics* in general. Some of the pieces of the puzzle here include Ferdinand de Saussure's *semiology*, which maintains that all signs indicating referents are composed of a material (or exterior) *signifier* and a mental (or interior) *signified*; Charles Peirce's *semiotics*, which maintains that signs are not just dyadic (signifier and signified) but rather triadic (as he put it, "an action, or influence, which is, or involves, an operation of *three* subjects, such as a sign, its object, and its interpretant, this trirelative influence not being in any way resolvable into an action between pairs"); *speech-act theory* of J. L. Austin and John Searle; *communicative action theory* of Habermas; *developmental structuralism* (e.g., Piaget); and traditional *hermeneutics*—to mention a prominent few. Although "semiotics" in the narrow sense refers to Peirce's approach to the topic, it is common to use that term to refer to the entire field of signs and symbols.

Given the failure of the empiricist, positivist, behaviorist, and representational paradigms to account for the generation of the many varieties of linguistic meaning, the central issue of semiotics (and knowledge in general) has become where exactly to *locate the referents of utterances*. To give a simple example, when I say, "I see the dog," we can all look and point to the real dog, assuming it's there. The real dog has simple location in empirical space, and thus locating that referent is fairly easy. But when I say, "George is green with envy because John has already shown that he has more courage," then where exactly are we to locate "envy" and "courage"? They don't have simple location in physical space, and thus we can't point to them empirically. We can't "put our finger" on them.

Just so, we can't put our finger on most of the referents of mathematics (where is the square root of a negative one?), nor poetry, nor logic, nor any of the virtues—we can't point to honor or valor or compassion or spiritual knowledge.

But the fact that most of the important issues in our lives do not have simple location does not mean they aren't real or do not exist. It only means that they cannot be found in physical space with simple location: they cannot be found in the sensorimotor worldspace.

But in addition to the sensorimotor worldspace, there is the emotional, the magical, the mythical, the rational, the existential, the psychic, the subtle, the causal, and the nondual worldspaces. *And all of those worldspaces have their own phenomenologically real referents.* A dog exists in the sensorimotor worldspace, and can be seen by any holon with physical eyes. The square root of a negative one exists in the rational worldspace, and can be seen by anyone who develops to the dimension of formal operational awareness. And Buddha-nature exists in the causal worldspace, and can be easily seen by anybody who develops to that very real dimension of their own structural possibilities.

In other words, *the real referent of a valid utterance exists in a specific worldspace*. The empiricist theories have failed in general because they ultimately recognize only the sensorimotor worldspace (and thus cannot even account for the existence of their own theories, which do not exist in the sensorimotor worldspace but in the rational worldspace).

In short, the *signifier* (e.g., the material word "dog," "negative one," or "Buddha-nature" as they are written on this page or spoken by a person) is the Upper-Right quadrant, the actual material mark. The *signified* (that which comes to mind when you read the word "dog" or "negative one" or "Buddha-nature") is the Upper-Left quadrant, the interior apprehension. This is what Saussure meant by the material mark (signifier) and the concept it elicits (signified), both of which are different from the actual referent. And the actual *referent* of a valid utterance, to the extent it is valid, exists in a given worldspace—in the intersubjective space, opening, or clearing within which all referents arise (the Lower-Left quadrant).

Because all signifiers are by definition material, they can be seen by any animal with physical eyes (my dog can see the physical marks on this page). But the *signified* can only be seen *if the appropriate level of interior development* has been attained. Thus, my dog can see the signifier "dog," but that word has no meaning for him, no signified for him, and thus he cannot know what the referent of that word actually is. Likewise, a six-year-old can read the words "the square root of a negative one," but those signifiers don't have any meaning (nothing is signified), and thus the six-year-old cannot grasp the actual referent (the mathematical entity that exists only in the rational worldspace).

Thus, because referents exist only in particular worldspaces, if you have not developed to that worldspace—if you do not possess the *developmental signified*—then you cannot see the actual referent. Thus, anybody can read the words (the signifiers) that say "Buddha-nature," but if the person has not developed to the causal dimension, then that word will basically be meaningless (it will not elicit the correct signified, the developmental signified, the interior apprehension or understanding), and thus that person will not be able to perceive Buddha-nature, just as the six-year-old cannot perceive the square root of a negative one.

Thus, all referents exist in worldspaces (the Lower Left); all signifiers exist in the material and empirical domain (Upper Right); and all signifieds are actually developmental signifieds, and exist in the Upper Left.

But signifiers (Upper Right) and signifieds (Upper Left) do not exist in a vacuum. They each have their collective forms. The *collective signifiers*—the form or structure that governs the rules and the codes of the system of signifiers (the Lower Right)—is simply *syntax*. And the *collective signifieds*—the actual meaning generated by cultural intersubjectivity (the Lower Left)—is simply *semantics*.

This gives us a chance to bring together the various semiotic schools I mentioned at the beginning of this summary. For example, by seeing that the signified (Upper Left) arises only in the space of the collective worldview or cultural semantic (Lower Left)—which will serve as the necessary background context for the individual interpretation—Peirce's triadic and Saussure's dyadic structure of the sign can be brought into close accord (Peirce's sign is Saussure's signifier; Peirce's object is Saussure's referent; Peirce's interpretant is Saussure's signified).

We can likewise find room in this integral approach for the important discoveries of postmodernism on the nature of the materialities of communication and the chains of sliding signifiers (Derrida), and on the importance of transformative codes in selecting which signifiers will be deemed serious and which marginal (Foucault). Even more important, I believe, we can honor Paul Ricoeur's "structuralist hermeneutics," a bold (and partially successful) attempt to integrate *formalist explication* (structural system or syntax of Lower Right) with *meaningful interpretation* (cultural hermeneutics and semantics of Lower Left). Ricoeur: "If, then, the intention is the intention of the text, and if this intention is the direction that it opens for thought, it is necessary to understand the deep semantics in a fundamentally dynamic sense; I will hence say this: to explicate is to free [or expose] the structure, that is to say, the internal relations of dependence which constitute the static of the text [the formalist syntax]; to interpret is to set out on the path of thought opened by the text, to start out on the way to the orient of the text [deep semantics]." Also, by emphasizing the fact that all signifieds are actually developmental signifieds, we can honor the important contributions of the developmentally oriented theorists (such as Habermas on the development of communicative competence).

In short, individual *signifiers* are Upper Right (material marks); *signifieds* are Upper Left (interior apprehensions); *syntax* is Lower Right (collective systems and structural rules of language accessed in an objective fashion); *semantics* is Lower Left (the actual referents of linguistic signs, referents which exist *only* as disclosed in particular worldviews or worldspaces). If we add ten or so levels of development in each of those quadrants, I believe we will have the beginnings of a truly comprehensive or integral theory of semiotics.

Finally, this integral approach—almost as a bonus—sets *spiritual referents* on precisely the same general footing as any other valid referent (sensory, rational, mathematical, etc.) To my mind, the grounding of spiritual referents is *the* crucial issue in this field, and so far virtually no work has been done in this area at all. But an integral semiotics puts both "dog" and "God" on the same footing.

This is why we can say that "Buddha-nature" is a material word (the *signifier*) whose semantic *referent* exists only in a *worldspace* (in this case, the causal worldspace) that is disclosed only as a *developmental signified* (the interior apprehension of someone who has actually developed or evolved to that worldspace). This is true of any signifier, signified, and referent, and thus, when coupled with the genuine methodology of spiritual knowledge (i.e., injunction, data, fallibilism), grounds spiritual knowledge in a justifiable and demonstrable fashion.

To my knowledge, this is a novel overall approach, with few precedents in the world's modern or ancient traditions, although what I have presented is a brutally simplified summary and outline. As I earlier indicated, a future work is devoted entirely to this topic.

13. Emerson, *Selected Prose and Poetry.*

Chapter 6: The Recaptured God

1. I have elsewhere presented a sustained critique of Michael Washburn's position (Wilber, 1990), and I will not repeat those arguments. I will here specifically address the revised, second edition of *The Ego and the Dynamic Ground.*

2. Other important enduring structures include what I call talents, such as artistic, mathematical, musical, dance, and so on. I have in mind Howard Gardner's important work on multiple intelligences, which I discuss in chapter 11. As we will see, each of these talents (as a relatively independent developmental line) unfolds through the same general levels of the spectrum of consciousness.

3. The self-needs, self-identity, and morals I call the *self-related stages* (other self-related stages include interpersonal, defense mechanisms, and object-relations). They are all generated, as we will see, when the proximate self-sense identifies with a particular level of consciousness.

   The basic structures of consciousness are the general (cross-line, cross-domain) levels or waves of development, through which almost two dozen developmental lines or streams proceed. The basic structures are mostly enduring structures (although they do have some transitional features associated with their phase-specific emergence). The developmental lines include both enduring and transitional structures, but they are mostly transitional. Examples of developmental lines include the self-stages, worldviews, affective development, various talents (music, art, dance), and so on. In this and the next few chapters, we will explore all of these topics in detail.

4. The distinction between enduring and transitional structures is not well known. Flavell (1963) is a rare exception; he points out this crucial distinction, only to note that almost nobody has done anything with it.

The difference between the enduring structures and the transitional structures can easily be seen in a comparison of, say, Piaget (cognitive) and Kohlberg (moral). With cognitive development in general, each stage is *incorporated* into subsequent stages, so that the junior is a crucial *component* of the senior. Once images emerge, for example, the individual has full and constant access to the capacity to form images. And images themselves will be an indispensable ingredient in the higher symbolic, conceptual, and formal thought. But with moral development, the process is quite different: higher structures do not so much incorporate as *replace* previous ones. Thus, a person at moral stage 3 does not have open access to moral stage 1, for those stages are mutually incompatible (a conformist does not simultaneously act as an egocentric rebel). In fact, a moral stage-3 person cannot even think in the terms of moral stage 1; those earlier structures have long ago dissolved and been replaced (barring fixation, repression, etc.).

At the same time, this is not a rigid and stark distinction, but more of a continuum between purely enduring and purely transitional (as idealized end limits). We see the distinction most clearly in terms of conscious access. Previous enduring structures are almost always fully present and available to consciousness (such as sensorimotor, images, symbols, etc.), but previous transitional structures are largely deconstructed and are not fully available to awareness, even if some of their core competences have indeed been differentiated-and-integrated. The need for food remains; the oral stage does not (barring fixation, repression, etc.). This will become more obvious as we proceed.

Since I first published an article on these two different types of development ("Ontogenetic Development: Two Fundamental Patterns," 1981), I have stressed the importance of this distinction, simply because the entire notion of *transcendence* depends upon it. Development might indeed follow the pattern of "transcend and include" or "negate and preserve." But what is negated, and what is preserved? What remains, and what is replaced? What endures, and what must go? Buddhas transcend the separate-self sense, but even Buddhas must eat. Some things go, and some things stay! And my point is that higher development (like all development) includes and incorporates basic structures but replaces and deconstructs transitional structures, and to confuse these two is effectively to abort development.

As I indicated, for the most part the basic levels are enduring structures—they are the waves in the Great Holarchy of Being. And the various developmental lines or streams are mostly transitional structures—they are replaced by their successors as consciousness continues its ever-expanding evolution. In the text I will focus on the basic levels and lines, but their respectively enduring and transitional natures might be kept in mind.

5. Wilber, 1984, 1996c; Wilber et al. 1986.
6. When describing it in Right-Hand (or it) language, I refer to the self as the self-system. In Left-Hand terms, I refer to it as the self-sense (and self-identity). Both are equally valid languages and equally important aspects of the holon that is the self.

As we will see, I divide the overall self-sense into the anterior self (experienced as I-I), the proximate self (experienced as "I"), and the distal self (experienced as "me" or even "mine").

So technically we say, when the proximate self-sense identifies with a particular basic structure, the exclusivity of that identification generates (or supports) the corresponding transitional structures of the self-stages (identity, needs, morals). Not all transitional structures are generated this way; only the self-related stages. Exactly what that means will become clear, I believe, as the discussion unfolds. [See *Integral Psychology* for a further discussion of this topic.]

7. Further, at each of those levels of pathology, there are specific subtypes, determined by the actual events in the phases of the particular fulcrum itself, because development can miscarry at any of those crucial phases. For example, a failure to leave the fusion phase of a fulcrum means that the self remains fully embedded at that level (developmental arrest, attachment, indissociation, fusion). A failure in the differentiation phase means that the self begins to differentiate and transcend that level but fails in crucial ways, and thus remains partially split and stuck to various aspects of that dimension (fragmentation, fixation), often with a consequently fragile self boundary (splitting). A failure in the integration phase means that the self refuses to include aspects of the previous basic structures in its makeup; it doesn't just differentiate, it dissociates (repression); it doesn't transcend and include, it transcends and alienates, denies, represses, distorts.

In *Transformations of Consciousness*, I suggest specific examples of each of those subtypes for each of the nine fulcrums (i.e., twenty-seven types of specific developmental pathologies). I also suggest the types of therapy that seem best suited to dealing with each of these pathologies. That is still a very introductory and generalized discussion, but I believe it is a useful step toward a more comprehensive overview of psychopathology. [See also *Integral Psychology*.]

8. Wilber, 1984, 1995, 1996d; Wilber et al., 1986. See also chapter 11, especially section "Integral Therapy." [See also *Integral Psychology*, chap. 8.]

9. In contrast to both the enduring and transitional structures of consciousness, states of consciousness tend to be discrete and temporary. This differentiates them from even the transitional structures in the developmental streams, because transitional structures, for as long as they are in place, are fully and continuously available, as are the enduring structures themselves; but states come and go, and rarely last more than a few hours.

Further, basic structures are inclusionary (they directly include their predecessors), but states are usually exclusionary (you cannot be drunk and sober at the same time), which is why all of the strict NOSC (nonordinary states of consciousness) models have proven incapable of conceptualizing the development and evolution of consciousness.

The three most important states are waking, dreaming, and deep sleep, said by the traditional psychologies to correspond with gross, subtle, and causal realms. The human being, beginning in the first months of prenatal life, is immersed in all three states (and thus has access to gross, subtle, and causal realms, although not in any permanent or adapted capacity). Growth will consist in a gradual conversion of these alternating and temporary states into enduring structures and traits. The mechanism of that conversion is the central story of the growth and development of consciousness in humans and evolution at large. [This topic is further discussed in *Integral Psychology*.]

10. This Plotinian approach can be directly applied to general Buddhist studies, thus securing one of the simplest and most durable integrations of East/West approaches. See *A Brief History of Everything* for an elaboration of this theme.

11. 1995, p. 38.

12. The *type of defense* depends upon the *level of development* at which the dissociation occurs (the hierarchy of defenses), even into the transpersonal domains with their own specific defenses and pathologies. In technical terms, almost any of the surface structures of the basic structures and the developmental lines can be dissociated, repressed, sublimated, or otherwise defended against; it is those surface structures, not the deep structures, that are repressed. The major *dynamic* of defense at any level is death-seizure; defenses finally drop only when all deaths have been died, all subjects have been killed, at which point only Emptiness reigns, which is not threatened with death because it was never born; the great Unborn, radiant to infinity, is radically undefended precisely because there is nothing outside it that could hurt it, harm it, push it, pull it. (For a further discussion of those themes, see *The Atman Project, Up from Eden, Transformations of Consciousness*, [and *Integral Psychology*].)

13. Here are the five:

1. *How central a role does pre-egoic conflict play?* According to Washburn, I give almost no importance to pre-egoic conflict. On the contrary, as we saw, the first four fulcrums of the pre-egoic period are in many ways the most crucial, and conflict in the subphases of those fulcrums is a central theme of early development. (As we will see, the real issue here is *what* is being repressed, not whether repression occurs.)

2. *Transition to the egoic stage: Are pre-egoic potentials lost or retained?* Washburn maintains that my model cannot accommodate the loss and repression of pre-egoic potentials. Once again, he is focusing merely on basic structures, which are incorporated, not lost. But the self-system is involved in extensive defensive measures, and thus many pre-egoic potentials are indeed lost.

(The real disagreement, again, is about the exact nature and characteristics of these pre-egoic potentials that are lost. For Washburn, these pre-egoic potentials are a form of the Dynamic Ground, which are originally in *full consciousness* in the infantile self but are then, in the first year or two, repressed and disconnected from awareness. For me, the pre-egoic potentials are general bodily vitality, sensual awareness, diffuse prana, and emotional-sexual energy in general—as we will see.)

3. *The egoic stage: Is the mental ego alienated from its sources and its foundations?* Washburn (1995) states that my model "sees the mental ego as remaining in touch with its foundations. Pre-egoic basic structures are preserved within the more inclusive boundaries of egoic life" (pp. 40–41). Once again, Washburn

focuses only on the basic structures and totally ignores the self-system and the self-fulcrums with their pathologies, repressions, dissociations. Of course the ego can alienate and repress aspects of its pre-egoic potentials (differentiation can go into dissociation at any of the fulcrums!).

4. *Transition to the transegoic stage: Straight ascent or spiral movement through origins?* By focusing on the basic structures alone, and ignoring the self-system and the many uneven developmental lines (not to mention altered states), Washburn can present a caricature of my model as a "straightforward ascending movement."

Not only does that ignore the entire movement of descending and involutionary energies, which I clearly described at great length in the sources cited by Washburn, it completely trivializes the dialectical and spiraling nature of self-development. (Once again, the real disagreement here concerns the nature of the infantile structure that is supposed to be the lost "source" and the "origin" to which the mature self *must* regress in order to gain spiritual awakening.)

5. *The transegoic stage: Are there two selves or none?* In this discussion Washburn seems to ignore everything I have written about the ego being *both* negated and preserved, and he simply presents his view as a correction to my errors.

Looking at those five points, which are supposed to be deficiencies in my model that then recommend Washburn's, it appears that none of them are very sound. As to the nature of the "dynamic ground," about which Washburn and I definitely disagree, see the text.

14. Wilber, 1979b. This view (that libido is a limited version of spirit) also makes sense from an involutional view, which derives the lower from the higher ontologically (in involution), not chronologically (in evolution), and therefore does not have to elevate the pre-egoic structure to transegoic God-consciousness. The involutional stance is my view, whereas Washburn (and my earlier stance) is essentially the Romantic orientation.

15. Wilber, 1978a, 1978b, 1978c, 1979a. I also published another article which summarized this overall position (Wilber, 1979b).

16. Wilber, 1982a.

17. Wilber, 1980.

18. 1995, p. 249.

19. 1995, pp. 48, 50, 49. I will discuss Stan Grof's view in the next chapter, but it should be noted that, despite certain vague similarities, the views of Washburn and Grof on the perinatal and neonatal state are often quite diametrically opposed. For Washburn, the real loss of the Ground doesn't congeal until around eighteen months; whereas for Grof, that drama is basically ended around birth. This is a crucial and altogether divisive wedge separating their views; if one of them is right, the other is very wrong.

Thus, in Grof's data, when people relive the agony of being born as a separate-self, they don't relive the events that occurred at eighteen months. But they would have to, according to Washburn's model. Likewise, Grof and Washburn do not agree on a common point that indicates the introduction of existential tragedy into human consciousness, and that would therefore accommodate both of their models. Grof and Washburn support each other only from a misty distance; up close, they are some of each other's greatest antagonists.

In my view, Grof is dealing basically with fulcrum-o and Washburn with fulcrum-1, and I believe the data from both of them strongly supports that conclusion. I will return to this in the next chapter.

20. These three great realms are exactly why Western philosophy has always had three broad currents: Sensory, Rational, and Idealistic, depending on whether emphasis was given to body, mind, or spirit.

And the pre/trans fallacy explains why Sensory/Romanticism and Idealism were always in strange and bizarre mixtures and alliances against their common "enemy," Rationalism. Schelling, in my opinion, did a fair job of integrating all three great domains, which is why he balances Romanticism and Rationalism and Idealism (and is claimed by all three movements); but subsequent Romantics all too often headed in a purely prerational and sensory-emotional direction, which is why Fichte and Hegel were forced to launch virulent attacks, not against reason, *but against the Romantics*, who were often busy elevating prerational infantilisms to transrational glory.

The entire German tradition itself is a study in the pre/trans fallacy, producing now a Hegel, now a Hitler. Precisely because the German tradition strove so nobly and so mightily for Geist and Spirit (which is to its everlasting credit), it was open more intensely to confusing prerational bodily and emotional enthusiasms with transrational insight and awareness. Blood and soil, return to nature, and noble savages flourished under the banner of a Romantic return to spirit, a recapture of the lost Ground, a return of the hidden God, a revelation written in blood and etched in the flesh of those who would stand in the way of this noble-savage, ethnic-blood purity, and the gas chambers waited as the silent womb of the Great Mother to receive all of those who corrupted this purity.

21. Of course, Washburn is too careful a theorist to actually believe his own two-pole reductionism, which is why he sneaks back the correct three-part model with his notion that Ground can appear as libido (gross), free psyche (mind), and spirit (causal). This is the correct three-tiered traditional view, and once we see that Ground is equally the Ground of all three, it drops out of the developmental equation, and the novel aspects of Washburn's presentation likewise disappear, leaving us with a Wilber-II type of model.

Failing to acknowledge this, the road is then wide-open for Washburn to follow through on his reductionism (and subsequent elevationism). Washburn states that in the "original embedment" of the infantile state, "the newborn is absorbed in the Dynamic Ground and in the numinous power resident in the Ground" (p. 48). The central characteristic of this state is "the unrestricted circulation of the power of the Ground within the newborn . . ." (p. 48). It is important that Washburn maintains this, as we saw, because if Ground is not fully present and *fully unrestricted* in the infantile state, then the spiritual awakening of the transegoic stage could *not* be an actual reunion with something lost in development (spiritual awakening would instead be an *emergent*, which is indeed a reunion, not with something lost in early evolution but in the prior movement of involution; which, of course, is the Plotinus/Aurobindo/Wilber-II view).

Given that the Ground supposedly exists "fully unrestricted" in the newborn, let us look at the actual characteristics of the infantile self in order to see what this Ground might actually consist of. Does the neonate have the capacity to cognitively take the role of other? No, that capacity doesn't emerge until around year six or seven. But without the capacity to take the role of other, there is no corresponding capacity for actual compassion, altruistic love, or intersubjective care; there is no concernful ethics or moral virtue, and no service to others. In fact, this infantile state is, by virtually unanimous agreement, a state of extreme egocentric and narcissistic involvement.

The ego then eventually emerges—especially, says Washburn, with concrete and formal operational thought—and this emergence, he maintains, *necessarily* involves the "primal repression" of the Ground (it is forced out of consciousness). Yet this is the very same period, researchers agree, that conventional and postconventional morality can develop—the period where the self learns to take the role of other, learns to develop intersubjective love, compassion, mercy, service, and care.

In Washburn's model, then, when the Ground is fully present and unrestricted, the self lacks love, lacks compassion, lacks virtue, lacks service. But when the Ground is repressed, the self develops love, compassion, virtue, and care. This is a very strange Ground. (It is, I suggest, a Ground shot through with pre/trans fallacies.)

Incidentally, Washburn's "ptf-3" is indeed a fallacy: it is simply another name for Washburn's refusal to recognize the Trikaya (the existence of gross, subtle, and causal realms). His collapse of tripartite into bipartite forces him to view any renormalization as a fallacy.

22. 1995, p. 171.
23. Ibid.
24. 1995, p. 201.
25. 1995, p. 74.
26. 1993, p. 67.

Chapter 7: Born Again

1. 1985, p. 16.
2. In Miller, 1993, p. 52.
3. Jungian "archetypes" are essentially monological, even if collective. That is, they are basically collective subjective, not collective intersubjective, structures. Thus, for example, the subjective image of the Great Mother arises within intersubjective patterns that are themselves found in none of the lists of archetypes ever given by the Jungians, precisely because these intersubjective patterns are not objects of monological phenomenology and are thus never disclosed by any of the techniques of Jungian or neo-Jungian inquiry. Jung and his many follow-

ers remain within the monological tradition, even if, as I indicated, they have fruitfully extended the content and range of that phenomenology. See chapter 11 for a fuller discussion of Jungian archetypes.

4. 1985, p. 435.
5. 1988, p. 9.
6. Ibid.
7. 1985, p. 99.
8. 1988, p. 9.
9. 1985, p. 99.
10. 1985, pp. 140, 99.
11. 1988, p. 10.
12. 1985, p. 99.
13. Smith 1976, p. 165.
14. Of course, the gross bodymind itself, and all of its competences and enduring structures, *will be included* in the higher organizations of the subtle and transpersonal domains. But the *exclusive* restriction and identification of consciousness to the gross bodymind must be released, and this is in every way a genuine and often brutal life/death struggle. Precisely because consciousness is leaving the biologically oriented worldspace (the gross bodymind in general), it is indeed a death to the extensive network of biological identifications—that is, a death to the *exclusive* identification with the gross mechanisms of life and vital force in general, not to mention the entire structures of conventional meaning and relationships that have developed around the gross bodymind itself.

    Grof maintains that my existential level is rather anemic because it doesn't contain a confrontation with biological death (which Grof, using his dual definition, tends to capitalize as Death, because he will insist that perinatal death is the only real death there is). But Grof's objection is clearly unfounded. Deconstructing the gross bodymind is altogether a biological death. When consciousness breaks the identification with the biological domain in general, this can be, on occasion, as dramatic and as physiologically intense as Grof maintains. The model I have presented is capable of accounting for that intensity and the genesis of that intensity. Furthermore, as we will see, my model fully accepts the possibility that this might involve a conscious reliving of the biological birth trauma. On both these counts, I do not believe that Grof's criticism is sound.

15. In *Eye to Eye*, and again in *Sex, Ecology, Spirituality*, I try to outline several ways in which "death" and the "death-instinct" have been used by different theorists. This is a semantic nightmare of unparalleled proportions. Let me here simply say that there are at least two very different types of "death" that have been recognized from Plato to Freud, East and West—and which I will call horizontal death and vertical death.

    Horizontal death is what I just described in the text: the death to any of the elements on any given level. This can have negative consequences (as in dissociation), but it can also be part of positive growth (the mechanism of disidentification and transcendence in general, which dialectically runs into vertical death).

Vertical death usually means—in Freud, for example—the regressive movement whereby a higher structure is lost altogether and there is a regression toward the lowest of all levels, insentient matter (and hence "death"). In this usage (Freud's final formulation, which is not in the least the way Grof portrays it), Freud contrasts the death instinct with Eros; the aim of Eros, he says, is to join together; the aim of the death instinct, to take apart or destroy. This shifting down to a lower level is one type of vertical death (this is Thanatos proper, the actual drive toward the death that is insentient matter, or total regression).

In that formulation, and as far as it goes, Freud was actually very much in the Neoplatonic tradition, which sees manifestation operating in a vertical ascending movement (Reflux, Eros) and a vertical descending movement (Efflux), which is not a linear notion but refers instead to spirals between shallower and deeper dimensions within the nested holarchy of being.

But I then pointed out that what Freud saw as Thanatos, the Neoplatonic tradition saw as Agape. And this allowed me to reach the following conclusions: Agape split from Eros appears as Thanatos; Eros split from Agape appears as Phobos. The repercussions of those formulations are carefully discussed in SES. Grof ignores all of them in his discussion of my views of death.

16. Grof protests that they aren't that similar, and therefore fulcrum-o will not in any fashion serve the same purposes as the BPMs. This strikes me as old-fashioned nitpicking. Fulcrum-o refers to the stencils surrounding biological birth; the BPMs refer to the stencils surrounding biological birth—how different can they be?

The fulcrums and their subphases, as I have described them, are general processes, simple milestones to help us orient ourselves in the overall developmental process. Moreover, they are based on significant amounts of clinical, therapeutic, empirical, and phenomenological evidence. In the general sweep of differentiation-and-integration, we can divide and subdivide that process in many fruitful ways. I have found that a fourfold division—which I usually shorten to the even simpler threefold fusion/differentiation/integration—works just fine as a theoretical summary of this extensive evidence (Wilber et al., 1986).

Grof's BPMs are based on the specific contours of actual clinical delivery, and so of course they will vary in specific details. But the fact remains: Grof's four stages of clinical childbirth and my fulcrum-o refer to *identical processes*. The very essence of Grof's criticism collapses under that simple fact.

Here are the correlations: Subphase 1 of fulcrum-o is the initial state of oceanic fusion, indissociation, merger, embeddedness; this is quite similar to the amniotic and oceanic oneness of BPM I (and refers in general to the entire prenatal period). Subphase 2 is the overall differentiation process, where the infant's body is differentiated and propelled from the mother's. At the beginning of this differentiation, there is "engulfment and no exit" (BPM II), eventually giving way to separation and differentiation through the birth canal (BPM III). The last subphase, that of resolution and integration, is birth itself and the neonatal state (BPM IV), which is then the *beginning* phase of fulcrum-1.

Stan maintains that fulcrum-o is an "ad hoc" addition on my part, hastily tacked on to my model to account for his data. Not so. When I first advanced the fulcrum idea fifteen years ago, not only was the perinatal fulcrum included (and yes, it was then included to acknowledge Stan's data, as well as other sources), but even earlier bardo realms were all described as fulcrums. I believe all of that is still very true, because a fulcrum simply describes any fusion-differentiation-integration sequence.

The reason that fulcrum-0 (and to some extent fulcrum-1) looks different from the other fulcrums is that they are the only physical-level fulcrums with *simple location*, whereas the other fulcrums are interior (such as emotions, concepts, existential dilemma, psychic occasions, and so on), none of which have simple location (and so they "look" different at first glance). But all of these fulcrums, first to last, are forms of Spirit and its developmental growth, a growth that occurs—in all domains, gross to subtle to causal—via the fulcrum (or transcend-and-include) process. There is nothing ad hoc about this.

All that remains, in terms of genuine disagreement, is the actual importance of these fulcrum-0 imprints as they play themselves out in adult development, transpersonal experiences, clinical pathology, and psychotherapy. I maintain that most of those events actually involve fulcrum-6, but that they might, under certain circumstances, involve fulcrum-0, just as Grof describes it. Grof, on the other hand, is locked into a perinatal/birth position, which recognizes only fulcrum-0, not also fulcrum-6.

17. This does not have to occur in a "linear" fashion, however, because the enduring imprints of past fulcrums are enfolded into the self-system—the compound individual—as complex nests of past actuals, holarchically available to present consciousness under specific circumstances, including LSD and holotropic sessions.

18. Aurobindo's overall model of consciousness consists basically of three systems: (1) the surface/outer/frontal consciousness (typically waking state), consisting of physical, vital, and mental levels of consciousness; (2) a deeper/psychic/soul system "behind" the frontal in each of its levels (inner physical, inner vital, inner mental, and innermost psychic or soul; typically dream state); and (3) the vertical ascending/descending systems stretching both above the mind (higher mind, illumined mind, intuitive mind, overmind, supermind; typically deep sleep state) and below the mind (the subconscient and inconscient)—all nested in Sat-Chit-Ananda.

I have sometimes been accused of omitting Aurobindo's system #2, the depth or soul system, but I do not (as the last chapter of *The Atman Project* makes clear). Nonetheless, I can certainly understand why a few Aurobindo followers believed I had, in that *Atman Project* is a simple outline of Wilber-II (and doesn't dwell on too many details), and in other outlines, such as *Transformations*, I do not mention it for space considerations. Nonetheless, from my first study of Aurobindo, it has been the very rare occasion that I find myself in disagreement. I generally accept all three of the above points of Aurobindo's model, and they have been fully incorporated into Wilber-II and its subsequent refinements.

For simplicity's sake, I sometimes use the "frontal" to mean not only system #1, but #3 if and when it breaks into frontal development in this life (in other words, my general use of frontal often means the entire vertical Great Chain as it might manifest in any individual's given lifetime: physical to vital to mental to higher mental to illumined mental to intuitive mental to overmental to supermental). Again, this does not imply any rigidly "linear" development; the deeper psychic being "behind" the frontal can often "peak" into the frontal; but developmental adaptation does indeed proceed holarchically on balance, because earlier competences form the platform on which higher ones will rest. This, too, is in general agreement with Aurobindo.

(This use of "frontal" should not be confused with Adi Da's use of that word, which usually means the descending spiritual force coming down the front line of the body; frontal in that sense means higher involutionary force that purifies the frontal line. I agree with that usage, but the two semantic meanings should not be confused.)

Finally, the soul (for Aurobindo and myself) is not to be confused with pure Atman. The ego is that which evolves in this lifetime; the soul is that which evolves between lifetimes (or, if you prefer, evolves to the superconscient in this lifetime; the entire "bardo" is occurring right now, moment to moment); but the pure Atman does not evolve or involve at all. The pure Atman is pure Witness, unmanifest, unevolving, unborn, undying. The *evolving soul* is superseded by the *Unborn Spirit* (pure Atman-Brahman). Technically, in my model, the soul is the psychic/subtle to low-causal, and thus, being of manifestation, it evolves; the pure Atman is high causal, and being unmanifest, does not evolve, is not born, does not die: it does not enter the stream at all, but embraces it fully as a mirror embraces its every reflection.

With reference to the Tibetan model and the "indestructible drop," I return to this topic yet again in *Sex, Ecology, Spirituality*, and discuss it at length (note 1 for chapter 14).

19. The existence of these prenatal, perinatal, and early infancy states, supported by Grof's data—should it be verified—is actually a severe blow to the Washburn/Wilber-I model, because that model rests entirely on the notion that the ultimate Ground is in some sense fully present in the infantile state. Yet, even in these models that are the most "far out" (such as Aurobindo and Vajrayana), the *highest level* that is present in the *pre-egoic period* is still just the psychic/soul, which not only is *not* Spirit, but is in fact the final dualistic barrier to Spirit.

This cripples the Washburn/Wilber-I model at its most crucial tenet: nowhere during the pre-egoic period is there anything that is in fact an unrestricted Ground of Being (nor Spirit-as-Spirit); there is at best the soul, at worst, chaotic impulses. Those two options—one "far out" (the soul) and one conventional (chaotic impulses)—are *both* equally and completely fatal to the Washburn/Wilber-I model, because spiritual realization, in that model, must be a *resurrection* and *recontacting* of something fully present in the pre-egoic period, and by both of those alternatives, that model fails; nowhere is there anything ultimate or nondual in the pre-egoic period. This, to my mind, is a strong argument against the viability of the Washburn/Wilber-I model.

20. [See *Integral Psychology* for a full elaboration of these sources, from premodern to modern to postmodern.]

Stan has a tendency to describe his research as being *the* clinical data. He has criticized my work for ignoring evidence, saying that it is necessary "to test theoretical adequacy against the clinical data." I agree totally. But by "the clinical data" Grof means basically *his* data (hallucinogens and hyperventilation), whereas the vast majority of researchers I have relied on are exactly those who pioneered direct clinical and experimental evidence—not to mention the vast phenomenological evidence presented by the contemplative wisdom traditions themselves. *The Atman Project*, for example, was directly based on the empirical, phenomenological, and clinical evidence of over sixty researchers from numerous approaches (and hundreds of others in an informal way)—the bulk of which cannot be adequately handled in Stan's model. And yet Stan keeps saying that my approach cannot handle "the" clinical evidence, a stance that certainly seems odd.

Because my model is evidence-driven, not theory-driven, I have not included astrology in it, which disappoints Stan. Or rather, I have completely included astrology, but in ways unacceptable to Stan. Namely, based on the total web of present evidence, I find that astrology is an accurate interpretation of the interior of the mythic-membership worldspace (i.e., the Lower-Left quadrant at its mythic level of development). This implies, of course, that astrology will fail in tests of accuracy when compared with methodologies derived from the mental (and higher) stages of development.

So far, as Roger Walsh has summarized the available evidence (*Gnosis*, Spring 1996), astrology has indeed repeatedly failed to pass experimental tests, even those arranged by astrologers themselves. Until astrology passes at least several such tests, I have no choice but to remain agnostic. And, in all cases, I believe it is still a *quite accurate hermeneutic of the interior of the mythic worldspace*.

Also, I believe that astrology can be very useful as an interpretive tool, rather like a Rorschach test; but that is rarely how it is presented, which is as a reading of an ontological reality with predictive capabilities, a claim that, the evidence to date suggests, is mythic-membership in its contours and its embrace. [See *One Taste*, July 29 and Dec. 21 entries, for recent studies on the validity of astrology and their disappointing results.]

Chapter 8: Integral Feminism

1. Peggy Wright has published two feminist essays about my work, which are unfortunately some of the most extensive distortions of my work that I have seen published. I can only warn readers that, in my opinion, she does not in any adequate fashion report my actual view, nor, therefore, does she offer a believable critique of it. Many other feminists have responded to my work with an appreciative, constructive criticism, which I value [see, for example, the contri-

butions of Elizabeth Debold, Kaisa Puhakka, and Joyce Nielsen in Jack Crittenden et al. (eds.), *Kindred Visions,* forthcoming from Shambhala.]

Wright's two essays were published in *ReVision Journal.* Because Jack Crittenden and I cofounded that journal, I am often asked my opinion of it, and
unfortunately I must say that both Jack and I are disappointed in the course it
has taken. We believe that it displays many deep-seated prejudices, and that a
balanced, fair overview of alternative conceptions is rarely found in its pages
(Wright's articles being typical). We are no longer associated with the journal.

When *ReVision* decided to run a three-volume series based on my work ("Ken
Wilber and the Future of Transpersonal Inquiry"), I was perforce drawn back
into its pages. A few of the essays were superb, but many were academically
anemic and quite a few of them distorted my work in significant ways. The
essays were later drawn together into a book, which purported to be a dialogue
with my work, but which, most critics were quick to point out, was mostly a
showcase for alternative conceptions, such as those of Grof, Washburn, various
primitivists, and agenda-driven authors such as Wright. In presenting viable
alternative conceptions such as Grof's and Washburn's, I believe the series and
the book were a success. In presenting my own work, the series/book contained
a host of misleading and damaging inaccuracies, as students of my work immediately noted. As one critic put it, "This is a model of how to treat a scholar
unfairly." For those interested in a summary, presentation, or explication of my
work, this series/book is not a reliable source.

The presentations by theorists such as Grof and Washburn I have responded
to in the previous two chapters. In this endnote, I will address Wright's essays,
and try to answer each of her misrepresentations. It is unfortunate that this has
to happen, but I suppose it needs to be done for the record.

This is typical of a Wright argument: "Representing any theory as describing
deep invariant human structures rather than culturally shaped experience involves the responsibility to identify the cultural assumptions inherent in the
model itself" (1995, 3). But I do not portray, and have never portrayed, my
model as describing invariant structures *rather than* culturally shaped experiences. I have frequently used the analogy of the human body; it has 206 bones,
2 lungs, 1 heart—those deep structures appear to be universal—but societies
everywhere differ on the modes of play, sex, culture, and work engaged in by
the body—those surface structures are contingent, historically molded, and culturally relative. I have consistently called for an understanding that carefully
balances universal deep features with culturally variant surface features.

But Wright ignores this explicit balance in my work; she presents a very lopsided and at times ludicrous caricature of my views; and she then triumphantly
corrects them with a "more balanced view" that is often nothing but a variation
of my actual view before Wright distorted it. She simply reintroduces my actual
conclusions, changing terminology if necessary to hide the sleight of hand, and
then presents this as a "feminist" correction of my "androcentric" views.

Take, for example, her critique of my use of the terms "hierarchy" and "heterarchy" in SES. These terms have a long and established usage in the literature, which I represent carefully and fairly. I then add the understanding that each of these modes of governance has a *pathological* form. My entire discussion concerns all four modes: normal and pathological hierarchy, normal and pathological heterarchy.

I point out that "in a heterarchy, rule or governance is established by a pluralistic and egalitarian interplay of all parties" (chap. 1). Wright immediately claims that I am therefore "setting up heterarchy as incapable of establishing priorities," that I am in effect denying that heterarchy has *any* priorities at all. But of course "rule or governance" means a set of directions, guidelines, or priorities, or else there would be no rule or governance whatsoever (which would in fact be *pathological* heterarchy, as I make quite clear). But normal heterarchy's governance or priority, I point out, is based on "pluralistic and egalitarian interplay of all parties."

Wright will then "correct" my view by saying, No, heterarchy doesn't mean no rule or governance, as Wilber says, it really means "rule with," which is governed by "mutual relations and intercommunion of parts"—in other words, she defines heterarchy exactly the way I actually define it.

Wright thus totally caricatures my view as saying that natural heterarchy has no governance at all, and as examples of this, she gives what I clearly identify as *pathological* heterarchy, which is indeed a failure of priorities altogether. She then claims that I have ridiculed heterarchy by proclaiming it to be incapable of any governance or priorities or rules at all, and then she sets about to fix my faulty and demeaning (and "androcentric") thesis.

She does this by simply *renaming* my heterarchy (which I define as "mutual equivalence and communion of all parties") as "synarchy" (which she defines as "mutual relations and intercommunion of parts")—the same idea, but Wright will now claim it all for herself by simply giving it her own term. And then she will tie synarchy to females, so that all of a sudden we are on a strange Gilligan's Island where there all the nice linking and communion and healing connections belong to females and all the nasty ranking and dominance belong to males. Males will then be the major possessors of hierarchy—which Wright narrowly interprets, quite against the massive literature on the subject, as being power "concentrated in the hands of a few" (which is in fact *pathological* hierarchy)—and females are the main bearers of the wonderful synarchy. This is called correcting androcentrism.

My actual conclusion in that discussion was stated very clearly: "Beware any theorist who pushes solely hierarchy or solely heterarchy, or attempts to give greater value to one or the other in an ontological sense. When I use the term 'holarchy,' I will especially mean the balance of normal hierarchy and normal heterarchy. Holarchy undercuts both extreme hierarchy and extreme heterarchy, and allows the discussion to move forward with, I believe, the best of both worlds kept firmly in mind" (from the section "Pathology").

The fact that I point out that hierarchy originally meant "sacred rule" does *not* mean, as Wright claims, that I think heterarchy is *not* sacred (I was rehabilitating hierarchy from theorists such as Wright, and so I needed a more accurate historical reconstruction). My actual conclusion was that the sacred exists in and as a balance and partnership of hierarchy (traditionally male) and heterarchy (traditionally female).

But that conclusion, of course, Wright simply co-opts under the name synarchy, and so again she has simply taken my conclusion, presented it first inaccurately as androcentric, then added the gynocentric aspects of my view that she herself has ignored or distorted, and then presented my conclusion, renamed, as her contribution to the discussion.

Other of Wright's distortions: I do not, as Wright maintains, exclude children from transpersonal experiences (nor have I ever done so). The point, rather, is that as a rule children do not develop *enduring* structures of transpersonal adaptation (the bardo fades and the frontal structures are all pre-egoic). There has been no evidence whatsoever presented (by Armstrong or feminists or anybody else) for the assertion that children develop stable and enduring transpersonal structures, and so naturally I do not include it in my model. But children can have a variety of fleeting transpersonal *peak experiences* or altered states for a number of reasons.

As we saw in chapter 7, human beings, starting from the earliest months after conception, have access to the three broad states (of waking, dreaming, sleep), and they therefore have general access to the three great domains of gross, subtle, and causal (although not in any permanently accessible and continuous fashion). But influx from these states can therefore occur at any developmental (frontal) stage, simply because all individuals wake, dream, and sleep. Moreover, every individual, at almost any age, goes through an entire "round" every twenty-four hours, plunging from waking (gross) into dream (subtle) into deep sleep (causal), and then around again. The self can be "all over the place," and this is true for children as well. The question, rather, is one of stable frontal adaptation, which clearly proceeds from preconventional to conventional to postconventional to post-postconventional. (See chapters 9 and 10 for a further discussion of these themes.) Wright blithely ignores everything I have written on this topic.

Wright accuses me of "invidious monism," a stunning misreading. My "highest" reality, as I have often stressed, is not a stage set apart from other stages, but is rather the Suchness or Thatness or empty Ground that is *equally present* in and as all stages and all phenomena. The metaphor I have repeatedly used is that Suchness is not the highest rung in a ladder but the wood out of which the entire ladder is made. That is, when Spirit is realized as Spirit (what we called "spirit-as-spirit"), then what is realized is simply the entire Ground of Being, which is equally and fully present in every single thing and event in the entire Kosmos. It is radically all-inclusive and all-embracing, the primordial Emptiness that is one with all Form whatsoever. Wright's discussion of this issue (and her critique based on "invidious monism") is irrelevant because it misreports my view.

Wright maintains that I confuse the "permeable self" of females with prepersonal structures, which she calls the "pre/perm fallacy." "Wilber has essentially taken the pre/perm fallacy . . . and carried it into transpersonal theory." As the following discussion in the text (under the section "The Permeable Self") makes obvious, I clearly distinguish between prepersonal permeable, personal permeable, and transpersonal permeable, so that I do not in any fashion equate prepersonal with permeable, which is the entire crux of Wright's charge that I commit the "pre/perm" fallacy, the centerpiece of her implied charge of sexism. The fact that I clearly do no such thing does not stop Wright from making this bizarre charge.

(Incidentally, pathology in the prepersonal stages—in both male and female—involves self boundaries that, *within the context of their own gender standards,* are fragile, noncohesive, broken, and fused—not simply permeable, but fractured. A weak and noncohesive boundary in the permeable self is judged to be so within its own standards; it is not judged to be so with reference to the agentic self. This is all very clear in the literature, and Wright is rather badly missing some very important theory and research by her insistence on seeing androcentrism under every rock.)

Which she certainly seems to do. In SES I mention that Janet Chafetz has made the significant point that women who operated a heavy plow had higher rates of miscarriage, and therefore it was to their Darwinian advantage not to engage in such activity. Chafetz herself does not cite a source for this information. Wright leaps at this as evidence that I often use "unsubstantiated secondary sources." But the fact that heavy physical labor in the third trimester increases the rates of miscarriage—sometimes dramatically—is a common medical fact. It is uncontested, and therefore Chafetz does not need to reference a source for this, nor do I. But Wright offers this as evidence that I don't cite sources well and that they are often "secondary."

Wright especially jumps on my use of the term "centaur." The meaning of a word, semanticists agree, is simply how you use it. Jane Loevinger's highest stage of development, for both men and women, is one that she summarizes (with reference to Broughton) as: "both mind and body are experiences of an integrated self." Hubert Benoit, Jane Alexander, and Erik Erikson had used the term "centaur" to describe such an integrated state, because the human (mind) is not a rider divorced from the horse (body) but one with it. I thought that was an interesting use of the term, and so I adopted it, and defined it precisely, using Jane Loevinger's summary. The way I define and use the term is, of course, precisely its actual meaning.

But Wright pounces on the fact that in ancient Greek mythology, the centaurs were male. Wright takes this as yet further evidence that my approach is androcentric. But why not go all the way? In ancient Greek mythology, the centaurs were male, it is true; but many were also filthy, stupid, vulgar, and general idiots. Why not be consistent and accuse me of male bashing at the same time?

If it were widespread knowledge that centaurs were male, and if the use of that term could be shown to disenfranchise women in some significant ways, then its continued use might be sexist. But not only does the fact that centaurs were male come as news to most people, but to claim its use is sexist, based on archaic mythology, is like claiming that since Gaia is female, the very use of the germ "Gaia" is sexist, biased, and prejudiced.

Wright divides her overall critique of my position into three main sections. The first is her "hierarchy/heterarchy" discussion, which I dealt with above. The second she calls "ecological," and it concerns two main issues. One is her claim that, because I commit the pre/perm fallacy, my discussion of ecological issues is flawed. But I do not commit the pre/perm fallacy, as we just saw. This misconstrual is directly related to the other major ecological issue Wright focuses on. She feels, for example, that I underrate the contributions that rationality itself can make to world healing. But in truth, I make it quite clear that all of the positive contributions of all of the previous stages need to be honored, integrated, and incorporated, and this most definitely includes both prerational and rational modes. Wright incomprehensibly maintains that my view "overlooks, or at best minimizes, the importance of the positive, integrative actions [that can] take place within the cognitive levels of the rational. . . ." But in fact, after pointing out the extraordinary integrative capacity of rationality and reasonableness, here is my actual conclusion: "Thus, the single greatest world transformation would simply be the embrace of a global reasonableness and pluralistic tolerance—the global embrace of egoic-rationality . . ." (chap. 5, the section "Multiculturalism"). Once again, Wright has reached a similar conclusion—the importance of what can be achieved within rationality—claimed it for herself, denied it to me, and then presented my position as androcentric, outmoded, and fallacious.

Wright's third main area of critique is the claim that my anthropological sources are "outmoded." She points to my use of Habermas as an example. But I did not rely on Habermas as a main anthropological source. The bibliography of SES contains almost one hundred contemporary anthropological sources (and volume 2 contains over five hundred), all of which are listed for a reason. Thus, Wright claims that my earliest technological stage is hunting and gathering, and she says this conception is outmoded because scavenging was quite prevalent. Actually, my earliest technological stage is *foraging,* which includes scavenging, hunting, gathering. I clearly list the actual stages as "foraging, horticultural, agrarian, industrial, informational" (chap. 5, the section "Male Advantage and Female Advantage"), and I explicitly tie this discussion to Lenski, not Habermas (for a long discussion of these technological stages in my model, see Wilber 1996d). For Wright to claim that my approach is based on outdated anthropological research is irresponsible in the extreme.

Wright's biases, her extensive misrepresentations, and *ReVision's* publication of them are perhaps their own comment: this is publishing with an agenda.

2. Gilligan's (1982) three hierarchical stages are what she calls (1) "selfish" (preconventional), (2) "conventional ethical" or "care," (3) "postconventional metaethical" or "universal care." They are hierarchical because they are invariant; none can be bypassed; each transcends but includes (differentiates and inte-

grates) the competences of its predecessor(s); each is thus ranked as more inclusive and more encompassing, capable of exerting power over its own lesser engagements; so that each stage is developmentally higher than its predecessor(s). Gilligan has also suggested a fourth stage that hierarchically integrates the justice and care perspectives (see below). Alexander et al. ("Introduction") have an excellent discussion of the centrality of hierarchy in Gilligan, and a contribution by Gilligan herself that highlights this importance.

3. C. Alexander et al. (1990), p. 10. Gilligan refers to this higher stage of moral integration as involving "a cognitive transformation from a *formal* to a *dialectical* mode of reasoning that can encompass the contradictions out of which moral problems often arise" (my italics, ibid., p. 223), which is what I have called the shift from formop to vision-logic, a vision-logic which Gilligan also calls "more encompassing," "dialectical," and "polyphonic"—a vision-logic that will "reunite intelligence and affectivity" (centauric) and, especially, integrate "the different voices of justice and care" (p. 224)—that is, achieve a balance within each individual of male and female, which Gilligan also calls a "paradoxical interdependence of self and relationship" (agency and communion) (p. 224). All of those points have been explicitly mentioned in my definition of centauric vision-logic, a stage that includes the beginning integration of masculine and feminine within each individual, and thus I am obviously in substantial agreement with Gilligan on these particular points.

Nonetheless, as Gilligan points out, this is never a simple, clean, and seamless integration; there still remains an (unresolvable) tension between these two voices, even though, relatively speaking, they are brought much closer together in vision-logic than in formal operational. This is why I believe that we continue to take the male and female dispositions with us even into the higher stages, although they increasingly find a relatively more harmonious stance within each soul. Spirit is neither male nor female; and as Spirit, we are neither. But as embodied and manifesting beings, we have roots in the bodily dispositions with their different value spheres, through which communication joyfully flows in any event, and those chords of the body still sing in different voices, all the way to God and Goddess, who are themselves manifestations of pure Emptiness.

Specifically, we might say that spirit-as-matter is sexless; Spirit has thrown itself outward into even the least sentient forms, too simple to reproduce themselves, untouched by sex. As Spirit evolves from matter to body, Spirit-as-body grows into its own sexuality in order to reproduce itself on that level. Spirit-as-body is thus profoundly sexed, male or female. As Spirit evolves from body to mind, the bodily differences, so pronounced, tend to influence the mind as well, so that Spirit-as-mind continues the sexual orientation (as seen in the different voices of moral orientation, for example), although with the higher mental stages (centauric) these voices are increasingly integrated. As the soul emerges through the mind, Spirit-as-soul contains the lingering "evolutionary traces" of the sexual dispositions found so heavily in the body and in a lesser degree in the mind; the soul is the last reach of sexual differentiation, which lingers as a faint but fine perfume. Finally, Spirit-as-spirit is again sexless—the pure Emptiness that, when it manifests, embraces (Agape) its own sexuality freely.

4. Even if we start *entirely* with Gilligan's model and with Jane Loevinger's model (which was originally developed using *women only*), we will still arrive at something very much like the model I have presented, because this model explicitly incorporates both Gilligan's and Loevinger's linking *and* ranking aspects and stages. (In fact, several aspects of my model were explicitly taken from Loevinger's early model, developed with women. I later "de-feminized" it—and "de-masculinized" it—to arrive at the gender-neutral basic structures of consciousness, through which men and women tend to develop with different emphasis.)

5. For an extended discussion of this theme, see chapter 1 of *Sex, Ecology, Spirituality*.

6. That is, the basic structures are essentially identical and gender-neutral, but the self-related stages tend to manifest with different orientations in the sexes, precisely because the self-system (which mediates between basic structures and self-stages) tends to operate with a different emphasis in male and female, namely, the self of males tends to operate more agentically, whereas the female self is constructed more relationally or communion-oriented. Thus, if we take the gender-neutral basic structures, apply the enzyme of self-system with its identification process (which itself is generally of the form male/agentic or female/communion), we will generate respectively the Kohlberg and Gilligan transitional moral stages. All of this is incorporated into the gender model that I have presented.

That is simply an example of what I believe is a larger process at work in development, namely: if you take the six or so major characteristics of the self-system, and allow each of them to work on the basic structures, you will generate the major lines of the self-related stages, such as morals, self-identity, self-needs, and so forth. Thus, the characteristic of the self known as identification, when applied to successive basic structures, generates the stages of self or ego development. The characteristic of defense, applied to the basic structures, generates the hierarchy of defense mechanisms. The characteristic of metabolism, applied to the basic structures, generates the hierarchy of self-needs, and so on. If, in each of these cases, the self takes a more predominantly agentic or communal voice, that will similarly color each of the translations.

7. Wright maintains this distortion in both of her essays.

8. I intentionally say "select from *male* and *female* value spheres" because different aspects of these biological givens are variably *selected* (e.g., plow societies select for male physical strength). I always refer to the male and female value spheres (not masculine and feminine), for these are biologically based and thus quasi-universal. "Masculine" and "feminine" are not so much "selected for" as "constructed from"—i.e., upon the selection from biological factors will be built culturally specific styles of masculine and feminine. Both cultural worldviews and techno-economic factors will play a hand in the selection from the male and female value spheres, which will then be elaborated and constructed in culturally specific ways to generate particular masculine and feminine styles.

Some of these masculine and feminine styles might (or might not) be fairly universal; those that are, are grounded more directly in the biological sphere.

9. In volume 2, I outline and summarize these various factors and the extensive evidence for each of these conclusions.

10. On the possible meanings of "Gaia" and its actual role in living systems, see SES, chapters 4 and 5.

Chapter 9: How Straight Is the Spiritual Path?

1. When I was doing research for *The Atman Project,* I was faced with a difficult choice: I had literally thousands of pages of notes, summarizing and cross-referencing the works of several hundred theorists, East and West. Should I try to publish all of this material, or simply present a brief outline?

At that time (*Atman* was written in 1976 and published in book form in 1980), I could find no publishers even vaguely interested in all this research material, and so I took the only available course: I presented several dozen tables that simply listed the stages given by some of the more prominent of these theorists, as well the overall correlations with the seventeen-stage "master template" that I had culled *from all of their combined efforts,* using all of them to fill in the gaps in the others.

I gave rather brief but fairly comprehensive summaries of each of the seventeen stages. I especially focused on the changes in motivation, cognition, sense of self, modes of space and time, affect, types of wholeness, self-control, socialization, morality, angst-guilt, perceptual clarity, and death-terror as they all developed and evolved through the seventeen stages. Using this summary approach, I brought the whole book in at two hundred pages, which was rather quickly accepted for publication in that "friendly" form.

My hope, in publishing this abbreviated outline, was that graduate students would pick this up, use the tables and the outlines, go to the original sources, and start cranking out the details themselves, which otherwise lay languishing in pages of research notes. This indeed began to happen, and many subsequent researchers went to the original sources and began filling in the details of this general template.

These seventeen stages, I suggested, dealt with the evolution of consciousness in the manifest individual human being (i.e., frontal evolution). In addition to those stages of evolution, there were the entire bardo (and involutionary) realms, according to the Tibetan model, which I adopted more or less in toto for those realms (since it is by far the most complete, and in some facets, the only, model of those states). I especially focused on the three bardo or "in between" states that start immediately postlife (with a direct immersion in the ultimate Goal and Ground that is Dharmakaya) and eventually end up in the conception or prenatal state—an overall trajectory that involves a stepping down from causal to subtle to gross, resulting finally in rebirth in the prenatal gross bodymind—thus covering the entire sweep of involution (ultimate to causal to subtle to gross).

According to the Tibetan model, each of these involutionary bardo "step-downs" is followed by a "forgetting" (amnesia) as the self steps down into increasingly denser forms, causal to subtle to gross. The early prenatal and neonatal self thus does indeed come "trailing clouds of glory," but, I continued, these involutionary realms and sources are increasingly forgotten as evolution in the gross realm begins, moving through its seventeen stages. Each of these evolutionary stages "unfolds" that which was "enfolded" in the involutionary movement, and thus each developmental unfolding is a widening and deepening of consciousness via a "remembrance" (anamnesis) of the higher and transcendental realms "lost" in involution. This also means that the entire seventeen-stage sequence is driven by the overarching desire to recapture the Goal and Ground of Dharmakaya, which was experienced directly, not at the mother's breast, but in the prior Clear Light Emptiness. The entire evolutionary sequence was driven, in other words, by the Atman project.

But, I suggested, this involutionary bardo sequence is not simply (or even predominantly) something that happens after life and before rebirth. *It is in fact—and most importantly—the very structure of this moment's experience:* we are constantly contracting away from infinity into forms of grasping and experiencing and knowing and willing. As I put it in *The Atman Project:* "Not only did the whole involutionary series occur prior to one's birth, one reenacts the entire series moment to moment. In this moment and this moment and this, an individual *is* Buddha, is Atman, is the Dharmakaya—*but,* in this moment and this moment and this, he ends up as John Doe, as a separate self, as an isolated body apparently bounded by other isolated bodies. At the beginning of *this* and every moment, each individual *is* God as the Clear Light; but by the *end* of this same moment—in a flash, in the twinkling of an eye—he winds up as an isolated ego. And what happens In Between the beginning and ending of *this* moment is identical to what happened In Between death and rebirth as described by the *Tibetan Book of the Dead.*"

As we saw in chapter 7, we can also state this overall model using Aurobindo's terminology: there is what Aurobindo calls the deep self or psychic being, which transmigrates, and there is the frontal self, which develops or evolves in each manifest life. The seventeen stages are fundamentally stages of the frontal being (using "frontal" in the broad sense as overall evolution in this life [see note 18 for chapter 7]); they unfold in a developmental sequence over the course of a manifest individual life (although they also reflect enduring ontological levels of being—the Great Chain of Being, in fact).

Behind the frontal, and capable of "transmigrating" (in whatever sense you would like to give that, from microgenetic—in this moment—to actual life-to-life rebirth), there is the deeper or psychic being, which fundamentally partakes of the psychic/subtle level itself, and thus partakes of a profoundly (if still intermediate) transcendental and witnessing capacity (which is also the ultimate foundation of the self-system in manifest evolution). The Tibetans, as we saw, describe this deeper psychic being as an "indestructible drop" (the psychic/subtle level as it appears in each individual, which is also how I specifically use the term "soul"), an essence or "tigle" that carries karma from birth to birth, until reunited with the ultimate Clear Light Emptiness.

Thus, any "witnessing" memories from the prenatal and neonatal state are due, not to the actual structure of the infantile frontal consciousness embedded with the mother, but with the "trailing clouds of glory" that the psychic being might still intuit. The "glory" of this "recollection" is not the glory of the suckling infant and the "dynamic ground" of the mother/infant union, but the glory of the In Between through which it has just passed. In other words, as we saw, any trailing clouds of glory in the pre-eogic *period* are not due to pre-egoic *structures* (or "physicodynamic processes").

Likewise, this model (Tibetan/Aurobindo/Wilber-II) locates the *subject* of these memories in the psychic being, not in the frontal consciousness, which has little or no neuronal foundation at this stage anyway. According to the Tibetan model, access to this psychic being is increasingly lost as evolution in the gross bodymind gets under way (which, in my model, occurs via the basic waves and fulcrums of frontal evolution, during which, at the actual psychic stage—fulcrum-7—the deeper psychic being will begin to stand forth in consciousness, eventually standing as the causal Witness itself, which was *implicit* at every previous stage as the core of the self-system, its actual consciousness at any given level, but does not stand forth as a stable adaptation until the psychic/subtle level of development, and does not stand as its own condition until the causal level, which is ultimately subsumed in the Nondual).

Likewise, the radical Unity which is lost and whose recapture is so fervently desired—the radical Unity that is the single and ultimate longing in the heart of every holon—is the prior Unity of the Dharmakaya, not the neonatal unity at the mother's breast (which, as we saw, is not one with the "whole" world at all). The Atman project is driven by the desire to actualize in evolution that which was lost in involution, and that actualization, via the frontal consciousness, fluidly unfolds in numerous waves—with all their ups and downs.

Such is a brief summary of the model (the Wilber-II model) presented in *The Atman Project*. During that period-II (whose books also included *Up from Eden, Quantum Questions, A Sociable God,* and *Eye to Eye*) I added the notions of peak experiences and altered states of consciousness, and I distinguished between levels of self (or waves of consciousness) and levels of reality (or realms of existence), so that this was a model of levels, states, and realms. Thus, a person at virtually any stage of development can have an altered state or peak experience of the psychic, subtle, causal, or nondual realms (which gives us a grid of numerous *types* of spiritual experiences, e.g., a magic-, mythic-, or rational-level peak experience of a psychic, subtle, causal, or nondual realm; this grid was outlined in *A Sociable God*). But, as always, for these altered states to become permanent traits, temporary states must be converted to permanent structures via development (so that, e.g., subtle states become subtle traits or permanently realized structures). All of those concepts were taken up and included in Wilber-III, with the addition of an explicit differentiation between levels and lines—as will be explained in the text.

2. Wade treats fulcrum-7 and fulcrum-8 as one stage, which she simply calls "transcendent," and she subdivides fulcrum-5 into two equivalent levels, Achieve-

ment and Affiliative, based on such items as hemispheric dominance (which often also means male and female versions of the same level, although some individuals experience both in sequence).

Wade does not clearly distinguish between basic levels and the self-stages traveling through those levels, nor does she distinguish clearly between levels and lines. But those are easily remedied [subsequent conversations with Jenny indicate that she is comfortable with such distinctions]. As presented in the book, her nine basic levels are thus an amalgam of those various items.

With regard to male and female, as I explained earlier, I believe that, for the most part, biological/constitutional factors predispose the male and female to develop through each and every stage with a somewhat different emphasis (agency and communion, achievement and affiliative), so I do not believe that this is a difference that jumps out at stage 5 and disappears at stage 7. The Graves model—and also that of Kegan and others—tends to see each stage as dialectically alternating from an individualistic emphasis to a collective or communal emphasis—e.g., stage 1 is self-assertive (or individualistic), stage 2 is self-sacrificing (or communal), stage 3 is self-assertive, stage 4 is communal, and so on. I believe there is some truth to that idea, but I believe it needs to be refined by taking into account the native dispositions of male and female (Upper Right), the cultural backgrounds in which individual development occurs (Lower Left), and the techno-economic mode of the social system itself (Lower Right), because all of those factors influence whether a stage is "individualistic" or "communal."

3. Many mystical and transpersonal models include at least four to six stages in the transpersonal domain, but Wade settles for two stages. She openly leaves room for other transpersonal stages, but it brings her account rather quickly to an end. As Daniel Brown, Jack Engler, and I attempted to show in *Transformations of Consciousness*, there is abundant cross-cultural material to construct at least a six-stage model of transpersonal-realm development (which I usually simplify to four stages: psychic, subtle, causal, and nondual). Still, these refinements are easily incorporated into Wade's model if she feels the evidence warrants it.

Incidentally, Wade maintains that I do not recognize prebirth or postbirth states. This is incorrect.

4. The first summary of Wilber-II was published in 1979 ("A Developmental View of Consciousness," *Journal of Transpersonal Psychology* 11, no. 1 [1979]). The full-length *Atman Project* appeared in 1980. Work from period-II continued to be published for the next few years: *Up from Eden* (1981), *A Sociable God* (1983), *Eye to Eye* (1983), and *Quantum Questions* (1984).

Wilber-III was first published in "Ontogenetic Development: Two Fundamental Patterns," *Journal of Transpersonal Psychology* 13, no. 1 (1981); this was followed by a two-part series in the same journal, "The Developmental Spectrum and Psychopathology: Part 1, Stages and Types of Pathology; Part 2, Treatment Modalities" (Wilber, 1984). These papers were then included in *Transformations of Consciousness* (Wilber et al., 1986). Wilber 1984 was probably the strongest statement of the difference between enduring and transitional structures; and Wilber 1990 was the strongest statement about the difference between levels and lines, although this present volume updates both. [See *Integral Psychology* for the most recent and comprehensive presentation of this model.]

5. With Wilber-III, I was once again faced with the choice of publishing pages of research notes or simply an abbreviated outline. This time, personal factors (my wife's illness) forced me to publish only the abbreviated outline (first as an article in the *Journal of Transpersonal Psychology,* then in *Transformations of Consciousness,* co-authored with Jack Engler and Daniel P. Brown; see note 4). And once again I did so with the hope that some bright grad student or subsequent writer would pick up the ball and run with it.

At the same time, it was becoming increasingly obvious that the "secret" to the psychological, noetic, or consciousness dimension could not be found in that dimension alone. In fact, the spectrum of consciousness only covered the Upper-Left quadrant, and thus my interest was increasingly drawn to the much more challenging issue: not just elucidating the states and stages of consciousness, but how those phenomena intermeshed with the other quadrants in an "all-level, all-quadrant" approach: in other words, Wilber-IV, which is the model presented in *Sex, Ecology, Spirituality* and *A Brief History of Everything,* as well as in this book. See chapter 11, section titled "An Integral Theory of Consciousness," for a summary of Wilber-IV. [See also *Integral Psychology* for the most recent overview.]

6. The need to distinguish between enduring and transitional structures becomes obvious when we attempt to correlate interior structures of consciousness with organic brain structures, because many of the former are transitional (and disappear), whereas most of the latter are permanent (and endure). The need to correlate interior (Left-Hand) with exterior (Right-Hand) structures is an important part of any integral approach, as Jenny Wade makes clear in her own terms, and this is one of the very useful aspects of her book.

As I would put it, brain structures are the exterior (Upper Right—brain stem, limbic system, neocortex, etc.) correlates of the interior structures (Upper Left—sensations, impulses, images, symbols, concepts, rules, and so forth). With reference to the interior stages, as consciousness evolves through the basic structures, it generates various transitional structures. Wade's nine stages are essentially stages of *transitional* structures (they are essentially the nine fulcrums of self development and associated worldviews), which is why when consciousness is at, say, her authentic level, it does not generally have simultaneous access to the naive level. But the correlative brain structures are still active and still fully functioning (they are enduring, not transitional). Wade's correlations between consciousness structures and brain structures are superb, I think, but she does not discuss why evolution deconstructs the former but not the latter, which becomes more apparent if we clearly distinguish between enduring and transitional structures.

Because Wilber-II is essentially consonant with Aurobindo, Wilber-III/IV constitutes my criticism and critique of Aurobindo (and Chaudhuri) as well. Again, this is not a repudiation but a refinement. Likewise, since the Great Chain of Being (the Great Holarchy) is essentially identical to Wilber-II, Wilber-III/IV constitutes a significant part of my overall criticism and refinement of the perennial philosophy itself (including the basic psychology of Vedanta, Mahayana/ Vajrayana Buddhism, the Kabbalistic sefirot, Plotinus and the Neoplatonic tradition, and so on). I believe that these III/IV refinements (waves, streams, self, realms, and states, as they manifest in all four quadrants) are especially important as we begin the actual and specific details of integrating Eastern and Western models.

7. Confusions in these types of reductionistic models especially show up when they attempt to treat the nondual domain, which is often equated with "the Implicate Order." And precisely because the implicate order is in some sense different from the explicate order, this actually results in a hidden dualistic view. In other words, because of the implicate/explicate distinction, theorists like Bohm must assign *characteristics* to the implicate order, an order they also tend to identify with the *unqualifiable* absolute, Ground of Being, Emptiness, etc. Qualities that Bohm and others have assigned to the implicate order include: perpetual flux, parts merge and unite in a constant flow, an order of fluid energy, dynamic and holographic flux, a frequency realm, a seamless whole, and so on.

But, as Nagarjuna pointed out, as soon as you qualify the Absolute—in any fashion whatsoever, including "wholeness" and "nondual"—you in fact create a dualistic model. Washburn, for example, must *qualify* the Ground in order to *set it apart* from the ego, which immediately creates a strong dualism, which he then attempts to overcome with his "psychic whole," which makes the Ground a *subset* of something else, and thus not much of a Ground to begin with. According to Nagarjuna and the nondual mystics, all of this comes from the confused attempt to qualify Emptiness.

8. *ReVision*, Summer 1996.

9. The exact relation of these developmental lines to each other is a matter of empirical and phenomenological research. Most evidence to date suggests that, for example, physiological development is necessary but not sufficient for cognitive development, which is necessary but not sufficient for interpersonal (and self) development, which is necessary but not sufficient for moral development. (We return to this topic in detail in chapter 10.)

In my model, the major axis on which all of these are measured is consciousness (the levels of the spectrum of consciousness, the levels of basic structures). This "consciousness axis" is vaguely similar to cognitive development, but they are not simply the same thing, especially given the biases in cognitive research, which include: (1) an almost exclusive emphasis on it-knowledge, which is called "cognition," and which in fact leaves out the I and we aspects of consciousness; (2) a consequent overemphasis on the acquisition of scientific it-knowledge as the central axis of development, with a concomitant attempt to (3) define a central axis in terms of Piagetian logico-mathematical competence;

(4) a consequent failure to count emotions (and prana) as a mode of consciousness; (5) an almost total ignoring of the transrational structures of consciousness. This is why I do not simply equate the basic structures of consciousness with the cognitive line of development, although there is a closer overlap with this line than with most others. If I sometimes refer to the basic structures as cognitive, it is with all these major qualifications in mind; in almost all cases, I refer to them separately. [See *Integral Psychology*, chap. 1.]

10. P. 81. All quotes in this section are from Gardner et al. (1990).

11. Ibid.

12. Ibid, my italics.

13. P. 87, my italics.

14. P. 93.

15. P. 95. In my opinion, there is a "metaphysical" basis for the existence of levels and lines, or waves and streams, and the fact that their essential contours are universal (even if they often manifest with quite different surface features). The different lines of development are all variations on the four quadrants, each of which unfolds in levels of development or manifestation. All holons possess (at least) the four quadrants, or simply the "big three" of I, we, and it: subjectivity or self (self-expression, self-talents, aesthetics, self-identity, ego structure, self-needs, etc.); we or communal intersubjectivity (including moral development, ethics, justness and justice, care and responsibility); and it (or objective realities, cognition in an it-mode, object permanence, etc.). Each of those four quadrants unfolds through the basic levels of its own manifestation: thus, lines and levels, streams and waves. [See *Integral Psychology*, chap. 14.]

16. P. 95.

    We might also note that, following Aurobindo's lead, we can treat gross (frontal), subtle (psychic), and causal (higher and superconscient) development as three broadly distinct lines, which means that, within certain limits, they can each develop quasi-independently. This means that individuals (ontogenetically and phylogenetically) might make strides in psychic/subtle development while still being relatively undeveloped in frontal structures (ego, rationality, conventional verbal, etc.). This further points up why I believe these various streams are not stacked linearly on top of each other like bricks, but rather alongside each other like columns—and further, why progress in some lines might run ahead of, or lag behind, others.

17. P. 95.

    Two other similar approaches deserve mention. Diane McGuinness, Karl Pribram, and Marian Pirnazar (1990) agree with Piaget that there is a universal sequence of cognitive development from the sensory level to concrete schemas/operations to abstract subtleties, but they point out that research does not support the Piagetian notion that this logico-cognitive scheme occurs across all domains (nor always in an age-related fashion). Rather, that general progression *recurs with each new learning experience or developmental line (at any age)*. I quite agree. This "continuous state transformation model" is "nevertheless hierarchical in terms of microdevelopment in the acquisition of any specific skill. The states . . . form an invariant sequence, and each successor integrates its predecessor" (Alexander et al., 1990, p. 14). Note that the progression from sensory to concrete schema to abstract/subtleties is essentially preconventional, conventional, postconventional (although they recognize no post-postconventional).

Kurt Fischer, Sheryl Kenny, and Sandra Pipp (1990) begin by pointing out that the Piagetian notion of synchronous development across domains has not held up to further research. As we are putting it, different lines develop at different paces. The authors point out that a Piagetian stage is a *capacity* that must be fleshed out with *competency*, which varies with different skills, and which depends especially on actual *practice*. Although these skills differ, sometimes dramatically, they all nevertheless fall into three general hierarchical levels of acquisition, based on complexity, which the authors call: sensorimotor (cf. preconventional), concrete representations (cf. conventional), and abstractions (cf. postconventional).

The authors subdivide the abstract level into four more hierarchical stages: early and late formal operations (formal rational or formop), and then two postformal stages, that of systems and then systems of systems (i.e., two stages of vision-logic).

Fischer et al. also note the importance of biological/brain maturation schedules for these various cognitive developments, thus rightly emphasizing, I believe, the intimate connection of the Left- and Right-Hand aspects of each holon of human awareness.

Those important models are all consistent with the general notion of different streams progressing through the same general waves (for me, different developmental lines unfolding through the same general levels of consciousness, all held together, not by a single and synchronous Piagetian line, but by the self-system juggling the entire lot of quasi-independent lines, levels, stages, and states).

We should also note that, in addition to vertical or transformative developments, there are horizontal or translative developments. Any basic structure, since it remains in existence (even if subsumed), can be further exercised, developed, and trained within its own domain. The oral stage might emerge in the earliest months of life, but a great chef is a thing of adult wonder.

Thus, we can investigate the *horizontal* or *translative* developments of any number of lines, streams, or domains. Moreover, once major vertical transformations come to rest for any given individual, there remains only translative growth, if that. These translative unfoldings are both enduring and transitional; some are hierarchically integrated, others are more "the seasons of a person's (adult) life," which Daniel Levinson has so wonderfully documented.

One of the difficulties of studying higher vertical transformation is that society's force as a pacer of transformation drops out (at this stage in evolution) around the formal level, and thus with any postformal and post-postconventional developments, not only are you on your own, you are sometimes actively discouraged. Most studies, from Loevinger to Kohlberg to Piaget, show that major vertical transformations tend to end by late adolescence/early adulthood, and all that is left, from that point on, are variations on horizontal or translative development.

Thus, the center of gravity of a given culture tends to act as a "magnet of development": if you are below that average, the magnet pulls you up; if you try to go beyond it, it pulls you down.

At this point in evolution, it appears that there are only a relatively few practices that can act as higher and postformal pacers of development. These include most especially meditation and integral transformative practices; also a few forms of psychotherapy; intense artistic or athletic accomplishment (the intense exercise of any talent or developmental line); rare cases of psychedelics; holotropic breathwork and other yogic manipulations of the gross bodymind; life-threatening illness or accident; grace.

18. In *A Sociable God*, for example, I trace the spiritual/religion line through magic religion, mythic religion, rational religion, psychic religion, subtle religion, causal religion, and nondual religion (each of which is a level or wave of the spiritual line or stream). I further differentiated between translative spiritual *legitimacy* (on any given level) versus transformative spiritual *authenticity* (capacity for transformation to a higher/deeper level). [See *Integral Psychology*, chap. 10.]

19. The technical correlations (given in SES) for these various terms are as follows:

The *preconventional* realms refer specifically to the sensorimotor (the basic structures of matter, sensation, and perception), and in a more general sense to the overall preoperational realms (impulse, image, symbol, and concept, and early to middle conop)—and all of the developmental lines associated with those basic structures (e.g., protective needs, precon morality, impulsive self-sense, etc.). The associated worldviews include archaic, magic, and magic-mythic.

The *conventional* realms in general refer to the basic structures of late conop (rule/role), early and middle formop—and all of the developmental lines associated with those basic structures (conformist self, mythic-membership, belong-ingness needs, etc.). The worldviews include mythic and mythic-rational.

The *postconventional* realms in general refer to the basic structures of later formop and all of vision-logic—and all the developmental lines associated with those basic structures (formal, postformal, centauric, integrated, social contract and universal principles, etc.). The worldviews include rational and existential (integral-aperspectival).

The *post-postconventional* realms in general refer to the basic structures of psychic, subtle, causal, and nondual—and all the developmental lines associated with those basic structures (post-postformal, including the four corresponding moral stages in those realms [see SES, note 59 for chap. 8]). Worldviews include shamanic/yogic, saintly, sagely, and nondual (nature mysticism, deity mysticism, formless mysticism, nondual mysticism).

20. Fowler's empirical and phenomenological research, executed as a reconstructive science, found that individuals move through six or seven major stages of the development of spiritual faith (or spiritual orientation); his findings match very closely the map I am here presenting.

Briefly: Stage o is "preverbal undifferentiated" (our archaic); Stage 1 Fowler calls "projective, magical" (our magical), which he also correlates with preop.

Stage 2 he calls "mythic-literal," correlated with early conop, where faith extends to "those like us." Stage 3 is "conventional," which involves "mutual role taking" and "conformity to class norms and interests," late conop and early formop (stages 2 and 3 being our mythic and mythic-rational, respectively, with both stages being our overall mythic-membership).

Stage 4 is "individual-reflexive," as "dichotomizing formop" (and the ego) emerges, and involves "reflexive relativism" and "self-ratified ideological perspective." Stage 5 is "conjunctive faith," as "dialectical formop" emerges and begins to "include groups, classes, and traditions other than one's own"; this involves "dialectical joining of judgment-experience processes with reflective claims of others and of various expressions of cumulative human wisdom." (Postconventional, universal rationality and universal pluralism, mature ego, beginning of worldcentric orientation).

Stage 6 is "universalizing," which is "informed by the experiences and truths of previous stages" (centauric integration of previous stages, which Fowler also calls "unitive actuality" and "unification of reality mediated by symbols and the self"—that is, the integrated centauric self). This self is "purified of egoic striving, and linked by disciplined intuition to the principle of being," involving a "commonwealth of being" and a "trans-class awareness and identification," correlated with "synthetic formop" (our vision-logic, the fruition of the world-centric orientation, and the beginning of transpersonal intuition; the higher contemplative stages themselves were not investigated by Fowler, given their rarity, but the fit up to that point is quite close, often exact). Fowler, *Stages of Faith*.

21. There are, of course, many different definitions of "spiritual" (and "religious"); in fact, in *A Sociable God* I outline nine quite different but common uses of those terms. In this discussion we are focusing on the two most common uses that occur in this general discussion of the development of spirituality and its relation to psychological development.

In that regard, there is another usage of "spiritual" that is also fairly common, namely, spirituality is that which profoundly integrates all the other levels and lines. In this usage, it is quite similar to how I use the "overall self" (as the locus of integration), and readers who prefer this usage can make the necessary correlations. [See *Integral Psychology*, chap. 10.]

22. More specifically: In the transpersonal psychology textbook that I have been not-writing for fifteen years [*Integral Psychology*], I divide the "overall self" into two general aspects, the *proximate self* and the *distal self*. The proximate self is the intimately subjective self, the self that is experienced as an "I." The distal self is the objective self, which is experienced as a "me" or "mine." (There is also the *anterior self*, which is experienced as "I-I," which is whatever intuition of the Witness is present prior to its full causal unfolding.) The sum total of these (three) selves I call the overall self.

The proximate self is indeed *a separate developmental line*—it is the developmental line of the self-sense or proximate self-identity (often called "ego development"), but which in my model runs the entire spectrum, from the pleromatic self to the uroboric self to the typhonic self to the persona to ego to centaur to psychic/subtle soul to causal spirit. And for simplicity's sake, I often refer to this as the self or self-sense, without getting involved in further distinctions.

But the overall self is the proximate self plus the distal self (plus its own intuition of the anterior I-I), plus anything else that comes into the self's orbit: I, me, and mine, the great juggling act that is the overall self.

In the development of the proximate self-identity or self-sense line, the proximate self of one stage becomes part of the distal self of the next. That is, what is intimately *subject* at one stage becomes an *object* of awareness of the next ("I" becomes "me" or even "mine"), which is exactly how the basic structures are stripped of self-sense, how identification becomes disidentification, how attachment becomes detachment. Death to a proximate self converts it to a distal self, which is eventually dropped altogether in the Great Death of radical Enlightenment, where the I-I alone stands forth as the ultimate Self of all subjects and all objects.

That is the developmental line of the specific or *proximate self-sense*, which is indeed a developmental sequence of relatively invariant stages. *These stages of the proximate self-sense are exactly the fulcrums of self-development* (which I usually give as nine or ten in number).

But the overall self, which I sometimes loosely refer to as the "center of gravity" of consciousness, is an amalgam of the proximate self-sense plus distal self plus all the other items the overall self is juggling. This includes unconscious aspects split off in the development of the proximate self-sense (unconscious impulses, dissociated personae, etc.), as well as the balancing act of all the other transitional stages, traits, states, and talents. [See *Integral Psychology*, chap. 3, 8.]

Thus, when you have a sense of your overall self (simply as you exist right now), it is not just your I and your me, but also somehow all of the other concerns floating through your awareness at any given time—your possessions, your talents, your relationships, family, friends, your wishes, your goals, your fears, and so forth (including unconscious intentions that exert their own influence, whether consciously perceived or not).

And that is why the overall self does not follow an invariant (or universal) sequence of stages. Being an amalgam, it is indeed "all over the place." On the long haul, of course, the self, to the degree it continues to unfold, will show a broad progression through the major waves of consciousness, simply because all of the lines that it is juggling are themselves making their way through those waves.

Thus, this center of gravity, to the extent development in any of the lines continues, will show a slow and progressive developmental unfolding (but not in any set sequence). This means that *this overall-self development might therefore be initiated by any number of different lines during this process.* At one point, the overall self might develop—that is, increase its overall depth—through its cognitive growth; at another point, growth in the affective line might take the lead; at another, its artistic growth might explode and drag the self with it; at yet another, its spiritual growth; at yet another, it might be the proximate self itself that yearns for the light and drags everything it can with it. That overall growth will not follow a set sequence, even though almost all of the developmental lines within it will; and yet depth on the whole will increase, and increase in a specific direction (namely, toward spirit-as-spirit, pushed by the crane of Eros and pulled by the skyhook of Agape).

This is also why overall growth cannot be conceptualized as due primarily to cognitive structures nor to cognitive dissonance; nor to ego growth nor psycho-sexual growth; nor interpersonal growth nor emotional growth nor spiritual growth. At any point in development, in any given individual, any of those lines might take the lead in overall development, until that line lags and any other line or lines pick up the pace. None of this shows invariant (nor hierarchical) stagelike progression, and yet all of them have their eye on the same prize, namely, God.

23. Washburn raises the issue of whether vision-logic (and the centaur) is an ad hoc and perhaps unnecessary addition. Couldn't rationality simply integrate the body, since each level transcends and includes its predecessors? Why add the allegedly extra stage of vision-logic and make that necessary for the mind/body integration?

I have postulated each and every stage in my model based specifically, not on philosophical assumptions, but on substantial amounts of empirical, phenome-nological, clinical, or contemplative evidence. The same is true for the centaur and its vision-logic.

A cognitive stage beyond Piaget's formal operational—a stage of "higher rea-son," as it were, or in some sense a generally *postformal* realm—has been sug-gested now by at least two dozen major theorists and researchers, whom I have carefully cited. When I was first pondering the existence of vision-logic (in "The Spectrum of Consciousness," *Main Currents in Modern Thought*, 1974), I could only find one or two mainstream researchers (such as Arieti) and a few philosophers (such as Schelling, Hegel, Gebser) who concurred. But those now proposing postformal stage(s) include Arlin; Cowan; Souvaine, Lahey, and Kegan; Koplowitz; Fischer, Kenny, and Pipp; Richards and Commons; Pascual-Leone; Kohlberg and Ryncarz; Habermas; Bruner; Cook-Greuter; Basseches; L. Eugene Thomas; Sinnott; Kramer; Gilligan, Murphy, and Tappen; Alexander et al.

Francis Richards and Michael Commons (1990) have given one articulation of this general postformal stage. They see vision-logic as consisting of four sub-stages (systematic, metasystematic, paradigmatic, cross-paradigmatic); I recom-mend their work.

But whatever we decide on the fine details, the existence of something like vision-logic is now accepted by a very significant number of theoreticians and researchers, and is backed with a considerable amount of evidence. That, in-deed, is why I present it; there is nothing ad hoc about this.

Likewise, I suggested the existence of the centauric self-sense based on various substantial research results, especially those of Loevinger, Broughton, Maslow, Rogers, Gilligan, Graves, and others, whose research shows that, beyond and quite distinct from the individualistic ego stage is a bodymind integrated stage. I have often used Loevinger's summary of Broughton's research: "At this stage, mind and body are both experiences of an integrated self."

Why do I say that it is only vision-logic that can integrate mind and body? This is, of course, a relative affair and a matter of degrees. One might even make the argument that the mind and body are not truly integrated until radical Enlightenment, and I would not argue with that. But generally speaking, I describe the centaur as the integration of mind and body because (1) this directly follows the evidence of Loevinger, Broughton, Graves, and others; and (2) the centaur, as the great transition from the gross bodymind to the subtle bodymind, represents the "final" integration of that gross bodymind.

More technically: because vision-logic is on the edge of the transmental, the self of vision-logic is increasingly disidentifying with the mind itself. Because vision-logic transcends formal rationality, it can more easily integrate formal reason and body.

It is true that each stage generally transcends and includes its predecessors, but that refers most specifically to the basic structures themselves (which are without inherent self-sense). But we must never forget that the basic structures are negotiated by the self, and the leading edge of self-development is the home of the death-terror. Thus, whatever the leading level of development with which the self's center of gravity is identified, just that level is the central nexus of the death-seizure. While the basic structures can be rather cleanly integrated, the self-stages, with their boundary of death-terror, cannot. Only as each basic structure is transcended and stripped of self-identify, can the self cease defending it against death. Thus, when the self is identified with formop, it cannot let go of formop and effect a "clean" integration with previous levels. This is nothing new with formop, but is true of every level appropriated by self-development (this is, in fact, the dynamic of the repression barrier at each and every level of development: the boundary of defenses, in their many forms and levels, is instituted from the embedded-unconscious of any level, with its inherent death-terror).

The first stage beyond identification with formop is, of course, vision-logic, at which point the formop mind, now basically stripped of self-sense, can be more cleanly integrated with the previous levels, including the bodily realms. And this, whatever the explanation, is what the actual clinical evidence shows at this level, where "mind and body are both experiences of an integrated self."

(One other contributing factor to the integration of the centaur is the significant loosening of the repression barrier that occurs at this stage. See chapter 7 for a discussion of this topic.)

The evidence, in short, clearly shows that this postformal integrated personal stage (centaur) is significantly distinct from the previous, formal, egoic stage. As I said, there is nothing ad hoc in any of this. [See *Integral Psychology,* chap. 8.]

24. 1990, p. 8.

Chapter 10: The Effects of Meditation

1. This is not to overlook what appear to be some valid criticisms of some of the TM research, including occasional bias in the researchers, inadequate methodology, and obliviousness to negative effects on practitioners. But even when those inadequacies are taken into account, what's left of the research is still quite impressive.

   For example, 1 percent of a college control sample scored at Loevinger's highest two stages (autonomous and integrated), whereas in a similar sample of regular meditators, 38 percent reached those stages. Moreover, "A review of over twenty published studies (involving approximately seven thousand subjects) indicated that the highest average ego development level obtained in any adult sample was the 'conscientious' stage [above which are individualistic, autonomous, and then integrated]. Furthermore, no interventions to facilitate ego development have succeeded in stimulating growth beyond the conscientious level." That 38 percent broke through this ceiling with meditation is quite extraordinary. Moreover, if the Loevinger test is slightly modified to be more sensitive to those at the higher stages, 87 percent in one meditating population broke the conscientious barrier, with 36 percent scoring autonomous and 29 percent integrated. Alexander et al. (1990), p. 333.

2. 1990, p. 339.

3. Alexander et al. refer to their seven or so basic levels of consciousness as "mental levels," which is perhaps not the best term, since there are submental and supramental levels in their scheme. They point out that "mental" in a broader sense means "the overall multilevel functioning of consciousness," and so I will usually refer to their basic levels as *levels of consciousness*; these, as I said, are essentially similar to my basic structures of consciousness.

   In the text I mention that this is more properly "Vedantic" rather than specifically "Vedic," because in the Vedas you actually find no mention of the koshas or sheaths of awareness; no mention of the three great realms (gross, subtle, causal); no doctrine of the three great states (waking, dream, sleep); no psychology of Atman and its relation to Brahman. Those are all tenets found in the much later Upanishads, which were then codified in Vedanta. It is common in India to claim "Vedic" authority for anything you want taken seriously.

4. P. 319.

5. The basic levels of consciousness are also their own lines, but not all lines come from those levels (in fact, the most important ones do not). That is, as each basic structure emerges, it remains in existence, and thus it can be developed indefinitely: as a level, it is also its own line. But the basic structures do not define the other major lines of development, nor in any way account for them (except by being necessary but not sufficient for their development).

   On page 296, Alexander et al. equate the "rows" on their diagram with "domains" (lines). But the rows are also the levels of consciousness—exactly the problem (i.e., levels used as the major lines). Of course, this by default leaves room for the other domains (such as moral, artistic, etc.), but there is no actual place for these domains on any of their rows. The authors therefore, at one point, are forced to put these domains into their "columns" or "faculties," but these are already *defined* as developmental *periods*, which in fact leaves no actual room for specific domains either.

6. Here is their central dynamic: "In accordance with the orthogenetic principle of development (Werner), the postrepresentational stages [post-postconventional] should become differentiated from and hierarchically integrated with the representational level. Thus, the capacity for conceptual thought would not be abandoned. Instead, the entire representational system . . . would take on the status of a subsystem within, rather than executor of, mental life" (p. 289).

I agree entirely—*but only for the enduring structures*; the transitional structures are *not* functional subsystems; their functionality comes precisely from their phase-specific *exclusivity*, and when that exclusivity is broken, that stage is broken with it.

It is precisely this confusion (of enduring and transitional) that forces the authors to list two of their six levels as "functional"—in their diagram they put these in "broken lines" to contrast them with the solid/structural nature of the other levels; but in fact all six levels are supposed to be structural—a move that effectively erases one-third of their model. Explicitly differentiating between enduring (solid lines) and transitional (broken lines) would rectify that problem, I believe.

7. P. 22.

8. P. 295.

9. Ibid.

10. The embedded-unconscious—created by the proximate self's exclusive identification with a particular basic structure of consciousness—plays an extremely important role in development and pathology, because the embedded-unconscious is the home of most of the self's defenses at any given level. Precisely because the self is identified with a level, it must defend that level against threats—and ultimately, defend it against death (until the self "dies" to that level, differentiates from it, disembeds from it, turns it from proximate to distal, from attachment to detachment). Prior to that point, the self-system will dissociate, repress, displace, project, distort, or otherwise alienate any aspects of self or other that threaten this identity, that threaten its life, that threaten its present level of development and adaptation. This is the "horizontal" battle of life and death that occurs on every level of development, until all deaths have been died, all subjects have been transcended, all selves disembedded, and there stands instead the radiant Self that is the Kosmos at large.

11. *The Evolving Self*, p. 31. Notice likewise that my point #5 in "The Form of Development" was: "What is *subjective* becomes *objective*." This ceaseless conversion of the subject of this moment into the object of the subject of the next moment is, of course, one of Whitehead's central contentions. This has always been one of the easiest entries into Whitehead's profound philosophy, and certainly one of the many points of my agreement with his views. In *Eye to Eye* (chapter 6), I gave a long appreciation of Whitehead's work, with several of its correlations with my own work. SES contains several endnotes doing the same.

My major criticisms of Whitehead are basically two. The first is that his essentially monological orientation severely limits the application of his metaphysics. In assuming an essentially subjectivist stance (the subject becomes the object of the next subject), he fails to grasp the extensive significance of intersubjectivity (his societies are interobjective, not genuinely intersubjective; that is, they are societies of monological occasions), so that he fails to see that actual occasions are not merely subjective/objective, but all-four-quadrant (holons). This is why Whitehead's stance, to give only one example, has never been able to generate a coherent and comprehensive linguistic theory, despite the claims to the contrary by his followers. Whitehead has taken the modern monological collapse of the Kosmos and made it paradigmatic for reality at large.

Second, although some theorists believe that Whitehead fits the bill as *the* great transpersonal philosopher, I believe Whitehead fails that task in the most essential respects (much as I admire him otherwise). To give only the most obvious example: in order to actually awaken to the nondual Kosmos, as we have seen, one must attain subject permanence (the unbroken continuity of awareness through waking, dream, and sleep states). Without that as an actual yogic or contemplative accomplishment in consciousness, *there is no corresponding mode of knowing that will disclose the Real*. This yogic injunction, exemplar, or practice is the real *transpersonal paradigm*, and without it (or something similar to it), you have no authentic transpersonal anything. At the very least, you must incorporate the necessity for this injunction into your system. Notice that Shankara, Nagarjuna, Aurobindo, Plotinus (and Alexander and Wilber) can pass this test; Whitehead does not. This is not a secondary issue; it is at the precise heart of the matter, a heart that Whitehead lacks.

Thus, the notion of "Whitehead as exemplary transpersonal philosopher" is based mostly on a translative language game, in my opinion, and not on transformative injunctions that actually disclose the transpersonal and post-postconventional domains. I myself have always found Whitehead's account to be an excellent place to begin, but it simply does not go nearly far enough. Certain of his notions are nonetheless indispensable, I believe, such as prehension and prehensive unification, actual entities and societies, creativity (as absolute and universal subjectivity), concrescence, presentational immediacy, causal efficacy, "the many become one and are increased by one"—the list is endless, and in that regard I am an enthusiastic Whiteheadian.

But all of those notions, without exception, take on dramatically different forms as you move from the gross domain (which Whitehead covers) into the subtle and causal domains, themselves disclosed only by higher yogic injunctions, and thus domains that, at best, are only vaguely postulated by Whitehead (e.g., eternal objects). Whitehead's philosophy remains a dilution of these principles as they appear, filtered and thinned, in the gross domain, where Whitehead first spots them (and quite accurately reports them at that level). But of their higher forms and functions, let alone the injunctions and exemplars that will disclose them, Whitehead has at best second- and third-hand intimations— and precisely no way, in his entire philosophy, to introduce you directly to those higher domains.

Nevertheless, Whitehead's beginning orientation is infinitely preferable to most other contenders, such as logical positivism, mere empiricism, scientific materialism, etc. This is why I continue to find myself sympathetic with so many Whiteheadians, including the wonderful John Cobb, Charles Hartshorne, and the many superb books by David Ray Griffin.

12. Summary by Alexander et al. (1990), p. 19.

13. In this book, Kegan addresses one of the limitations of *The Evolving Self*, namely, the exact nature and relation of line and level, or stream and wave, or specific domain and cross-domain principle. Here, he identifies the "general underlying principle" that similarly organizes the different lines (cognitive, affective, etc.) of "the same order of consciousness" (i.e., the same level or dimension of consciousness). His *three orders of consciousness* are essentially preconventional, conventional, and postconventional (readers are urged to consult his actual formulations), which, again, is quite consistent with my view, except that Kegan still is reluctant to acknowledge a post-postconventional wave, although his model can easily handle it.

14. P. 34.

15. P. 363.

16. Pp. 297, 295.

17. Note also that because they call their level 6 "the ego" (meaning the individual self), they cannot easily see that the self is instead that which navigates all levels, until it is subsumed in and by the Self (which was the implicit source of awareness or I-I in all previous levels, and the implicit core of the self-system at those levels), a Self which in turn steps out of itself and into the radiant Emptiness of the Nondual.

Their approach blocks them, in my opinion, from the more adequate conception of the self-system as that which balances all the various lines, and is not itself merely another line alongside others, which would leave the psyche an incoherent jumble of noncommunicating lines.

Thus, I believe the only viable view is this: (1) the proximate self (at whatever level) is the *locus of identification* ("the dominant locus of functional awareness," the "bounded I"); (2) the proximate self successively identifies with each emerging basic structure (or level of consciousness) and thus becomes embedded at that level (or at that wave); (3) which generates a stream of transitional self-related stages (self-sense, self-needs, morals) supported by the *exclusiveness* of the proximate identification; (4) these exclusivity structures, due to the "looseness" of the overall self, can develop in a quasi-independent fashion, though they tend to be held together in a bundle by the self; these remain in place until (5) the self de-embeds or dis-identifies with that level, (6) embeds at the next level, (7) which *integrates* the previous *enduring* structures but *negates* the previous exclusivity/transitional structures—and so on until developmental arrest (or Enlightenment, with its own post-Enlightenment dynamic).

Incidentally, Alexander et al. divide overall development into three very broad and major stages: the prerepresentational (the preconventional), the representational (conventional and postconventional), and the postrepresentational (post-

postconventional). I agree entirely; those are the gross, subtle, and causal realms. I also agree, as I said, with the authors' novel and important point that the transition from the first to the second is via object permanence, and from the second to the third via subject permanence. They would probably agree that the fourth (turiya) is yet another major transition, which we might call "nondual permanence."

18. I am in this book using "meditation" in a generic sense. Different types of meditation will produce different specific effects, and the generic conclusions can be adjusted accordingly.

19. The farther apart the developmental lines are in the "necessary but not sufficient" relations, the more independently they can develop. Thus, there can be severe disjunctures between cognitive and moral, with cognitive running quite ahead of moral, but interpersonal and moral tend to develop closer to each other. I maintain that the self-related stages (or simply the self-streams) tend to develop as a "bundle" held together by the proximate self-sense, but even these can develop somewhat independently because the self-sense can be all over the place, and can, in worst-case scenarios, interiorly dissociate and fragment, allowing the self-lines to splinter.

20. 1990, p. 289.

21. The integral psychograph can also include any horizontal typology the particular therapist finds useful. For example, a popular horizontal typing is the Enneagram, consisting of nine major types of personality with associated wisdom and defense. As I suggested in *Brief History*, those nine Enneagram classifications are not vertical levels but horizontal types, which can therefore appear on all levels (except the upper and lower reaches, where they fade out). Accordingly, if we wish to work with the Enneagram, we would have the spectrum of levels of each of the nine types. It is not enough to know that you are a "6" on the Enneagram. Are you a precon 6, a con 6, a postcon 6, or post-postcon 6? Thus, both horizontal and vertical analysis would be part of the integral psychograph. (The Enneagram as commonly used now does not foster transformation but merely translation.)

One of the reasons that I do not particularly emphasize horizontal typologies, whether Jungian, Enneagram, astrological, etc., is that empirical evidence for them is almost always lacking, because it is virtually impossible to demonstrate that *everybody* fits into the various types. (I am including astrology, not because I necessarily believe it, but because, even if it were shown to possess some sort of validity, it would still be a horizontal typology, which I maintain is intrinsically impossible to verify as characterology.)

The situation is quite different with vertical levels—such as the spectrum of basic structures—because, to the extent that those levels are accurate, virtually *everybody* passes through them, and this can be empirically demonstrated with a great deal of confidence. Thus, barring severe disturbances, everybody develops images, symbols, concepts, and rules. The vertical levels are precisely those universal structures through which virtually everybody passes, as cross-cultural evidence has consistently demonstrated. In order to develop concepts, you must first develop images, and there are no known exceptions.

Not so with horizontal typologies, because you may—or may not—fit into their stereotypes. This is why, as I said, I have not been much of an advocate of horizontal typologies, from astrology to Jungian to the Enneagram. At the same time, if you find them useful in an interpretive fashion, I have no objections whatsoever. Just do not suppose they are universal, comprehensive, or all-inclusive, because research does not support that claim.

Don Riso, in my opinion, is doing an excellent job of using the horizontal Enneagram with the vertical spectrum of consciousness. See *Personality Types* and *Understanding the Enneagram*.

22. Each of the nine or ten fulcrums of self development have a corresponding type or class of pathology. See chapter 4, The Spectrum of Psychopathology, in Wilber et al., *Transformations of Consciousness*. Bryan Wittine, in his review of SES (see chapter 11), presents my view as if it maintained clear-cut levels of pathology and clear-cut treatment modalities, which is not the case at all. Precisely because the self is "all over the place," so is pathology and its treatment. "Levels," as usual, are simply abstract landmarks that help orient us in the ongoing stream of consciousness unfolding.

23. I have left out a great number of types of therapies, including relational therapies (such as family therapy, group therapy, couples therapy, or sangha-oriented practices), simply because this is a list of individually oriented approaches. But I do not mean to exclude them from consideration. By definition, integral therapy is all-level, all-quadrant, engaging the intentional, behavioral, cultural, and social in all of their relevant dimensions.

24. Jack Engler, who first used the phrase "You have to be somebody before you can be nobody" (Wilber et al., 1986), was referring specifically to *the self-development line*, and I believe he is quite right in that regard. This is why Engler says that he is convinced that meditation increases ego strength, and I agree entirely ("ego strength" technically means the capacity for disinterested witnessing).

Engler's important point—a point I also suggested in "The Pre/Trans Fallacy"—has often been lost on his critics, perhaps because he did not clearly separate the spiritual line from the self line. Let us do so; his important point about the self line still remains (as the discussion in the text will make clear, I believe).

Nor can his point be dislodged by the ersatz feminist criticism of Peggy Wright. The permeable self *also* develops from precon to con to postcon to post-postcon modes of permeability, and Engler's point (and certainly my point) is that "You have to be con before you can be postcon."

25. I am referring to frontal development. If you map the ontogenetic development of, for example, "witnessing consciousness"—as Jenny Wade expertly does in *Changes of Mind*—you often find a U-shape development, reflecting (possibly) the "trailing clouds of glory" of the psychic/subtle soul-drop (see likewise Grof's data). But the first leg of that U is simply the *end* of the *involutionary* line, which is not to be confused with the evolutionary and frontal development line, which is just getting started and is here at its lowest and most primitive

level, where ultimate concern—the form of frontal spirituality—is oral: one's ultimate concern is food, survival, bodily safety, and so on. The ultimate concern of the "original embedment" is simply food, and that is exactly the form of the "dynamic ground" at that stage—God is oral, the spirit is all mouth.

26. When we use the second general definition of "spirituality" and maintain that spiritual development is a separate line of development that runs alongside the others (all held together by the self-system), that spiritual stream itself, evidence (such as Fowler's) suggests, runs from preconventional to conventional to post-conventional to post-postconventional waves. That particular stream is "linear" (which means nested), holarchical, and largely invariant, moving through those waves in a sequence that, according to available evidence, cannot be altered by social conditioning. Although that particular spiritual line, in my opinion, is composed mostly of transitional structures, those structures still build upon the competences and skills of the earlier structures, even as certain of their central elements are replaced. Gilligan's linear and invariant hierarchy, for example (which, as a hierarchy of care, is very close to the hierarchy of ultimate concern), runs from selfish (egocentric, preconventional) to care ("conventional ethical") to universal care ("postconventional meta-ethical")—to, I would add, transpersonal compassion (post-postconventional).

As Gilligan notes, none of those stages can be bypassed or fundamentally altered, and, as far as we can tell, that applies as well to any specific spiritual line, in *both* its more agentic/male modes and its more communion/female modes (because both of them progress through the same waves—the same gender-neutral basic structures of consciousness—but with a different emphasis or "in a different voice"). And, as I suggested, meditation can be expected to accelerate—but not alter—that sequence of spiritual unfolding, in both male and female modes.

The actual details will depend upon the specific type of meditation; upon the level to which the meditation aims; upon whether the focus is predominantly ascending or descending; and upon whether the practitioner is male or female. But as a generalization, this conclusion ("meditation can be expected to accelerate—but not alter—that sequence of spiritual unfolding, in both male and female modes") is quite accurate, I believe. The central core of meditative development consists of the unfolding of the gender-neutral structures of consciousness, so that the differences between the male and female modes, although very significant, are still secondary in this regard.

The major constraint on the relation of "psychological" and "spiritual" lines (considered as separate lines) would be the "necessary but not sufficient" relation that we find between the various lines themselves. For the most part, this is something that only empirical research can determine. [See *Integral Psychology*, chap. 10.]

Chapter 11: Heading toward Omega?

1. In the first printing of SES, several ellipses were incorrectly used in a handful of long quotes; this was corrected in subsequent printings. But even in the first

printing, the endnotes still listed all the different page numbers that the different quotes were taken from. Thus, for example, in one long Emerson quote, where the ellipses are missing, if you look at the endnote, it gives five different sources: in other words, nobody was trying to pretend that these quotes were all from one place. As I said, these ellipses were restored in subsequent printings.

2. My interpretation of Emerson included the notions that (1) nature is not Spirit but a symbol of Spirit (or a manifestation of Spirit); (2) sensory awareness in itself does not reveal Spirit but obscures it; (3) an Ascending current is required to disclose Spirit; (4) Spirit is understood only as nature is transcended (i.e., Spirit is immanent in nature, but fully discloses itself only in a transcendence of nature—in short, Spirit transcends but includes nature).

Since I had claimed these interpretations could be found in most college texts, and since Smoley and diZerega claimed otherwise, I decided to check the standard college *Cliffs Notes on Emerson* (Lincoln, Neb.: Cliffs Notes, 1975), known for their uncontroversial stances (they are written by a team of internationally recognized authorities—six of them, in this case), and found the following, point by exact point:

(1) "Emerson . . . used nature as a symbol of the realm of spirit. . . . Nature [is] a symbol of Spirit" (pp. 15, 16). Nature is a form or expression of Spirit, but is not Spirit itself in its fullness. The authors point out the essential similarity with Plotinus: "Here we have again Plotinus's idea of cosmic movement. There are two movements, one of out-going or descent [Efflux, Agape], the spontaneous creativity of the higher which generates the lower. This is the movement by which the various levels of reality are eternally brought into being. Then there is the movement of return, ascent [Eros, Reflux] by which Soul passes up through all the stages of Being [which Emerson often calls "platforms"] to final union with the First Principle [the nondual One]" (pp. 63-4). "So," the authors continue, "in Emerson's 1836 epigraph, nature is described as 'the last thing of the soul,' the last emanation from God" (p. 9). And thus the lowest expression of God, but an expression of God nonetheless. For Emerson, nature is the starting point of the soul's remembrance of Spirit, but not the stopping point! Nature worshippers and neopagans, of course, do not take kindly to this; they are welcome to their views, but they simply cannot claim Emerson in their camp.

(2) "Man's reliance on the senses and the unrenewed Understanding alone lead to a frustration of his spiritual desires" (p. 14). There is a "further knowledge, a knowledge not accessible by means of sensory experience or by the reflection based on this experience" (p. 40).

(3) "So, for Emerson the idea of ethical ascent involves the activity of man's higher powers" (p. 14). "Good and life for Emerson are realized in our ethical ascent toward Soul" (p. 11).

(4) "We see the unmistakable tendency of Emerson's mind to move to ever higher levels of reality" (p. 19), which occurs through "a hierarchy of faculties" (p. 24). "The central argument is one of ethical ascent: Nature teaches man the proper use of nature—to transcend it" (p. 16). Thus, nature is to be transcended (and included) in Spirit, since nature is simply a lower expression of Spirit, but

an expression nonetheless, and a fitting and sublime starting point for the return journey. But of anyone who remains at the level of nature worship, Emerson says: "His mind is embruted, and he is a selfish savage. . . ."

As I said, all of these Emersonian points are largely uncontested, and they are exactly the points I represented in SES.

3. A few scholars asked me about my choice of Inge's translation of Plotinus, and so perhaps a brief explanation is in order.

In presenting Plotinus's ideas, I consulted the works of Turnball, Brehier, Rist, O'Daly, Wallis, and Karl Jaspers (who was perhaps my favorite commentator), and I focused especially on three major translations of his works: A. H. Armstrong's seven-volume series in the Loeb Classical Library, Harvard University Press (published in 1966–88); William Ralph Inge's two-volume series, originally the Gifford Lectures of 1917–18, published in 1929 (and reprinted in 1968); and Stephen MacKenna's translations, which he undertook from 1917 to 1930 (now available in a Penguin Classics edition and the wonderful Larson Publication edition).

For various reasons, which I will explain in a moment, I decided that, of all these translations, William Inge's had certain advantages. The other translations seemed to understand better the letter, but not as well the spirit, of Plotinus, and so even where they excelled technically, they were sometimes rather thin in their interpretive sweep.

Nonetheless, Inge's translation is usually not listed among the various translations of Plotinus, simply because he included only large, representative tracts of Plotinus; he did not publish a complete translation. For that, I relied primarily on Armstrong. As O'Meara (1995) recently pointed out, "Armstrong's translation supersedes that of S. MacKenna . . . , which, although a work of great literary quality, is less reliable and less clear" (p. 127).

Many critics still love MacKenna's beautiful style, as do I. Inge actually consulted MacKenna's translations (except for the very last parts, which MacKenna had not completed at the time), and Inge spoke very highly of them. Nonetheless, where Inge's translations deviated from MacKenna, he had his own sufficient reasons, and these sorts of deviations are explained at length in Inge's extensive notes, which scholars can easily consult and adjudicate for themselves.

Instead of getting involved in this battle of technical details and technical debate, and instead of performing a mixing and matching and juggling act between three translations, I simply chose to go with Inge's translations. Since the main points—the identical main points—could be made with any of these three translations, why did I choose Inge? I already gave one reason: I found Inge to have a deeper spiritual resonance than the others. I love MacKenna's translation; it is often quite beautiful and always moving, and I don't mean to detract from his wonderful and loving effort; and Armstrong's is technically exquisite. Nonetheless, Inge seems to intuit a profound depth of realization that comes across clearly in his work, and I was drawn to this depth.

The second reason is that Inge was himself an accomplished philosopher, and it is often the case that such accomplishment can bring a greater depth and wider range of perceptions to an interpretive task, only one of whose elements is technical proficiency. Again, I do not wish to detract from MacKenna, but he was a bank clerk and a journalist; his sheer love of Plotinus is evident and altogether moving; but I also appreciated the background and commentary that Inge was able to bring to the task.

The third main reason I chose Inge is that, for a very long time, William Inge was the only respected academic scholar—or at least, one of the very, very few—who *actually believed in the truth of what Plotinus was saying*. He was not interested in Plotinus as a merely historical curiosity, but rather as the representative of a profound worldview that still possessed abundant truth and goodness and beauty. So respected was Inge that, when Bertrand Russell was writing his chapter on Plotinus in *A History of Western Philosophy*, Inge was the only decent philosopher Russell could think of who believed in Plotinus: "A philosophical system," says Russell, "may be judged important for various different kinds of reasons. The first and most obvious is that we think it may be true. Not many students of philosophy at the present time would feel this about Plotinus; William Inge is, in this respect, a rare exception." Russell goes on to refer to Inge's book as "invaluable," and points out that "it is impossible to disagree with what Inge says on the influence of Plato and Plotinus."

And that was exactly the topic of the section about Plotinus in my book; namely, the historical influence of Plotinus. Inge's undisputed expertise in this area was yet another reason I chose him.

And finally, I simply wanted to pay homage to this rather extraordinary man, who for so long kept the light of Plotinus burning when few, if any, were interested. So I chose Inge. I made it very clear that all quotes were from Inge, and thenceforth, I gave careful citations: the page numbers given in Inge contain the exact references to the specific Plotinus material (usually the *Enneads*). All that is required of a scholar who makes such choices is that he carefully indicate what his sources are, and I did so.

(In the first printing, several ellipses were omitted; these were restored in subsequent printings. And the "four satoris" versus "often" refers to Plotinus; this was also corrected in subsequent printings. But Karl Jaspers's conclusion remains precisely the same, which is why I quoted it in the first place: "What, according to Porphyry, would seem to have been a rare, anomalous experience, is, in the statement of Plotinus, the natural reality.")

There were two minor errors in the Emerson and Plotinus sections. With Plotinus, I indicated that all quotes were from Inge unless otherwise indicated, and then I gave Plotinus's last words as "the divine-in-us departs to the divine-in-all," which was actually Jaspers's translation, not Inge's, which is "the divine in me departs to unite itself with the Divine in the universe." With Emerson, I deleted a reference to "nature" in one quote because Emerson uses "nature" in several different ways, which becomes obvious only later in the narrative. Both errors were subsequently corrected, and neither of them affected the conclusions, which were exactly as outlined in note 2 above.

4. Walsh, R. 1995. The spirit of evolution. A review of Ken Wilber's *Sex, Ecology, Spirituality*. *Noetics Sciences Review*, Summer, 1995.

5. See also M. Commons, J. Sinnott, F. Richards, and C. Armon (eds.) *Adult Development,* vol. 1, *Comparisons and Applications of Adolescent and Adult Developmental Models* (New York: Praeger, 1990.)

    M. Commons, C. Armon, L. Kohlberg, F. Richards, T. Grotzer, and J. Sinnott (eds.), *Adult Development,* vol. 2, *Models and Methods in the Study of Adult and Adolescent Thought* (New York: Praeger, 1990.)

    J. Sinnott and J. Cavanaugh (eds.), *Bridging Paradigms: Positive Development in Adulthood and Cognitive Aging* (New York: Praeger, 1991.) Also J. Sinnott (ed.), *Interdisciplinary Handbook of Adult Lifespan Learning.* (Greenwich, Conn.: Greenwood Press, 1994.)

    Transcendence and Mature Thought in Adulthood: The Further Reaches of Adult Development, edited by Melvin E. Miller and Susanne R. Cook-Greuter, is an excellent and accessible anthology. Charles Tart's *Transpersonal Psychologies* is still a fine reference work, as is Seymour Boorstein's *Transpersonal Psychotherapy.* And *Transformations of Consciousness* (Wilber et al., 1986) remains a useful text in transpersonal developmental psychology.

    Perhaps the most accessible transpersonal anthology is *Paths beyond Ego,* edited by Roger Walsh and Frances Vaughan. (My only caveat is that the authors have continued to reprint the rough-draft version of my essay "Eye to Eye," which, for semantic reasons, denied that a higher or transpersonal "science" was possible—simply because "science" and "empirical" were so closely wedded. I subsequently decided this was a losing semantic quibble, and, in the published version of "Eye to Eye," defined exactly what we could mean by a higher, nonempirical science, which has remained my stance. Inexplicably, the editors are still using the original rough draft [pp. 184–89]). Aside from that, this anthology remains the finest introduction to the field, and is highly recommended. [See *Integral Psychology* for an extensive list of references to the field.]

6. Incidentally, as I always point out, I agree with Jung on the nature of these archaic images *qua* archaic images: I believe they are collectively inherited, a type of phylogenetic heritage (a point Freud also accepted); they are important in certain types of pathology; they can be found abundantly in the world's mythologies; they often appear in dreams; and so on. But those archaic images have little if anything to do with post-postconventional development. One of Jung's pre/trans fallacies was that he confused collective with transpersonal, whereas there are collective prepersonal, collective personal, and collective transpersonal structures.

7. There are many ways to describe the archetypes as used by the perennial philosophy. If you are in formless meditation (cessation or nirvikalpa samadhi), the first phenomena that you see as you come out of cessation are exactly the archetypes. They are subtle forms, sounds, illuminations, affects, energetic currents, and so on. Likewise, each night, as you come out of deep dreamless sleep and begin dreaming, the first forms you see are archetypes. In anuttaratantra yoga, as you descend out of black near attainment, the first forms you see are archetypes.

    What all of those have in common is that the archetypes are the primordial forms lying on the boundary between the causal unmanifest and the first subtle-level manifestation. They are thus the first and earliest forms in involution or manifestation (or movement away from causal Source), and the last or highest forms in evolution, or return to Source (and thus the final barriers as well).

These archetypes, as I said, are subtle forms, illuminations, energetic currents, sounds, extremely subtle affects, and so on—the first forms of being, on which all lesser being will be modeled; the first forms of affect, of which all lesser feelings will be a dim reflection; the first forms of manifest consciousness, of which all lesser cognition will be a pale reflection; the first forms of luminosity, of which all lesser understanding will be a hazy hint; the first forms of sound, of which all lesser sounds will be a hollow echo. And thus the archetypes, the true archetypes, are the Forms of our own highest potential, the Forms of our own true nature, calling to us to remember who and what we really are. And in their last action, they are set aside and deconstructed—the ladder that, having served its purpose, is discarded—and there stands instead the radiant infinity that was always already shining through and beyond those Forms altogether.

8. Most problematic is the fact that the mechanisms of inheritance are not even vaguely the same for these two types of "archetypes." Archaic images are inherited from common experiences of yesterday. But the higher deep structures (or higher archetypes) were never a common past experience, and thus do not have the same origin. (The reason is that the "high archetypes" are lost in early involution; the "low archetypes" or archaic images are lost in early evolution. I have seen no Jungian make that distinction, and this hobbles the entire thrust of "archetypal" psychology, constantly plaguing even its more sophisticated variants with pre/trans fallacies.)

9. *Essence*, p. 20.

10. For a discussion of this, see Anthony, Ecker, and Wilber, *Spiritual Choices*.

11. The Diamond Approach of Hameed Ali (who writes under the pen name A. H. Almaas) is, in my opinion, a superb therapeutic/transformative discipline. Within this broad appreciation, which I will reiterate in a moment, I have a few criticisms.

What is most interesting in Ali's theoretical development is his eventual move from a classic Romantic/Wilber-I model to an Aurobindo/Wilber-II model. But the problem, we will see, is that he nonetheless continues to wobble, in an often self-contradictory fashion, between these two models.

In his early book *Essence* (1986), we find a very strong Romantic/type-I presentation. The infant is born fully in contact with Essence or Being: "Babies and very young children not only have Essence, they are in touch with their Essence; they are identified with their Essence; they are the Essence" (p. 83; in his later books, Ali always capitalizes *Essence*; I have done so in these quotes as well). But then, through the emergence and development of the ego and its object constancy, Essence is lost. "So we can conclude that people are born with Essence but end up without it later on" (p. 84).

The various aspects of Essence, which Ali identifies as Platonic Forms (including Will, Strength, Joy, Self, Personal, Compassion, Merging, Love, Intelligence,

Peace) *are slowly lost as the ego develops*, because the ego is the great enemy, so to speak, of Essence and Being. "Because Essence has various aspects, and different aspects dominate at different times [of early development], Essence is lost aspect by aspect" (p. 89).

By the time of late childhood, Essence is for the most part thoroughly buried and rendered only vaguely available. In its place are various "holes"—the empty psychic spaces created by the repression or loss of the various aspects of Essence. Thus, early development (according to "Ali-I") consists of (1) the profound and widespread loss of Essence, aspect by aspect, leaving (2) various holes, inadequacies, or absences in the being of the individual, holes that (3) the individual then compensates for with various further defense mechanisms. Individuals, with virtually no exceptions, thus arrive at adulthood as a bundle of holes and defense mechanisms dedicated to the avoidance of Being and Essence.

Therapy, for Ali-I, thus consists in the actual *retrieval* of the aspects of Essence that were present in infancy but later repressed, denied, or abandoned. "This understanding of the loss of Essence is of paramount importance when it comes to the question of techniques of retrieval of Essence" (p. 89). By bringing nonjudgmental awareness to one's present symptoms, distresses, inadequacies, or "holes," one ceases to defend against the lack, but instead simply experiences it. This direct awareness eventually discloses a sense of experiential emptiness, and if one stays with that emptiness and fully enters it, the corresponding aspect of repressed Essence will emerge and "fill" that hole. The retrieval of Essence thus allows postformal development to proceed apace.

That is obviously a very strong Romantic model. In many ways, it parallels Wilber-I; it even maintains that the infant is fully realized as Atman itself! "The Hindus call it the Atman. The child had it to start with, but its loss led to the development of the ego sense of identity . . ." (p. 169). We saw that not even the Tibetans (nor the Hindus, for that matter) believe that the child is fully realized or fully in touch with Atman, and that Atman is lost as one grows up. Rather, Atman is lost in prior involution, not in early evolution!

But at this point Ali is committed to a very strong Romantic model. "Our understanding of how Essence arises in children and then is put aside in favor of ego identifications is a new and rather surprising set of observations." Of course, it is neither new nor surprising, but the two-centuries-old Romantic developmental scheme.

Nonetheless, sensing a problem with this scheme, Ali begins to revise his stance toward the end of *Essence*, and we can see the start of the slow shift from a Romantic/Wilber-I to a Wilber-II type of model. He points out that there are two ways to look at the emergence of Essence, which he calls *uncovering* versus *development*, the former being the actual retrieval of something present in infancy but lost, the latter being the growth and development of something only minimally present in infancy. Ali says that he has been presenting an uncovering view, but he says that both views are probably true, and in fact, the most important part of the story is actually *development*. "Seeing the process as a development applies more accurately to an aspect of Essence that is in a sense more central" (p. 161). This central aspect of Essence "goes through a process of development, growth, and expansion. . . . This true personality [true Self, Atman, Personal Essence] grows, expands, and develops in a very specific sense" (p. 163). In other words, it primarily grows and develops rather than being lost and restricted.

Poised thus on the verge of a truly type-II model, Ali begins *The Pearl beyond Price—Integration of Personality into Being: An Object Relations Approach*, which is one of the genuinely superb contributions to East/West psychology and psychotherapy. The only major problem with the book, in my opinion, is that although it marks a shift from a type-I to a type-II model, Ali wobbles back and forth between them in some very self-contradictory ways.

On the one hand, Ali comes down decisively on the side of an overall developmental process (a strong Aurobindo/Wilber-II model), in which ego development is not a repression of Essence but a growth toward Essence, all part of a single overall developmental or evolutionary process. Thus, he says, Personal Essence "is the ultimate product of ego development. In other words, ego development and spiritual enlightenment are not two disjoint processes but parts of the same process" (p. 154). He makes that point time and again, and in very clear language. "It is more correct to consider ego development and spiritual transformation as forming one unified process of human evolution. . . . Inner evolution [moves] from birth, through ego development, to the realization of the Personal Essence. So it is one process of evolution from the beginning of ego development to the final stages of spiritual enlightenment" (p. 161). "This point is a radical departure from the understanding of both traditional spiritual teachings and modern psychology," he writes. "It unifies these two fields into one field, that of human nature and development" (p. 154).

That "unification," of course, was the central message of *The Atman Project*, and of Aurobindo, and before that, of Fichte and Schelling, among others. This shift to a full-fledged Aurobindo/Wilber-II orientation allows Ali to make some truly important contributions to the techniques of spiritual transformation (and postformal development) by working with the very early traumas to the self (particularly, as we will see, with fulcrum-2). If self development and spiritual development are part of the same spectrum of consciousness and not simply antagonists, then early damage to the former can cripple the emergence of the latter. That is the essence of the Diamond Approach (and of Wilber-II).

But throughout *The Pearl beyond Price* are scattered strong remnants of the "Ali-I" (Romantic/Wilber-I) approach. I want to give a few extended examples of these, both to show what is actually involved and to indicate why this issue is so important.

Start with the true Self or Atman or Essential Self. Is it fully realized in the infant? As we saw in chapter 6, the Romantic, neo-Jungian, Washburn, Wilber-I view is that the Essential Self is fully present in infancy, but the development of the ego denies, represses, or obscures this Ground. The ego becomes alienated from Ground, but later it can retrieve this Ground ("in a mature form" or "at a higher level") and so find a re-union with God, Ground, Being, or Essence. Thus, at the start of evolution, the self is one with Ground; in the middle of evolution, the self becomes alienated from Ground; at the further reaches of evolution, the self and Ground reunite, which is a retrieval of that which was fully present in the earlier stages of evolution but was subsequently lost. Such is the standard Romantic model in any of its forms.

The more typical perennial philosophical view is that the self becomes alienated from spirit during *involution*, not during anything that happens in *evolution*. Involution is the prior (but also timeless) movement whereby spirit goes out of itself to create soul, which goes out of itself to create mind, which goes out of itself to create body (prana), which goes out of itself to create matter. Each junior level is a restriction, manifestation, or stepped-down expression of its senior dimension, so that all waves are ultimately manifestations of the ocean of Spirit itself. But each lower wave "forgets" its senior dimension (amnesia), so that the end product is the world of matter, lying around all by itself and wondering how it got there.

Evolution then proceeds to *unfold* and *remember* that which was *enfolded* and *forgotten*: out of matter arises life; out of life evolves mind; out of mind emerges soul; out of soul emerges spirit, which is both the Ground and the Goal of the entire sequence. The infant, in this view, is indeed born "trailing clouds of glory," because (to use the Tibetan version), it has just involved from spirit to soul to mind to take on a material body. But in no sense is the infant *fully* in touch with Dharmakaya or Spirit (except insofar as Spirit is the Ground of all things, including infants). Rather, the infant stands basically at the end of the involutionary line (the primary alienation has already occurred)—and at the beginning of the evolutionary line, which is now at its *lowest* and starting point: the infant is primarily a bodyself, instinctual, vital, impulsive, narcissistic, egocentric; living for food, its God is all mouth.

Precisely because the infant is at the lowest level in its *frontal* development and evolution, it is merged with and embedded in the lowest dimension of Spirit: it is one with the material and physical world (as Piaget put it, "The self is here material, so to speak"). This is the undifferentiated state of protoplasmic awareness that dominates the early infantile state (the fusion subphase of fulcrum-1). There are no differentiated emotions nor emotional object constancy; there are no mental concepts, symbols, or rules; no logic, no narrative, no poetry, no mathematics, no art, no music, no dance, no capacity to take the role of other, and therefore no genuine love, no compassion, no mercy, no tolerance, and no benevolence.

In other words, the Romantics' idea of Ground. Precisely because the Romantics lacked any genuine understanding of involution, they took this early infantile physical fusion state, and, simply because it was "undifferentiated," imagined that it was the great Ground of Being itself.

The self, of course, will very soon differentiate and transcend this crude physical fusion, in order to identify with the emotional body, then the mind, then the soul, then spirit itself, transcending all, embracing all. This transcendence of the physical fusion state is a painful awakening to the separate being of the bodyself (fulcrum-2). This awakening is not the loss of spirit or essence, but the bitter-sweet first step to the full awakening of spirit itself.

The Romantics, by contrast, reached the understandable but naive conclusion that the pain and alienation of the emerging ego occurs because God has just been lost (whereas the ego is simply the first painful step back to God). Thus we arrive at the *traditional* Romantic view, which is that (1) the infant self starts out one with the Ground but in an unconscious fashion; (2) that union is then necessarily lost or repressed by the emerging ego; (3) the ego, having necessarily crushed the Ground, can then return to, retrieve, or otherwise recapture the Ground, but now in a fully conscious fashion, thus effecting a spiritual reunion. Where the infant is one with Ground in an unconscious fashion, the mature self is one with Ground in a conscious realization.

But even the Romantics began to realize that their own scheme was incoherent, because the second step is inherently impossible. All things are one with Ground; if you lose that oneness, you cease to exist. Rather, you can either be conscious or unconscious of that union. If you are already unconscious of the union, you can't get any lower. And since the Romantics had already conceded that the infantile self is unconscious of the union, that actually meant that the infantile self is *already* fallen. But this put the Romantics in an untenable situation. If the early, primitive state is already fallen, then enlightenment *cannot* be a recapture of yesterday, and the entire impulse of the traditional retro-Romantic disposition was exploded at its roots.

(Historically, Romanticism then either evolved to a Hegelian/Aurobindo/Wilber-II approach, or it faded as a coherent movement, although, of course, retro-Romanticism continues to arise as a common pre/trans fallacy, which we will return to later.)

The only way to attempt to salvage a specifically retro-Romantic agenda is to take the course outlined by Washburn. If enlightenment is going to be the recapture of something present in the infant but lost, then that infantile state must be one with Ground and that oneness must be "unrestrictedly present" in some sort of fully conscious fashion. As I tried to show in chapter 6, this is untenable; nonetheless, it is the only possible way to proceed with the retro-Romantic agenda.

With that theoretical background, we return to Ali. Is the Essential Self or Atman fully present in the infant? And here Ali runs into the Romantic Waterloo. In order to make the model work at all, the infant must be conscious of the Self, must be genuinely Self-realized, else there is nothing worth *recapturing*. And so that is exactly what Ali does. "When the Essential Self is present then, in a sense, the child is born; he is self-realized. He is his true Self. . . . The child is self-realized, in some sense, at this early age. He is completely the Essential Self" (p. 266, 278–79). The young child, then, is completely Self-realized, and this enlightened child will then "lose" its Self-realization as the ego develops.

Let us then ask, is this Self-realized child motivated by compassion, or mercy, or selfless service, or tolerance, or benevolence? In fact, as Ali acknowledges, the self at this point is actually extremely egocentric, narcissistic, impulsive, utterly ego-absorbed—in many ways, the antithesis of all things spiritual. Up close and in fine detail, the young child is simply not looking very consciously Self-realized at all.

As a result, Ali begins the retreat from this Romantic confusion by reverting to the traditional Romantic oxymoron: the child is fully Self-realized but is *not conscious* of the Self-realization. "The child is not aware that he is being the Essential Self. He is not conscious of his self-realization" (p. 278). Oxymoron, because "Self-realized" means conscious of the Self; you cannot be unconsciously consciously realized.

To complete the reversion to the old Romantic model, all that is necessary would be for Ali to further claim that the child will then actually *lose the unconscious Self-realization* (an ontological impossibility, but the only route left open for the traditional Romantic agenda). Sure enough: "The perception of vulnerability, limitation and dependency, without the ability to separate these from the experience of the Essential Self, leads to the abandonment of identity with the latter. The child loses his unconscious self-realization" (p. 279).

(Of course, if it's actually unconscious, the loss has already occurred— namely, in prior involution, which Romanticism always confuses with the first steps in evolution.)

But Ali's own analysis shows that the Essential Self is never *actually* experienced by the infant. "There is a true and timeless Self, an Essential Self, a Self that is not constructed in early life" (p. 265)—all very true. "The Essential Self feels like a concentrated presence, a precious and pure presence of consciousness, with the characteristic sense of self. The self of definiteness, singularity, uniqueness and preciousness are lucid and complete. . . . It is a source of pure love and knowledge" (pp. 272, 277).

Does the infant then have all of that as a direct and undistorted experience? No, says Ali, the infant or young child does not. "Clearly, since he is not aware of the Essential Self in an objective way, he cannot but connect this sense of Self to the representation"—that is, the intuition of the Self is applied to the limited and separate bodyself. Ali says that in the infant the *grand* qualities of the Self appear distorted as the *grandiose narcissism* of the infantile self. "The grand qualities belong to the Essential Self, but they become grandiose when attributed to the body and mind. The delusion is in attributing them to the body-mind" (p. 278).

The central question then becomes, is the infant *ever* undistortedly aware of the grand qualities of the true Self, or is it always in touch only with the delusion? Ali answers that the grand qualities of the Essential Self are *always* confused and deluded by the infant self, that it has no choice but to do so. Thus at all times, "these feelings of grandeur and omnipotence are false" (p. 278). It follows that the infant is never undistortedly in touch with the Essential Self per se, but only with confused and deluded intuitions of that Self.

Moreover, it will do no good to say that the infant during the narcissistic (practicing) subphase intuits the Self but misapplies that intuition to its present and limited stage of development, because *all stages of development do exactly that*, in their own specific way (that's the "Atman project": the everpresent intuition of Atman mistakenly identified with the present and limited self).

It follows from Ali's own presentation that, either way, the infant is not undistortedly in touch with any of the grand qualities of the Essential Self—and thus, those grand qualities are not there to be "lost" in the first place. (They are lost in involution, not evolution, and thus their remembering is an emergence in evolution, not an uncovering in evolution.)

What *is* lost during childhood, or what might be lost, are any of the various forms of Essence-at-that-stage. As we put it in our discussion of Washburn, what is lost or repressed by the infant and young child is basically spirit-as-prana, not spirit-as-spirit. Just so, Essence manifests in various forms at each and every stage of its own development and growth (an overall growth that Ali has already agreed is the central axis of development), but any of the aspects of Essence-at-that-stage can be repressed, denied, lost, or distorted. This loss, not of Essence proper but of Essence-at-that-stage, does indeed leave "holes," against which the self will construct further defenses.

These defenses were originally instituted, in my opinion, not because of the actual loss of Essence proper, but because of malformations in the development of the self on the way toward Essence proper. These early defenses are often constructed to ward off dangerous impulses, desires, libidinal drives, élan vital (spirit-as-prana), emotions and feelings, and these defenses more often than not remain firmly in place well into adult development. Thus, as Essence proper (of the psychic level) begins to emerge in consciousness, *these defenses will defend against that as well*. A rigid boundary is a rigid boundary. A wall that keeps out id is a wall that can keep out God as well.

Thus, with regard to spiritual growth, understanding and deconstructing these early defenses is an important endeavor, not because we are then retrieving a pure Essence that was present in infancy but repressed, but because we are dissolving the same blocks that prevent the higher emergence of Essence per se.

Thus, these "holes" are a dual absence, so to speak, sealing out both the lower and the higher. They harbor the submergent as well as the emergent (generated by the embedded self and the embedded-unconscious at any of its stages of development). They are not, however, compensations for a pure Essence present but lost in infancy. As Plotinus used to say, most of our problems involve not a "no" but a "not yet." The holes are in part a "no" said to earlier feelings, emotions, desires, and impulses; but they are also, and most significantly, a "not yet" of Essence proper waiting to be born, a higher state struggling to come down, not an infantile state struggling to come up.

Thus, if one experientially approaches a hole with accepting awareness, one might initially be drawn to the repressed-submergent aspect of that emptiness or lack or absence; one might actually recover a specific memory of the earlier event(s) contributing to the repression or loss. But as that actual loss is negotiated, the emptiness gives way to some form of Emptiness itself, Essence per se, Essence proper, Essence of the psychic or subtle dimension (which was never, as Ali inadvertently demonstrated, directly present in the infantile structure). The hole contains, not simply a repressed past actual, but the emptiness on the edge of a future potential about to emerge in development for the first time. Analyzing the defenses against past actuals helps with the emergence of future potentials because the same defenses screen both (the embedded-unconscious, as we saw, hides both lower and higher from its narrow gaze).

This experiential aspect of the hole is thus not the emptiness of something once present but repressed, but of something new struggling to emerge. The experiential emptiness is a profound yearning for the greater tomorrow, not a lament at the loss of a lesser yesterday.

Ali says that, with enlightened awareness, you can see that the young child is radiating Essence. In fact, with enlightened awareness you can see Essence radiating from dirt; that's not the point. The point is, what is the actual form of Essence that can manifest at any given stage? If the infant *necessarily* experiences Essence as "grandiose," "faulty," "narcissistic," "delusional," and "deformed," then it is most definitely not "Self-realized," and thus development does not consist in its actual loss.

Ali can get caught in these confusions because, in a typical Romantic move, he covertly uses a dual definition of Essence, one horizontal and one vertical, as it were. Discussing the infant of the practicing phase (subphase 1 of fulcrum-2), Ali notes that, according to Margaret Mahler's superb research, the infant is "full of himself." As Mahler puts it, "Narcissism is at its peak!" She goes on to say that "The world is the junior toddler's oyster. . . . The chief characteristic of this practicing period is the child's great narcissistic investment in his own functions, his own body, as well as in the objects and objectives of his expanding 'reality'. . . . He is exhilarated by his own abilities, continually delighted with the discoveries he makes in his expanding world, and quasi-enamored with the world and his own grandeur and omnipotence."

Ali quotes those passages and then excitedly adds that "We could not have described the experience of the Essential Self more eloquently. Mahler here shows her exquisite perception of the manifestations of the true Self" (p. 271).

Actually, Mahler here is describing the subphase from which the narcissistic personality disorders originate. This subphase is actually the height, not of the true Self, but of egocentricity, the precise opposite of the true or essential Self. If this phase of development, just as it is, lasted into adulthood, the result would be a person absolutely incapable of taking the role of other, of showing any concern or care for other human beings or sentient beings in general, a narcissistic monster for whom others are mere extensions of its grandiose self, a person utterly lacking in compassion, love, care and concern. This is the formal opposite of Self-realization, not an "exquisite" example of it.

This is the constant danger in the merely monological approaches, here exemplified by the Diamond Approach. The I-me-mine becomes the central axis of reality, and then *anything* that radiantly shines in that line is actually perceived as "enlightened" or manifesting "Essence." If instead we track developments in all four quadrants (and especially in the Lower-Left or intersubjective domain), we would immediately see how impoverished the infantile awareness is.

Ali points out, correctly I believe, that "The capacity for integration exists on all levels of functioning: physical, mental, emotional, and on the Being level. But since the Being level is the deepest, when it is present it enhances all dimensions of integrative capacity" (p. 171). I agree entirely. There is horizontal integration—any integration of any particular level—and there is the vertical integration of the very highest level—that of Being or Essence per se, which can enhance all types of integration.

But Ali simply tends to confuse these two types of "fullness," and whenever he spots any sort of fullness on any level, he tends to immediately identify it with the Being level, when it usually is nothing but an exuberant horizontal fullness and integration. It is not Essence proper, but simply Essence-at-that-stage.

Thus, referring to the narcissistic and egocentric infant, Ali says that it exists in a state of pure Love and essential Being. "Babies exist in this state of Being a great deal of the time. It is this state that we are perceiving when we see a baby as cute and adorable. This aspect is experienced as a gentle and soft presence that feels fluffy, pure and sweet" (p. 320). But if sweet, cute, adorable, and fluffy are characteristics of pure Love and essential Being, then kittens are totally Self-realized. Again we see the confusion of Essence per se with any merely horizontal "fullness" (or Essence-at-that-stage).

In all of Ali's reversions to the Romantic model, we see the classic and defining Romantic confusion. The Romantics (past and present), to their everlasting credit, were looking for ways to transcend ego and discover Spirit or pure Being or holistic Ground. And in order to discover Being, one must surrender an exclusive identification with the ego or the separate-self sense. That is also what it experientially feels like: you relax the mind and let go of the ego, and more spacious, liberated, open, and spiritual modes of being become available.

So far, so good, and the Romantics made some very profound observations about all that. But then the Romantics made their characteristic mistake: they simply divided the world into Being versus ego. Anything that was ego (or rational, or analytical, or conceptual, or personal, or linear) was viewed as "bad," and *anything else*—anything that lacked ego—was thought to be God, or Ground, or Glory. Ego was sin, Non-ego was Being or Ground or God or Essence.

But the "Non-ego" world actually includes the pre-egoic and the transegoic, the former of which is infantile, the latter of which is highly evolved, and the Romantics simply lumped them both together. The result was most unfortunate. Nobly aiming for the transegoic, the Romantics ended up glorifying anything that was non-egoic, nonconceptual, nonrational—and this often included intensely prerational and preconventional modes: they were regressing in search of their God and Goddess.

Likewise, it was simply assumed that in evolution (whether ontogenetic or phylogenetic), prior to the emergence of the ego there *must* have been Essence, Being, Ground, Eden. Some sort of angels must have walked the earth prior to the nasty emergence of the ego. But developmentally prior to the ego was not angels but apes; and prior to that, worms; and prior to that, ferns; and to that, dirt. The ego was not a Fall down from Ground, but a major step up and toward the actual emergence of Ground as a superconscious state and realization.

In other words, the primordial Fall occurred in involution, not in early evolution. And the ego is not the extreme point of alienation and loss, but halfway back to the Source. The ego is a major increase in Essence, not a major loss of Essence. The glass is half-full, not half-empty.

But all of this was lost on the Romantics, because of their simple notion that "there is either ego or Being" (which opened them to massive pre/trans fallacies). And I mention all of this because, every time Ali regresses from his type-II model to his earlier Romantic/type-I model, he does so precisely under this "Being or ego" notion.

Thus, Ali will divide the world into "ego states" and "Being states," and anything lacking the former must possess the latter. "Being is always there. That it is not a conscious experience indicates the presence of defenses against it" (p. 138). But rocks do not have a conscious experience of Being, and they are *not* defending against it. Again, Plotinus was right on the money: the rock's problem is not a "no" but a "not yet." The rock is not repressing anything. The rock does not have to *undo* its defenses, *uncover* its Essence, and *retrieve* a oneness with it. Rather, in order to consciously realize Essence, the rock will have to grow and evolve into a plant, which will evolve into a horse, which will evolve into an ape, which will evolve into a human, which will take up the Diamond Approach and realize Essence. Not uncovering, but development.

Just so, most of the infantile pre-egoic states are not defending against Essence proper, but simply have not yet grown into a capacity to consciously contain Essence per se. But Ali constantly makes the assumption that there is ego or Being, and thus the pre-egoic states get a massive elevation to Essence proper (as we saw with his glorification of the narcissistic monster of the practicing subphase). His confusion is summarized in his technical statement: "To believe that one's boundaries coincide with the external contours of the body indicates that one has not only cathected [identified with] the body, but also decathected Being" (p. 398).

But that is not so. The choices are not ego or Being. The choices are pre-ego, ego, or Being. And the move from pre-ego to ego (and a cathecting of the body) is a move toward Being, not a move away from it. But once that pre/trans fallacy is made, then every step in the evolution of the self or ego will have to be interpreted as a destruction of Being: the oak is a violation of the acorn. The retro-Romantic slide.

If Ali were presenting a simple Washburn/Romantic/Wilber-I model, as he did in *Essence*, then he could at least be consistent. But, as I pointed out at the beginning of this review, in *The Pearl beyond Price*, Ali moves clearly and decisively to an Aurobindo/Wilber-II model, and he says so in unmistakable terms. But these terms contradict the remnants of his Romantic/type-I model.

Thus, in most of his presentation in *The Pearl beyond Price*, ego development is correctly seen as an increase in Essence, not primarily a loss of Essence. "The ego becomes less defensive as it grows and develops, acquiring more flexibility, pliability, and hence openness to essential [Essence] perceptions" (p. 136). "Of course [Essence] manifests more often as the child grows in years" (p. 159). "So it is one process of evolution from the beginning of ego development to the final stages of spiritual enlightenment" (p. 161). And there is his basic, Aurobindo/ Wilber-II type model, with which I am in substantial agreement. (Of course, these can be refined into type-III and -IV models, but that is a secondary issue at this point.)

(As for the "trailing clouds of glory" that are increasingly forgotten as ego development or frontal development gets under way, that psychic/soul awareness will fade *of necessity*. Nothing the ego does, or can do, does or does not do, will stop or prevent that amnesia. In other words, that very specific loss is not due to the ego or to ego development. According to the Tibetans, that loss is foregone; as the Christian mystics put it, the infant is born in sin—it is not born in Essence and then has sin done to it by Mommy. Rather, this is a prior loss instituted in involution, by the separate self's contracting in the face of infinity. That contraction will play itself out right down to the material body in the prenatal period. Since there is *nothing* that can happen in ego development to stop this process, it is nothing that can be blamed on ego development itself. The frontal ego is part of the climb back to a recovery of Source. The ego becomes a "sin" only when it stays beyond its allotted time. That is, the ego is the *hero* from the pre-egoic to egoic leg of development. Only in the postformal and transegoic stages—starting in early adulthood—does the ego become "the problem." But to simply call the ego a "disease" is like calling an acorn a diseased oak. Its problem is not "no" but "not yet.")

I have a few other (but minor) criticisms, which I will briefly mention before turning to a positive assessment of the major strengths of the Diamond Approach.

- By focusing primarily on fulcrum-2 and the early separation-individuation phase of development, Ali tends to ignore or downplay the importance of the other intermediate fulcrums, in both individual and collective modes. By focusing on object relations, all the "major action" seems to be over by age three. But this overlooks the truly crucial fulcrums and developments still to come (especially fulcrums 3, 4, and 5).

- For a similar reason, the Diamond Approach seems to ignore the Piagetian revolution, which taught us that major psychological earthquakes keep occurring quite past age three. One of Piaget's classic experiments, for example, demonstrated that the young child cannot clearly take the role of other until around age six or seven. Genuine love, of course, involves caring and respecting the perspective of another. Ali might not have been so fast to equate the practicing narcissism of age two with Essential Love had he taken Piaget into account.

- Ali might be a little more generous in his recognition of the many transpersonal theorists who preceded him (Washburn, Engler, Alexander, for example). Many of Ali's major tenets were in print a decade or two before him.

That said, I would like to end with an appreciation of the Diamond Approach.

The modern West has made two profound discoveries vis-à-vis the unconscious mind and its relation to psychopathology and psychotherapy. The first runs in a line that starts with Plotinus and reappears in Fichte and Schelling, then Schelling's students Schopenhauer and Nietzsche, and was summarized in Eduard von Hartmann's *Philosophy of the Unconscious* (1869; it went into eight editions in ten years, an unprecedented popularity for an academic work), was brilliantly given clinical and theoretical grounding by Pierre Janet, and was eventually codified by Sigmund Freud. The insight, in its various forms, is simply that the mind can repress the body, that concepts can suppress instincts, that will can smash feelings, and the result of this interior civil war is emotional sickness, neurosis, inner division, and alienation. And the cure, by any name, is *uncovering*: relaxing the repression, recontacting the repressed feeling or emotion or drive, befriending that impulse, and reintegrating it with the self.

This first major discovery, in other words, was of the specific dynamics of fulcrum-3.

The second major discovery is more recent. It is much harder to discern and thus took longer to spot. It was the discovery of the even deeper dynamics of fulcrum-2, the actual process whereby the "protoplasmic" and "material fusion state" differentiates and individuates to produce a cohesive, unified, functional self. In other words, this is the beginning of the development from pre-ego to ego. The dynamic here is not that the ego represses the body, but that there is not yet an ego strong enough to repress much of anything.

The pathology at this early fulcrum therefore involves, not repression, not the Oedipus/Electra complex, not an interior civil war, but the very growth of a cohesive self to begin with. Problems with this fulcrum-2 therefore involve narcissistic personality disorders, borderline pathology, borderline psychosis, and other serious disturbances. Therapy aimed at this deep level does not attempt to *uncover* anything (there is little to uncover because the self is not strong enough to repress in the first place), but instead involves what is called *structure building*, or ways to help the self differentiate from the material fusion state.

This second major discovery runs in a line from Schelling to Jung (and his notion of individuation), but awaited the more precise theory and research of Edith Jacobson, D. W. Winnicott, Heinz Kohut, Otto Kernberg, and Margaret Mahler (to name a prominent few). It has revolutionized our understanding of the early development of the Upper-Left quadrant, and in its own way is every bit as groundbreaking as the first line leading to Freud and an understanding of fulcrum-3.

In Wilber-III, I included extensive references to this pioneering work, and indicated how absolutely crucial I felt it to be, not just for understanding ego development, but for the continuation of that development into postformal and spiritual domains. And yet, alas, apart from such important exceptions as Jack Engler, very little work has been done to integrate these pioneering insights with methods of spiritual development.

That is where the Diamond Approach excels, in my opinion. Hameed Ali (particularly in his "Ali-II" model in *The Pearl beyond Price*) has succeeded in powerfully utilizing the findings about fulcrum-2 to help individuals move into postformal and post-postconventional development. In my opinion, his understanding is precise, extensive, and accurate; and his use of this understanding to open access to the transpersonal domains is superb and in many ways unprecedented.

Ali has several stages of growth beyond the discovery of Personal Essence (but they all remain appropriately grounded in Personal Essence). These higher stages include Personal Essence proper, the discovery of which leads to realms beyond the personal, roughly in this general order: the impersonal Witness, cosmic consciousness, then pure Being manifested as dual unity with Personal Essence via Love; then Absence (or cessation), a Void within which Loving Presence spontaneously arises and takes the form of Personal Essence; the Nameless, nondual with Personal Essence in all realms; and the Absolute (which still spontaneously manifests as Personal Essence for appropriate, spontaneous functioning).

There is no indication in the writings of the Diamond Approach that subject permanence is achieved (which is a hallmark of stable causal-level adaptation); nor that permanent lucid dreaming constancy is reached (a hallmark of stable subtle-level adaptation). The Diamond Approach, in other words, seems to remain grounded in psychic-level adaptation, even as it powerfully intuits higher domains. This, nonetheless, is an extraordinary achievement, and certainly ranks it as one of the premiere transformative technologies now available on any sort of widespread scale.

The Pearl beyond Price is one of the truly great and pioneering books of the East/West dialogue. The criticisms that I have raised are all in the context of much admiration. It remains to be seen, of course, just what fate our culture will deal a postformal and post-postconventional approach. Historically—and in almost any country—postformal consciousness has been crucified. Once a group, grounded in such, starts to become "popular" and "noticed," a whole host of background cultural forces swing into play, even in pluralistic, tolerant societies that share the values of the Western enlightenment. It is thus with the very best wishes and encouragement, and slight trepidation, that I watch the future unfolding of the Diamond Approach.

12. This entire section is one summary of the Wilber-IV model, which is the model presented in *Sex, Ecology, Spirituality*; *A Brief History of Everything*; and this book. The Wilber-III aspects in this model are virtually unchanged, but they are set in a context ("all-quadrant, all-level") that renders their constitutive elements more visible. Neither consciousness, personality, individual agency, nor psychopathology can be located simply or solely in the individual organism.

The subjective domain is always already embedded in intersubjective, objective, and interobjective realities, all of which are partly constitutive of subjective agency and its pathologies: thus the shift from Wilber-III to Wilber-IV.

13. [A more complete version of this endnote is the article "An Integral Theory of Consciousness," contained in this volume.]

The Left-Hand dimensions are the realm of interior consciousness, it is true; but the Right-Hand domains are the exterior forms of consciousness, without which the interior forms do not, and cannot, exist. As for the "location" of consciousness, and for those who read chapters 4 and 5, it amounts to the same thing to say—and I do say—that manifest consciousness is "located" in exactly the same place art is.

In other words, the Upper-Left quadrant is simply the functional locus of a distributed phenomenon. Consciousness is not located inside the brain, nor outside the brain either: those are physical boundaries with simple location, and yet a good part of consciousness exists not merely in physical space but in emotional spaces, mental spaces, and spiritual spaces, none of which have simple location, and yet all of which are as real as (or more real than) simple physical space.

That is why we say that manifest consciousness is distributed across all quadrants with all their levels and lines. The Right-Hand domains all have simple location (location in physical spacetime) and can be "pointed to" with your finger; but the Left-Hand domains are located in spaces of intention, not spaces of extension, and so you cannot put your physical finger on them. And yet consciousness is anchored in those intentional spaces every bit as much as in the extensional spaces, whether those extensional spaces are of the external world or of the nervous system or anything in between. The Right Hand reductionists (subtle reductionists) attempt to reduce intentional spaces to extensional spaces and then "locate" consciousness in a *hierarchical network of physically extended emergents* (atoms to molecules to cells to nervous system to brain), and that, I believe, will never work. It gives us, more or less, only half the story (the Right-Hand half).

David Chalmers (1995) recently caused a sensation by having his essay "The Puzzle of Conscious Experience" published by *Scientific American*, bastion of physicalist science. Chalmers's conclusion was that subjective consciousness continues to defy all objectivist explanations. "Toward this end, I propose that conscious experience be considered a fundamental feature, irreducible to anything more basic. The idea may seem strange at first, but consistency seems to demand it" (p. 83).

Chalmers makes a series of good points. The first is the irreducibility of consciousness, which has to be "added" to the physical world in order to give a complete account of the universe. "Thus, a complete theory will have two components: physical laws, telling us about the behavior of physical systems from the infinitesimal to the cosmological, and what we might call psychophysical laws, telling us how some of those systems are associated with conscious experience. These two components will constitute a true theory of everything" (p. 83).

This attempt to reintroduce both Left- and Right-Hand domains to the Kosmos has been considered quite bold, a testament to the power of reductionism against which so obvious a statement seems radical. Chalmers moves toward a formulation: "Perhaps information has two basic aspects: a physical one and an experiential one. . . . Wherever we find conscious experience, it exists as one aspect of an information state, the other aspect of which is embedded in a physical process in the brain" (p. 85). That is, each state has an interior/intentional and exterior/physical aspect. My view, of course, is that all holons have not just those two, but rather four, fundamental and irreducible aspects, so that every "information state" actually and simultaneously has an intentional, behavioral, cultural, and social aspect. An "all-quadrant, all-level" view is much closer to a theory of everything, if such even makes any sense.

Chalmers goes on to point out that all of the physicalist and reductionist approaches to consciousness (including Daniel Dennett's and Francis Crick's) only solve what Chalmers calls "the easy problems" (such as objective integration in brain processes), leaving the central mystery of consciousness untouched. He is quite right, I believe. The funny thing is, all of the physicalist scientists who are sitting there and reading Chalmers's essay are already fully in touch with the mystery: they are already directly in touch with their lived experience, immediate awareness, and basic consciousness. But instead of directly investigating that stream (with, say, vipassana), they sit there, reading Chalmers's essay, and attempt to understand their own consciousness by objectifying it in terms of digital bits in neuronal networks, or connectionist pathways hierarchically summating in the joy of seeing a sunrise—and when none of those really seem to explain anything, they scratch their heads and wonder why the mystery of consciousness just refuses to be solved.

Chalmers says that "the hard problem" is "the question of how physical processes in the brain give rise to subjective experience"—that is, how physical and mental interact. This is still the Cartesian question, and it is no closer to being solved today than it was in Descartes's time, and for a simple reason: it is a dilemma that is solved only in the postformal realms. (See chapter 3 for an extended discussion of this theme [see also *Integral Psychology*, chap. 14, for an extended discussion of the mind-body problem].)

For example, in the simple hierarchy physical matter, sensation, perception, impulse, image, symbol . . . , there is an *explanatory gap* between matter and sensation that has not yet been satisfactorily bridged—not by neuroscience, nor cognitive science, nor neuropsychology, nor phenomenology, nor systems theory. As David Joravsky put it (in his review of Richard Gregory's *Mind in Science: A History of Explanations in Psychology and Physics*), "Seeing is broken down into component processes: *light*, which is physical; excitation in the neural network of eye and brain, which is also physical; *sensation*, which is subjective and resists analysis in strictly physical terms; and *perception*, which involves cognitive inference from sensation and is thus even less susceptible to strictly physical analysis." Gregory himself poses the question, "How is sensation related to neural activity?" and then summarizes the precise state-of-the-art knowledge in this area: "Unfortunately, we do not know." The reason, he says, is that there is "an irreducible gap between physics and sensation which physiology cannot bridge"—what he calls "an impassable gulf between our two realms." Between, that is, the Left and Right halves of the Kosmos.

But, of course, it is not actually an impassable gulf: you see the physical world right now, so the gulf is bridged. The question is, how? And the answer, as I suggested in chapter 3, only discloses itself to postformal awareness. The "impassable gulf" is simply another name for the subject/object dualism, which is the hallmark not of Descartes's error but of all manifestation, which Descartes simply happened to spot with unusual clarity. It is still with us, this gap, and it remains the mystery hidden in the heart of samsara, a mystery that absolutely refuses to yield its secrets to anything less than post-postconventional development.

I have repeatedly had people explain to me that the Cartesian dualism can be solved by simply understanding that . . . and they then tell me their solutions, which range from Gaia-centric theories to neutral monism to first-third person interactionism to systems theory. I always respond, "So this means that you have overcome the subject-object dualism in your own case. This means that you directly realize that you are one with the entire Kosmos, and this nondual awareness persists through waking, dream, and deep sleep states. Is that right?" "Well, no, not really."

The solution to the subject-dualism is not found in thought, because thought itself is a product of this dualism, which itself is generated in the very roots of the causal realm and cannot be undone without consciously penetrating that realm. The causal knot or primordial self-contraction—the ahamkara—can only be uprooted when it is brought into consciousness and melted in the fires of pure awareness, which almost always requires profound contemplative/meditative training. The subject-object duality is the very *form* of the manifest world of maya—the very beginning of the four quadrants (subject and object divide into singular and plural forms)—and thus one can get "behind" or "under" this dualism only by immersion in the *formless* realm (cessation, nirvikalpa, ayn, nirvana), which acts to dissolve the self-contraction and release it into pure nondual awareness—at which point, the traditions (from Zen to Eckhart) agree, you indeed realize that you are one with the entire Kosmos, a nondual awareness that persists through waking, dream, and deep sleep states: you have finally undone the Cartesian dualism.

As we will see below, the methodology of an integral theory of consciousness would thus have to include two broad wings: one is the simultaneous tracking of the various levels and lines in each of the quadrants, and then noting their correlations, each to all the others, and in no way trying to reduce any to the others.

The other is the *interior transformation of the researchers themselves*. This is the real reason, I suspect, that the Left-Hand dimensions of immediate consciousness have been so intensely ignored and aggressively devalued. Any Right-Hand path of knowledge can be engaged without a demand for interior transformation; one merely learns a new translation. (More specifically, most researchers have already, in the process of growing up, transformed to formop or vision-logic, and no higher transformations are required for empiric-analytic or systems theory investigations.)

But the Left-Hand paths demand, at some point, transformations of consciousness in the researchers themselves. You can master 100 percent of quantum physics without transforming consciousness, but you cannot in any fashion master Zen without doing so. You do not have to transform to understand Dennett's *Consciousness Explained*; you merely translate. But you must transform to actually understand Plotinus's *Enneads*. You are already adequate to Dennett, because you both have already transformed to rationality, and thus the *referents* of Dennett's sentences can be easily seen by you (whether or not you agree, you can at least see what he is referring to, because his referents exist in the rational worldspace, plain as day).

But if you have not transformed to (or at least strongly glimpsed) the causal and nondual realms, you will not be able to see the referents of Plotinus's sentences. They will make no sense to you. You will think Plotinus is "seeing things"—and he is, and so could you and I, if we both transform to those worldspaces, whereupon the referents of Plotinus's sentences, referents that exist in the causal and nondual worldspaces, become plain as day. And that transformation, it seems to me, is an absolutely unavoidable part of the paradigm (the injunction) of an integral approach to consciousness.

So those two wings—the "simultracking" of all quadrants and the transformation of researchers themselves—are both necessary for an integral approach to consciousness.

Thus, I do not mean for an integral theory of consciousness to be an eclecticism of the dozen or so major approaches I summarized in the text, but rather a tightly integrated approach that follows intrinsically from the holonic nature of the Kosmos.

The methodology of an integral approach to consciousness is obviously complex, but it follows some of the simple guidelines we have already outlined: three strands, four validity claims, ten levels of each. To briefly review:

The three strands operative in all valid knowledge are injunction, apprehension, confirmation (or exemplar, evidence, confirmation/rejection; or instrumental, data, fallibilism). These three strands operate in the generation of all valid knowledge—on any level, in any quadrant, or so I maintain.

But each quadrant has a different architecture and thus a *different type of validity claim* through which the three strands operate: propositional truth (Upper Right), subjective truthfulness (Upper Left), cultural meaning (Lower Left), and functional fit (Lower Right).

Further, there are nine or ten major levels of development in each of those quadrants, and thus the knowledge quest takes on different forms as we move through those various levels. The three strands and four claims are still fully operating in each case, but the specific contours vary.

Take, as an example, a specific researcher, whose individual consciousness is the Upper-Left quadrant, itself a spectrum of nine or ten levels, which we have sometimes summarized as matter, body, mind, soul, and spirit. As we saw in chapter 3, we can further simplify that as body, mind, and spirit, which is the traditional "three eyes" of knowing: the eye of flesh, the eye of mind, and the eye of contemplation. (This is just a simplification, and all of the points I am about to make apply across all ten levels, not just the simplified three.)

Now the eye of mind itself can, as it were, look up, look down, or look sideways. That is, the mind (reason and vision-logic) can accept data from the senses, data from the mind itself, or data from contemplation. In the first we get empiric-analytic knowledge (i.e., symbolic knowledge of presymbolic forms, whose referents exist in the sensorimotor worldspace); in the second we get hermeneutic, phenomenological, and mathematical knowledge (symbolic knowledge of symbolic forms, whose referents exist in the mental and formal worldspaces); and in the third we get mandalic sciences (symbolic maps of trans-symbolic occasions, whose referents exist in the postformal worldspaces).

All of those different modes of knowing (at all ten levels) nonetheless follow the three strands of valid knowledge accumulation, and thus each of them is anchored in a genuine and justifiable epistemology. (For an extended discussion of this theme, see chapter 3.)

The three strands, four claims, and ten levels thus present us with a fairly comprehensive methodology of knowledge acquisition, and this relates directly to an integral theory of consciousness. I'll run through some of the major approaches mentioned in the text and very briefly indicate what is involved.

The *emergent/connectionist* cognitive science models (such as Alwyn Scott's *Stairway to the Mind*) apply the three strands of knowledge accumulation to the Upper-Right quadrant, the objective aspects of individual holons. Statements about these are guided by the validity claim of propositional truth tied to empirically observable events, which means that in this approach the three strands will acknowledge only those holons that register in the sensorimotor worldspace (i.e., holons with simple location, empirically observable by the senses or their extensions). Nonetheless, all holons are holarchic, or composed of hierarchical holons within holons indefinitely, and so this emergent/connectionist approach will apply the three strands to objective, exterior, hierarchical systems as they appear in the individual, objective organism (the Upper-Right quadrant).

All of this is fine, right up to the point where these approaches overstep their epistemic warrant and try to account for the other quadrants solely in terms of their own. In the case of the emergent/connectionist theories, this means that they will present a valid Upper-Right hierarchy (atoms to molecules to cells to neural pathways to reptilian stem to limbic system to neocortex), but then consciousness is somehow supposed to miraculously jump out at the top level (the Left-Hand dimensions are treated as a monolithic and monological single entity, and then this "consciousness" is simply added on top of the Right-Hand hierarchy, instead of seeing that there are levels of consciousness which exist as the interior or Left-Hand dimension of every step in the Right-Hand hierarchy).

Thus, Scott presents a standard Upper-Right hierarchy, which he gives as atoms, molecules, biochemical structures, nerve impulses, neurons, assemblies of neurons, brain. Then, and only then, out pops "consciousness and culture," his two highest levels. But it appears that consciousness and culture are not levels in the Upper-Right quadrant, but significantly different quadrants each of which has a correlative hierarchy of its own developmental unfolding (and each of which is intimately interwoven with the Upper Right, but can in no way be reduced to or explained by the Upper Right). So in an integral theory of consciousness, we would include the Upper-Right hierarchy and those aspects of the emergent/connectionist models that legitimately reflect that territory; but where those theories overstep their epistemic warrant (and are thus reduced to reductionism), we might move on.

The various schools of *introspectionism* take as their basic referent the interior intentionality of consciousness, the immediate lived experience and lifeworld of the individual (the Upper-Left quadrant). This means that, in these approaches, the three strands of valid knowledge are applied to the data of immediate consciousness, under the auspices of the validity claim of truthfulness (because interior reporting requires sincere reports: there is no other way to get at the interiors). Introspectionism is intimately related to interpretation (hermeneutics), because most of the contents of consciousness are referential and intentional, and thus their meaning requires interpretation: What is the meaning of this sentence? of last night's dream? of *War and Peace*?

As we have seen (introduction, chapters 3, 4, 5), all valid interpretation follows the three strands (injunction, apprehension, confirmation). In this case, the three strands are being applied to symbolic/referential occasions and not merely to sensorimotor occasions (which would yield only empiric-analytic knowledge). As everybody knows, this interpretive and dialogical knowledge is trickier, more delicate, and more subtle than the head-banging obviousness of the monological gaze, but that doesn't mean it is less important (in fact, it means it is more significant).

The introspective/interpretative approaches (from depth psychology to phenomenology to contemplation) thus give us the *interior contours of individual consciousness*: the three strands legitimately applied to the interior of individual holons under the auspices of truthfulness. This exploration and elucidation of the Upper-Left quadrant is an important facet of an integral approach to consciousness.

Developmental psychology goes one step further and inspects the stages of the unfolding of this individual consciousness. Since it usually aspires to a more scientific status, developmental psychology often combines an examination of the interior or Left-Hand reports of experience (the *semantics* of consciousness, guided by interpretative truthfulness and intersubjective understanding) with a Right-Hand or objective analysis of the structures of consciousness (the *syntax* of consciousness, guided by propositional truth and functional fit). This *developmental structuralism* traces most of its lineage to the Piaget revolution; it seems an indispensable tool in the elucidation of consciousness and an important aspect of any integral approach. (It is rare, however, that these approaches clearly combine both the semantics and syntax of the stages of consciousness development, which is a pragmatic integration I am especially attempting to include.)

Eastern and nonordinary states models point out that there are more things in the Upper-Left quadrant than are dreamt of in our philosophy, not to mention our conventional psychologies. The three strands of valid knowledge are here applied to states that are largely nonverbal, postformal, and post-postconventional. In Zen, for example, we have a primary injunction or paradigm (zazen, sitting meditation), which yields experiential data (kensho, satori), which are then thrown against the community of those who have completed the first two strands and tested for fallibility. Bad data are soundly rejected, and all of this is open to ongoing review and revision in light of subsequent experience and further communally generated data. These approaches are quite right: no theory of consciousness can hope to be complete that ignores the data from the higher or deeper dimensions of consciousness itself, and this exploration of the further reaches of the Upper-Left quadrant is a central aspect of an integral theory of consciousness.

Advocates of *subtle energies* (prana, bioenergy) bring an important piece of the puzzle to this investigation, but they often seem to believe that these subtle energies are the central or even sole aspect of consciousness, whereas they are merely one of the dimensions in the overall spectrum itself (prana is sometimes subdivided into astral and etheric energies, but all of them are lower to intermediate levels).

For the Great Chain theorists, East and West, prana is the link between the material body and the mental domain (see chapter 1), and in a sense I believe that is true enough. But the whole point of a four-quadrant analysis is that what the traditions tended to represent as disembodied, transcendental, and nonmaterial modes actually have correlates in the material domain (every Left-Hand occasion has a Right-Hand correlate), and thus it is much more accurate to speak of the physical bodymind, the emotional bodymind, the mental bodymind, and so on. This simultaneously allows transcendental occasions and firmly grounds them. And in this conception, prana is simply the emotional bodymind in general, with correlates in all four quadrants (subjective: proto-emotions; objective: limbic system; intersubjective: magical; interobjective: tribal).

The investigation of these subtler pranic energies is hampered, of course, by the fact that, as a "step up" from the physical dimension, they cannot be empirically perceived in the sensorimotor worldspace (they exist in the emotional worldspace, and can be easily seen there—for example, any time you get angry, happy, or hungry; and these can be intersubjectively shared and confirmed, following the three strands). Moreover, the objective aspects of these energies are likewise open to investigation, first, in the standard empirical studies of the brain and limbic system using everything from PET to EEG (the three strands applied to the empirical correlates); and second, in the somewhat more delicate attempt to detect their field influences on the denser material domain, also following the three demands of instrumental, data, confirmation (e.g., by research-ers from Tiller to Motoyama; see Murphy [1992] for an outstanding overview). What is not helpful, however, is to claim that these energies alone hold the key to consciousness.

Likewise with the *psi approaches*, which are clearly some of the more contro-versial aspects of consciousness studies (telepathy, precognition, psychokinesis, clairvoyance). I believe that the existence of some types of psychic phenomena is now beyond serious dispute. I have discussed this in the book *Eye to Eye* (along with the application of the three strands to psi events), and I won't repeat my observations here. I would simply like to emphasize that, once it is realized that the sensorimotor worldspace is merely one of at least ten worldspaces (the ten or so basic waves of existence from matter to body to mind to soul to spirit), we are released from the impossibility of trying to account for all phenomena on the basis of empirical occasions alone. At the same time, precisely because the sensorimotor worldspace is the anchor of the worldview of scientific materi-alism, as soon as some sort of proof of non-sensorimotor occasions (such as psi) is found, it can be excitedly blown all out of proportion. Psi events indeed cannot be unequivocally located in the sensorimotor worldspace, but then nei-ther can logic, mathematics, poetry, history, meaning, value, or morals, and so what? There is still substantial evidence that some psi phenomena exist, and if there can be found no sensorimotor explanation, the conclusion is *not* that psi do not exist, but that we must look to other worldspaces for the phenomenol-ogy of their operation. I believe that any integral theory of consciousness would take seriously these phenomena and the substantial evidence of their existence.

Of the dozen or so major approaches to consciousness studies that I listed in the text, the *quantum approaches* are the only ones that I believe lack substan-tial evidence at this time, and when I say that they can be included in an integral theory of consciousness, I am simply holding open the possibility that they may eventually prove worthwhile. In *Eye to Eye* I review the various interpretations of quantum mechanics and its possible role in consciousness studies, and I will not repeat that discussion, except to say that to date the theoretical conclusions (such as that intentionality collapses the wave function) are based on extremely speculative notions that most physicists themselves find dubious.

The central problem with these approaches, as I see it, is that they are trying to solve the subject/object dualism on a level at which it cannot be solved; as I suggested above, that problem is (dis)solved only in *postformal* development, and no amount of *formal* propositions will come near the solution. Nonethe-less, this is still a fruitful line of research, if for no other reason than what it demonstrates in its failures; and more positively, it might help to elucidate some of the interactions between biological intentionality and matter.

All of those approaches center on the individual. But the *cultural approaches* to consciousness point out that individual consciousness does not, and cannot, arise on its own. All subjective events are always already intersubjective events. There is no private language; there is no autonomous consciousness (short of spirit-as-spirit, which isn't individual anyway). The very words we are both now sharing were not invented by you or me, were not created by you or me, do not come solely from my consciousness or from yours. Rather, you and I simply find ourselves in a vast intersubjective worldspace in which we live and move and have our being. This cultural worldspace (the Lower-Left quadrant) has a hand in the very structure, shape, feel, and tone of your consciousness and of mine, and no theory of consciousness seems complete that ignores this crucial dimension.

In these cultural approaches, the three strands are applied to the intersubjective circle itself, the deep semantics of the worlds of meaning in which you and I collectively exist. These cultural worldspaces evolve and develop (archaic to magic to mythic to mental, etc.), and the three strands applied to those worldspaces, under the auspices of mutual understanding and appropriateness, reveal those *cultural contours of consciousness*, which is exactly the course these important approaches take. This, too, seems to be a crucial component of an integral theory of consciousness.

Likewise for the *social sciences*: the materialities of communication, the techno-economic base, and the social system in the objective sense also reach deep into the contours of consciousness to mold the final product. The three strands, under the auspices of propositional truth and functional fit, yield these social determinants at each of their levels. A narrow Marxist approach, of course, has long been discredited (precisely because it oversteps its warrant, reducing all quadrants to the Lower Right); but the moment of truth in historical materialism is that the modes of production have a profound and constitutive influence on the actual forms and contents of individual consciousness, and thus an understanding of these social determinants seems crucial for an integral theory of consciousness.

I hope that this outline, abbreviated as it is, is nonetheless enough to indicate the broad contours of a methodology of an integral theory of consciousness, and that it sufficiently indicates the inadequacy of any approaches less comprehensive. The *integral* aspect enters in simultaneously tracking each level and quadrant in its own terms and then noting the correlations between them. This is a methodology of phenomenologically and contemporaneously tracking the various levels and lines in each of the quadrants and then correlating their overall relations, each to all the others, and in no way trying to reduce any to the others.

Thus, as I mentioned above, an integral approach to consciousness has two broad wings: one is the "simultracking" of events in "all-quadrant, all-level" space; the other is the interior transformation of the researchers themselves. (This is the integral model that I have also been referring to as Wilber-IV.) And each of the dozen or so approaches that I listed in the text finds an important and indispensable place, not as an eclecticism, but as an intrinsic aspect of the holonic Kosmos. For an extended discussion of these themes, see Wilber, "An Integral Theory of Consciousness," in *Journal of Conscious Studies* 4, no. 1 (1997), pp. 71–92 [contained in this volume].

14. 1989, p. 173.

15. 1994, p. ix, his italics.
16. McDermott chastises me for several polemical endnotes in SES. For various reasons I did indeed decide that a certain polemical stance was required in a few cases. After consultation with several editors, publishers, and colleagues, I decided to include several endnotes with a polemical/humorous tone, sharply critical of perhaps nine or ten theorists (out of several hundred discussed). These theorists themselves often use polemical, and in some cases even vitriolic, prose. They aggressively condemn entire cultures and civilizations, or engage in unrelenting male bashing, or declare, without irony, that they alone boast the new paradigm. Those who disagree with them are often viciously dismissed. I simply chose in these endnotes to address their arguments by using a bit of their own polemical medicine.

    Specifically, from each of the dozen or so movements that are, in my opinion, particularly regressive or flatland—or that are merely Descended or merely Ascended—I chose one or two typical representatives. These fractious movements include some of the merely Descended aspects of ecofeminism, deep ecology, ecoholism, and eco-primitivism; some of the regressive aspects of Jungian, archetypal, and mythopoetic movements; astrology and astro-logic as mythic-membership; monological physics equals mysticism; monological systems theory; positivism; and merely Ascended gnosticism (East and West).

    I chose a representative example from each and responded polemically. McDermott laments this; I consider it an integral part of the book, without which it would have abdicated its duty. At the same time, I am more than willing to meet any of these theorists in dialogue, as witness the three-volume *ReVision Journal* discussion. *Sex, Ecology, Spirituality* has become a focal point for just this discussion, and the good in all this, as I see it, is that indeed the conversation has been jolted into high gear. This has also forced certain theorists to actually show their cards. McDermott opines that the tone of these endnotes has hindered the conversation, whereas exactly the opposite is the case. People have been galvanized, both for and against, pro and con, and this is a profound good, it seems to me.

Chapter 12: *Waves, Streams, States, and Self*

1. "An Integral Theory of Consciousness" was first outlined in an endnote in *The Eye of Spirit*; it was expanded and published, under that title, in the *Journal of Consciousness Studies* 4, 1 (1997). That essay was revised, with an addition by Roger Walsh, for its inclusion in volume 7 of my *Collected Works* (2000), which is the version I am referring to in this chapter.
2. See *Integral Psychology* for several dozen of versions of this spectrum of consciousness presented by ancient and modern sources.
3. For a discussion of the Great Nest of Being, see *The Marriage of Sense and Soul, Integral Psychology, One Taste*, and *A Theory of Everything*. See also Huston Smith's superb *Forgotten Truth* (1976), Roger Walsh's *Essential Spirituality* (1999), and Michael Murphy's *The Future of the Body* (1992). Arthur Love-

joy's *The Great Chain of Being* (1964) remains the authoritative historical over-view, although, again, "Great Chain" is a misnomer.

4. Research (e.g., summarized by the references in this paragraph) suggests that some of these psychological structures are universal, some are culture-specific, and some are individual. All three are important; but clearly, I do not believe that all structures are universal. However, since I am presenting a cross-paradigmatic model, the structures (basic and transitional) that I usually focus on are those for which we have substantial evidence that they are generally universal and cross-cultural wherever they appear (i.e., they do not necessarily appear in all cultures, but when they do appear, they show a similar pattern). These basic levels or basic structures are: matter, sensation, perception, impulse, image, symbol, concept, rule, formal, vision-logic, psychic, subtle, causal, and nondual, which I often group into nine or ten functional units as: sensorimotor, emotional-sexual, rep-mind, rule/role mind, formal-reflexive, vision-logic, psychic, subtle, causal, nondual. See *Integral Psychology* (Wilber, 2000b).

5. These lines or modules are *relatively* independent because they seem to be inter-twined in certain "necessary but not sufficient" patterns. For example, empirical research has already demonstrated that physiological development is necessary but not sufficient for cognitive development, which is necessary but not suffi-cient for interpersonal development, which is necessary but not sufficient for moral development, which is necessary but not sufficient for ideas of the good (Loevinger, 1976; Commons et al., 1989, 1990). Further, because the self inher-ently attempts to *integrate* these various lines (see below), their independence is dampened by the binding power of the self-system. (See this volume [2002b] and *Integral Psychology* for a further discussion of these themes.)

   The idea of relatively independent lines of development is similar to the widely accepted notion of independent *modules* (linguistic, cognitive, moral, etc.), ex-cept that in my view these modules, as they develop, are all subject to the same general levels or waves (preconventional to conventional to postconventional to post-postconventional), and they are all balanced and integrated by the self. But my model does allow us to use the important contributions of module theo-rists, set in what I believe is a more adequate framework.

6. There is moderate to strong evidence for the existence of the following develop-mental lines: cognition, morals, affects, motivation/needs, ideas of the good, psychosexuality, kinesthetic intelligence, self-identity (ego), role-taking, logico-mathematical competence, linguistic competence, socio-emotional capacity, worldviews, values, several lines that might be called "spiritual" (care, open-ness, concern, religious faith, meditative stages), musical skill, altruism, commu-nicative competence, creativity, modes of space and time perception, death-fear, gender identity, and empathy. Much of this evidence is summarized in this vol-ume (2002b) and in Wilber, 2000b.

7. In my own system, the "body/energy" component is the Upper-Right quadrant, and the "mind/consciousness" component is the Upper-Left quadrant. The inte-gral model I am suggesting therefore explicitly includes a corresponding subtle energy at *every* level of consciousness across the entire spectrum (gross to subtle

to causal, or matter to body to mind to soul to spirit). Critics have often missed this aspect of my model because the typical four-quadrant diagram shows only the gross body in the Upper-Right quadrant, but that is only a simplified summary of the full model presented in my work.

In the traditions, it is often said that these subtle energy fields exist in concentric spheres of increasing embrace. For example, the etheric field is said to extend a few inches from the physical body, surrounding and enveloping it; the astral energy field surrounds and envelops the etheric field and extends a foot or so; the thought field (or subtle body energy field) surrounds and envelops the astral and extends even further; and the causal energy field extends to formless infinity. Thus, each of these subtle energy fields is a holon (a whole that is part of a larger whole), and the entire holonic energy spectrum can be easily represented in the Upper-Right quadrant as a standard series of increasingly finer and wider concentric spheres (with each subtler energy field transcending and including its junior fields). Each subtle energy holon is the exterior or the Right-Hand component of the corresponding interior or Left-Hand consciousness. In short, all holons have four quadrants across the entire spectrum, gross to subtle to causal, and this includes both a "mind/consciousness" and a "body/energy" component.

For a discussion of body/realms—e.g., gross body (Nirmanakaya), subtle body (Sambhogakaya), causal body (Dharmakaya)—as the energetic support or "body" of each of the consciousness levels and states, see *Sex, Ecology, Spirituality*, note 1 for chap. 14. I often use the words "body," "realm," and "sphere" interchangeably; see *Integral Psychology*.

8. Even though it is said by, e.g., the Tibetan tradition, that subtle consciousness/energy or the subtle mind/body can detach from the gross mind/body, as in the chonyid bardo realm following death; and the causal mind/body can detach from both the subtle and gross mind/body, as in the chikhai bardo or the clear-light emptiness post-death experience (Deutsch, 1969; Gyatso, 1986). This conception allows consciousness to extend beyond the physical body (and survive physical death) but never to be merely disembodied (since there are subtle and causal bodies). In my opinion, this is a profound body/mind (or matter/consciousness) nonduality at every level, a conception I have incorporated into my own system. Whether or not these higher, subtle energies and their corresponding states actually exist in any fashion that can be satisfactorily verified is, of course, part of an integral research agenda. I have provisionally included them in the "master template" simply because the cross-cultural evidence for them is strong, if not conclusive, and until more definitive studies can be done I believe it would be premature to reject them.

9. I am indebted to my friend Allan Combs for the notion of "states of mind," although Allan and I have a mild disagreement as to their specific relationships with states and structures of consciousness. Allan has also independently devised a grid of religious experiences. See his *Radiance of Being* and my *Integral Psychology* for an overview. It should be noted that Allan would like to do a second revised edition of *Radiance* to bring his own thoughts up to date. Allan

acknowledges that his presentation of my work only covers phase-2 and does not deal with my present model; but the book is otherwise highly recommended.

10. States of consciousness are in one sense experienced by subjects—the dream state, for example—but usually what is actually experienced is some specific, if different or altered, phenomenal state. The individual then compares many similar phenomenal states and concludes that they all belong to a broad state of consciousness (such as dreaming, or intoxication, or some such). Thus, both broad states and basic structures tend to be missed by phenomenology's adherence to phenomenal states. See note 11.

11. On the limitations of phenomenology, see several long notes in *Sex, Ecology, Spirituality*, such as note 28 for chap. 4; and several notes in *Integral Psychology*, such as note 21 for chap. 14.

First-person phenomenological investigations of consciousness can easily spot *phenomenal states* and even first-person *phenomenal stages*. For example, in the "highest yoga" school of Tibetan Buddhism (anuttaratantra yoga), there are ten major stages of meditation, each marked by a very specific phenomenological experience: during meditation, a person experiences first a mirage-like appearance, then smoke-like, then fireflies, then a flickering lamp, then a steady lamp (all of these stages are said to result from the progressive transcendence of the gross bodymind); then the individual begins to experience the subtle realms: an expanse like a clear autumn moonlight, then clear autumn sunlight, which takes one to the causal or unmanifest realm, which is an experience like "the thick blackness of an autumn night," and then the breakthrough to the nondual (Gyatso, 1986). Those specific experiences appear to be genuine stages in this particular meditative line (they are all said to be necessary, and none can be skipped), and any individual, sitting in meditation, could indeed see or spot these stages by him- or herself, because they present themselves as successively perceived phenomenal states. This is why I maintain that the phenomenological method can register phenomenal states and phenomenal stages in the "I" (or Upper-Left quadrant). And this is why the world's contemplative literature is full of these types of states and stages.

However: although the phenomenological method can spot phenomenal states and phenomenal stages, it cannot easily spot subjective *structures* (i.e., psychological structures in the Upper-Left quadrant, such as those discovered by Graves, 1970; Piaget, 1977; Loevinger, 1976; etc.), nor can it spot *intersubjective structures* and *intersubjective stages* (in the Lower-Left quadrant, e.g., Gebser's worldviews, Habermas's stages of communicative competence, interpersonal moral stages, Foucault's interpretative-analytic side of the structures of power). As suggested in the main text, no amount of introspection by individuals will disclose social structures of oppressive power (e.g., Foucault), moral stages (e.g., Carol Gilligan), linguistic structures (e.g., Chomsky), stages of ego development (e.g., Jane Loevinger), stages of values (e.g., Clare Graves), and so on—all of those are inherently invisible to mere phenomenology. This is why phenomenological approaches tend to be strong in the "I" components but weak in the "we" components. (Cultural phenomenologists, such as some ethnomethodologists, are strong in the "we" or intersubjective components, but not in stages or structures of intersubjectivity. When those stage-structures are presented, phenomenology shades into neostructuralism; both of those approaches thus appear to be useful aspects of a more integral approach.)

The general inadequacy of phenomenology for spotting intersubjective structure-stages seems to be the major reason that the world's contemplative literature is virtually silent on these important intersubjective aspects of consciousness. This also appears to be why research into nonordinary states of consciousness, such as Grof's holotropic model of the mind (Grof, 1985, 1998), produces very partial and incomplete cartographies (both psychedelic research and holotropic breathwork are very good for spotting experiential, phenomenal, first-person states, but fare less well in spotting intersubjective and interobjective patterns; hence the lopsidedness of such cartographies and their inadequacy in dealing with many important aspects of consciousness in the world [Wilber 2000c, 2002b]).

This might also be why many contemporary meditation theorists are hostile to structure-stage conceptions—their phenomenological methodology does not spot them, so they assume they are imposed on consciousness for suspect reasons by categorizing theorists.

In short, it appears that phenomenological methods tend to excel in spotting (in the UL) individual phenomenal states and phenomenal stages, but not individual structures; and while they excel in spotting different cultural and intersubjective patterns, they miss virtually all of the intersubjective structures and intersubjective stages (of the LL; not to mention the Right-Hand patterns, which are not discussed in this note). A more integral approach would likely result from a combination of I, we, and it dimensions, using research methodologies that are "all-quadrant, all-level" (see below).

12. Nonetheless, using the same terms (psychic, subtle, causal, nondual) to cover both the transpersonal structures and the transpersonal states was perhaps an unhappy choice; in my defense, I would say that three decades ago, there were only so many terms to go around, and we used them as parsimoniously as possible. For example, in Vedanta, as previously mentioned, the subtle body/realm or *sukshma-sharira* (experienced in, e.g., the dream state, the chonyid bardo state, and savikalpa samadhi) includes or supports three *structures* or levels—the prana-maya-kosha or emotional-sexual level, the mano-maya-kosha or mental level, and the vijnana-maya-kosha or higher-mental/soul level—and I have, from the beginning, used the world "subtle" to refer to both the *overall* subtle state/realm (the prana-, mano-, and vijnana-maya-kosha) *and* the highest structure in it (the vijnana-maya-kosha); the context usually indicates which is meant. In Vedanta, the causal state/realm has just one structure, the ananda-maya-kosha, so there is less semantic problem.

There is a substantial amount of agreement in the traditions (e.g., contemplative Christianity, Kabbalah, Vajrayana, Sufism, Vedanta) about these transpersonal realms, structures, and states—but the terminology used by different scholars to translate them is indeed a semantic nightmare. So let me just say that I use four major terms (psychic, subtle, causal, and nondual) to refer to the various transpersonal occasions, including transpersonal *states* (e.g., subtle, causal, and nondual states of consciousness, experienced in dream state, savikalpa samadhi, deep sleep, nirvikalpa samadhi, jnana samadhi, sahaja, etc.); *realms*, bodies, or spheres of being (e.g., gross body/realm, subtle body/realm, causal body/realm); and *structures*, waves, or levels of consciousness (e.g., psychic level or illumined mind, subtle level or intuitive mind, causal level or overmind, and nondual or supermind, to use Aurobindo's terminology for the corresponding levels). For those concerned with these intricacies, the context will usually indicate which is meant. See *Integral Psychology* for a further discussion of these technical issues.

13. For the definitive cross-cultural study of meditative stages, see Daniel P. Brown, "The Stages of Meditation in Cross-Cultural Perspective," chap.8 in Wilber et al., *Transformations of Consciousness*. For charts comparing a dozen meditative systems containing stages, see *Integral Psychology*.

14. For integral spiritual practice, see *One Taste* (Wilber, 1999) and Murphy and Leonard, *The Life We Are Given* (1995).

A final point about the word "integral" and about Jean Gebser's structures. Although I am a long-time admirer of Gebser, I believe his work is now hindering the field of consciousness studies. First, Gebser does not have a clear understanding of the quadrants, so he tends to conflate different phenomenological languages, different validity claims, and different evidential data. Second, his "archaic structure" is, in my opinion, charged with the retro-Romantic (and pre/trans) fallacy. Third, and most troublesome, his "integral structure" actually contains *at least* five structures (namely, vision-logic, psychic, subtle, causal, and nondual; or, to use Aurobindo's terms, higher mind, illumined mind, intuitive mind, overmind, and supermind—all of which are clumsily collapsed into "the" integral structure by Gebser. Although there is evidence that he realized this later in life, he did not live to adequately correct it). Even according to more conventional maps, such as Spiral Dynamics, what Gebser calls "integral" actually contains green, yellow, turquoise, and coral structures. In short, I believe Gebser's investigation of "the" integral structure was pioneering but is now outdated.

Nonetheless, I continue to refer to the entire vision-logic realms (and second-tier thinking) as "integral," simply because it has become a very common usage. But clearly, the truly integral "level" is the nondual, which is not actually a level or state but the ever-present ground of all levels and all states (see, e.g., chap. 13 of the present work).

Lastly, there is the issue of levels of consciousness and levels (planes, realms, axes, spheres) of reality; for a discussion of this theme, particularly in reference to postmodern, postmetaphysical epistemologies, I refer the reader to a series of long endnotes in *Integral Psychology* (Wilber, 2000b), beginning with note 3 for chap. 1.

15. See note 14.

16. Any of the widely accepted developmental lines can be used to create and re-

search these types of grids. For example, in the cognitive line we have preoperational (preop), concrete operational (conop), formal operational (formop), and postformal (which has various levels, up to and including the transpersonal waves, but this simple division will work for this example). An individual at preop can temporarily experience a psychic, subtle, causal, or nondual state; so can an individual at conop, formop, and postformal. In each case, it appears that the individual interprets those states largely in the categories of the cognitive level at which he or she is currently adapted. For instance, a conop experience of a subtle state tends to be interpreted in very literal-concrete terms (just as mythic symbols at that stage are also taken very literally; e.g., Moses actually did part the Red Sea) and often very ethnocentrically ("only those who believe in my God will be saved"); whereas a person at postformal cognition interprets a subtle-state experience in pluralistic, metaphorical, and aperspectival terms ("I experienced a ground of being that is present in all sentient beings but is expressed differently by each, with no expression being better than another"); and someone directly at the transpersonal waves experiences these realms in their self-transcending immediacy, beyond conceptualization, pluralistic or otherwise.

As suggested, any of the more dependable models of developmental lines can be used to research these types of grids, such as the self-stages (including research tools) presented by Jane Loevinger, Susanne Cook-Greuter, or Robert Kegan; the Graves values scale; Gebser's structures; Maslow's needs hierarchy; Bill Torbert's stages of action-inquiry, and so on. This offers a series of fruitful empirical, phenomenological, and structural research strategies for mapping states onto structures.

17. In this simple example I have used Gebser's structures, which cover the lower-to-intermediate structures (up to centauric vision-logic). But there are higher, transpersonal structures that need to be added to the grid (see note 14), and there are also more sophisticated maps of the lower-to-intermediate structures, such as Spiral Dynamics—e.g., there can be a purple, red, blue, orange, green, yellow, and turquoise peak experience of a psychic, subtle, causal, or nondual state. Also, as a person permanently evolves into higher structures, such as the psychic or subtle, they can still peak-experience yet higher realms, such as causal and nondual.

If we use a general scheme—of, say, twelve levels and four states—that gives us around forty-eight types of transpersonal peak experiences and nonordinary states, although in actuality some of the squares in that grid do not occur (e.g., once at the psychic level, one no longer has psychic peak experiences, for that is now a permanent acquisition). But by and large, those forty or so types of nonordinary and spiritual experiences are very real—and very easy to spot using this grid. I believe that this approach enriches and advances our understanding of these phenomena, the study of which seems to have stalled.

There has been a great deal of research and models based primarily on altered and nonordinary states (Grof, 1985; 1998; Tart, 1972; Fisher, 1971; Wolman, 1986; White, 1972, etc.), and a great deal of research and models on various structures of consciousness (Graves, 1970; Loevinger, 1976; Piaget, 1977; Gilligan, 1982; 1990; Fowler, 1981; Selman, 1974; etc.), but virtually no proposals for an "all-quadrants, all-structures, all-states" model that combines the best of both. I will return to the importance of this more integral research agenda in the main text.

18. Individual psychopathology is actually an all-quadrant affair (see below), and thus important aspects of its genesis can be found in all four quadrants: there are contributing factors from the Upper-Right quadrant (e.g., brain physiology, neurotransmitter imbalance, poor diet); Lower-Right quadrant (e.g., economic stress, environmental toxins, social oppression); and the Lower-Left quadrant (cultural pathologies, communication snarls). Treatment likewise can involve all four quadrants (including psychopharmacology [UR] where appropriate). I am here focusing only on some of the important factors in the Upper-Left quadrant. For the contributions of all four quadrants to pathology, see *Sex, Ecology, Spirituality* (Wilber 2000c); *A Brief History of Everything* (1996c); *The Eye of Spirit* (2002b); and *Integral Psychology* (2000b).

19. To say that the self "identifies" with a level is not to picture this in an all-or-none fashion. Even with the proximate self-sense (e.g., as investigated by Loevinger), research indicates that individuals tend to give around 50 percent of their responses from one level and 25 percent from the level above and below it. As suggested in the main text, the self is more a *center of gravity* than a monolithic entity. This also appears to include the existence of numerous subpersonalities (Rowan, 1990; Wilber 2000b).

20. These are not the only four definitions of spirituality. In *A Sociable God*, I outline nine different definitions. But these four are some of the most common and, I believe, most significant. In *A Sociable God*, I also distinguish between *legitimate* (or translative) spirituality, which seeks to fortify the self at its present level of development, no matter how high or low; and *authentic* (or transformative) spirituality, which seeks to transcend the self altogether (or at least transform it to a higher wave of consciousness). The first three uses of "spirituality" (given in the main text) are different definitions of authentic spirituality, in that all of them include, at least in part, the idea that real spirituality involves a change in level of consciousness (either temporary, as in #1, or permanent, as in #2 and #3). The fourth usage is a good definition of legitimate spirituality, in that it seeks to promote the health of the self at whatever level it is at, without vertically changing consciousness. As suggested in the main text, all four of these uses of spirituality are valid, in my opinion, and all four of them seem to represent very real and important functions that spirituality can perform. The difficulty appears to be that some religious and spiritual theorists (and movements) latch onto just one narrow aspect of the spiritual impulse in humans and claim it is the only impulse worth acting on, which seems to distort both legitimate an authentic spirituality and often sets the self in a spiral of deception and deceit.

21. This phenomenon (i.e., a person can be highly developed in certain spiritual traits but poorly developed in others, such as psychosexual, emotional, or inter-

personal skills) can be believably explained by three of the four definitions (e.g., #1: if spirituality is defined as an altered state, those states can certainly occur in a personality that is dysfunctional; #2: if spirituality is the highest levels in any of the lines, a person can be highly developed in some lines and poorly or pathologically in others; #3: if spirituality is a separate line itself, then individuals can be highly advanced in that line and poorly or pathologically developed in others). This uneven mixture (of spiritual and pathological) is not easily explained by definition #4 (i.e., if spirituality is something that either is or is not present at any stage, then the only way to get uneven and mixed development is to revert to one of the other definitions, but that "developmental ranking" is what this definition claims to avoid). Nor can uneven development be explained by single ladder models of development (according to which, a person failing a lower stage could not advance to a higher).

22. This discussion earlier suggested a "grid of religious experiences." Notice that that grid is simply what we see if we combine factors 1 and 2/3—that is, if we map the various states of consciousness on the various structure-stages. Thus, even that grid recognizes some of these major uses, suggesting again their widespread importance.

23. Technically, "we" is first-person plural, and "you" is second person. But I include first-person plural ("we") and second person ("you/Thou") as *both* being in the Lower-Left quadrant, which I refer to in general as "we." The reason I do so is that there is no distinctive second-person plural in English (which is why Southerners have to say "you-all" and Northerners say "you guys"). In other words, when "we" is being done with respect, it implicitly includes an I-Thou relationship (I cannot truly understand thee unless WE share a set of common perceptions).

Both the Lower-Left quadrant and the Upper-Left quadrant are postulated to exist "all the way down"; that is, this is a form of modified panpsychism ("pan-interiors"), which seems to be the only model capable of faithfully rendering this "master template" (See Addendum B; see also Wilber, 2000b). This implies that intersubjectivity also goes "all the way down" and that humans, as "compound individuals," contain all the prehuman forms of intersubjectivity as well. Thus, in humans, intersubjectivity is not established merely by exchange of linguistic signifiers, which is the commonly accepted notion. Rather, humans contain prelinguistic intersubjectivity (established by, e.g., emotional or prereflexive co-presence with and to the other); linguistic intersubjectivity (established by the co-presence of interiority whose exteriors are linguistic signifiers but cannot be reduced to those exteriors); and translinguistic intersubjectivity (established by the simple presence of Presence, or nondual Spirit). In short, intersubjectivity is established at all levels by an interior resonance of those elements present at each level, a resonance that appears to span the entire spectrum of consciousness, prelinguistic to linguistic to translinguistic. The suggestion that I limit intersubjectivity to the exchange of linguistic signifiers is quite off the mark (see *Sex, Ecology, Spirituality*, 2nd ed. [Wilber, 2000c]).

24. Here is one example of the importance of taking the four quadrants into ac-

count when dealing with states and structures. We saw that all individuals have access to the three great realms/states of gross, subtle, and causal, simply because everybody wakes, dreams, and sleeps. Thus, even an infant has access to these three great realms. But the way in which the infant (or anybody) interprets these *states* depends in part upon its *stage*-structure of development (e.g., a subtle state can be experienced by the archaic, magic, mythic, rational, etc., structures, with a different "flavor" in each case). Moreover—and of crucial importance—all of the states and stages are firmly set in the four quadrants (intentional, behavioral, cultural, and social). Thus, an infant is often plunged into the subtle/dream state, but it will not have the dream thought "I must go to the grocery store and buy some cereal," for those specific sociocultural items have not yet entered its awareness. The infant definitely has access to a subtle state, but it has not yet developed the specific structures (of language, cognition, and cultural perceptions) that will allow it to have those specific thoughts in the subtle/dream state.

Thus, it appears that the three general states are largely *given*, but the various structure-stages *develop*. And because all of them are set in the four quadrants, even the states (which are given prior to culture) are nonetheless firmly molded by the particular culture in which they unfold (because they are molded, in fact, by all four quadrants—intentional, behavioral, cultural, and social).

This allows us to see how an infant can definitely experience a subtle or causal state, but that state is nevertheless unpacked only by a preconventional, egocentric, preformal structure, not a postconventional, global, worldcentric structure (which has not yet developed). This more integral view allows us to steer a course between those who maintain that infants are directly in touch with a pure spiritual reality, and those who maintain that infants are narcissistic and preconventional. (See *Integral Psychology*, chap. 11, "Is There a Childhood Spirituality?")

As the infant develops through the various levels/structures/waves of consciousness, with all of their various lines, those structures will increasingly provide the content for much of the subtle states (in addition to any truly archetypal material that might be given as part of the subtle itself; but even the latter will be molded in its existence and expression by the four quadrants). Thus, at some point, the young child might indeed develop the conventional thought, "I must go to the grocery store," and that thought, molded by all four quadrants, might then invade the dream state. A child in a different culture might dream in French or Chinese; not "cereal" but "baguettes," and so on. In this way, the *development* in the structures (levels and lines) profoundly influences the content of the general states, which nonetheless are *given* in their general form.

This also allows us to see how all individuals can have access to the three great realms of being (gross, subtle, and causal), and yet still show stage-like development that colors these realms, for the development in the structures will often give content and form to the states. A four-quadrant analysis of states and structures thus allows us to incorporate the best of the ancient models of consciousness with more modern and postmodern research. For further discussion of these themes, see *Integral Psychology* (Wilber, 2000b) and the websites www.worldofkenwilber.com, www.IntegralAge.org, www.enlightenment.com, and iKosmos.com.

25. Even though the Upper-Right quadrant is today of such importance (as evidenced by the increasing dominance of cognitive science, evolutionary psychology, neuroscience, biological psychiatry, etc.), it is the one about which I have written the least. The reasons for this are simple: (1) this quadrant is investigated by the scientific method, or empiric-analytic inquiry, which is fairly straightforward in its operation and interpretation; (2) there is an enormous amount of work already being done in this quadrant; (3) the data collected in this quadrant, once verified, tend to be stable and trustworthy, requiring only modest amounts of interpretation (unlike the interior quadrants, which are made of interpretations). In short, I have written the least about this quadrant not because it is the least important but because it needs the least attention. In chap. 14 of *Integral Psychology* I give an overview of this quadrant and its investigation by the field of consciousness studies—particularly discussing the mind/body or Left/Right "hard problem" of consciousness (as summarized in Addendum B), and I cite several dozen books that have begun the crucially important endeavor of mapping Upper-Left and Upper-Right correlations, a mapping on which any truly integral psychology will depend.

26. An integral approach also lends itself to a more comprehensive understanding of the various types of unconscious processes. The question regarding any sort of unconscious is: can an event occur that is part of the existence of an individual but that does not register in consciousness? The answer appears to be definitely yes; but an integral model can be more precise. Evidence suggests that aspects of virtually any level in any line in any quadrant can in fact be unconscious—and can to some degree be made conscious (directly or indirectly) through various techniques. This making conscious the unconscious is said to be connected with various types of liberation. For the kinds of unconscious processes (and liberation) in each of the four quadrants, see *Sex, Ecology, Spirituality*, 2nd ed., note 28 for chap. 4 and note 1 for chap. 14. For the types of the unconscious in the Upper-Left quadrant, see *The Atman Project* (CW2) and *The Eye of Spirit* (chaps. 6, 7, 9, 10, and 11 above). I still believe that the five types of unconscious in the UL (first outlined in *The Atman Project*) are of considerable importance for individual psychology.

27. All four of the quadrants have various types of waves, streams, and states (among other items). That is, all four quadrants possess levels of development and lines of development (e.g., grades and clades in biological evolution; technological lines of development through the levels of foraging, horticultural, agrarian, industrial, informational, etc.); and all four quadrants also show various types of states (brain states, states of material affairs, gaseous states, etc.). Thus, all quadrants have waves, streams, and states (in addition to aggregates, heaps, etc). But in the Left-Hand quadrants, these are all ultimately related to consciousness itself (levels of consciousness, lines of consciousness, and states

of consciousness—both individual and collective), whereas in the Right-Hand quadrants, we find that levels, lines, and states primarily involve matter (physiological brain states, biomaterial grades and clades, technological modes, etc.). The Left-Hand quadrants are the interiors, the Right-Hand quadrants the exteriors, of each and every holon (Wilber, 2000c, 1996c, 1998). See Addendum B.

28. By "existing entity" I mean "holon." See Wilber, 2000b, 2000c.

29. This specifically happened with the publication of *A Sociable God*. My previous two books, *The Atman Project* and *Up from Eden*, were subtitled, respectively, *A Transpersonal View of Human Development* and *A Transpersonal View of Human Evolution* (they were written as a two-volume set). *A Sociable God* was originally subtitled *A Brief Introduction to a Transpersonal Sociology*. But even by that time, the transpersonal field had become, to my mind, problematic. I certainly did not harbor any ill-will toward the field, but at the same time, what I was doing was not confined to transpersonal psychology or transpersonal anything, for that matter. I changed the subtitle to *A Brief Introduction to a Transcendental Sociology*, and within a few years of that date (1983), I never again used the word "transpersonal" to describe my work (although I do still use it to describe the supramental realms of consciousness).

There are numerous gifted scholars and researchers who continue to publicly define themselves as "transpersonal," including Stan Grof, Richard Tarnas, Brandt Cortright, Jorge Ferrer, Donald Rothberg, Peggy Wright, Michael Washburn, Frank Lawlis, Jurgen Kremer, and many others. I think those writers represent the field of transpersonal fairly well, and I think that their research needs to be continued within the rubric of the transpersonal paradigm as it has developed within their collective body of work (with all its many variations and nuances).

Scholars who have publicly identified themselves as "integral" (and have presented integral models or are moving toward such) include Michael Murphy, George Leonard, Roger Walsh, Frances Vaughan, Allan Combs, Don Beck, Susann Cook-Greuter, Francisco Varela, Jenny Wade, Bert Parlee, Tony Schwartz, Robert Forman, Marilyn Schlitz, Antony Arcari, Raz Ingrasci, Keith Thompson, Michael Zimmerman, and many others. Although I can speak for none of those writers, I think it is safe to say that they all are strong supporters of the transpersonal field, but they are also trying to introduce more comprehensive theories and models that build more bridges to the conventional and orthodox world. At this time it seems prudent that both of these schools, integral and transpersonal, while continuing their mutually beneficial dialogue and occasional joint ventures, also focus on their own maps and models and begin applying them in the real world, so that the actual fruits of these various models, and their usefulness in real-world situations, will begin to speak for their relative merits.

30. Thus, even after 1983, I remained on the editorial board of both the *Journal of Humanistic Psychology* and the *Journal of Transpersonal Psychology*. I published something like eight articles in the former and nine articles in the latter. I had, and have, an enormous respect for the respective editors, Tom Greening

and Miles Vich, who both moved their journals toward a more integral approach. It is just that, at least in the case of transpersonal, it continued to close in on itself and its growing ideology, and I found the field less and less grounded in research, evidence, and cogent interpretations, to the point that it had not built more bridges to the conventional world, but simply burned them. Therefore, when Miles stepped down as editor, it was appropriate for me to step down as well.

31. In order to survive, especially economically, it is likely that humanistic and transpersonal will be forced to coalesce into an awkward hybrid, so that transpersonal can ride the coattails of Humanistic Psychology, Division 32 of APA, which is nonetheless regarded as a rather weak division compared to the others. My point is that unless both of these interior psychologies more consciously move toward an AQAL framework, they will increasingly be selected against in the new currents that demand more integral responses.

Chapter 13: Always Already

1. Kunsang, 1986.
2. Most Nondual schools trace several stages of post-Nirvanic development leading to nondual Enlightenment, and then several stages of post-Enlightenment development, as ever-present awareness realigns the entire bodymind top down (rather like building a suspension bridge). Here is a typical classification of the post-Nirvanic and post-Enlightenment waves of development (I believe there is sufficient evidence for each of these waves to be included in an integral model):

We start at the point of nirvana itself. Classical nirvana is permanent access to nirvikalpa samadhi or cessation—that is, to the pure, causal, formless, unmanifest realm (nirodh, nirvikalpa, nirvana: the prefix *nir* in each case means "without" or "absent" or "cessation"). But the Nondual schools claim this is actually a *conditional* state, set apart as it is from the entire realm of manifestation. This is why, for example, the state of conditional nirvikalpa samadhi is merely the eighth of the ten Zen ox-herding pictures depicting post-postconventional development (the eighth picture is an empty circle, "nir").

Beyond conditional nirvikalpa samadhi, the various Nondual traditions describe a series of stages or waves of development, leading eventually to a continuous and spontaneous recognition of the always already state (namely, the intrinsic, brilliant, simple, naked, ever-present awareness itself), a spontaneous and continuous recognition often referred to as sahaj samadhi.

These post-Nirvana developments move from conditional nirvikalpa samadhi to sahaj samadhi, usually in a series of three or so major waves, including (1) the recognition of subject permanence (continuous recognition through waking, dream, and deep sleep states); (2) the uprooting of the very subtlest of the subject-object tensions that surround the causal Heart and hold the separate-self sense in place; so that (3) the last remnants of dualism are illumined by ever-present awareness; and (4) the nondual state of sahaj is effortlessly recognized under all changes of state.

Sahaj itself is "nondual Enlightenment," beyond which lie the post-Enlightenment developments or waves leading to bhava samadhi, or the outshining and transfiguration of the entire manifest and unmanifest worlds. These post-Enlightenment developments are the events that unfold in the space of sahaj, in the nondual space of simple, ever-present awareness, once the bodymind is self-liberated from the tortures of the self-contraction; that is, once it is recognized that the self-contraction does not exist, never did exist, and never will exist. Under that realization, the bodymind is transfigured into its own primordial condition, the naked luminosity that is its own remark, self-evidently, eternally.

Bibliography

Adi Da (Da Free John). 1977. *The paradox of instruction*. Clearlake, Calif.: Dawn Horse Press.

———. 1979. *The enlightenment of the whole body*. Clearlake, Calif.: Dawn Horse Press.

Alexander, C., and E. Langer, eds. 1990. *Higher stages of human development*. New York: Oxford University Press.

Alexander, C., et al. 1990. Growth of higher stages of consciousness: Maharishi's Vedic psychology of human development. In Alexander and Langer (eds.), 1990.

Almaas, A. H. 1986. *Essence*. York Beach, Maine: Weiser.

———. 1988. *The pearl beyond price*. Berkeley: Diamond.

Anthony, D., B. Ecker, and K. Wilber, eds. 1987. *Spiritual choices*. New York: Paragon.

Apel, K-O. 1994. *Selected essays*, vol. 1. Atlantic Highlands, N.J.: Humanities Press International.

Arieti, S. 1967. *The intrapsychic self*. New York: Basic Books.

Aristotle. 1984. *The complete works of Aristotle*, vols. 1 and 2, edited by J. Barnes. Princeton: Princeton University Press.

Arlin, P. 1975. Cognitive development in adulthood: A fifth stage? *Developmental Psychology* 11: 602–606.

———. 1990. Wisdom: The art of problem finding. In Sternberg (ed.), 1990.

Assagioli, R. 1965. *Psychosynthesis*. New York: Viking.

Aurobindo, Sri. 1990 (1939). *The life divine*. Wilmot, Wisc.: Lotus Light Publications.

———. n.d. *The life divine* and *The synthesis of yoga*. Pondicherry: Centenary Library, XVIII-XXI.

Austin, J. L. 1962. *How to do things with words*. Cambridge: Harvard University Press.

———. 1979 (1961). *Philosophical papers*. Oxford: Oxford University Press.

Baldwin, J. M. 1973. *Dictionary of philosophy and psychology: Bibliography of philosophy, psychology, and cognate subjects*. Peter Smith Publishers.

———. 1975. *Genetic theory of reality*. Philosophy in America Series. New York: AMS Press.

———. 1990a. *Fragments in philosophy and science: Being collected essays and addresses*. New York: AMS Press.

———. 1990b, Development and evolution: Including psychophysical evolution, evolution by orthoplasy and theory of genetic. New York: AMS Press.

Barthes, R. 1982. *A Barthes reader*. Edited by S. Sontag. New York: Hill and Wang.

Basseches, M. 1984. *Dialectical thinking and adult development*. Norwood, N.J.: Ablex Press.

Bataille, G. 1985. *Visions of excess*. Minneapolis: University of Minnesota Press.

Beck, D., and C. Cowan. 1996. *Spiral dynamics: Managing values, leadership, and change*. London: Blackwell.

Berry, J., Y. Poortinga, M. Segall, and P. Dasen. 1992. *Cross-cultural psychology: Research and applications*. Cambridge: Cambridge University Press.

Bertalanffy, L. von. 1968. *General system theory*. New York: Braziller.

Birch, C., and J. Cobb. 1990. *The liberation of life*. Denton, Tex.: Environmental Ethics Books.

Blanck, G., and R. Blanck. 1974. *Ego psychology: Theory and practice*. New York: Columbia University Press.

———. 1979. *Ego psychology II: Developmental psychology*. New York: Columbia University Press.

———. 1986. *Beyond ego psychology*. New York: Columbia University Press.

Bohm, D. 1973. *Wholeness and the implicate order*. London: Routledge.

Boorstein, S., ed. 1980. *Transpersonal psychotherapy*. Palo Alto, Calif.: Science and Behavior Books.

Broughton, J. 1975. The development of natural epistemology in adolescence and early adulthood. Doctoral dissertation, Harvard University.

Brown, D. P. 1977. A model for the levels of concentrative meditation. *International Journal of Clinical and Experimental Hypnosis* 25: 236–73.

———. 1981. Mahamudra meditation: Stages and contemporary cognitive psychology. Doctoral dissertation, University of Chicago.

Brown, D. P., and J. Engler. 1980. The stages of mindfulness meditation: A validation study. *Journal of Transpersonal Psychology* 12 (2): 143–92. Part I and II. Also in *Transformations of consciousness*, by K. Wilber, J. Engler, and D. Brown. Boston: Shambhala Publications, 1986.

Brown, L., and C. Gilligan. 1992. *Meeting at the crossroads*. New York: Ballantine.

Brown, N. O. 1959. *Life against death*. Middletown, Conn.: Wesleyan University Press.

Bruner, J. 1983. *In search of mind*. New York: Harper & Row.

———. 1986. *Actual minds, possible worlds*. Cambridge: Harvard University Press.

Buddhaghosa, B. 1976. *The path of purification*. 2 vols. Boulder: Shambhala Publications.

Capra, F. 1997. *The web of life: A new understanding of living systems*. New York: Doubleday.

Chafetz, J. 1984. *Sex and advantage*. Totowa, N.J.: Rowman and Alanheld.

———. 1990. *Gender equity*. Newbury Park, Calif.: Sage.

Chalmers, D. 1995. The puzzle of conscious experience. *Scientific American*, December.

———. 1996. *The conscious mind: In search of a fundamental theory*. New York: Oxford University Press.

———. 1997. Moving forward on the problem of consciousness, *Journal of Consciousness Studies* 4 (1).

Chaudhuri, H. 1981. *Integral yoga.* Wheaton, Ill.: Quest Books.

Combs, A. 1995. *The radiance of being: Complexity, chaos, and the evolution of consciousness.* St. Paul, Minn.: Paragon House.

Commons, M., C. Armon, L. Kohlberg, F. Richards, T. Grotzer, and J. Sinnott, eds. 1990. *Adult development.* Vol. 2, *Models and methods in the study of adult and adolescent thought.* New York: Praeger.

Commons, M., F. Richards, and C. Armon. 1984. *Beyond formal operations.* New York: Praeger.

Commons, M., J. Sinnott, F. Richards, and C. Armon, eds. 1989. *Adult development.* Vol. 1, *Comparisons and applications of developmental models.* New York: Praeger.

Cook-Greuter, S. 1990. Maps for living. In *Adult Development,* vol. 2, edited by Commons et al.

Cook-Greuter, S., and M. Miller, eds. 1994. *Transcendence and mature thought in adulthood.* Lanham, Md.: Rowman & Littlefield.

Coomaraswamy, A. 1943. *Hinduism and Buddhism.* New York: Philosophical Library.

Cowan, P. 1978. *Piaget with feeling.* New York: Holt.

Crews, F. 1975. *Out of my system: Psychoanalysis, ideology, and critical method.* New York: Oxford University Press.

Crittenden, J., ed. Forthcoming. *Kindred visions.* Boston: Shambhala Publications.

Culler, J. 1982. *On deconstruction.* Ithaca, N.Y.: Cornell University Press.

de Man, P. 1971. *Blindness and insight.* New York: Oxford University Press.

Dennett, D. 1991. *Consciousness explained.* Boston: Little, Brown.

Derrida, J. 1976. *Of grammatology.* Baltimore: Johns Hopkins.

———. 1978. *Writing and difference.* Chicago: University of Chicago Press.

———. 1981. *Positions.* Chicago: University of Chicago Press.

———. 1982. *Margins of philosophy.* Chicago: University of Chicago Press.

Deutsche, E. 1969. *Advaita Vedanta.* Honolulu: East-West Center.

Dewey, J. 1981. *The philosophy of John Dewey,* edited by J. McDermott. Chicago: University of Chicago Press.

Diamond, I., and G. Orenstein. 1990. *Reweaving the world: The emergence of eco-feminism.* San Francisco: Sierra Club Books.

Douglas, M. 1982. *In the active voice.* London: Routledge.

Dreyfus, H., and P. Rabinow, 1983. *Michel Foucault: Beyond structuralism and hermeneutics.* Chicago: University of Chicago Press.

Eccles, J. 1984. *The human mystery.* London: Routledge.

———. 1994. *How the self controls its brain.* Berlin: Springer-Verlag.

Edinger, E. 1992. *Ego and archetype.* Boston: Shambhala Publications.

Eisler, R. 1987. *The chalice and the blade.* San Francisco: Harper.

Emerson, R. W. 1969. *Selected prose and poetry.* San Francisco: Rinehart Press.

Engler, J. 1984. Therapeutic aims in psychotherapy and meditation: Developmental stages in the representation of self. *Journal of Transpersonal Psychology* 16 (1): 25–61.

Fischer, K., S. Kenny, and S. Pipp. 1990. How cognitive processes and environmental conditions organize discontinuities in the development of abstractions. In Alexander et al., 1990, pp. 162–90.

Fisher, R. 1971. A cartography of the ecstatic and meditative states: The experimental and experiential features of a perception-hallucination continuum. *Science* 174, pp. 897–904.

Fish, S. 1980. *Is there a text in this class?* Cambridge: Harvard University Press.

Flavell, J. 1963. *The developmental psychology of Jean Piaget*. Princeton, N.J.: Van Nostrand.

Flavell, J., P. Miller, and S. Miller. 1993. *Cognitive development*. Englewood, N.J.: Prentice-Hall.

Forman, R. 1998a. *Mysticism, mind, consciousness* Albany, N.Y.: SUNY Press.

———. 1998b. What does mysticism have to teach us about consciousness? *Journal of Consciousness Studies* 5 (2): 185–201.

———, ed. 1990. *The problem of pure consciousness*. New York: Oxford University Press.

Foucault, M. 1970. *The order of things*. New York: Random House.

———. 1972. *The archaeology of knowledge*. New York: Random House.

———. 1975. *The birth of the clinic*. New York: Random House

———. 1978. *The history of sexuality*, vol. 1. New York: Random House

———. 1979. *Discipline and punish*. New York: Vintage.

———. 1980. *Power/knowledge*. New York: Pantheon.

Fowler, J. 1981. *Stages of faith: The psychology of human development and the quest for meaning*. San Francisco: Harper & Row.

Fox, W. 1990. *Toward a transpersonal ecology*. Boston: Shambhala Publications.

Gadamer, H. 1976. *Philosophical hermeneutics*. Berkeley: University of California Press.

———. 1992. *Truth and method*. 2nd ed. New York: Crossroad.

Gardiner, H., J. Mutter, and C. Kosmitzki. 1998. *Lives across cultures: Cross-cultural human development*. Boston: Allyn and Bacon.

Gardner, H. 1972. *The quest for mind*. New York: Vintage Books.

———. 1983. *Frames of mind*. New York: Basic Books.

Gardner, H., E. Phelps, and D. Wolf. 1990. The roots of adult creativity in children's symbolic products. In Alexander and Langer (eds.), 1990, 79–96.

Gebser, J. 1985 (1949). *The ever-present origin*. Athens: Ohio University Press.

Gedo, J. 1979. *Beyond interpretation: Toward a revised theory for psychoanalysis*. New York: International University Press.

———. 1981. *Advances in clinical psychoanalysis*. New York: International University Press.

Geertz, C. 1973. *The interpretation of cultures*. New York: Harper & Row.

Gerson, L. 1994. *Plotinus*. London: Routledge.

Gilligan, C. 1982. *In a different voice*. Cambridge: Harvard University Press.

Gilligan, C., J. Murphy, and M. Tappan. 1990. Moral development beyond adolescence. In Alexander and Langer (eds.), 1990, pp. 208–28.

Goleman, D. 1988. *The meditative mind: Varieties of meditative experience.* Los Angeles: Tarcher.

Graff, G., and G. Gibbons, eds. 1985. *Criticism in the university.* Evanston, Ill.: Northwestern University Press.

Graves, C. 1970. Levels of existence: An open system theory of values. *Journal of Transpersonal Psychology* 10, pp. 131–55.

Gregory, R. 1982. *Mind in science.* Cambridge: Cambridge University Press.

Grof, S. 1985. *Beyond the brain: Birth, death and transcendence in psychotherapy.* Albany: SUNY Press.

———. 1988. *The adventure of self-discovery.* Albany: SUNY Press.

———. 1998. *The cosmic game: Explorations of the frontiers of human consciousness.* Albany: SUNY Press.

Grof, S., with H. Bennett. 1992. *The holotropic mind.* San Francisco: HarperCollins.

Gyatso, K. 1986. *Progressive stages of meditation on emptiness.* Oxford: Longchen Foundation.

Habermas, J. 1979. *Communication and the evolution of society,* translated by T. McCarthy. Boston: Beacon Press.

———. 1984–1985. *The theory of communicative action,* translated by T. McCarthy. 2 vols. Boston: Beacon Press.

———. 1990. *The philosophical discourse of modernity,* translated by F. Lawrence. Cambridge: MIT Press.

Hartman, G., ed. 1979. *Psychoanalysis and the question of the text.* Baltimore: Johns Hopkins.

———. 1970. *Beyond formalism.* New Haven: Yale University Press.

Hayward, J., and F. Varela. 1992. *Gentle bridges.* Boston: Shambhala Publications.

Hegel, G. 1993. *Hegel's science of logic.* Atlantic Highlands, N.J.: Humanities Press International.

Heidegger, M. 1959. *Introduction to metaphysics.* New Haven: Yale University Press.

———. 1962. *Being and time.* New York: Harper & Row.

———. 1968. *What is called thinking?* New York: Harper & Row.

———. 1977. *Basic writings,* edited by D. Krell. New York: Harper & Row.

Hirsch, E. D. 1967. *Validity in interpretation.* New Haven: Yale University Press.

———. 1976. *The aims of interpretation.* Chicago: University of Chicago Press.

Hoy, D. 1978. *The critical circle.* Berkeley: University of California Press.

Hoy, D., and T. McCarthy. 1994. *Critical theory.* Cambridge: Blackwell.

Husserl, E. 1970. *The crisis of European sciences and transcendental phenomenology.* Evanston, Ill.: Northwestern University Press.

———. 1991 (1950). *Cartesian meditations.* Boston: Kluwer.

Inge, W. R. 1968 (1929). *The philosophy of Plotinus,* vols. 1 & 2. Westport, Conn.: Greenwood.

Irigaray, L. 1985. *This sex which is not one.* Ithaca, N.Y.: Cornell University Press.

Iser, W. 1974. *The implied reader.* Baltimore: Johns Hopkins.

Jackendoff, R. 1987. *Consciousness and the computational mind.* Cambridge: MIT Press.

Jakobson, R. 1980. *The framework of language.* Ann Arbor: University of Michigan Press.

———. 1990. *On language.* Cambridge: Harvard University Press.

Jantsch, E. 1980. *The self-organizing universe.* New York: Pergamon.

Jaspers, K. 1966. *The great philosophers.* New York: Harcourt.

Joravsky, D. 1982. Body, mind, and machine. *New York Review of Books,* Oct. 21.

Kant, I. 1949. *Kant's* Critique of Practical Reason *and other writings in moral philosophy,* translated by L. Beck. Chicago: University of Chicago Press.

———. 1951. *Critique of judgement.* New York: Hafner.

———. 1990. *Critique of pure reason.* Buffalo, N.Y.: Prometheus Books.

———. 1993. *Prolegomena.* Chicago: Open Court.

Kegan, R. 1982. *The evolving self.* Cambridge: Harvard University Press.

———. 1994. *In over our heads.* Cambridge: Harvard University Press.

Koestler, A. 1976. *The ghost in the machine.* New York: Random House.

Kohlberg, L. 1981. *Essays on moral development,* vol. 1. San Francisco: Harper.

Kohlberg, L., and C. Armon. 1984. Three types of stage models. In M. Commons et al.,1984.

Kohlberg, L., and R. Ryncarz. 1990. Beyond justice reasoning. In Alexander and Langer (eds.), 1990, pp. 191–207.

Kohut, H. 1971. *The analysis of the self.* New York: IUP.

———. 1977. *The restoration of the self.* New York: IUP.

Koplowitz, H. 1978. *Unitary thought.* Toronto: Addiction Research Foundation.

Kramer, D. 1983. Post-formal operations? *Human Development* 26: 91–105.

———. 1990. Conceptualizing wisdom. In Sternberg (ed.), 1990.

Kris, E. 1952. *Psychoanalytic explorations in art.* New York: IUP.

Kristeva, J. 1980. *Desire in language.* New York: Columbia University Press.

Kuhn, T. 1970. *The structure of scientific revolutions.* Chicago: University of Chicago Press.

Kunsang, E., trans. & ed. 1986. *The flight of the garuda: Five texts from the practice lineage.* Kathmandu: Rangjung Yeshe Publications.

LaBerge, S. 1985. *Lucid dreaming.* Los Angeles: Tarcher.

Lacan, J. 1968. *The language of the self.* Baltimore: Johns Hopkins.

———. 1982. *Feminine sexuality.* New York: Norton.

Laszlo, E. 1972. *Introduction to systems philosophy.* New York: Harper Row.

———. 1987. *Evolution: The grand synthesis.* Boston: Shambhala Publications.

Leibniz, G. 1990. *Discourse on method and monadology.* Buffalo, N.Y.: Prometheus.

Lenski, G. 1970. *Human societies.* New York: McGraw-Hill.

Lenski, G., P. Nolan, and J. Lenski. 1995. *Human societies.* New York: McGraw-Hill.

Levinson, D., et al. 1978. *The seasons of a man's life.* New York: Knopf.

Loevinger, J. 1976. *Ego development.* San Francisco: Jossey-Bass.

Lovejoy, A. 1964 (1936). *The great chain of being.* Cambridge: Harvard University Press.

Lyotard, J. 1984. *The postmodern condition.* Minneapolis: University of Minnesota Press.

Lyotard, J., and J. Thebaud. 1986. *Just gaming*. Manchester: Manchester University Press.

Mahler, M. 1968. *On human symbiosis and the vicissitudes of individuation*. New-York: IUP.

Mahler, M., F. Pine, and A. Bergman. 1975. *The psychological birth of the human infant*. New York: Basic Books.

Maslow, A. 1970. *Religions, values, and peak experiences*. New York: Viking.

———. 1971. *The farther reaches of human nature*. New York: Viking.

Masterson, J. 1981. *The narcissistic and borderline disorders*. New York: Bruner/Mazel.

———. 1988. *The search for the real self*. New York: Free Press.

Maturana, H., and F. Varela. 1992. *The tree of knowledge*. Rev. ed. Boston: Shambhala Publications.

McGann, J. 1985. *Historical studies and literary criticism*. Madison: University of Wisconsin Press.

McGuinness, D., K. Pribram, and M. Pirnazar. 1990. Upstaging the stage model. In Alexander and Langer (eds.), pp. 97–113.

Miller, J. 1993. *The passion of Michel Foucault*. New York: Simon & Schuster.

Miller, M., and S. Cook-Greuter, eds. 1994. *Transcendence and mature thought in adulthood: The further reaches of adult development*. Lanham, Md.: Rowman and Littlefield.

Murphy, M. 1992. *The future of the body*. Los Angeles: Tarcher.

Murphy, M., and S. Donovan. 1989. *The physical and psychological effects of meditation*. San Rafael, Calif.: Esalen.

Murphy, M., and G. Leonard. 1995. *The life we are given*. New York: Tarcher/Putnam.

Murti, T. 1970. *The central philosophy of Buddhism*. London: Allen and Unwin.

Naess, A. 1989. *Ecology, community and lifestyle*. Cambridge: Cambridge University Press.

Neumann, E. 1954. *The origins and history of consciousness*. Princeton: Princeton University Press.

Newton, J., and D. Rosenfelt, eds. 1985. *Feminist criticism and social change*. New York: Methuen.

Nietzsche, F. 1965. *The portable Nietzsche*, edited by W. Kaufmann. New York: Viking

———. 1968. *Basic writings of Nietzsche*, translated and edited by W. Kaufmann. New York: Modern Library.

Nucci, L., ed. 1989. *Moral development and character education*. Berkeley: McCutchan.

O'Meara, D. 1995. *Plotinus*. New York: Oxford University Press.

Parsons, T. 1951. *The social system*. Englewood Cliffs, N.J.: Prentice-Hall.

———. 1966. *Societies*. New York: Free Press.

Pascual-Leone, J. 1990. Reflections on life-span intelligence, consciousness, and ego development. In Alexander and Langer (eds.), 1990, pp. 258–85.

Passmore, J. 1991. *Serious art*. La Salle, Ill.: Open Court.

Peirce, C. 1931–1958. *Collected papers.* 8 vols. Cambridge: Harvard University Press.

——. 1955. *Philosophical writings of Peirce,* edited by J. Buchler. New York: Dover.

Piaget, J. 1977. *The essential Piaget,* edited by H. Gruber and J. Vonèche. New York: Basic Books.

Plato. 1956. *The works of Plato,* edited by L. Edman. New York: Modern Library.

Plotinus. 1966–1988. *Enneads,* vols. 1–7, translated by A. H. Armstrong. Cambridge: Harvard University Press.

——. 1992. *Enneads,* translated by S. MacKenna. Burdett, N.Y.: Larson.

Popper, K. 1974. *Objective knowledge.* Oxford: Clarendon.

Popper, K., and J. Eccles. 1983. *The self and its brain.* London: Routledge.

Puhakka, K. 1996. Restoring connectedness in the Kosmos: A healing tale of a deeper order. *The Humanistic Psychologist,* Fall 1996.

Richards, F., and M. Commons. 1990. Postformal cognitive-developmental theory and research. In Alexander and Langer (eds.), 1990, pp. 139–61.

Ricoeur, P. 1981. *Hermeneutics and the human sciences.* Cambridge: Cambridge University Press.

——. 1992. *Oneself as another.* Chicago: University of Chicago Press.

——. 1995. *The philosophy of Paul Ricoeur,* edited by L. Hahn. Chicago: Open Court.

Riso, D. 1987. *Personality types.* Boston: Houghton Mifflin.

——. 1990. *Understanding the enneagram.* Boston: Houghton Mifflin.

Robinson, L. 1986. *Sex, class, and culture.* New York: Methuen.

Rorty, R. 1979. *Philosophy and the mirror of nature.* Princeton: Princeton University Press.

——. 1982. *Consequences of pragmatism.* Minneapolis: University of Minnesota Press.

Rothberg, D. 1986a. Philosophical foundations of transpersonal psychology. *Journal of Transpersonal Psychology* 18: 1–34.

——. 1986b. Rationality and religion in Habermas' recent work. *Philosophy and Social Criticism* 11: 221–43.

——. 1990. Contemporary epistemology and the study of mysticism. In R. Forman (ed.), 1990.

——. 1992. Buddhist nonviolence. *Journal of Humanistic Psychology* 32 (4): 41–75.

——. 1993. The crisis of modernity and the emergence of socially engaged spirituality. *ReVision* 15 (3): 105–15.

Rowan, J. 1990. *Subpersonalities.* London: Routledge.

——. 1993. *The transpersonal.* London: Routledge.

Russell, B. 1945. *A history of western philosophy.* New York: Clarion.

Saussure, F. 1966 (1915). *Course in general linguistics.* New York: McGraw-Hill.

Schapiro, M. 1994. *Theory and philosophy of art: Style, artist, and society.* New York: Braziller.

Schelling, F. 1978 (1800). *System of transcendental idealism,* translated by P. Heath. Charlottesville: University Press of Virginia.

Schopenhauer, A. 1969. *The world as will and representation.* 2 vols. New York: Dover.

Schwartz, T. 1995. *What really matters: Searching for wisdom in America.* New York: Bantam.

Scott, A. 1995. *Stairway to the mind.* New York: Copernicus.

Scotton, B., A. Chinen, and J. Battista, eds. 1996. *Textbook of transpersonal psychiatry and psychology.* New York: Basic Books.

Searle, J. 1992 (1969). *Speech acts.* Cambridge: Cambridge University Press.

———. 1995. *The construction of social reality.* New York: Free Press.

Selman, R., and D. Byrne. 1974. A structural analysis of levels of role-taking in middle childhood. *Child Development* 45.

Shaffer, D. 1994. *Social and personality development.* Pacific Grove, Calif.: Brooks/Cole.

Shankara. 1970 (1947). *Crest-jewel of discrimination,* translated by C. Isherwood and Prabhavananda. New York: New American Library.

Shapiro, D., and R. Walsh, eds. 1984. *Meditation: Classic and contemporary perspectives.* New York: Aldine.

Sheldrake, R. 1989. *The presence of the past: Morphic resonance and the habits of nature.* New York: Viking.

———. 1990. *The rebirth of nature.* London: Century.

Showalter, E. 1985. *The new feminist criticism.* New York: Pantheon.

Siegler, R. 1991. *Children's thinking.* Englewood Cliffs, N.J.: Prentice-Hall.

Sinnott, J. 1984. Post-formal reasoning. In Commons et al. (eds.), 1984.

———, ed. 1994. *Interdisciplinary handbook of adult lifespan learning.* Greenwich, Conn.: Greenwood Press.

Sinnott, J., and J. Cavanaugh, eds. 1991. *Bridging paradigms: Positive development in adulthood and cognitive aging.* New York: Praeger.

Smart, N. 1984 (1969). *The religious experience of mankind.* New York: Scribner's.

Smith, H. 1976 (reissued 1993). *Forgotten truth.* New York: Harper.

Souvaine, E., L. Lahey, and R. Kegan. 1990. Life after formal operations. In Alexander and Langer (eds.), 1990, pp. 229–57.

Sroufe, L., R. Cooper, and G. DeHart. 1992. *Child development.* New York: McGraw-Hill.

Sternberg, R., ed. 1990. *Wisdom: Its nature, origins, and development.* New York: Cambridge University Press.

Strelka, J., ed. 1976. *Literary criticism and psychology.* University Park: Penn State University Press.

Suleiman, S., and I. Crosman, eds. 1980. *The reader in the text.* Princeton, N.J.: Princeton University Press.

Tannahill, R. 1992 (1982). *Sex in history.* London: Scarborough House.

Tannen, D. 1990. *You just don't understand.* New York: Morrow.

Tart, C., ed. 1972 (1969). *Altered states of consciousness.* New York: Doubleday.

———, ed. 1992. *Transpersonal psychologies.* New York: HarperCollins.

Taylor, C. 1985. *Philosophy and the human sciences: Philosophical papers 2.* Cambridge: Cambridge University Press.

Thomas, L., S. Brewer, P. Kraus, and B. Rosen. Two patterns of transcendence: An empirical examination of Wilber's and Washburn's theories. *Journal of Humanistic Psychology* 33 (3): 66–82.

Tompkins, J., ed. 1980. *Reader-response criticism.* Baltimore: Johns Hopkins.

Trungpa, C. 1988. *Shambhala: The sacred path of the warrior.* Boston: Shambhala Publications.

Vaillant, G. 1993. *The wisdom of the ego.* Cambridge: Harvard University Press.

Varela, F. 1979. *Principles of biological autonomy.* New York: North Holland.

Varela, F., E. Thompson, and E. Rosch. 1993. *The embodied mind.* Cambridge: MIT Press.

Wade, J. 1996. *Changes of mind: A holonomic theory of the evolution of consciousness.* Albany: SUNY Press.

Wallace, R. 1970. Physiological effects of Transcendental Meditation. *Science* 167, pp. 1751–54.

Walsh, R. 1989. Can Western philosophers understand Asian philosophies? *Crosscurrents* 34: 281–99.

———. 1990. *The spirit of shamanism.* Los Angeles: Tarcher.

———. 1995. The spirit of evolution: A review of Ken Wilber's *Sex, ecology, spirituality. Noetics Sciences Review,* Summer.

———. 1999. *Essential spirituality: Exercises from the world's religions to cultivate kindness, love, joy, peace, vision, wisdom, and generosity.* New York: John Wiley & Sons.

Walsh, R., and F. Vaughan, eds. 1993. *Paths beyond ego.* Los Angeles: Tarcher.

Washburn, M. 1995. *The ego and the dynamic ground.* 2nd ed., rev. Albany: SUNY Press.

White, J., ed. 1972. *The highest state of consciousness.* New York: Anchor Books.

Whitehead, A. 1967. *Science and the modern world.* New York: Macmillan.

Wilber, K. 1974. The spectrum of consciousness. *Main Currents in Modern Thought,* November/December.

———. 1978a. Spectrum psychology, part 1. *ReVision* 1 (1): 5–29.

———. 1978b. Spectrum psychology, part 2. *ReVision* 1 (2): 5–33.

———. 1978c. Microgeny. *ReVision* 1 (3/4): 52–84.

———. 1979a. Spectrum psychology, part 4. *ReVision* 2 (1): 65–73.

———. 1979b. Are the chakras real? In *Kundalini, evolution and enlightenment,* edited by J. White. Garden City, N.Y.: Doubleday Anchor, 1979.

———. 1979c. A developmental view of consciousness. *Journal of Transpersonal Psychology* 11 (1).

———. 1980. The pre/trans fallacy. *ReVision* 3 (2). Reprinted in Wilber, 1996c.

———. 1981a. Ontogenetic development: Two fundamental patterns. *Journal of Transpersonal Psychology* 13 (1): 33–58.

———. 1981b. *No boundary.* Boston: Shambhala Publications. Also in CW1.

———. 1982a. Odyssey. *Journal of Humanistic Psychology* 22 (l): 57–90.

———. 1982b. *The holographic paradigm.* Boston: Shambhala Publications.

———. 1983. *A sociable God: A brief introduction to a transcendental sociology.* New York: McGraw-Hill. Also in CW3.

———. 1984. The developmental spectrum and psychopathology: Part 1, stages and types of pathology. *Journal of Transpersonal Psychology* 16 (1): 75–118. Part 2, Treatment modalities. *Journal of Transpersonal Psychology* 16 (2): 137–66.

———. 1990. Two patterns of transcendence: A reply to Washburn. *Journal of Humanistic Psychology* 30 (3): 113–36. Reprinted in CW4, under the title "A Unified Theory of Development."

———. 1993 (1977). *The spectrum of consciousness.* Wheaton, Ill.: Quest Books. Also in CW1.

———. 1995. *Sex, ecology, spirituality: The spirit of evolution.* Boston: Shambhala Publications. Also in CW6.

———. 1996a (1980). *The Atman project.* 2nd ed. Wheaton, Ill.: Quest Books. Also in CW2.

———. 1996b (1981). *Up from Eden.* 2nd ed. Wheaton, Ill.: Quest Books. Also in CW2.

———. 1996c (1983). *Eye to eye: The quest for the new paradigm.* 3rd ed. Boston: Shambhala Publications. Also in CW3.

———. 1996d. *A brief history of everything.* Boston: Shambhala Publications. Also in CW7.

———. 1997. An integral theory of consciousness. *Journal of Consciousness Studies* 4 (1): 71–92. Also in CW7.

———. 1998. *The marriage of sense and soul: Integrating science and religion.* New York: Random House. Also in CW8.

———. 1999a. *One taste: The journals of Ken Wilber.* Boston: Shambhala Publications. Also in CW8.

———. 1999b. *The collected works of Ken Wilber,* vols. 1–4. Boston: Shambhala Publications.

———. 2000a. *The collected works of Ken Wilber,* vols. 5–8. Boston: Shambhala Publications.

———. 2000b. *Integral psychology: Consciousness, spirit, psychology, therapy.* Boston: Shambhala Publications. Also in CW4.

———. 2000c (1995). *Sex, ecology, spirituality.* 2nd ed. Boston: Shambhala Publications. Also in CW6.

———. 2000d. *A theory of everything: An integral vision for business, politics, science, and spirituality.* Boston: Shambhala Publications.

———. 2002a, forthcoming. *Boomeritis: A Novel That Will Change Your Life.* Boston: Shambhala Publications.

———. 2002b. *The Eye of Spirit: An Integral Vision for a World Gone Slightly Mad,* 3rd ed., expanded (Boston: Shambhala). The 1st edition was published in 1997, the 2nd in CW7.

Wilber, K., J. Engler, and D. Brown. 1986. *Transformations of consciousness: Conventional and contemplative perspectives on development.* Boston: Shambhala Publications.

Wimsatt, W. K., and M. Beardsley, The intentional fallacy. In *The verbal icon,* by W. K. Wimsatt. New York: Noonday Press, 1966.

Wittgenstein, L. 1961 (1921). *Tractatus logico-philosophicus.* London: Routledge.

———. 1965. *Philosophical investigations*. New York: Macmillan.

Wolman, B., and M. Ullman, eds. 1986. *Handbook of states of consciousness*. New York: Van Nostrand Reinhold.

Zimmerman, M. 1990. *Heidegger's confrontation with modernity*. Bloomington: Indiana University Press.

———. 1981. *Eclipse of the self*. Athens: Ohio University Press.

———. 1994. *Contesting earth's future*. Berkeley: University of California Press.

Zimmerman, M., ed. 1998 (1993). *Environmental Philosophy*, 2nd ed. Upper Saddle River, N.J.: Prentice Hall.

Index

Absolute/relative dualism, 73–75
  eye of contemplation and, 80–81
  satori and, 82–83
Adi Da, 57, 59, 332n.18
Aesthetic theory, contradictions within, 26
Affective stylistics, reaction to New Criticism, 89
Agape, 330n.15
  female transformation and, 178–82
Agency
  developmental stages and, 344n.2
  male moral development and, 170, 172, 178–80
  pathology of male, 171
Agency-in-communion concept, 170
  translation and transformation within, 177
  See also Agency; Communion
Alexander, Charles, 199, 204–5, 207–8, 339n.3, 347–48n.17
  confusion of states, structures, and stages in, 208–10, 217–18, 355n.6
  consciousness model of, 354n.3
  developmental stages of, 357–58n.17
  levels equated with lines in, 209, 217–18, 354–55n.5
  research on effects of meditation, 221, 222
  self-system of, 216–18, 357n.17
  unbounded Self in, 210–11
Alexander, Jane, 337n.1
Ali, Hameed, 240
  Diamond Approach of. See Diamond Approach

post-conventional approach of, 377n.11
"All-quadrant, all-level" (AQAL) model, 189–91, 274, 277, 281, 287–89, 391n.11, 394n.17, 395–98nn.24–27. See also Integral approach; Integral vision; Quadrants of development
Almaas, A. H. See Ali, Hameed
Altered states of consciousness, 132, 264
  spiritual development and, ix, 201, 229, 259
  See also Nonordinary states of consciousness
Alternative educational institutions, 309–10n.2
Ancient wisdom
  as past forms of Truth, 54–55, 58
  as radical Truth, 53–54, 58
Anterior self, 350n.22
Anthropic Principle, 7
Anti-evolutionary theorists. See Cultural evolution, theoretical objections to
Apel, Karl-Otto, 249–50
Apprehension strand of knowledge acquisition, 17, 77
  empiricist emphasis of, 77, 78
  satori as, 82–83
Aquinas, Saint Thomas, exterior approaches to theology, 7
Archaic images, 238–40, 364n.6
Archetypes
  as archaic image, 238–40, 364n.6, 365n.8

413